This detailed study contributes to an expanding field of interest: the social history of industrial employers. Using previously untapped primary sources, *Organised capital* explores the emergence of employers' organisations in northern England and analyses their policies during the heyday of collective activity. Arthur McIvor evaluates the impact of trade unionism, state intervention, war, economic recession and changing product markets on these organisations, charting their role and patterns of growth. He challenges notions of a monolithic employer group and crude economic determinism, while also rejecting 'revisionist' accounts of weak and ineffective employers. Instead, he reaches a more balanced appraisal of these institutions' role in capital–labour relations and the pursuit of employers' class interests. This book will be of interest both to historians and to students of industrial relations.

Organised capital

Employers' associations and industrial relations in northern England, 1880–1939

Organised capital

Employers' associations and industrial relations in northern England, 1880–1939

Arthur J. McIvor

University of Strathclyde

Published by the Press Syndicate of the University of Cambridge
The Pitt Building, Trumpington Street, Cambridge CB2 1RP
40 West 20th Street, New York, NY 10011-4211, USA
10 Stamford Road, Oakleigh, Melbourne 3166, Australia

© Cambridge University Press 1996

First published 1996

Printed in Great Britain at the University Press, Cambridge

A catalogue record for this book is available from the British Library

Library of Congress cataloguing in publication data

McIvor, Arthur J.
    Organised capital: employers' associations and industrial
relations in northern England, 1880–1939 / Arthur McIvor.
        p.   cm.
    Includes bibliographical references and index.
    ISBN 0 521 55094 7
    1. Employers' associations–England, Northern–History.
    2. Industrial relations–England, Northern–History.   1. Title.
    HD6948.E52N675   1996
    331'.09427–dc20   95-8504   CIP

ISBN 0 521 55094 7 hardback

For Brenda

Contents

Maps and tables

Acknowledgements

I owe a great debt to many people who have helped me in the writing of this book, not least all those who have researched, written and published on the history of industrial employers and on whose shoulders, metaphorically speaking, I have stood. Special thanks, however, go to Ted Musson who first suggested that I explore the history of employers' organisations and who supervised my doctorate at Manchester University. Thanks also to Derek Oddy, who not only gave me my first job in history, but who graciously tolerated my absences from his research project as I finished my Ph.D. I have also benefited considerably from the comments of Howard Gospel, Alan McKinlay, Joe Melling and Eleanor Gordon on previous manifestations of my work on organised employers. Alan Fowler and Andrew Bullen have also been of invaluable assistance, guiding me at critical junctures through the minefield that constitutes industrial relations in the Lancashire cotton industry. Irene Magrath provided stimulating contrasts with the wool and worsted millowners across the other side of the Pennines, whilst my late friend Steve Jones gave me much encouragement and inspiration. Of particular importance has been the support and camaraderie of colleagues in the history department at Strathclyde where I have worked over the past ten years. I count myself extremely fortunate to have settled in a department which manages to combine a friendly, warm atmosphere with an environment (or should I say a regime!) conducive to sustained research and writing. I have also benefited considerably from discussions with my students at Strathclyde, especially my postgraduates and those rash enough to take my third- and fourth-year labour history classes. I must also mention the labour history workshop at Strathclyde: historical research is usually a very solitary exercise and it has been most refreshing, as well as instructive, to work collectively, exchange ideas and discuss a whole range of industrial relations topics with participants and speakers in the workshop seminars which have run over the past six years or so.

The ESRC provided financial support (research grant F00232204) which helped this project along, whilst the history department at

Strathclyde kindly funded smaller research trips. I am also most grateful to the many employers' associations that allowed access to their records and to the local librarians and archivists throughout north-west England who responded with patience to my (sometimes desperate) pleas for material. In the latter respect those kind souls at Manchester Public Library, Manchester University Library, the Greater Manchester and the Lancashire County Record Offices deserve a special mention. Thanks also to Allison Armour for typing parts of the text and to colleagues Gordon Jackson and Brian Tomlinson for much needed technical assistance with the word-processing package.

I have been as guilty as many other writers – perhaps even more so – of neglecting family responsibilities whilst working on this book. So I would like to express both my apologies and my appreciation to my much-loved two children, Kieran and Tom, and my wife, Brenda, for bearing so reasonably my far too frequent absences and my preoccupation with this when I should have been concentrating on them. My parents, Joan and Arthur McIvor, provided incalculable support and encouragement, for which I was never really able to thank them properly. However, my greatest debt and deepest acknowledgement is to my partner Brenda to whom this book is dedicated. Her enthusiasm and her moral support over many, many years has been absolutely critical in the production of this book. I alone, of course, am responsible for any weaknesses and errors in the text.

List of abbreviations

AAOCS	Amalgamated Association of Operative Cotton Spinners
AEU	Amalgamated Engineering Union
ARSLO	*Annual Report on Strikes and Lock-Outs*
ASE	Amalgamated Society of Engineers
AUBW	Amalgamated Union of Building Trade Workers
AWA	Amalgamated Weavers' Association
BTEA	Building Trades Employers' Association (local)
BTLD	Board of Trade Labour Department
CAEOE	Central Association of Employers of Operative Engineers
CCB	Cotton Control Board
CEPA	Cotton Employers' Parliamentary Association
CSMA	Cotton Spinners' and Manufacturers' Association
CWA	Cardroom Workers' Amalgamation
EEA	Engineering Employers' Association (local)
EEF[1]	Engineering Employers' Federation
EL	Economic League
EPC	Employers' Parliamentary Council
ETU	Electrical Trades Union
FBI	Federation of British Industries
FMCSA	Federation of Master Cotton Spinners' Associations
GBA	General Builders' Association
ITEA	Iron Trades Employers' Association
JCCTO	Joint Committee of Cotton Trade Organisations
JSC	Joint Standing Committee (Lancashire engineering)
LCEL	Lancashire and Cheshire Economic League
LCFBTE	Lancashire and Cheshire Federation of Building Trade Employers
LMDA	Lancashire Masters' Defence Association (cotton)
MBA	Master Builders' Association (local)

[1] The Engineering Employers' Federation changed its name a number of times. For convenience, EEF has been used throughout the text.

MCSA	Master Cotton Spinners' Association (local)
NAMB	National Association of Master Builders
NAOP	National Association of Operative Plasterers
NCEO	National Confederation of Employers' Organisations
NCTTF	Northern Counties Textile Trades' Federation
NFAEL	National Federation of Associated Employers of Labour
NFBTE	National Federation of Building Trade Employers
NFBTO	National Federation of Building Trade Operatives
NFLA	National Free Labour Association
NWCC	National Wages and Conditions Council (building)
NWFBTE	North-West Federation of Building Trade Employers
PEC	Provisional Emergency Committee (cotton)
SMCP	Society of Master Calico Printers
UCSA	United Cotton Spinners' Association

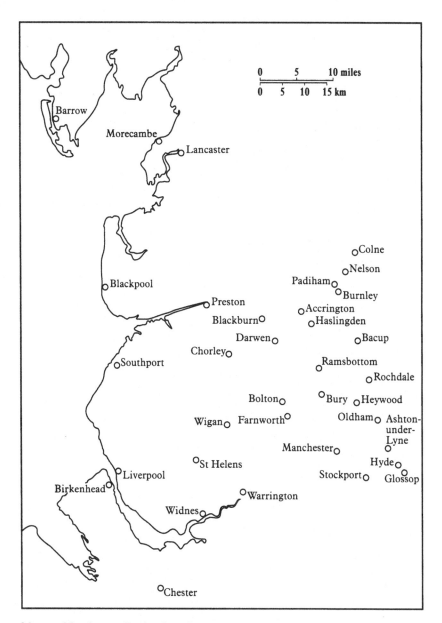

Map 1.1 North-west England: main towns

Introduction

The subject matter of this book lies within the intersection of business and labour history, emerging from a long-standing interest in the history of employer combinations, anti-labour organisations and management industrial relations strategies. For a relatively brief period, from the late nineteenth century to the Second World War, employers' organisations proliferated, and collectively formulated policies characterised the behaviour of most British employers in many spheres of industrial relations, social, economic and political activity. Before and after this phase, atomised, company-level bargaining and determination of labour relations predominated. Since the 1930s, the ability of employers' organisations in Britain to regulate industrial relations and control labour markets within their respective industries has significantly declined, and internalised, company-specific labour management structures and policies have become more important.[1] This book thus explores the heyday of delegated, multi-employer relations with trade unions and collective regulation of the labour contract and labour markets, examining the genesis and evolution of employers' associations, the formulation of multi-employer labour relations strategies and the changing role of such institutions in British industrial relations over the period 1880–1939.

Such a fundamental process of change – from individualism and the free market to collective employer action and market regulation – merits extensive analysis and prompts at least four primary clusters of questions which are taken up in the pages that follow: first, what are employers' organisations and what is distinctive about the British variant? Secondly, how were such organisations structured and how representative and powerful were they? Thirdly, what were the forces which encouraged an increasing number of British capitalists to eschew individualism, form and join collective associations and accept collectively formulated labour policies? Fourthly, what role did these collective organisations of

---

[1] For a discussion of such developments post-1945 see H. Gospel, *Markets, Firms and the Management of Labour in Modern Britain*, Cambridge: Cambridge University Press, 1992, pp. 103–68.

employers play in structuring industrial relations systems, reacting to market pressures, trade unionism, industrial conflict and state intervention? In other words, how and why did such institutions behave in the way that they did?

To address these questions this study draws upon the growing corpus of secondary literature relating to the labour policies of employers and the history of employers' organisations and engages with some of the prevailing interpretations of employer organisation development and strategies. However, it is anchored firmly within one region of England – the heavily industrialised north-west – and is informed by immersion in the surviving archival records of employers' organisations in three industries – cotton textile manufacturing (spinning and weaving), construction and engineering. The basic primary source material exploited for this book has, therefore, been the surviving minute books, annual reports, correspondence files, cash and account books, membership files and other documents generated by the employers' organisations in such industries. These include the records of the North-West Federation of Building Trade Employers, the Joint Standing Committee of Lancashire Engineering Employers' Associations, the Federation of Master Cotton Spinners' Associations and the Cotton Spinners' and Manufacturers' Association, together with the papers of a plethora of independent and affiliated local employers' associations covering most of the major industrial towns in north-west England. These extant records are a testimony to how employers' organisations became more extensive and representative in the period *c.* 1890–1920, with two notable bursts of organisational activity in the 1890s and between 1914 and 1920. Increasingly over these years individualistic and paternalistic employers broke with the tenets of popular *laissez-faire* anti-combination ideology. Informal consultation and tacit, clandestine combinations between employers gave way to *ad hoc* local, often temporary associations, which in turn were consolidated and superseded by stable and permanent industry-wide federations of local associations.

What is the justification for such a study and such an approach? There are three points worth making here: first, and most obviously, the book addresses a serious gap in the literature. The role of organised capital in British society has attracted interest, though in relation to the study of labour history this still remains a markedly underresearched theme.[2]

[2] See, for example, Chris Wrigley's note on the neglect of employers in industrial relations: C.J. Wrigley (ed.), *A History of British Industrial Relations*, vol. II: *1914–1939*, Brighton: Harvester, 1987, p. 19. Interest and research in this area is growing, though the continuing relative neglect of the labour management policies of employers is confirmed by even a cursory glance over the bibliographies compiled in the journals *Labour History Review* and *Business History*.

Industrial conflict, as Carter Goodrich perceptively commented in 1920, occurred over a fluid 'frontier of control'.[3] Labour encroached into managerial terrain during phases of tight labour markets and booming trade, whilst capital 'pushed the working classes back to their kennels', as Sir Philip Gibbs approvingly noted, during economic depressions.[4] Arguably, the labour side of this equation has been extensively (though certainly not exhaustively) investigated; trade union histories abound in great quantities and the surge of interest in working-class history from the early 1960s has resulted in a plethora of studies which focus on the role of labour in the workplace, in industrial relations and in society. By comparison, the history of employers' organisations and the evolution of capitalist labour relations strategies is an area of study which, whilst growing, is still in its infancy. Indeed, to date we lack a single academic monograph specifically on employers' organisations. Undoubtedly, this is partly because the defensive and conservative attitudes and policies of employers' organisations have proved less attractive to historians than the more militant political and social theories that lie at the foundation of trade union policy.

The secrecy and anonymity of employers' associations and their reticence to allow access to their records have been important additional factors accounting for the dearth of research in this area. Historically, employers' associations have tended to shun publicity, hence alternative sources beyond association records have serious limitations. When the Royal Commission on Labour appealed for copies of rules in 1890–1 it received more than five times the number of rules from trade unions than from employers' associations (377 to 70).[5] As late as 1937 the Ministry of Labour's annual digest of statistics included just one small table on employers' associations, compared to fifteen pages of detailed statistical data on trade unions.[6] Many employers' organisations had no need of the sort of large-scale delegate conferences which would attract media interest and often considered their functions as an extension of the internal business of their constituent members, which they regarded as of little interest to the public.

Attitudes have, however, changed considerably over time. An increasing number of organisations over the past twenty years or so have deposited their archives in public record offices or allow historians direct

[3] C. Goodrich, *The Frontier of Control*, new edition, London: Pluto Press, 1975 (first published 1920).

[4] Cited in J. Cronin, *Labour and Society in Britain, 1918–1979*, London: Batsford, 1984, p. 34.

[5] Royal Commission on Labour, *Rules of Associations of Employers and Employed*, c. 6795, London: HMSO, 1892, pp. vii; xxii.

[6] Ministry of Labour, *27th Annual Abstract of Labour Statistics, 1922–36*, Cmd 5556, London: HMSO, July 1937, pp. 136–52.

access to their private papers. Generally speaking, only organisations which have embarrassing or illegal activities to hide still continue to refuse access to their extant archival material. The Economic League, with its semi-clandestine political blacklisting operation, is a good example.

Secondly, why the three industries? The rationale here was that a comparative study would produce more meaningful results, allowing hypotheses to be tested across a few case studies, with different structures, technologies and product markets. The industries were chosen because they all had long traditions of collective organisation amongst both masters and men, they provided a good contrast in terms of industrial structure, and a range of product and labour markets. There were also practical considerations. The surviving source material was both relatively plentiful and readily accessible for these sectors.

Thirdly, the regional perspective provides an alternative point of reference to the national and international one which currently dominates the labour management literature. The text brings under closer scrutiny the activities of local employers' associations and regional federations and their relationships at two levels: with the organised labour movement and with their own constituency – millowners, building masters and engineering employers. At least pre-1914, the main focus of collective bargaining was the locality and region, and local autonomy was a particularly marked feature of British employers' associations. One of the more important hypotheses I hope to sustain in what follows is that those revisionist scholars who have argued for the relative weakness of British employers' associations (and commensurate strength of organised labour) over this period have overstated their case by concentrating excessively upon the national rather than the provincial level and by focusing predominantly upon relationships between employers and the minority of skilled craft workers rather than the majority of unskilled and semi-skilled employees. This, it seems to me, provides a rather skewed and somewhat distorted perspective upon industrial relations. Not that I am suggesting that north-west England is in any sense representative. That remains to be seen. But I do think that this study casts doubt upon the ability – given our present state of knowledge – of talking in terms of 'national models' of employers' organisations and of the British variant being intrinsically weak and ineffective. At the very least, more detailed regional and sectoral case studies are necessary to refine our understanding of employers' organisations and their role within British society. This book constitutes a contribution to this ongoing debate and if it stimulates further interest and additional empirical research into the role played by employers' organisations within British society it will have fulfilled its purpose.

The text is divided into three sections. Part 1 (chapters 1 and 2) sets the scene for what follows by providing an introduction to the historiography, sketching the context and outlining the origins and development of employers' organisations in Britain up to the 1880s. Theories of employer collectivism and behaviour are discussed and evidence offered to support the view that in north-west England, at least, employers maintained organisational continuity for very long periods and that employer organisations played a significant role in industrial relations at the local level from the mid-nineteenth century.

Part 2 (chapters 3 to 6) focuses upon the maturation of employer organisation, strikebreaking and the transition towards collective bargaining, c. 1880–1920. Chapter 3 analyses the structure and evolution of employers' associations over these years, setting this firmly within the prevailing economic, political and social context. Here an attempt has been made to reconstruct membership trends and levels of organisation and solidarity by cross-referencing membership lists and local trade directories. Such quantitative data, drawn from a series of organisations in north-west England and elsewhere, suggest that the period witnessed a quite remarkable surge in employer collectivism, tangibly indicated in expansion in the number and representativeness of employers' associations and in the trend towards inter-association collusion at the regional and national, industry-wide levels. Specific interest groups and divisions within organisations are also identified, developing the important theme of intra-class competition and fragmentation. British employers, it should be stressed at the outset, were no monolithic group. However, this should not obscure the fundamental point that divisions of interest between employers were increasingly being transcended in the common interest as the rules of the collective game were being incrementally absorbed. Within this chapter, the causes of increasing employer organisation membership and growing class consciousness, c. 1880–1920, are also discussed, moving from analysis of the national context to the specific economic and social circumstances that prevailed within north-west England.

Chapters 4 and 5 explore in some depth the industrial relations policies developed by employers' organisations over the 1880–1914 period. It is perhaps something of a paradox that the upsurge in employers' organisation which occurred from around 1890 provided the preconditions for both the accelerating commitment to institutionalised, procedural forms of control over labour, and the formalisation and consolidation of employers' coercive strikebreaking machinery. These were, however, two sides of the same coin: not mutually exclusive but alternative control strategies utilised where and when appropriate. Chapter 4 analyses the growing sophistication of the employers' arsenal of strikebreaking and union-busting machinery and the pivotal role employers' associations played in this process, discussing, in turn, the organisation of substitute labour for strikers, modes of victimisation, legal action, strike indemnity and compensation schemes and the utilisation of the multi-employer lock-out. One of the major functions of employers' organisations before 1914 was forcibly to break strikes, either as an initial reaction, or as a second line of defence when established procedures to settle disputes without a stoppage of work were either exhausted or ignored. Such coercive sanctions in turn served to strengthen trade union commitment to formal disputes and bargaining procedures.

The conjuncture of rising worker organisation and militancy – an ability and will to sustain resistance – with intensifying competition, more hostile product markets and changes in state and public attitudes towards industrial relations encouraged an increasing number of employers to seek alternative, less costly and less provocative strategies to maintain discipline and stabilise industrial relations. What remains unclear is the role employer organisations played in this process, their contribution to the evolution of a formalised collective bargaining system. How committed were employers to the jointly agreed or unilaterally imposed disputes procedures of their industries and why? Did employers gain disproportionately from such mechanisms? How were unions treated within disputes procedures? Did this switch in policy enable employers' organisations to stabilise costs effectively, limit craft control and autonomy and maintain managerial authority and control at the point of production? How did this formalised framework respond to changes in product and labour market circumstances? Chapter 5 addresses such questions, through a detailed analysis of the policies of local and regional employers' organisations in the cotton manufacturing and engineering industries in north-west England. This section will engage with the continuing controversies over the motivations and implications of this formalisation of industrial relations.[7]

War conditions provided a quite unique industrial relations experience, influencing employers' organisation and collectivist behaviour, attitudes and labour relations policies in many significant ways. The impact of war upon British employers' organisations forms the subject matter of chapter 6. The disruptions to product and labour markets imposed severe strains

[7] See H.A. Clegg, A. Fox and A.F. Thompson, *A History of British Trade Unions since 1889*, vol. I: *1889–1911*, Oxford: Clarendon Press, 1964, pp. 326–54, 471–5; K. Burgess, *The Origins of British Industrial Relations*, London: Croom Helm, 1975, pp. 309–11; J. Porter, 'Wage bargaining under conciliation agreements, 1860–1914', *Economic History Review*, 2nd series, 23 (1970), pp. 460–75; K. Sisson, *The Management of Collective Bargaining: An International Comparison*, Oxford: Clarendon Press, 1987; K. Sisson, 'Employers and the structure of collective bargaining: distinguishing cause and effect', in S. Tolliday and J. Zeitlin (eds.), *The Power to Manage?* London: Routledge, 1991, pp. 256–72.

upon employer cohesion, leading to a corrosion of authority as employers' organisations lost control over labour markets. On the other hand,
unprecedented government intervention in labour matters, combined
with a quite remarkable surge in trade union growth and shop-floor
labour militancy between 1914 and 1920, placed great pressure upon
individual employers, encouraging combination. Hence, these years witnessed a counter-surge in the number, representativeness and stability of
British employers' organisations, at almost all levels. Moreover, many
organisations acted, often quite aggressively, though with varying degrees
of success, to bring the destabilising influences, especially of the period
1914–17, under some control. This represented a consolidation of class
awareness by employers, a realisation that only through mutual support
could they offer a bulwark against an increasingly interventionist state,
tight labour markets (and the empowerment of labour that this implied),
rising labour costs, labour 'encroachments' and the wartime extension of
workers' control – as both an ideology and a reality – which struck at the
very heart of the notions of managerial prerogative, proprietorial rights
and executive decision-making.

Part 3 (chapters 7, 8 and 9) analyses organisational developments and
multi-employer labour relations policies during the inter-war economic
slump, focusing in turn upon developments in cotton manufacturing,
building and engineering. Research here has tended to focus upon the
central level, upon pivotal confrontations such as the 1922 engineering
lock-out and the general strike of 1926, or on attempts to forge a new
industrial relations concordat, through the abortive Mond-Turner talks.[8]
By shifting the focus to the regional level, the attitudes, tactics and policies of local employers' associations and their constituent members
during the recession will be brought into sharper relief, thus allowing
hypotheses within the literature to be tested. For example, how did the
conflict, identified by Garside and Gospel, between hawks and doves,
anti-unionist employers and conciliators during the recession resolve
itself in the staple sectors of the economy in north-west England?[9] And,

---

[8] Engineering and shipbuilding have been most thoroughly researched. See J. Zeitlin, 'The
internal politics of employer organization: the Engineering Employers' Federation,
1896–1939', in Tolliday and Zeitlin, *Power to Manage?* and A. Reid, 'Employers' strategies
and craft production: the British shipbuilding industry, 1870–1950', in Tolliday and
Zeitlin, *Power to Manage?* E. Wigham, *The Power to Manage*, London: Macmillan, 1973,
provides a broad, though now somewhat dated, survey of EEF history. See also J. Zeitlin,
The Triumph of Adversarial Bargaining: Industrial Relations in British Engineering, 1880–1939,
Oxford: Oxford University Press, forthcoming.

[9] W.R. Garside, 'Management and men: aspects of British industrial relations in the inter-
war period', in B. Supple (ed.), *Essays in British Business History*, Oxford: Clarendon Press,
1977; H.F. Gospel, 'Employers' labour policy: a study of the Mond-Turner talks,
1927–33', *Business History*, 21 (1979), pp. 180–97.

what role did the local employers' associations and regional federations play in this? Evidence suggests that the markedly altered economic circumstances triggered a major counter-attack, spearheaded by employers' associations, designed to roll back many of the gains made by labour during the decade of mass organisation and insurgency over 1910–20.[10] Pre-war and wartime co-operation and incorporation strategies gave way to the free play of economic forces and a more self-interested and coercive strategy amongst many employers, especially those most hard-pressed in the staple, export-orientated sectors of the economy. Evidence suggests a dual offensive to reimpose managerial prerogatives, authority and discipline on the shop-floor, whilst simultaneously reasserting firm control over wage bargaining and slashing labour costs. However, each industry pursued these common aims in different ways. Engineering employers were amongst the fiercest proponents of managerial prerogatives to organise production with minimal interference from trade unions. However, at the local level, in north-west England at least, engineering employers appear to have tempered their principles with a great deal of pragmatism and flexibility in the aftermath of the 1922 lock-out. In cotton manufacturing, the employers' organisations promulgated a vigorous costs reduction drive, invariably leading to an intensification of work, largely occurring within the parameters of the existing technology and the established division of labour.

Part 3 explores the parameters of this inter-war employers' counter-attack against labour, but also attempts to define its limits. Whilst the failure of the Mond-Turner talks showed that employers' organisations were drawing back from extending procedural control at the peak level, still, at the local level the employers' associations in engineering, cotton and building in north-west England remained firmly committed to stabilising industrial relations through collective bargaining and maintaining the formal disputes procedure. Employers' organisations in these industries were frequently operating as constraining agencies upon their more militant, confrontationist members, invariably insisting that collective agreements be honoured. This role created intense pressures within employers' organisations. Combined with product market fluctuations, structural divisions and intensified cut-throat competition between employers during the recession, this inevitably resulted in disaffection

---

[10] H.A. Clegg, *A History of British Trade Unions since 1889*, vol. II: *1911–33*, Oxford: Clarendon Press, 1985; K. Burgess, *The Challenge of Labour*, London: Croom Helm, 1980; A. McIvor, 'A crusade for capitalism: the Economic League, 1919–1939', *Journal of Contemporary History*, 23, no. 4 (1988); A. McIvor, 'Cotton employers' organisations and labour relations, 1890–1939', in J.A. Jowitt and A.J. McIvor (eds.), *Employers and Labour in the English Textile Industries, 1850–1939*, London: Routledge, 1988.

with association policy, a breakdown of consensus, membership haemorrhage and some undermining of employer solidarity. Some organisations
controlled breakaways more effectively than others. However, already in
the 1930s, it is possible to discern a diminution in the effectiveness of
employers' organisations, particularly their ability to regulate the labour
market. The initiative in industrial relations strategy began to drift notice-
ably back to the individual firm, a trend which was to be consolidated
after the Second World War.[11]

The conclusion will review the findings from north-west England and
draw together the various lines of enquiry pursued through the text, commenting on continuity, changing patterns and the determinants of
employers' organisation and multi-employer labour relations policies
prior to the Second World War. It will be argued that the period *c.*
1880–1920 witnessed the emergence of a complex network of employers'
organisations, stimulated by a triumvirate of external pressures from a
more competitive marketplace, an increasingly interventionist government, and a rapidly growing and increasingly militant labour movement.
These organisations accommodated themselves to the emergence of mass
unionism and, whilst wracked by internal divisions, nevertheless came to
play a pivotal role in the development of the British industrial relations
system and in defending employers' interests. My interpretation of the
strength, cohesion, power and influence of British employers' organisations differs significantly from that promulgated by some recent 'revisionist' historians of industrial relations, who have emphasised the weakness,
disunity and strategic impotence of such institutions.[12] The grounds for
arriving at such a view are expounded in the following pages of this book.

[11] See the *Report of the Royal Commission on Trade Unions and Employers' Associations, 1965–68*,
Cmnd 3623, London: HMSO, 1968.
[12] See the next chapter for a review of this literature.

Part 1

Setting the scene

1 Context and historiography

This chapter has two parts. The first aims to set the conceptual context for the text that follows, outlining what employers' associations are and what they do, briefly reviewing prevailing theories of employer organisation and behaviour, and the historiography of this topic. This will construct a framework of reference which will be returned to and fleshed out as key themes are interwoven within the text. The second section will narrow the focus to the geographical region of north-west England, providing some background information on the three industries chosen for intensive investigation: cotton manufacturing, engineering and building. Those readers who are familiar with this material might like to proceed directly to the next chapter. I start with some comments upon the nature of nineteenth-century British capitalism; the soil from which employers' organisations emerged.

Employers' organisations

As British industrialisation proceeded through the eighteenth and into the nineteenth centuries the dominant social figure was the aspiring capitalist entrepreneur: fiercely independent, individualistic and unequivocally committed to notions of unfettered free market competition. Within Victorian society private provision of capital was widely regarded as an act which conferred sacrosanct rights upon employers. Central to such prerogatives was the right to employ whom they thought fit, under terms of labour contract unilaterally determined by themselves, with the freedom to manage this labour without external interference or constraint. Such autonomy was deemed a fundamental prerequisite for the successful, profitable prosecution of a business. In reality, however, such control was rather more diffuse, and managerial prerogative could be interpreted in a wide variety of ways.[1] Many industrialists chose (or at least tolerated) a

[1] See A. McKinlay and J. Zeitlin, 'The meanings of managerial prerogative: industrial relations and the organisation of work in British engineering, 1880–1939', in C. Harvey and J. Turner (eds.), *Labour and Business in Modern Britain*, London: Frank Cass, 1989, pp. 32–47.

system whereby labour management was delegated to subcontractors and to craftworkers, enabling the latter workers to maintain a very high degree of discretionary power over their labour process.[2] This was the situation in engineering, shipbuilding, coal-mining, iron and steel, building, sections of textile manufacture and a whole range of other crafts. In the mill districts of northern England, as Joyce has demonstrated, older traditions of paternalism also survived into the mid-Victorian era, which worked to inculcate loyalty to the capitalist firm – and to the owner providing the largesse.[3] Whatever the prevailing control mechanism – authoritarian, delegated or paternalist – industrial relations were usually atomised, confined predominantly to the level of the company. Capital–labour relations were also relatively stable in the mid-Victorian period, c. 1850–80, at least compared to the prevailing scenario before and after.

This characteristic mode of nineteenth-century British capitalism – based upon relatively small-scale, family-owned private enterprise, free market competition, autocratic and paternalist labour control mechanisms, significant craft autonomy, decentralised industrial relations and limited but growing product markets providing (for the most part) secure profitability – faced a major challenge in the last quarter of the nineteenth century. The extension of international competition as other major nations industrialised created a much more hostile product market and a tightening squeeze on profits. The intensification of competition in the marketplace in the later nineteenth century coincided with other threats to the profitability of British capital. These were the implantation of a sustained trade union presence, both amongst and, for the first time, beyond the craftworkers (itself a product partly of tightening labour markets and a reaction to employer cost-cutting during the depression years of the 1870s and 1880s), the emergence of socialist political parties challenging the very concept of private ownership and a more openly interventionist (and accountable) state concerned primarily to maintain industrial efficiency and social stability, even if the achievement of the latter meant imposing additional costs upon capitalist enterprise.

The accumulation of such developments triggered a quite fundamental change in the attitudes of British industrialists, though the pace of such change varied significantly by sector and region commensurate with the varying intensity of external pressures. Employers increasingly eschewed individualism and sought solace and protection in collaboration. This took many forms, including company merger, amalgamation, the

---

[2] H. Gospel, 'Managerial structure and strategies: an introduction', in H.F. Gospel and C.R. Littler (eds.), *Managerial Strategies and Industrial Relations*, Aldershot: Gower, 1983, pp. 6–9; R. Price, *Masters, Unions and Men*, Cambridge: Cambridge University Press, 1980, pp. 55–93.
[3] See P. Joyce, *Work, Society and Politics*, new edition, London: Methuen, 1982.

formation of trade associations, chambers of commerce, cartels, specialist 'free labour' and political propaganda agencies functioning to propagate capitalist ideology (such as the Anti-Socialist Union and the Liberty and Property Defence League). Arguably, however, the industrial employers' organisations which proliferated in the late nineteenth century were the most significant of such institutions. Until the inter-war years, British companies remained relatively fragmented and small in scale. However, the level of associational activity was considerable. By the early 1920s there existed some 2,500 employers' associations and multi-employer agreements with trade unions covered more than half of Britain's working population.[4] The American Marxist Harry Braverman has postulated a transition towards *monopoly* capital.[5] In the British context, from the late nineteenth century to the Second World War, there was significant concentration within industry.[6] However, it would be equally if not more appropriate to talk in terms of the emergence of *organised* capital. Chapter 3 explores such organisational developments in more detail.

Before we consider the historiography, a working definition of employers' organisation is necessary. In essence, such bodies operated as employers' trade unions, representing, as best they could, the collective interests of capital. This involved creating, through representation of employers' interests within the political, ideological, social, economic and industrial relations spheres, an environment conducive to the maximisation of profit, hence ensuring an adequate return upon and the further accumulation of capital. Their actual form and structure defies generalisation – employers' organisations varied enormously in function, representativeness and power. In this respect they share the complexity of workers' collective organisations, operating at numerous levels: local, national, inter-industrial, political, ideological and the purely economic. However, the industry federations and their constituent local associations were the backbone of British employers' associations, and it is at this level where most of the real power and initiative lay prior to the First World War. Within this strand of collective activity considerable diversity in form and strategy also existed. A characteristic feature of these organisations, however, was the combination of industrial relations functions – intervening to regulate the labour contract and labour markets – with trade regulation and political activities. This was true, as I hope to demonstrate later, even for the EEF, an organisation which purported to be solely concerned with industrial relations. In any event, what is evident is that by the 1920s a formidable matrix of organised activity was firmly in place.

[4] Gospel, *Markets*, p. 84.
[5] H. Braverman, *Labor and Monopoly Capital*, New York: Monthly Review Press, 1974.
[6] See L. Hannah, *The Rise of the Corporate Economy*, London: Methuen, 1976.

Contrary to the views of some recent commentators, this effectively constituted an employers' movement, in the sense that such institutions
either implicitly or explicitly pursued an ideological crusade for free
enterprise capitalism, at the core of which was the campaign to preserve
managerial prerogatives and control in the workplace.[7]

The close relationship between employers' associations and trade unions
forms a central argument within the text that follows. However, employers'
organisations differed fundamentally from workers' organisations in one
very important respect. Individual companies already represent an aggregation of capital – a significant power base – and hence the intrinsic need for
collective organisation is diluted. In other words, it was somewhat more critical for workers to organise collectively to protect and advance their interests than employers. There was, therefore, a fundamental difference in
commitment to their collective institutions on the part of capital and labour.
The competitive relationship between employers undoubtedly made collaboration a rather difficult proposition. Thus industrialists required considerable pressure applied from external forces to act as a flux, facilitating
combination. The rules and regulations of employers' associations provide
some clues to the direction from which such cementing pressures
emanated, namely trade unions, politics and, in some cases, the market. Our
concern here is predominantly with the first of these, though in reality it is
difficult to divorce these related concerns. The major preoccupation of this
book is to analyse how employers in one particular region reacted to the
implantation and growth of trade unionism – how capital attempted to neutralise, or at least contain, the challenge of organised labour.

The real significance of employers' organisations lies in the way their
emergence fundamentally altered the nature of the labour contract, cus-
tomarily struck between individual master and worker, thus significantly
bolstering employers' power within the labour market. Frequently,
employers formed and joined organisations when they perceived their
ability to dominate the labour contract being undermined by the introduction of trade unionism in their workplace, or, alternatively, where the
labour contract was deemed to require renegotiation. This could occur as a
consequence of product market pressures, adversely affecting profitability,
or state intervention in working conditions which added significantly to
employers' costs and threatened profit margins. Patrick Joyce has
persuasively argued that the last two decades of the nineteenth century

---

[7] For the argument that at the peak level an 'employers' movement' existed see T. Rodgers,
'Employers' organisations, unemployment and social politics in Britain during the inter-
war period', *Social History*, 13, no. 3 (1988), p. 316. For the alternative view, see H. Phelps-
Brown, *The Origins of Trade Union Power*, 2nd edition, Oxford: Oxford University Press,
1986, pp. 102–34.

were a transitional period in English textile manufacturing between a phase characterised by individual contract bargaining between paternalist individual millowners and their employees, and a more collectivist, institutionalised phase of industrial relations.[8] This study really takes up where Joyce left off, exploring the collectively formulated labour relations strategies of northern employers from the late nineteenth century to 1939.

How did employers benefit from association? I hope that I can demonstrate in what follows that collectivism strengthened the employers' hands within the labour market, during both the peaks and troughs of the trade cycle. It is hardly by chance that a major spurt in employer organisation occurred in the late nineteenth century at just the point when a dwindling supply of labour into urban areas coincided with relatively heavy demand, thus increasing the potential value of such labour, and hence the cost to employers.[9] In such circumstances, organisation provided a vital defensive bulwark, particularly important because most employers failed to develop internal labour markets and remained wedded to neo-classical conceptions of the labour market.[10] Through organisation, individual employers gained access to associations' sophisticated strikebreaking and victimisation machinery which could be exploited to undermine industrial militancy during tight labour markets, restrict labour mobility and keep activists from the shop-floor. Moreover, tapping into the organisations' formal collective bargaining and disputes machinery also brought tangible benefits, choking off spontaneous industrial action and stabilising industrial relations (discussed in chapter 5). However, what needs to be recognised is that this delegation of the labour contract from the company to the association occurred in most cases only within a limited, though important, range of elements, notably basic wages and working hours. For employers, this provided the potential advantage of stabilised labour costs over a set period and a prescribed geographical region. It also took wages out of competition, controlling both the poaching of labour in tight labour markets and 'unfair' undercutting employers.

Collective bargaining, however, was conceded at a price. Joint regulation of prescribed elements of the labour contract was negotiated by employers as a quid pro quo for trade union acceptance of managerial rights to organise work at the point of production without trade union interference. This maintenance of sacrosanct managerial rights became a key strategy of employers' organisations, though it was emphasised publicly rather more vocally by some organisations (e.g. engineering) than

---

[8] Joyce, *Work, Society and Politics*, pp. 336–40.
[9] Derek Matthews, '1889 and all that: new views on the new unionism', *International Review of Social History* (hereafter cited as *IRSH*), 36, no. 1 (1991), pp. 43–51.
[10] Littler, 'A comparative analysis of managerial structures and strategies', p. 93.

others (e.g. building). The aim here was to keep trade unions firmly out of the workplace by prescribed collective bargaining on a limited range of issues on the employers' terms and to contain labour militancy by the formulation of stage-by-stage disputes procedures. By 1920, this, in essence, was the primary industrial relations remit of most British employers' associations – retaining control through procedural, and, to a rather lesser extent, substantive agreements. Employers' organisations thus strove to provide an environment conducive to profitability, adapting their policies to changing circumstances, notably the permanent presence of strong trade unions, a more hostile product market, an increasingly interventionist state, the disruption of war and violent fluctuations in labour markets and economic fortunes, particularly during 1910 to 1939. Initially, across many industries, this entailed the pursuit of autocratic policies designed to break strikes forcibly and extirpate trade unions. Gradually, however, this pattern altered and organised employer policy was reorientated to accommodate and work with trade unions. This process was most evident over the decade 1910–20, and, despite a concerted employers' counter-attack during the Depression, was sustained thereafter. The role played by employers' organisations in this quite fundamental transition is a key theme and will be explored further in subsequent chapters.

The relationship between organised capital and the state merits a brief comment at this stage. Increasing government involvement at a local and national level in social, economic and industrial matters clashed head on with a business ethos which stressed the prerogative of capital alone to make decisions which affected profitability. The Conciliation Act (1896), Workmen's Compensation Acts (1897; 1906), the Trade Disputes Act (1906), National Insurance (1911), Trade Boards (1909), Labour Exchanges (1909) and legal regulation of working hours and minimum wages in coal-mining (1908–12) are all examples of state encroachment into labour markets and the labour contract. The success of these elements of the trade union / social reform agenda were powerful stimulants upon individual employers to organise and provide a counterpoise. A clear lead from the state in promoting collective bargaining from the early 1890s undoubtedly also curtailed the options of employers, undermining the more coercive and authoritarian responses to strikes that characterised earlier years.[11]

The influence that organised capital attained in the corridors of political power in the twentieth century has been the subject of quite intense debate. Some commentators postulate that the state consists of an amalgam of interests and reject any inordinate influence for business

---

[11] McIvor, 'Strikebreaking'; S. Tolliday and J. Zeitlin, 'National models and international variations in labour management and employer organisation', in Tolliday and Zeitlin, *The Power to Manage?*, pp. 300–1.

(organised or unorganised) in the political sphere.[12] Other scholars have argued a more explicitly corporatist line, elevating both trade unions and employers' organisations to extra-parliamentary governing bodies, 'estates of the realm', with the government acting as a neutral and honest broker between these factions to assure social stability.[13] Marxists regard the state as a reflection of dominant economic interests, with businessmen calling the tune.[14] Given my regional perspective, I am not directly concerned here with organised capital in Westminster politics, nor the broader issue of how the state was governed. Such issues merit separate and intensive investigation.[15] However, I hope to sustain the argument that employers' organisations could influence policy, primarily through active involvement in the implementation process on the factory floor. Organised employer action could subvert the aims of legislation – for example Factory and Workmen's Compensation legislation[16] – whilst formal state intervention in labour markets could provide employers with additional leverage, neutralising the dominance of skilled, well-unionised groups of workers. The creation of labour exchanges from 1909 provided employers with an alternative mode of recruiting labour, bypassing skilled subcontractors such as the cotton spinners and the overlookers. Savage has demonstrated the importance of such developments and the ways in which some employer organisations in north Lancashire exploited state regulation of employment to undermine their reliance upon powerful clusters of craftworkers.[17]

Product and labour markets affected the relative power of organised capital and critically influenced the formulation of employers' labour management strategies. Howard Gospel has argued this case consistently and developed the most sophisticated models for understanding and

[12] See, for example, J. Turner (ed.), *Businessmen and Politics: Studies of Business Activity in British Politics, 1900–1945*, London: Heinemann, 1984; R. Lowe, 'The government and industrial relations, 1919–39', in C.J. Wrigley, *A History of British Industrial Relations*, vol. II, pp. 185–210. Richard Price, writing from a Marxist perspective, also subscribes to the view that organised capital was intrinsically weak in economic and political decision-making in Britain (though not in the struggle over work control). See R. Price, *Labour in British Society*, London: Croom Helm, 1986, pp. 210–11.

[13] K. Middlemas developed these ideas in *Politics in Industrial Society*, London: André Deutsch, 1979. See also G.R. Rubin, *War, Law and Labour*, Oxford: Clarendon Press, 1987.

[14] See, for example, Burgess, *Origins*; K. Burgess, *The Challenge of Labour*, London: Croom Helm, 1980.

[15] A recent detailed study of wool textile employers suggests that organised capital was far more important in the process of government than previous accounts have recognised. See I. Magrath, 'Wool textile employers' organisations: Bradford c. 1914–1945' (Ph.D. thesis, University of Hull, 1991).

[16] See P. Bartrip and S. Burman, *The Wounded Soldiers of Industry, 1833–1897*, Oxford: Oxford University Press, 1983, pp. 190–214; A.J. McIvor, 'Work and health, 1880–1914', *Scottish Labour History Society Journal*, 24 (1989), pp. 47–67.

[17] M. Savage, *The Dynamics of Working Class Politics*, Cambridge: Cambridge University Press, 1987, pp. 89–90.

conceptualising the interactions between employer strategy and markets.[18] Gospel adapts the theories of Alfred Chandler, arguing that Britain's characteristic nineteenth-century pattern of heterogeneous and fragmented product markets for manufactured goods facilitated entry and consolidated a pattern of large numbers of relatively small firms and a high degree of competition, and perpetuated family ownership. Overstocked labour markets also retarded technological innovation and the development of more sophisticated internal labour management systems, as occurred in the USA, Germany and Japan. Lacking resources and organisational structures, British firms were thus more likely to delegate labour management externally, to employers' associations whose ability to effectively regulate the labour contract and labour markets was critically influenced by the relative homogeneity or heterogeneity of the industry's product markets.

This is a sophisticated and persuasive model which goes a long way to explaining labour management policies. In the Lancashire context, differences in product market structures made the construction of consensus policies much more difficult in the engineering sector than in the much more homogeneous (in terms of technology and markets) building construction sector. The cotton industry lay somewhere between these two, with important product and process divisions, though there was much technological convergence and product specialism within particular towns (see next section, pp. 28–9).

Whilst I wish to avoid an overly deterministic approach, the evidence for Lancashire nevertheless clearly indicates that product market developments were a primary determinant of employer cohesion/division and multi-employer labour relations strategies and will thus figure significantly in the discussion that follows. My argument here merits further clarification. Four points are worth making. First, employer organisation and regulation of labour markets prior to the Second World War were undermined to a lesser or greater degree by the competitive relationship which existed between employers and the characteristic heterogeneity of British product markets. The latter have been the most significant centrifugal forces operating to undermine collective action amongst employers. This fragmenting tendency of markets and competition was overcome to a degree between *c.* 1880 and 1920, however, by the existence of other powerful cementing forces – notably trade union implantation and growth and encroaching state intervention in industrial relations. Conversely, dilution of both the latter forces led directly to a significant atomisation of industrial relations in the inter-war years. Secondly, employers' organisations thrive where a considerable number of competing units

[18] Gospel, *Markets*, pp. 1–36.

operate in relatively homogeneous product markets and rely on external labour markets. The cotton, coal and building industries are good examples. Thirdly, general shifts in labour and product market circumstances influence the power balance between capital and labour, determining, to a large degree, fluctuations between offensive and defensive strategic modes and the ability of employers' associations to defend successfully employers' prerogative to manage and keep trade unions out of the workplace. Fourthly, the growing importance over time of large companies, dominating particular product markets, with well-developed internal management structures and increasingly reliant upon internal labour markets, undermined employers' organisation and the prosecution of consensus labour relations policies. This part of the Chandler equation certainly has relevance in consideration of multi-employer solidarity and strategies. As markets became more standardised and firms became more concentrated and specialised, the need for strong collective organisations to regulate relationships with trade unions and bargain collectively over the labour contract dwindled. Centrifugal rather than centripetal tendencies were already discernible, in north-west England and elsewhere, prior to the Second World War. Thereafter, the decline of multi-employer regulation and atomisation of industrial relations accelerated markedly, as the Donovan Report documented in the mid/late 1960s.[19]

The argument developed below is that collectively formulated labour containment policies worked relatively well in the 1890s and 1900s, but floundered when labour markets tightened between c. 1910 and 1920, despite the development of state labour market regulation. The period immediately following the First World War represented the historical peak of employers' association influence. Product and labour market circumstances during the 1920s provided employers with the power to regain the initiative, neutralise the wartime campaign for an extension of workers' control, re-establish their authority and substantially cut labour costs. However, there were limits to the employers' counter-attack, with organised capital drawing back from an all-out offensive and a thoroughgoing transformation of the division of labour in the basic sectors. Most preferred to accommodate trade unionism in the later 1920s and the 1930s, rather than rooting it out. The role played by employers' associations during this period was a significant one and has been neglected within the literature. Whilst employers' organisations in north-west England spearheaded the drive to cut labour costs and recreate employers' authority on the shop-floor in the 1920s as the depression deepened, they

[19] See the *Report of the Royal Commission on Trade Unions and Employers' Associations*, pp. 196–202.

were also invariably the voices of reason and restraint. The task in hand was rarely articulated as the rooting out of trade unionism. Rather, the aim was to bolster moderate trade unionism and preserve the institution of collective bargaining, forging a more permanent accommodation with organised labour as a buffer against syndicalist militancy and socialist ideas.

This is not to suggest, however, that employers' organisations were omnipotent and monolithic entities. Pluralist theory suggests that employer organisations simply aggregate the interests of their constituent members. However, it cannot be assumed that the interests of individual employers and fractions of capital within employer coalitions necessarily or always converge – except perhaps at the very broadest level, i.e. the desire to maximise profits. Strategies to achieve profit maximisation and exert control over labour differ significantly. Many employers preferred the individual as opposed to the collective approach and simply refused to join associations. Hence, there coexisted, often with some tension, an organised and an unorganised segment of capital. Whilst the latter was growing, particularly in mining and manufacturing, prior to the First World War unorganised employers were undoubtedly the majority within the British economy. In essence, employers' organisations represented coalitions of interests, sometimes in broad agreement, sometimes in conflict. The competitive relationship and individualist ethos, combined with the heterogeneity of business structures provided significant restraints, made collective organisation amongst employers and the forging of a consensus strategy invariably difficult. In the north-west, divergent product market experience both between and within industries was probably the single most divisive factor undermining effective employer solidarity. However, this was less of a problem before the First World War than after, and less significant at the local/regional level than at the national level. Because of geographical specialisation, local associations and regional federations had a smaller range of divergent tendencies to reconcile. It follows that lack of centralisation – on the Swedish model for example – does not necessarily imply lack of power and influence.[20] Moreover, as Magrath and Bullen have demonstrated, British employers' organisations operated with a great deal of flexibility and pragmatism in order to reconcile conflicting interests.[21]

Collective organisation has to be seen to be in the economic interests of the constituent parties, otherwise solidarity will be fragile and associative

---

[20] For a detailed international comparative analysis of employer organisation and strategies see Tolliday and Zeitlin, 'National models', pp. 296–322.

[21] A. Bullen, 'Pragmatism vs. principle: cotton employers and the origins of an industrial relations system', in J.A. Jowitt and A.J. McIvor (eds.), *Employers and Labour*, pp. 27–43; I. Magrath, 'Protecting the interests of the trade: wool textile employers' organisations in the 1920s', in Jowitt and McIvor (eds.), *Employers and Labour*, pp. 44–63. See also Magrath, 'Wool textile employers' organisations'.

activity transitory. What might be termed the traditional deterministic view – held by Marxists and non-Marxists alike – argues that market forces prompted employer organisation and moulded collective strategies. Such views invariably emphasise the central role that employers' organisations have played in British industrial relations and see employers' organisations as an expression of class interests. Recently, a strand of revisionist historians have criticised this as overly deterministic, suggesting that employer policy was the product not just of external forces but of internal political processes. Employer organisations, according to this interpretation, were at least partially autonomous active agencies, formulating policy (rather than blindly reflecting market forces or other external pressures) and making 'strategic choices'.[22] Hence, similar external constraints produced a range of responses, not one given, predetermined strategy. I would not substantially argue with this aspect of the revisionist case. Indeed, the empirical evidence from north-west England suggests that employers' organisations developed their own internal dynamic and could formulate collective policies which appear contradictory in the light of market developments. This is evident, for example, in the markedly different responses of cotton employers in north and south Lancashire to the industrial relations crisis of 1910–14 and in the quite considerable (and ultimately decisive) pressure generated within employers' organisations to sustain collective bargaining during the inter-war years.

Employer organisation and labour management strategies are themes which have thus attracted the attention of a number of scholars, most of whom have tackled such issues from the perspective of the central federations of employers, though there have been some limited but revealing local studies.[23] The existing literature incorporates quite a wide range of

---

[22] S. Tolliday and J. Zeitlin, 'Employers and industrial relations between theory and history', in Tolliday and Zeitlin, The Power to Manage?, pp. 18–22; Zeitlin, 'Internal politics', pp. 52–76.

[23] See W.R. Garside and H. Gospel, 'Employers and managers', in C.J. Wrigley (ed.), A History of British Industrial Relations, 1875–1914, Brighton: Harvester, 1982; H. Gospel, 'Employers and managers', in Wrigley (ed.), A History of British Industrial Relations, vol. II; J. Zeitlin, 'The labour strategies of British engineering employers, 1890–1922', in Gospel and Littler (eds.), Managerial Strategies; Tolliday and Zeitlin (eds.), Power to Manage?; Phelps-Brown, Origins, pp. 102–34; Jowitt and McIvor (eds.), Employers and Labour; J.A. McKenna and R.G. Rodger, 'Control by coercion: employers' associations and the establishment of industrial order in the building industry of England and Wales, 1860–1914', Business History Review, 59, no. 2 (1985), pp. 203–31; A. Yarmie, 'Employers' organisations in mid-Victorian England', IRSH, 25 (1980), pp. 209–34; R. Bean, 'Employers' associations in the port of Liverpool, 1890–1914', IRSH, 21 (1976), pp. 358–76; J.C. Lovell, 'Collective bargaining and the emergence of national employer organisation in the British shipbuilding industry', IRSH, 36 (1991), pp. 59–91. Two very valuable unpublished theses are H. Gospel, 'Employers' organisations: their growth and function in the British system of industrial relations in the period 1918–1939' (Ph.D. thesis, London School of Economics, 1974) and I. Magrath, 'Wool textile employers' organisations'.

views and perspectives on employer organisation. One of the first texts to pay particular attention to the part played by employers' organisations in industrial relations was Clegg, Fox and Thompson's *A History of British Trade Unions since 1889*, vol. 1: *1889–1910* (1964). This account, together with several subsequent studies from markedly different perspectives, including the work of Burgess, Wigham, and Gospel, stressed the effectiveness of employers' associations and the important role they played in British industrial relations prior to the Second World War.[24] Rodgers has recently analysed the political activities of the National Confederation of Employers' Organisations (NCEO), arguing that between the wars the NCEO was 'one of the formative agents in modern British social policy'.[25] Richard Price has postulated in *Masters, Unions and Men* (1980) that powerful local employers' organisations in the building industry played a key role in undermining autonomous craft regulation, creating a niche for employers who contained labour costs and exerted control over work through joint regulation of the labour market by the late nineteenth century. Recently, in one of the most detailed and perceptive investigations of employer organisation within one industry, Magrath has convincingly demonstrated how 'wool textile employers enjoyed a degree of influence in British society which was out of proportion to their size'.[26] I have also argued elsewhere for the strategic importance of employers' organisations in strikebreaking in the late nineteenth century and in the dissemination of pro-capitalist political propaganda between the wars.[27] Middlemas possibly represents the extreme view of this positive interpretation, arguing that both employers' associations and trade unions were pivotal institutions within British society, incorporated by the state from the First World War into decision-making, thus creating a sort of equilibrium in social relations until the 1960s.[28]

Other commentators have emphasised the impotency of British employers' associations, the persistence of disunity between capitalists, fragmentation and fractured collective consciousness. Many of the most recent studies have been articulated in terms of the adverse impact of British industrial relations institutions upon economic performance. The argument essentially is that British competitiveness has been weakened

---

[24] Burgess, *Origins*; Gospel, 'Employers and managers'; Wigham, *The Power to Manage*.
[25] Rodgers, 'Employers' organizations', p. 341.
[26] Magrath, 'Wool textile employers' organisations', p. 390.
[27] See A. McIvor, 'Employers' organisations and strikebreaking in Britain, 1880–1914', *IRSH*, 29 (1984), pp. 1–33; McIvor, 'A crusade for capitalism'; A. McIvor and H. Paterson, 'Combating the left: victimisation and anti-labour activities on Clydeside, 1900–1939', in R. Duncan and A. McIvor (eds.), *Militant Workers: Labour and Class Conflict on the Clyde, 1900–1950*, Edinburgh: John Donald, 1992, pp. 129–54.
[28] See K. Middlemas, *Politics in Industrial Society*.

by a tradition of powerful craft trade unions facing divided and prevari-
cating employers' organisations. The scenario which emerges through the
work of Tolliday and Zeitlin, Reid, Bean, and Phelps-Brown is of weak,
ineffective employers' associations which were unable, except at brief
moments of crisis, to develop a consensus labour relations strategy
because of the diversity of product market experience, widely differing
attitudes to trade unionism, variations in company size and structure,
inter-firm competition and rivalry, and an individualist ethos promulgated by the persistence of the family firm, which, according to one
commentator, 'fostered an inward looking attitude'.[29] Employer combinations in Britain thus lacked centralised control and authority over their
members. Jonathan Zeitlin has been perhaps the foremost flagbearer for
this revisionism, commenting in a historiographical article in the
Economic History Review: 'Employers' associations in Britain typically
lacked the internal coherence and capacity for sustained offensive action
of their German, Scandinavian and American counterparts, whether at
the peak or the industrial level . . . British employers were rarely willing to
subordinate their individual autonomy to the demands of collective
action on a long-term basis.'[30] This interpretation is pursued further in
the recently published collection of essays by Steve Tolliday and Jonathan
Zeitlin, *The Power to Manage?* (1991). This book constitutes perhaps the
most comprehensive scholarly attack to date on the concept of a converg-
ing trend in industrial relations patterns across developed capitalist countries. The historical record, Tolliday and Zeitlin argue, confirms no
unilinear trajectories, but rather a wide variety of experience and divergent patterns in labour management and employer organisation both
through time and across the national boundaries of developed capitalist
nations. This scenario was the consequence, the authors suggest, of
employer behaviour being determined not solely by the vagaries of
markets and technology; nor was it the product of prevailing industrial
structure and national culture. Rather, divergent patterns existed because
of unique historical contingencies and because management, employers
and their organisations exercised conscious choice over strategy, albeit
influenced by structural factors and, most significantly, by the actions of
two key 'interlocutors' – the state and the trade unions. The notion and
dynamics of class, Tolliday and Zeitlin imply, have very little relevance as
explanatory tools. British employers, they assert, have failed to exert
direct control over the labour process, failed to develop sophisticated

[29] Phelps-Brown, *Origins*, p. 113. See also Tolliday and Zeitlin, 'National models'; Bean,
'Employers' associations in the port of Liverpool'; A. Reid, 'Employers' strategies'.
[30] J. Zeitlin, 'From labour history to the history of industrial relations', *Economic History
Review*, 40, no. 2 (1987), p. 175.

supervisory and managerial hierarchies and failed to construct powerful and effective employers' organisations to articulate their class interests. Class identities were not well developed amongst British industrial capitalists.

This revisionism is a necessary corrective to invalid, rather abstract and overly deterministic theoretical models and, especially, the conception of a monolithic and omnipotent employer class – as portrayed, for example, in Harry Braverman's *Labor and Monopoly Capital* (1974). However, a recognition of divisions of interest and sectional fragmentation within industrial capitalism should not necessarily imply a virtual rejection of the validity of class as an explanatory concept altogether, or prompt the virtual dismissal of organised capital as a force in British industrial relations. In this respect I think the revisionist interpretation rather oversteps the mark, exaggerating the weakness and disunity of British employers' organisations, presenting, in my view, an overly sanitised, negative view of such bodies. This is predominantly because such accounts concentrate upon the relationship between employers and their skilled, well-organised workers and because this interpretation has been too narrowly focused on the issue of economic performance. This has obscured a broader and more rounded analysis of the aims, activities, genesis and functions of employers' organisations. My own interpretation, which will be fleshed out in the pages that follow, is a significantly more positive one, stressing the pivotal role played by employers' organisations, in pursuit of class interests, within industrial relations and society. This conclusion has been arrived at as the consequence of close investigation of the prevailing situation within three industries – cotton, engineering and building – within the geographical region of north-west England. The next section briefly outlines the economic development of these industries within Lancashire, providing the necessary context to inform an evaluation of the genesis and effectiveness of employers' organisations and the labour relations strategies they formulated in the period 1880–1939.

Lancashire: cotton, engineering and building

Lancashire and cotton are virtually synonymous; indeed, British cotton manufacture was increasingly concentrated in the county in the nineteenth century. First in the domestic system and then in mechanised factory production, the early textile entrepreneurs felt their way towards industrial organisation and production and in so doing created a distinctive pattern of life with the mills physically dominating their communities and the millowners' control extending deep into the texture of everyday life.[31] Cotton towns witnessed quite spectacular growth in the nineteenth century. Oldham, for example, expanded from a community of some 10,000 inhabitants with 12 mills in 1794 to a large industrial town of around 80,000 inhabitants by 1866 with more than 120 cotton spinning mills.[32] By the mid-nineteenth century the industry was approaching maturity, in the sense that its main phase of technological change and innovation had been achieved. At this point around 300,000 found employment in the industry.[33] Growth in output and employment continued thereafter, characterised by multiplication of the well-established technological base and consolidation of the division of labour. Spinning by the mule, with an all-male work team of one minder and two helpers (piecers), and weaving by the power loom (with an average of four looms per weaver) characterised the industry in England. The newer, more capital-intensive methods of ring spinning (operated by women) and automatic loom weaving (with a potential staffing ratio of 20–30 looms per weaver) were practically unknown in Lancashire, though common enough elsewhere by 1900.[34] Ironically, the giant textile machinery manufacturing firm of Platts in Oldham produced this more efficient cotton spinning and weaving technology, but its markets were almost exclusively abroad.[35]

In the decade 1910–20 the industry reached its historic peak in terms of output, numbers employed and machine capacity. The annual consumption of raw cotton multiplied almost fourfold between 1850 and 1913, whilst over the same period the production of woven cotton cloth increased sixfold. The 1907 Census of Production recorded a total of 1.25

[31] For recent overviews of the structure of the industry and the industrial relations background see P. Joyce, *Work, Society and Politics*; Jowitt and McIvor (eds.), *Employers and Labour*; A. Fowler and T. Wyke (eds.), *The Barefoot Aristocrats*, Littleborough: George Kelsall, 1987; J.K. Walton, *Lancashire: A Social History, 1558–1939*, Manchester: Manchester University Press, 1987. The significant outpost of the cotton industry in Scotland collapsed to a rump based around thread manufacture by 1914. Recent studies include W.W. Knox, *Hanging by a Thread: The Scottish Cotton Industry, c. 1850–1914*, Preston: Carnegie, 1995; P. Bolin-Hort, 'Managerial strategies and worker responses: a new perspective on the decline of the Scottish cotton industry', *Scottish Labour History Society Journal*, 29 (1994), pp. 63–83.
[32] J. Longworth, *The Oldham Master Cotton Spinners' Association*, Oldham: OMCSA, 1966, p. 9.
[33] H.H. Lee, 'The cotton textile industry', in R. Church (ed.), *The Dynamics of Victorian Business*, London: Allen and Unwin, 1980, p. 161; A.E. Musson, *The Growth of British Industry*, London: Batsford, 1978, pp. 202, 207.
[34] The extent to which this relative technological obsolescence has been a factor in the subsequent decline of the industry has been a subject of intense debate. For a recent overview see W. Mass and W. Lazonick, 'The British cotton industry and international competitive advantage: the state of the debates', *Business History*, 32 (1990), pp. 9–65.
[35] R. Kirk and C. Simmons, 'Engineering and the First World War: a case study of the Lancashire cotton spinning machine industry', *Salford Papers in Economics*, 81/5 (1981).

million workers employed in the textile sector, 572,000 in cotton.[36] By 1914, employment in cotton preparation, spinning and weaving peaked at around 650,000, with a further c. 100,000 in the yarn and cloth finishing section. Cotton manufacturing was firmly export-orientated, with dominant product markets in the Far East, notably India. Indeed, 80 per cent of Lancashire-produced cotton cloth was exported on the eve of the First World War.[37]

Until the 1920s the cotton industry in Lancashire increased in scale, product specialisation intensified and a characteristic spatial pattern of development emerged. With the limited liability movement from the 1860s there was a trend towards increased unit size, which saw average numbers employed in cotton mills double between 1850 and 1900. However, in contrast to developments in the USA and Japan the privately owned family-run firm persisted longer in Lancashire, and, indeed, remained important in some areas of the county up to the First World War. Whilst the American textile industry was experiencing a transition towards an oligopolistic situation, with the integration of marketing and manufacturing and the development of large, vertically integrated mills, the cotton industry in Lancashire, consisting of over 2,000 separate and mostly medium-sized mills in 1914, remained characteristically fragmented (by international, not British standards) and specialised.[38]

There were, however, notable structural differences between product sections within the industry. In cotton spinning the joint stock limited company became the dominant type of enterprise by the late nineteenth century, a trend linked to the advancing specialisation in yarn ranges. The transition took place more rapidly in some towns, notably Oldham, than others (for example Bolton). However, by the time of the First World War only around 20 per cent of spinning firms were still privately owned and by 1924 only 10 per cent. In weaving, the limited company mode of organisation developed much more slowly, partly because of a relative lack of specialisation and the custom in the trade of renting loom sheds. In 1911 still half of all weaving enterprises remained privately owned, falling to around 30 per cent by the mid-1920s. Finishing, by contrast,

---

[36] Around 47 per cent of those employed were located in cotton preparation and spinning and around 53 per cent in weaving. In 1914, around 60 per cent of the cotton labour force were women.

[37] B.R. Mitchell and P. Deane, *Abstract of British Historical Statistics*, Cambridge: Cambridge University Press, 1962, pp. 60, 179, 182; J.L. White 'Lancashire cotton textiles', in Wrigley (ed.), *A History of British Industrial Relations, 1875–1914*, p. 210.

[38] See D.A. Farnie and S. Yonekawa, 'The emergence of the large firm in the cotton spinning industries of the world, 1883–1938', *Textile History*, 19 (1988), pp. 171–210; D. Farnie, *The English Cotton Industry and the World Market, 1815–1896*, Oxford: Clarendon Press, 1979, chs. 6–7; Walton, *Lancashire*, pp. 202–5.

was heavily concentrated as a result of combinations forged towards the end of the nineteenth century – the Calico Printers' Association (1898) and the Bleachers' Association (1900) – which dominated their respective segments of the market.[39] Overall, however, there is no doubt that by the First World War the limited liability company dominated the cotton industry.

Whilst product specialisation was never complete, within Lancashire there developed two quite distinctive product regions, with the more capital-intensive yarn spinning taking place in south Lancashire, in the towns surrounding Manchester, and cloth weaving concentrated in the northern Lancashire towns, notably Preston, Blackburn, Burnley, Nelson and Colne. To a degree, particular specialisms characterised towns within these zones. In the spinning region, Bolton and Manchester were the centres for fine spun yarns using mainly Egyptian raw cotton. Oldham mills mostly spun medium and coarse quality yarns from American cotton. Yarns were sold direct to the smaller and generally less capital-intensive north Lancashire weaving mills, which generally bought a mixture of these products to weave into cloth. Preston was a relatively diversified cloth producer, as Savage has shown, though in common with Chorley there was a tendency to produce all grades of fancy, high-quality goods, with an emphasis on the home market.[40] Blackburn concentrated on coarse goods, dhooties and shirtings, destined largely for export to India. Burnley focused on the inexpensive narrower ranges of cloth, whilst Colne and Nelson specialised in coloured goods. Finishing the cloth – bleaching and dyeing – was also a quite separate and distinct process predominantly located in Manchester and Bolton. This heterogeneity had important implications, as the 1928 textile industries survey noted: 'It is obviously possible for diverse conditions to exist simultaneously in the several sections and for severe depression in one or more sections to co-exist with a much more favourable situation in others.'[41] This differentiation had a significant impact on employer organisation development and policy-making, perpetuating a sectional rather than an industrial form of organisation.

As the cotton industry was a pace-setter in the process of industrialisation, so in the twentieth century it has also been in the forefront of the process of deindustrialisation. Industrial decline characterised the years after the First World War. The drop in world demand for cloth and the generally depressed trading conditions of the inter-war years hit the export-orientated cotton textile manufacturing industry particularly

[39] Committee on Industry and Trade, *Survey of Textile Industries*, London: HMSO, 1928, pp. 24–6.   [40] Savage, *Dynamics*, pp. 64–9.
[41] Committee on Industry and Trade, *Survey* (1928), p. 16.

Table 1.1 *Employment in Lancashire: major industries, 1881, 1911, 1931*

	1881	1911	1931
Textiles	488,363	573,339	422,712
Building	94,615	118,367	78,407
Engineering	64,619	182,158	189,598
Mechanical	35,564	95,247	66,527
Electrical	251	15,761	40,445
Vehicles	7,879	16,309	36,456
Metal manufacture	61,024	42,833	24,057
Mining and quarrying	76,198	111,171	82,846
Services	189,555	240,477	209,580
Transport and communications	121,803	220,297	174,900
Clothing	99,463	124,033	110,073
Agriculture	57,139	55,278	48,883
Food, drink, tobacco	68,310	36,463	83,041
Distribution	—	214,621	321,677
Total employment	1,636,223	2,330,773	2,153,658

Source: C.H. Lee, *British Regional Employment Statistics, 1841–1971*, Cambridge: Cambridge University Press, 1979.

hard. Britain's proportion of the world's cotton output was falling prior to 1914. After the war, this became an absolute decline, with output levels declining by 1938–9 to under 40 per cent of 1913 figures and cotton cloth exports tumbling to less than 25 per cent of 1913 levels. Contraction ensued, with total machine capacity reduced by scrapping 38 per cent of all installed spindleage and 43 per cent of looms.[42] Official unemployment figures during the worst phase of the recession, 1930–2, topped 45 per cent for cotton and, in all, over a quarter of a million jobs were lost in the cotton industry between the wars.[43] After a brief reprieve, the contraction of the industry, crippled by the flood of cheap Asian imports, gathered pace from 1950 and by the late 1980s less than 40,000 workers found employment in the remaining 203 mills in the British cotton industry.[44] Cotton thus provides a classic example of a declining industry in a

[42] J.H. Porter, 'Cotton and wool textiles', in N.K. Buxton and D.H. Aldcroft, *British Industry between the Wars*, London: Scolar Press, 1979, pp. 29, 44; M.W. Kirby, 'The Lancashire cotton industry in the inter-war years', *Business History*, 16, no. 2 (1974), pp. 145–59; Walton, *Lancashire*, pp. 325–32; J.H. Bamberg, 'Rationalisation of the British cotton industry in the interwar years', *Textile History*, 19 (1988), pp. 83–102.

[43] Board of Trade, *An Industrial Survey of the Lancashire Area*, London: HMSO, 1932, pp. 94–129; Porter, 'Cotton and wool', p. 28.

[44] Figures courtesy of Bob Stott of the Textiles Statistics Bureau, Royal Exchange, Manchester. For more detail see the Bureau's *Quarterly Statistical Review*. On the contraction of cotton since 1945 see J. Singleton, *Lancashire on the Scrap Heap: The Cotton Industry, 1945–70*, Oxford: Oxford University Press, 1991.

post-industrial society. Lancashire has had to adjust painfully to the loss of its staple industry since the First World War.

Cotton was clearly the dominant industry in Lancashire prior to the First World War, but was by no means the sole employer in what was quite a diversified economic region.

Lancashire can crudely be divided up into five major economic zones, all with their distinctive features. Cotton manufacturing was confined to the two zones already referred to: spinning predominated in south Lancashire and weaving in the north and north-east of the county. Other significant employers of labour in these regions were coal, engineering, agriculture and domestic service. Manchester and its environs was dominated by finance and services, was an important engineering centre, had a relatively large building construction sector and some limited cotton manufacturing, notably finishing processes. Merseyside was dominated by the port of Liverpool, which was the major import and export entrepôt for Lancashire cotton and other industries. Liverpool and its satellite Birkenhead were also significant centres of shipbuilding and marine engineering. In the immediate hinterland were important chemical and glass manufacturing centres (Warrington; St Helens). Cotton manufacturing was, however, negligible on Merseyside. Finally, a fifth zone comprised the Fylde coast region, probably the least significant in economic terms. However, this district consisted of a series of fishing ports, a major engineering centre at Barrow-in-Furness and the growing tourist centres of Southport, Morecambe and Blackpool. The development of the latter towns in the late nineteenth and early twentieth centuries provided a heavy demand for building workers, which in turn created some disequilibrium in the region's labour markets.

Engineering in Lancashire initially developed to service the expanding cotton industry, with each town having a significant textile machinery-making sector, producing mules, looms and other machinery for purchase by local millowners. Textile machinery manufacture remained an important Lancashire specialism right up to the Second World War, though over time important changes occurred in the structure of this sector. The older, traditional, smaller family-owned companies found it increasingly difficult to compete with the massively capitalised, joint-stock, mass-production manufacturers, like Platts of Oldham, which came to dominate the production of the mule spinning frame, capturing both internal and export markets.[45] As a consequence, in some areas, for example Preston, the endogenous textile machinery-making sector

---

[45] Walton, *Lancashire*, pp. 206–7. Before the First World War, Platts employed 10,000 and at least four other textile machine-making companies employed over 2,000 each.

atrophied.[46] Elsewhere, as in Burnley and Blackburn, a rump of loom manufacturers survived on the fringes of the industry, relying on lower labour costs, less technological sophistication and traditional ties with neighbouring firms to remain operational. Generally speaking, the textile machinery-making sector remained characterised up to the 1920s by a very high degree of competition between a large number of companies.[47]

Elsewhere in the north-west other product specialisms in engineering emerged. Merseyside evolved into a significant shipbuilding and marine engineering centre. Vickers provided Barrow-in-Furness with a shipyard which dominated the local economy. Within Manchester, the major engineering centre in the region, however, there was much diversification, initially to service the various nascent industries developing within its hinterland, although by the third quarter of the nineteenth century much of this industry was capital goods and export-orientated. At the turn of the nineteenth century, trade directories in Manchester indicate the existence of 325 engineering companies: 161 limited and 164 private firms.[48] These included ironfounders, machine tool manufacturers, locomotive, boiler and engine makers, motor vehicle builders, printing machinery makers, arms manufacturers, pumps, hydraulic, laundry and electrical engineers. However, over time the product emphasis of the area changed markedly. In the late nineteenth century it was the capital goods sector employing large proportions of time-served skilled craftsmen that dominated, with companies such as Nasmyth Wilson and Beyer Peacock (locomotives), Hetheringtons and Brooks and Doxey (textile machinery), Crossley (gas engines), Galloways (boilermakers) and the machine tool makers, such as Craven, Hulse, Muir and Smith and Coventry. Whilst the mechanical engineering sector grew over the period 1880–1920, the really dynamic sectors in north-west England were electrical engineering and vehicle manufacture.

The inter-war recession witnessed significant concentration in engineering and the collapse or merger of many companies, with locomotive manufacture, boilermaking and textile machinery being particularly hard hit. The staple sector of textile machinery manufacturing collapsed, with home demand halved and exports falling at the astonishing rate of 6.2 per cent per annum between 1921 and 1938.[49] By 1939 the total number of engineering firms operating in Manchester had been cut by over half to 156 and limited liability companies outnumbered private companies by a ratio of two to one.[50] However, the newer, more capital-intensive, mass-production, domestic market-orientated engineering firms, employing a large

[46] Savage, *Dynamics*, pp. 68–9.   [47] Gospel, 'Employers' organisations', p. 45.
[48] *Kelly's Trade Directory for Manchester and Salford*, 1899.   [49] Walton, *Lancashire*, p. 332.
[50] *Kelly's Trade Directory for Manchester and Salford*, 1939.

proportion of semi-skilled labour, fared better and dominated the industry by 1939. Witness, for example, the development of electrical engineering on the Trafford Park estate. Seven of the largest ten firms within the Manchester Engineering Employers' Association in 1939 were electrical, motor or aeronautical engineers, including such household names as Ferranti, Metropolitan-Vickers, A.V. Roe, Fairey Aviation, Mather and Platt and Crossley Motors.[51] Throughout the period 1880–1939, roughly half of Lancashire's entire engineering capacity was located in Manchester, so it is not surprising that the city developed as the fulcrum region in terms of wage setting and the formulation of labour relations policies.[52]

Relatively speaking then, engineering in Lancashire was characterised by product and technological diversity, though textile engineering was a dominant specialism up to the First World War. Engineering was also a sector where employers were having to square up to rapid technological innovation (and some more limited organisational change) in the late nineteenth century (in marked contrast to cotton), with the development of new automatic and semi-automatic machine tools and the first echoes of scientific management drifting across the Atlantic in the 1900s.[53] These radical innovations in production methods and labour utilisation, combined with the heterogeneity of what was effectively a cluster of separate and distinct industries, had important implications for industrial relations, for the development of employers' organisation and for the forging of consensus labour relations stategies in engineering.

The building industry, which employed almost 120,000 in Lancashire in 1911, was markedly different from engineering and cotton manufacture in a number of respects. First, there was a much larger number of competing production units, geographically scattered throughout the towns of the region, roughly proportionate to the size of centres of population. In the early 1920s there were something in the region of 12,000–15,000 individual building employers and 50 or so separate and distinct local master builders' associations in Lancashire.[54] Secondly, the average size of building firms (around ten workers per employer) was extremely small by cotton and engineering standards. Sixty per cent of

[51] Manchester EEA, *Journal*, 1897–1953. In 1900 there were only two firms representing these 'new sectors' in membership of the association, both electrical engineers (Ferranti and P.R. Jackson).
[52] EEF, Levy Registers, Annual Subscriptions and Numbers Employed Files.
[53] Burgess, *Origins*, pp. 1–2; Wigham, *Power to Manage*, pp. 29–30; McKinlay and Zeitlin, 'The meanings of managerial prerogative', pp. 34–5.
[54] This is an estimate based upon calculation of the number of building firms in three Lancashire towns, Manchester, Bolton and Preston (2,126), calculated from local trade directories, 1920–2.

the members of the North-West Federation of Building Trade Employers
in 1913 employed less than 7 workers and only 20 building companies in
membership employed more than 100.[55] Thirdly, ease of entry, low
capital requirements, and labour intensiveness characterised the construction industry. Building employers remained dependent to a much
larger extent than did cotton and engineering masters upon the time-
served skills of the well-unionised male craft artisans – the mason, brick-
layer, joiner, plasterer, slater, plumber and painter. Fourthly, the industry
was almost totally dependent upon the domestic market, hence relieved
of pressure upon profitability caused by fluctuations in overseas demand.
Consequently, product market trends in building could be markedly out
of synchronisation with the manufacturing sector. For example, whilst
cotton experienced a relative recession during the 1890s, the building
industry in north-west England was quite buoyant. Demand from housebuilding in the post-war period also delayed the onset of retrenchment in
construction for several years, until the mid-1920s.

Whilst the pace of organisational and technological change in construction was slow in contrast to engineering, this was not a static scenario. The increasing utilisation of prefabricated material – ready-cut
timber, dressed stone and concrete, for example – created points of
potential conflict between masters and men. Within the industry there
were also quite fundamental divisions which affected industrial relations,
not least the relationships between municipalities and the building industry and between the two quite distinctive types of firm in the industry –
the general and the subcontractors. The difficulties inherent in combining
the interests of the latter plagued the master builders' associations in
north-west England. Nor was this a problem that diminished significantly
in importance, at least up to the Second World War. Whilst the average size
(in employment terms) of building firms in Lancashire roughly doubled
between the wars, the evidence for three major towns suggests that the
number of competing general contractors stabilised during these years,
whilst the number of competing subcontractors fell, but only by a relatively marginal 10 per cent or so.[56] The small-scale and highly competitive
nature of this industry continued to be a characteristic feature right up to
(and indeed beyond) the Second World War.

Finally, it is worth making the point that there were tensions between
(and even within) the economic/social zones identified in Lancashire.
Conflicts of interest are evident between north and south Lancashire

[55] NWFBTE, *Yearbook*, June 1914, p. 46.
[56] Figures derived from comparing local trade directories. See *Kelly's Directory of
Manchester*, 1920 and 1939; *Barrett's Directory of Preston*, 1922 and 1940; *Tillotson's
Directory of Bolton*, 1922; *Aubrey's Directory of Lancashire*, 1938.

millowners, and between Merseyside and Manchester/south Lancashire. The interests of industrial capitalists across these areas could and did converge, as for example during the 1897–8 engineering lock-out. However, centrifugal forces coexisted with centripetal ones. This was the result partly of historical economic and social relations and partly of individualistic motives linked to attaining competitive advantage. For example, the minority of north Lancashire spinning mills gained a strategic advantage in not combining with the south Lancashire mills prior to 1914, being able to run their machinery during strikes and lock-outs, thus temporarily benefiting from price rises for yarn caused by an artificial glut in demand. Bitter rivalries developed between Liverpool merchants and Manchester cotton masters, exacerbated by the opening of the Manchester Ship Canal and Manchester's attempt to displace Liverpool as the port of entry for raw cotton. Grim economic and social conditions on Merseyside spawned a more aggressive, volatile labour force, influenced by pre-war syndicalism, which had succeeded in designating the area a relatively high-wage region by 1914. By contrast, the engineering and cotton workers of south Lancashire were more openly economistic and conservative, notably less willing to challenge the hegemony of capital along the lines of their Merseyside counterparts. In south Lancashire this germinated more class-collaborationist social relations. Indeed, one social historian of Lancashire has commented on the way cotton workers absorbed the political economy of their employers before 1914 and how the Lancashire working class as a whole 'was remarkably thoroughly assimilated into the economic and political systems of industrial Lancashire'.[57] On Merseyside industrial relations remained more unstable and employer authority and control more tenuous.[58] Here, however, we are being drawn inexorably into relationships between employers and workers. This is the focus of subsequent chapters, starting with an evaluation of the genesis of organisations of industrial employers in the eighteenth and nineteenth centuries.

[57] Walton, *Lancashire*, pp. 268–9, 283.
[58] See J. Smith, 'Labour tradition in Glasgow and Liverpool', *History Workshop Journal*, 17 (1984), pp. 32–56. For a discussion of regional divergences in social relations see A. Reid, *Social Classes and Social Relations in Britain, 1850–1914*, London: Macmillan, 1992, pp. 60–2.

2   The legacy: origins of employers' associations

Employers' organisations have been around for a very long time, indeed, such organisations pre-dated the industrialisation process in Britain. Adam Smith, in his classic treatise, *The Wealth of Nations* (1776), was amongst the earliest of commentators to identify the existence of semi-clandestine masters' committees. Such combinations, Smith argued, operated across a number of trades and industries, working to regulate product prices, lower wages and control working hours.[1] The master tailors, for example, formed a number of alliances throughout the second half of the eighteenth century, ostensibly to combat industrial action by their workers, who developed (in the London Society of Journeymen Tailors) one of the most militant of eighteenth-century unions. Draconian union-bashing and violent strikebreaking tactics were often resorted to by such combinations. In one dispute in 1764, 23 master tailors imported over 1,000 strikebreakers, including 230 from outside Britain.[2] The master tailors' combination dissolved rapidly after breaking this strike. This pattern of brief, temporary, ephemeral combinations of masters to address specific industrial relations crises characterised the eighteenth and early nineteenth centuries. Rarely, during this period, were employers' associations sustained for any length of time. Presumably, in most instances, individual capitalists could effectively discipline and control their labour force without the necessity for forging wider class alliances.

Nevertheless, the extent of employer organisation, even in this early period, should not be underestimated. As the work of Yarmie, Musson, Coleman and Turner has shown, formal employers' combinations dealing with labour relations existed in the cotton, printing, coal, shipbuilding,

[1] A. Smith, *The Wealth of Nations*, new edition, Harmondsworth: Penguin, 1974, book 1, chapter VIII, p. 169.
[2] C.R. Dobson, *Masters and Journeymen: A Pre-History of Industrial Relations, 1717–1800*, London: Croom Helm, 1980, pp. 44–5, 60–73; see also J. Rule, *The Experience of Labour in Eighteenth-Century Industry*, London: Croom Helm, 1981, pp. 173–4; J. Rule, *The Labouring Classes in Early Industrial England, 1750–1850*, London: Longman, 1986, pp. 260–1.

worsted, cutlery and paper trades during the period of illegality under the multifarious individual trade and general Combination Acts in the late eighteenth century and during the first quarter of the nineteenth century.[3] Prosecutions of employers, though extremely rare, did take place under this legislation. If this drove employers' organisations underground, then undoubtedly many more such combinations existed within other industries, operating under the cover of secrecy.[4]

As industrialisation developed apace during the nineteenth century, so did the collective organisations of both masters and men. With the emergence of industrial capitalism, the factory system and related processes of urbanisation, a clearer division crystallised between wage-earning, propertyless workers and those who owned and controlled the tools and the means of production. The process of class formation and intensification of class consciousness, so brilliantly evoked by E.P. Thompson and E. Hobsbawm, found its organisational manifestation in the proliferation of trades unions and masters' organisations.[5] As Kirby and Musson have commented, these were 'separate and mutually hostile organisations backed by opposing and conflicting philosophies'.[6] Whilst the gestation of such organisations remains shrouded in mystery, several stimulants appear to have worked upon employers of labour over this period, encouraging them occasionally and for relatively short periods of time to combine their interests. The first was pressure from workers and their unions – perhaps seeking wage rises or protesting against wage cuts – constituting what most classical economist-influenced employers regarded as undue interference in their managerial functions and independence, and thus distorting the natural mechanism of the market. The second catalyst was a squeeze on profit margins caused by changes in product market circumstances, cyclical depressions and declining trade. A third factor which came increasingly into play from the second quarter of the nineteenth century was government intervention, most notably through Factory Acts and industrial relations legislation. The cotton textile industry provides clear evidence of all of these pressures at work.

[3] H.A. Turner, *Trade Union Growth, Structure and Policy*, London: Allen and Unwin, 1962, pp. 370–1; D.C. Coleman, 'Combinations of capital and labour in the English paper industry, 1789–1825', *Economica* (February 1954), pp. 32–53; A.E. Musson, *Trade Union and Social History*, London: Cass, 1974, pp. 137–55; Yarmie, 'Employers' organisations', p. 211.
[4] Dobson, *Masters*, pp. 124–6.
[5] E.P. Thompson, *The Making of the English Working Class*, London: Victor Gollancz, 1963; E.J. Hobsbawm, *The Age of Revolution: Europe 1789–1848*, London: Weidenfeld and Nicolson, 1962
[6] R.G. Kirby and A.E. Musson, *The Voice of the People: John Docherty, Trade Unionist, Radical and Factory Reformer, 1798–1854*, Manchester: Manchester University Press, 1975, p. 12.

The first evidence of combination amongst employers preceded the creation of trade unions in the cotton industry.[7] In 1745 a group of cotton manufacturers in Manchester combined to force a reduction of wages upon the operative weavers to help pay for the reparation demanded by the Young Pretender and the invading Scots when they passed through the city. Several years later Manchester merchants and employers combined, this time to deal with a strike of checkweavers. Some collective organisation of employers must also have been party to both the weavers' wage list of 1769 and the fine weavers' agreement of 1792. The resumption of the Napoleonic wars in 1803 initiated a trade crisis and Manchester cotton employers again organised together, raising a fighting fund of £20,000, to neutralise strikes by their operative spinners for wage rises. Moreover, there is some evidence to suggest that the cotton employers of the Manchester region maintained a degree of continuity in their organisation in the early nineteenth century. A cotton textile worker lamented in 1818: 'There is an abominable combination existing amongst the masters, first established at Stockport in 1802, and it has since become so general as to embrace all the great masters for a circuit of many miles around Manchester, though not the little masters, they are excluded.'[8] In Oldham – a predominantly coarse-spinning centre to the north of Manchester – a formal employers' organisation emerged early in the 1830s representing the larger, 'dynastic' family firms (the Oldham Cotton Masters' Association) which embarked on a wage-cutting drive. The newer entrants to the trade, hiring power, room and often even machinery (and employing a large proportion of kin) were excluded from this organisation. However, these smaller firms convened public meetings and debated policy in response to the economic downturn of the mid–late 1830s, and on at least one occasion in 1838 entered into a tacit agreement to curtail production systematically, around forty firms adopting the short-time scheme.[9]

The labour relations strategy of most early employers' associations operating in the first half of the nineteenth century was simply and unequivocally to suppress nascent trade unions. In response to the surge in trade union membership amongst the operative cotton spinners in the late 1820s (linked with the organisations led by John Docherty), employers organised and crushed the union at Manchester in 1829 and Ashton in 1830. Later defeats inflicted by organised masters all but destroyed trade

[7] Turner, *Trade Union Growth*, pp. 370–1.
[8] 'A journeyman cotton spinner, 1818', cited in Thompson, *The Making*, p. 219.
[9] J. Foster, 'Combinations amongst Oldham cotton masters, 1830–1870' (unpublished paper, c. 1964); E. Butterworth, *Historical Sketches of Oldham*, Oldham: J. Hirst, 1856, p. 118.

unionism amongst the spinners in Preston and Glasgow in 1837, and enabled the Glasgow masters to proceed with the replacement of male mule spinners with female operatives.[10] A wide range of coercive weapons was utilised to break strikes and crush trade unions. Advertising for and introducing an alternative, 'free', non-unionist labour force, protected by police, army or privately hired thugs was a common tactic, especially in smaller, localised strikes. Such attempts provoked some of the most violent and bloody incidents in industrial relations history. In larger strikes and at the peak of the trade cycle, however, the importation of blackleg labour was more difficult. Attempts were thus also made to prevent strikers and trade union organisers from obtaining work elsewhere. Blacklists were commonly circulated amongst members of employers' associations and more broadly, and many employers utilised the 'enquiry note' or the 'discharge note' system. The 'enquiry note' was a managerial reference back to a previous employer requesting details of a job applicant's history. The 'discharge note', common in coal and shipping, was a character testimonial which a worker obtained on leaving an employer and which needed to be presented elsewhere to get work.[11] Employers' organisations played an important role in popularising the use of such victimisation tactics and sometimes incorporated within their rules a proviso that forbade the employment of striking workers. They also encouraged and financed prosecutions in the law courts to intimidate workers, bringing actions for breach of contract, picketing ('molesting and obstructing') and against combination. A cotton trade union official, Thomas Banks, later recalled these hard times:

To be known as a trade unionist at that day was to be outlawed. A black ticket was sent around, thus every avenue was blocked and every door shut against the applicant for labour. These were the days of tyranny and oppression. Anyone who left off work without giving notice according to the rules of the mill was liable to be summoned before a bench of magistrates, and that bench had the discretionary power to give the poor factory operative from one to three months' imprisonment with hard labour.[12]

To enhance employer solidarity further during an industrial stoppage employers' organisations developed various financial compensation

---

[10] Kirby and Musson, *The Voice*, pp. 56–7, 59–60, 73–9, 119, 128–9; H.A. Turner, *Trade Union Growth*, pp. 74–5, 371; W. Hamish Fraser, 'The Glasgow cotton spinners, 1837', in J. Butt and J. Ward (eds.), *Scottish Themes*, Edinburgh: Scottish Academic Press, 1976; W. Hamish Fraser, *Conflict and Class: Scottish Workers, 1700–1838*, Edinburgh: John Donald, 1988.

[11] On the discharge note see J.H. Morris and L.J. Williams, 'The discharge note in the South Wales coal industry, 1841–1898', *Economic History Review*, 2nd series, 10 (1957–8), pp. 286–93.

[12] T. Banks, *A Short Sketch of the Cotton Trade of Preston over the Last Sixty Seven Years*, Preston: Toulain, 1888, p. 1.

schemes, counterbalanced by sanctions and disciplinary mechanisms. Individual member firms hit by a strike could often draw payments from a central fund created out of levies or alternatively could face the imposition of heavy financial penalties for disloyalty and setting a damaging precedent. In the Preston strike of 1853 such a financial 'guarantee' or penalty was fixed at the considerable sum of £5,000.[13] Occasionally such tactics were reinforced by threats of commercial embargoes and organised price undercutting. During a textile strike in 1829, for example, an employer settled terms with his men and then was subsequently forced to renege on these. According to a witness at the Committee on Combinations in 1838 he addressed his workers thus:

Men I am extremely sorry that I cannot stand to the arrangement which I have made . . . I have been to the masters' association today, and I must tell you that we were bound together by a bond of £500 if any one master should deviate . . . They have further told me that if I consent to give the list, they will throw their goods into the same market to which I go with my yarn at a price that will utterly ruin me.[14]

Perhaps the major weapon in the employers' arsenal of anti-union and strikebreaking tactics was the use of the lock-out. Lock-outs were organised with impunity in the first half of the nineteenth century and, of course, some form of collective organisation or committee of employers was a necessary prerequisite for any such action which extended beyond the individual firm. In 1829 when the Manchester fine spinners went on strike the employers retaliated by locking out all the fine and coarse spinners in the region.[15] Similarly, the 18 member firms in the Oldham Cotton Masters' Association locked out all their 4,000 or so workers from November 1836 to January 1837 in order to curb the demands of the operative spinners at various selected mills.[16] The general objective was to break the union's finances, undermine morale and the will to resist, and, in effect, starve workers into submission. What the multi-firm or regional lock-out did was to neutralise the effectiveness of the single firm strike and the 'rolling strike' tactic of trade unions, where successful precedents were pressed subsequently from firm to firm.

Re-employment after an industrial stoppage was also often selective – activists not being re-engaged. Employers' combinations made use of the non-unionist pledge, or what became known as 'the document', which

[13] See H.I. Dutton and J.E. King, *Ten Per Cent and No Surrender: The Preston Strike, 1853–4*, Cambridge: Cambridge University Press, 1981.
[14] S. Chapman, 'A historical sketch of the masters' associations in the cotton industry', *Proceedings of the Manchester Statistical Society* (1901), p. 74.
[15] Kirby and Musson, *The Voice*, pp. 73–9; Turner, *Trade Union Growth*, p. 371.
[16] Foster, 'Combinations'.

entailed workers signing a statement that they were not, and would not become, a member of a union. The widespread use of the document indicates the extent of employer anti-unionism in the first half of the nineteenth century. It was used to break building strikes in Liverpool, Manchester, London, Leeds and elsewhere in 1833–4; in the cotton strikes in Ashton in 1826, across Lancashire and West Scotland in 1837 and in Preston in 1853; in an attempt to smash the nascent Amalgamated Society of Engineers in the engineering lock-out in London and Manchester in 1852; and in the London building strike of 1859.[17] Only in the latter dispute were the organised employers forced to back down and abandon their demands that strikers sign the non-unionist pledge.

Thus the early, *ad hoc*, ephemeral, largely local combinations of employers in the first half of the nineteenth century usually developed an autocratic, exclusionist and coercive anti-trade unionist policy, backed up by a range of violent counter-strike measures. Paradoxically, perhaps, individual employers were forced on occasions to combine with their fellow capitalists and competitors in order to retain their capacity for individual bargaining between master and worker. This is not to imply, however, that trade unionism was everywhere rooted out by force. Already, a segment of industrial capital had accommodated itself to the existence of craft artisan societies, especially where such organisations effectively controlled entry to the trade. Hence the reluctance to prosecute many such societies under the anti-combination legislation between 1799 and 1824.

It is important, however, not to exaggerate the significance of employers' organisations before the middle of the nineteenth century or to overestimate the role they played in industrial relations. With few exceptions, employers' associations were neither strong, nor representative, nor stable over these years. To reiterate, they were established to deal with particular, specific crisis situations and usually faded out of existence soon after a particular dispute or stoppage had been settled. The life span of early nineteenth-century employers' organisations was extremely short, and any continuity in organisational structures extremely rare. For most of the time, the individual firm remained the focal point of industrial relations. A whole range of factors militated against continuous, strong multi-employer organisation in this period, including poor communications and spatial segregation. Effective employer organisation was undermined by the competitive relationship that existed between firms operating in similar markets, whilst internal divisions – differences in type and size of firm and product markets – could further dilute common interests and

---

[17] Rule, *The Experience of Labour*, p. 295; Wigham, *Power to Manage*, p. 279.

erode group solidarity. Moreover, external pressures were hardly in evidence. The government retained, for the most part, a *laissez-faire* strategy in relation to capital–labour relations. Moreover, outside the peaks of the trade cycle, trade unionism remained an insignificant 'threat' to capital, touching only a very small minority of almost exclusively male, skilled British workers. Moreover, in a period when many individual, paternalistic employers dominated local communities and when the views of capital were well represented in the judiciary, local municipalities, chambers of commerce and within the very fabric of society and politics, there was far less intrinsic need for employers to combine to protect and promote their interests.[18]

The mid-Victorian period witnessed a degree of consolidation and growth amongst employers' organisations, with combinations appearing at all levels and maintaining much more organisational continuity than previously.[19] Local associations of employers emerged on a permanent basis across a number of industries, whilst in others (cotton, building and engineering included) umbrella federations combining firms and local associations were constructed at the regional and national levels. More effective formal confederations of employers and parliamentary pressure groups also emerged in the 1870s and 1880s. Most notable of the latter were the National Federation of Associated Employers of Labour (established in 1873 ostensibly to counterbalance the role of the Trades Union Congress) and the Liberty and Property Defence League (founded in 1882 by the Liberal Earl Wemyss and integrating a number of MPs, employers' associations and companies).[20] The roller-coaster, fluctuating growth of trade unions, especially in coal and cotton, and across the skilled, artisanal trades, provided perhaps the major stimulant to employers in this period (*c.* 1850–80) to extend their organisations. The catalytic effect of unionism on employers' organisation was noted in the Report of the Royal Commission on Trade Unions in 1868–9 and in the Final Report of the Royal Commission on Labour: 'Formal organisations of employers usually make their appearance at a later date than those of the workmen, and arise for the purpose of joint resistance when individual employers find themselves too weak to cope with the growing strength of the trade unions.'[21] Wide divergences in the implantation of

---

[18] Joyce, *Work, Society and Politics*. See also A. Howe, *The Cotton Masters, 1830–1860*, Oxford: Oxford University Press, 1984.   [19] Yarmie, 'Employers' organisations', pp. 209–15.

[20] Ibid., pp. 226–33; A. Yarmie, 'British employers' resistance to "grandmotherly" government, 1850–80', *Social History*, 9, no. 2 (May 1984), pp. 141–69.

[21] Royal Commission on Labour, *Final Report*, pt 1, 1894, p. 31. See also the 1868 Report cited in J. T. Ward and W. H. Fraser, *Workers and Employers: Documents on Trade Unions and Industrial Relations in Britain since the Eighteenth Century*, London: Macmillan, 1980, pp. 94–5.

employers' organisation within and between industries continued, however, and sectional divisions of interest weakened collective initiatives by capital, as the experience of the engineering, building and cotton masters illustrates.

In the engineering industry, the first evidence of any employers' combination which was representative of more than a single town and its environs came in December 1851 when the Central Association of Employers of Operative Engineers (CAEOE) was formed. This organisation combined masters in London and the north-west of England and was created as a response to the formation of the Amalgamated Society of Engineers (1851), specifically to defeat the union-imposed embargo on piecework and overtime by initiating a lock-out of union members.[22] Thirty-six firms spread across Lancashire joined the CAEOE and locked out over 10,000 of their operatives in January 1852.[23] The objects of the organised employers were spelt out in their 'ukase' – a vitriolic manifesto against trades unionism and collective bargaining:

1. That no member of this association shall engage, admit into or continue in his service or employment, in any capacity whatever, any member of any trades' union or trades' society which takes cognisance of, professes to control, or practices [sic] interference with, the regulations of any establishment, the hours or terms of labour, the contracts or agreements of employers or employed, or the qualification of terms of service.

2. That no deputations of workmen, of trades' unions, committees or other bodies, with reference to any objects referred to in Article 1, be received by any member of this association on any account whatever; but that any person forming part of, instigating or causing such deputation, shall be dismissed forthwith; it being still perfectly open to any workman, individually, to apply on such subjects to his employer, who is recommended to be at all times open and accessible to any personal representation of his individual operatives.[24]

The lock-out was successfully sustained, the dispute terminating with the union withdrawing its overtime and piecework ban and accepting the employers' refusal to recognise trade unions, whilst members were forced to submit to the 'document'. Internal divisions amongst the employers re-emerged, however, once the cementing pressure of union militancy and encroachments into areas considered to be the domain of management receded. The CAEOE disintegrated shortly after the lock-out terminated. There is no evidence of further collaboration amongst the engineering employers beyond their local associations for twenty years thereafter.

---

[22] Burgess, *Origins*, pp. 23, 35; Wigham, *Power to Manage*, p. 3.
[23] J. Ward, *Workmen and Wages at Home and Abroad, or the Effects of Strikes, Combinations and Trade Unions*, London: Longmans, Green and Co., 1868, pp. 87–93.   [24] Ibid.

The Iron Trades Employers' Association (ITEA) emerged in 1872 ostensibly as a reaction against the successes of engineering workers on Tyneside who had achieved the nine-hour working day.[25] The ITEA was primarily a strikebreaking agency, which formalised the victimisation of strikers by popularising the use of the enquiry note and the blacklist amongst engineering employers. It also spearheaded campaigns during the trade downturn of 1876–9 to reduce wages (as at Liverpool) and increase working hours (as at Glasgow), and provided an insurance scheme whereby member employers were financially compensated for resisting labour demands during strikes. In 1873 the ITEA created a Registry Office for unemployed, non-unionist workmen and this pool of labour was utilised to break a number of strikes over the subsequent twenty years.[26] For example, during the long strike by the ASE in Bolton during 1886–7 (for wage rises and improved overtime pay rates), the ITEA filled the strikers' places with blacklegs, engaging special trains, boarding the replacees in the works and arranging a massive police escort.[27]

Unfortunately, few details have come to light regarding the coverage or membership of the ITEA, which maintained a continuous existence until the end of the nineteenth century, when it was superseded by the Employers' Federation of Engineering Associations. The ITEA was formed in Manchester and its main base of support lay in Lancashire and Yorkshire.[28] Some prominent local engineering employers' associations remained aloof, including the Clydeside master engineers. Whilst the ITEA provided strikebreaking services and counselled uncompromising anti-unionism, a number of local engineering employers' associations in the 1870s and 1880s were extending recognition to local branches of trade unions, creating joint committees which were formulating local joint working rules, covering such issues as minimum wages, working hours, local holidays and overtime rates.[29] Support for the ITEA appears, in fact, to have been fairly narrow and it is doubtful whether it was ever in any way representative of the engineering industry. However, in its own retrospective analysis of its role produced when it was wound up in 1900, the ITEA claimed to have played a significant part in extending the concept of collective organisation, asserting that it:

[25] J.B. Jefferys, *The Story of the Engineers*, London: Johnson reprint, 1970, pp. 94–5; Burgess, *Origins*, p. 25; Wigham, *Power to Manage*, pp. 14–20.
[26] See the Iron Trades Employers' Association (ITEA), *Record*, London: ITEA, 1900, pp. 25, 36. The ITEA free labour registry was also exploited by non-members, the Taff Vale Railway Company, for example, being assisted in strikes in 1876–7 and 1895–6 (*Record*, pp. 39, 130).   [27] Ibid., pp. 84–5.   [28] Burgess, *Origins*, p. 43.   [29] Ibid., p. 48.

educated engineering employers in the art of combination and taught them to know each other, to see each other's point of view, to merge the opinions of individuals in those of the collective body, and to diffuse information throughout the whole trade as to the best way of looking upon and combating labour questions and other matters which affect employers.[30]

There may be a grain of truth here, though in the light of the evidence, this constitutes a somewhat exaggerated claim, overstressing the significance and role of the ITEA.

In the building industry there were two short-lived attempts to widen the base of employer organisation in the late 1850s, with the Lancashire-based National Association of Master Builders and the Central Association of Master Builders. Little is known about the strength or activities of either organisation. They were established, according to Price and Burgess, to spearhead the employers' counter-attack against the building craft unions and, like the engineering employers' combination of 1851–2 (CAEOE), refused to consider collective bargaining or employ union members.[31] In 1865 a new organisation emerged, the General Builders' Association, formed 'especially for protecting the masters from the evils resulting from strikes'.[32] The GBA survived until 1872 and its longevity can partly be explained by the fact that, unlike previous central combinations, the GBA recruited local employers' associations direct, rather than individual firms. Moreover, in its definition of the respective roles of central and local groups, the GBA indicated clearly that its genesis was intimately linked with attacks on the autonomy and profitability of builders from two sources – the client and the unions:

These [local] associations should have for their object the promotion of the trade interests of their own districts by making trade rules; by settling rates of wages and trade prices; by taking common instead of individual action in all questions whether arising from the men on the one hand or the Architects on the other; by cultivating that mutual feeling of good faith which alone can obviate the evils of competition; and by loyally assisting the General Association. The General Association, without unduly interfering with their independence, should assist them in the promotion of the above objects and should endeavour as far as possible to secure uniformity in the best rules and customs, by using its influence to abolish the arbitrary trade rules at present enforced by the men, and the equally arbitrary conditions imposed by architects and by introducing arbitration for the settlement of trade disputes.[33]

The first statement of accounts of the GBA indicated that 36 local associations in England and Scotland had affiliated. By the end of 1866, 50 local associations were members, and by mid-1867 84 towns were

[30] ITEA, *Record*, p. 152.   [31] Price, *Masters*, pp. 40–2,53; Burgess, *Origins*, p. 112.
[32] General Builders' Association, Minutes, Annual General Meeting, 10 August 1865.
[33] Ibid.

46   Setting the scene

affiliated, including 22 from Lancashire. The organisation was crucially weakened, however, by a failure to recruit the London association, and by divisions within the trade between general contractors, speculative builders and the mass of small subcontracting firms.[34] The volatility of the product market only served to exacerbate such divisions.

In their recent analysis of building employers' associations McKenna and Rodger have stressed the conciliatory role of the GBA, contrasting this with the more militant anti-unionist stance of other organisations in the period.[35] The GBA professed a commitment to arbitration, and proposed to the Royal Commission on Trade Unions in 1867 that permanent disputes tribunals be established in all local associations consisting of an equal number of delegates from both employers and operatives, with an independent chairman, to settle all trade questions that led to stoppages. However, this was largely public posturing and there is no evidence to suggest that such conciliation boards were actually established. On the contrary, the evidence in the minutes of the GBA over the period 1866–71 clearly indicates that the organisation remained violently anti-unionist and that it settled disputes by resort to force rather than negotiation. There was, however, a difference in tactics, the GBA preferring to localise rather than escalate conflict:

that lock-outs be avoided; and instead that the branch association with the assistance of the general secretary attempt to fill the shops affected by the strike with men from other localities, it being understood first that the men thus introduced are to be considered as 'old hands' and guaranteed work as such, and not dismissed at the end of the strike.[36]

Between 1866 and 1871, labour replacement and selective re-employment, the provision of financial compensation during strikes, use of the enquiry note, blacklisting and the encouragement of company unions were all common GBA labour relations policies. Indeed, in 1867, labour replacement was institutionalised by the creation of a GBA Labour Registration Scheme, whereby local member firms kept registers of non-unionist workers for strikebreaking purposes.[37] The professed commitment to conciliation was superficial and evidently little more than a diversionary public relations exercise. In the event, as Price has argued, the more effective organisation and aggressive policies of the building employers in the 1860s succeeded in critically diluting the 'autonomous regulation' of the building craftsmen, significantly enhancing employer control over the labour process.[38]

[34] McKenna and Rodger, 'Control by coercion', pp. 213–14.   [35] Ibid.
[36] General Builders' Association, Minutes, 11 September 1866.
[37] Ibid., 9 October 1867; 30 June 1868; 26 July 1871.   [38] Price, Masters, pp. 105–28.

The GBA accumulated large debts and was formally disbanded in 1872. It had, however, clearly illustrated the advantages to such a heterogeneous, fragmented industry (characterised by relatively small business units and a large number of local associations) of an umbrella federation combining local employers' associations. In 1878, in response to a strike of carpenters in Lancashire, a number of local associations re-established the central federation under the new title of the National Association of Master Builders. The NAMB combined centralised strikebreaking functions with some encouragement to member associations to negotiate uniform local working rules *jointly* with the building unions. The main work of the organisation in the late 1870s and the 1880s, however, was as a pressure group for the building trade, dealing with such issues as factory, trade union and employers' liability legislation, forms of contract, direct labour and relations with clients, architects and municipalities. Such issues as these (rather than capital–labour relations) could be sufficient to spur a local master builders' association into existence, as the example of Oldham indicates.[39] By 1886, sixty local master builders' associations affiliated to the NAMB, representing most of the major British cities. However, these associations retained a large degree of autonomy and prior to the widespread adoption of the intertrading rule in the 1890s constituted in their membership only a small minority of those involved in the construction trade.[40]

Because of the centrality of the cotton industry in the industrialisation process it is perhaps not surprising to find what was probably the most extensive and effective network of employers' associations in Britain in this sector in the mid-Victorian period. Strong and representative local associations of employers existed in all of the main cotton producing towns and in both the spinning and the weaving sector federations of local associations had emerged in the 1850s and 1860s. The expanding level of trade unionism amongst cotton workers undoubtedly stimulated such counter-organisation.[41] However, growing government involvement in working conditions through factory legislation and a desire amongst employers to regulate competition amongst themselves were significant additional catalysts prompting cotton employers to combine.

---

[39] See J. Denver, *Fifty Years History of the Manchester, Salford and District Building Trades Employers' Association*, Manchester: MBTEA, 1951, pp. 20–3; Oldham Building Trades Employers' Association, Minutes, 1889–90; Burgess, *Origins*, p. 129.

[40] McKenna and Rodger, 'Control by coercion', pp. 220–7.

[41] On cotton trade unionism in the nineteenth century see Turner, *Trade Union Growth*, in conjunction with the more recent union-commissioned histories: Fowler and Wyke, *Barefoot Aristocrats*; A. Bullen, *The Lancashire Weavers' Union*, Manchester: Amalgamated Textile Workers' Union, 1984; A. Bullen and A. Fowler, *The Cardroom Workers' Union*, Manchester: Amalgamated Textile Workers' Union, 1986; A. and L. Fowler, *The Nelson Weavers*, Manchester: Amalgamated Textile Workers' Union, 1984.

It has been suggested that the success of the engineering employers in the 1852 lock-out was influential in persuading cotton magnates of the utility of strong collective organisations.[42] Rather more convincingly, however, Andrew Bullen has shown how a series of industrial disputes, strikes and lock-outs within the cotton industry, predominantly linked with wage issues, encouraged higher levels of collective organisation amongst both masters and men in the north Lancashire weaving towns in the 1850s.[43] The movement for wage increases across Lancashire in 1853 triggered a series of strikes which were resisted by the Preston employers, who initiated a town lock-out. A broader employers' amalgamation, the Lancashire Masters' Defence Association, then emerged, ostensibly to establish a 'defensive fund' to support the Preston employers and finance the importation of blacklegs.[44] Later the LMDA organised a sympathetic lock-out within the region. The action of the employers at Preston and the solidarity of the LMDA was ultimately successful in rolling back the initial victories of the weavers' unions, though only after a long and bitter eight-month stoppage of the Preston mills. Thereafter, the LMDA appears to have maintained a shadowy existence through 1854–5, fell into abeyance thereafter, and was revived in 1859 by the Burnley employers during the twenty-six-week weavers' strike at Padiham.

Whilst the LMDA clearly had some muscle, its effectiveness was limited by the failure to integrate Blackburn, the largest weaving town in north Lancashire. Labour costs in cotton weaving formed a large proportion of total costs and in an attempt to take wages out of competition between masters, and to minimise industrial disputes over wage payment, the Blackburn Cotton Masters' Association initiated and fleshed out in 1853–4 (in negotiation with an *ad hoc* committee of workers' representatives) what became known as the Blackburn Standard Wage List. This was a significant watershed because the list incorporated provision for a stage-by-stage disputes procedure (regarding wage rates and working conditions) at the factory and local level, thus providing the basis for collective bargaining between union and employers' association.[45] Those firms not paying according to the list were refused any support from the Blackburn masters' association. This is indicative of the positive role employers' organisations could perform in the formulation of an institutionalised

---

[42] Dutton and King, *Ten Per Cent*, pp. 34, 88–9.
[43] Bullen, 'Pragmatism vs principle', pp. 27–43. This section is largely based on Bullen's work, to which the author would like to acknowledge his debt.
[44] S. Chapman, *The Lancashire Cotton Industry*, Manchester: Manchester University Press, 1904, p. 239; Yarmie, 'Employers' organisations', p. 214; Dutton and King, *Ten Per Cent*, p. 86; Banks, *A Short Sketch*, p. 7.   [45] Burgess, *Origins*, pp. 263–4.

industrial relations system. In his study of cotton masters during the period 1830–60, Howe has asserted that the Blackburn Standard List and the settlement of the Padiham strike (1859) and the strike at Garnett and Co. of Clitheroe (1860) by conciliatory methods heralded a shift to recognition and acceptance of trade unions in cotton. This was dependent on and further stimulated counter-organisation by employers: 'These associations reveal the Lancashire textile capitalist not as the heroic individual who par excellence subscribed to the Anti-Corn Law League but as a member of a defined occupational community, integrated into a network of temporary and permanent associations for the defence of economic and class interests.'[46]

The difficulty, however, was that the Blackburn list provided for a considerably higher wage than was customary in north Lancashire and precipitated industrial action elsewhere to achieve the 'Blackburn Standard'. This created a bitter rift between cotton manufacturers, exacerbated by the actions of the Blackburn masters in implicitly supporting the agitation of the weavers' unions directed towards raising wages outside their own town. Product market specialisms created further divisions between cotton capitalists and for their part the Blackburn millocracy resented what they regarded as the unfair competition of other employers, especially those in Preston and Burnley, who benefited from undercutting their labour costs.

It took the trauma of the cotton famine of 1861–5 and the virtual collapse of trade unions and employers' associations to heal these divisions between high wage and low wage-paying employers.[47] In 1866, the three major cotton weaving employers' organisations in Blackburn, Preston and Burnley came together to establish the North and North-East Lancashire Cotton Spinners' and Manufacturers' Association (CSMA). This was an extremely powerful combination. As early as 1868, firms representing 53 per cent, 61 per cent and 72 per cent of the total looms in existence in Blackburn, Burnley and Preston respectively were affiliated to the CSMA.[48] One of the main objectives of this umbrella organisation was to standardise labour costs throughout the industry by creating a Cotton Weaving Uniform List. However, because of conflicts of interest within the employers' federation (largely between Burnley and Blackburn), such a uniform wage list did not become reality until 1892. The CSMA is also responsible for pioneering the creation of a two-stage (local and central) disputes settlement procedure with the weavers'

[46] Howe, *The Cotton Masters*, pp. 162–3, 171–8. Joyce places the crucial changes in employers' attitudes to unions and collective bargaining in the 1860s. See Joyce, *Work, Society and Politics*, p. 71.   [47] Bullen, 'Pragmatism vs principle', pp. 39–40.
[48] CSMA, Committee Minutes, 26 February 1868.

unions in 1881, pre-dating the more notorious Brooklands procedure in spinning (discussed in chapter 5) by more than a decade.

The multiple pressures on the cotton millocracy of growing trade unionism, intensification of competition and government intervention in working conditions through factory legislation encouraged a collective response. All of the large cotton spinning towns, including Oldham, Bolton, Preston and Ashton, saw local employers' associations emerge around mid-nineteenth century, and there is evidence of a growing degree of inter-association collaboration. The Preston Master Cotton and Flax Spinners' Association paid a levy to a central millowners' federation in February 1846, and another of one shilling per horsepower in March 1855.[49] The object of the 1855 organisation was to represent the interests of power machinery owners in the courts and in Parliament – Dickens referred to it as 'the Association for the Mangling of Operatives'.[50] It campaigned to minimise the impact of factory legislation on the millowners and neutralise the role of the Factory Inspectorate, creating a fund amounting to £5,000 which financed the defence of 'all cases of prosecution which they consider fairly to come within the sphere of the association'.[51] The Preston association also kept its own vigilance over factory legislation and other external constraints on their members' profitability, forming, for example, special committees to examine the progress of public health legislation and to make representations to local authorities over poor rate assessments. Deputations from Preston presented the owners' case to Robert Peel in 1845 on the issue of duties on cotton, and to George Grey on the Factory Act in 1855. Indeed, it is significant that the Factory Act Amendment of 1855 was the issue that prompted the revival of the Preston association (after several years of inactivity), thirty-nine local employers combining to agree to resist proposals to enforce the fencing of horizontal shafts in cotton factories, the source of innumerable serious injuries to workers.

Oldham occupied a dominant position in the cotton spinning trade similar to that held by Blackburn in weaving. By the 1860s, Oldham was the largest spinning centre in Britain, producing predominantly medium and coarse grade yarns and it became a pivotal wage setting area, with its agreements influencing the whole south Lancashire cotton spinning region. In 1866 an Oldham Master Cotton Spinners' Association was formed, the immediate stimulus being the need to resist the demands of the reorganised mule spinners' union for a 10 per cent wage rise after the

---

[49] Preston Master Cotton and Flax Spinners' Association, Minutes, 31 March 1855.
[50] Referred to in Joyce, *Work, Society and Politics*, p. 69.
[51] Preston Master Cotton and Flax Spinners' Association, Minutes, 31 March 1855. See also Minutes, 29 September 1856.

deprivations of the cotton famine period.[52] The objects of the association were made explicit in their Rules:

The association is established for the purpose of consulting upon and from time to time determining the rate of wages or prices paid to workmen for their work in the Oldham district, and the hours or time in any cotton manufacture, trade or business carried on within such district; and also for the purpose of affording aid and assistance to the members of the association in cases of combinations, strikes, coercion and intimidation by workpeople; and taking cognisance of any matters affecting the interests of the cotton trade in the district.[53]

The Oldham association maintained a continuous existence from 1866, and through the 1870s and 1880s consolidated its position as the representative voice of the town's millocracy. In 1869 91 firms were members, and by 1890, 115 constituent firms represented almost 70 per cent of potential machine capacity in the Oldham region.[54] The association became actively involved in the formation of the Oldham Chamber of Commerce over the period 1879–81, made deputations to the government on factory legislation, the India imports duties and the Employers' Liability legislation, and organised systematic short-time working throughout the trade during cyclical product market depressions.[55] The Oldham masters were also represented in the Cotton Spinners' Association, a broad-based trade association and parliamentary pressure group in existence from 1866 to the early 1890s. The CSA initially recruited firms direct, but was reorganised into the United Cotton Spinners' Association in 1888, with affiliation from local cotton employers' associations. At this point employers' associations representing 266 firms and almost 45 per cent of the spinning capacity in Lancashire affiliated to the UCSA.[56]

The Oldham cotton masters' association also became actively involved in labour relations. On the one hand the organisation strengthened the ability of individual millowners to resist trade union demands and pressure via rolling strike tactics by creating a reserve fund from levies raised on member firms and by making the lock-out weapon more effective.

---

[52] A. Bullen, 'The founding of the Amalgamation', in Fowler and Wyke, *Barefoot Aristocrats*, p. 61. Local associations of master spinners were also created at this time in Bury, Hyde and Stockport.   [53] Cited in Longworth, *Oldham Master Cotton*, p. 35.

[54] 1869 figures in Foster, 'Combinations', p. 6. Figures for 1890 derived by comparing *Worrall's Cotton Spinners' and Manufacturers' Directory*, 1891, with the Oldham MCSA, *Annual Report* and List of Members, 1891–2.

[55] See the manuscript Oldham MCSA, *Annual Reports*, 1881–9, including the 1884 Report (2 February 1885), for an example of successful organisation of short-time working across the trade.

[56] Cotton Spinners' Association (CSA), Membership List, 1888, compared with *Worrall's Cotton Spinners' and Manufacturers' Directory*, 1888–9; CSA, *Annual Report and Rules*, presented to the Annual General Meeting, 16 August 1887; CSA, *Annual Report and Rules*, presented to the Annual General Meeting, 4 September 1888.

Financial compensation was paid from the levy fund to employers during a strike to induce loyalty and prevent the concession of embarrassing precedents. On the other hand, the Oldham MCSA played an initiating role in the formulation of the Oldham Piece Price (wage) List in 1876, which incorporated an innovative disputes procedural clause allowing for grievances to be jointly discussed between the secretaries of the local union and employers' association before a stoppage of work took place. J.H. Porter has shown how this crude procedural mechanism succeeded in resolving innumerable mill disputes over wage calculations and has argued that it worked predominantly in the employers' favour.[57] This point will be returned to later (see chapter 5). The Oldham wage list also provided explicit, if somewhat limited, trade union recognition and, as at Blackburn, led the way towards full collective bargaining on a wide range of substantive issues. The formalised piece price lists in Lancashire cotton became the key component in a successful wage-for-effort bargaining system which, because of their flat rate payments, provided cotton workers in the north-west with an 'inner incentive' to maximise their production.[58]

Nevertheless, bitter industrial conflict characterised industrial relations in Oldham in the 1870s and 1880s. Four lengthy lock-outs and one long strike (26 weeks) took place in the town between 1871 and 1885. This deterioration in industrial relations was primarily employer-initiated (as the number of lock-outs suggests), with the Oldham MCSA in the vanguard of a labour cost reduction offensive, which incorporated a drive to intensify and 'speed up' work as profit margins in the coarse yarn sector narrowed. Indeed, the 'speed clause' in the Oldham list directly encouraged firms to intensify workloads.[59] From the commercial depression of 1873, the cotton industry experienced a declining rate of growth, increasing overseas competition and relative technological stagnation, with yarn prices falling by 50 per cent between 1873 and 1896.[60] The Oldham MCSA forced through wage reductions in response to the decline in trade, and neighbouring employers' associations and non-organised employers used the Oldham settlements as precedents, thus obtaining reductions in labour costs without a struggle. Indeed, in Rochdale, Bury, Heywood, Stockport and Hyde the local masters' associations formulated official agreements with local unions to abide by the results of wage movements in Oldham.

[57] J.H. Porter, 'Industrial peace in the cotton trade, 1875–1913', *Yorkshire Bulletin of Economic and Social Research*, 19 (1967), pp. 49–59.
[58] For a discussion of the genesis of the Oldham list and the implications for industrial relations see Fowler and Wyke, *Barefoot Aristocrats*, pp. 71–3; Burgess, *Origins*, pp. 241–3.
[59] Burgess, *Origins*, pp. 242, 278; Fowler and Wyke, *Barefoot Aristocrats*, p. 73.
[60] Turner, *Trade Union Growth*, pp. 40–1.

By the mid-1880s, the Oldham MCSA was finding its isolated position onerous, particularly as the operative mule spinners' amalgamation consolidated itself and unionisation became more firmly established within the cardroom. Consequently, the association began a concerted campaign to form a broader based federation of all local cotton spinning employers' associations. Initial attempts to forge co-operative action to reduce wages further by 10 per cent in 1885 were, however, unsuccessful. Of neighbouring towns only Ashton agreed to support the movement, and only to the extent of running short-time whilst the Oldham mills were closed.[61] To some extent, commercial self-interest was clearly at work here, and, as with the north Lancashire masters, pragmatism diluted the appeal to solidarity.[62] In the event, the position of the Oldham masters was weakened and they were forced to compromise and settle for a 5 per cent wage reduction.

Divisions in strategy amongst the employers were also based, however, on clear differences in product market experience and business structure. The Bolton Master Cotton Spinners' Association (formed 1861) refused to co-operate with Oldham because many large Bolton firms were experiencing buoyant, even expanding, trade, with little foreign competition, at a time when profit margins in the Oldham coarse spinning sector were being seriously squeezed. The Bolton employers specialised in fine, high-quality yarns, using Egyptian raw cotton, and feared the possibility of being drawn into the internecine industrial relations conflicts which characterised Oldham. Bolton firms also tended to be smaller scale, family dominated and privately owned, and there developed some antagonism between them and the large-scale, limited-liability cotton concerns in Oldham, particularly as the latter began to encroach into the higher counts/finer yarn product markets traditionally monopolised by Bolton.[63] Unlike the north Lancashire weaving masters, therefore, the local master spinners' associations (whilst individually being extremely powerful) failed to create an umbrella federation which regulated wages, negotiated on labour conditions or provided a final disputes procedural stage. Local autonomy and independence amongst cotton spinning employers prevailed, with the town and the individual firm remaining the focal points in industrial relations before 1890.

Conclusion

Much more research is required to flesh out the genesis, evolution and role of employers' associations in industrial relations in the eighteenth

---

[61] Oldham MCSA, *Annual Report*, 1885.
[62] The 'pragmatism' argument is fully developed by Bullen, 'Pragmatism vs principle', pp. 27–43.   [63] Joyce, *Work, Society and Politics*, pp. 68–9.

and nineteenth centuries. To this end, more industrial and regional case studies would be particularly helpful. This short contextual overview, setting the scene for a more detailed analysis of the period from c. 1880 on, suggests, however, a number of tentative hypotheses. First, that a tradition of intermittent employer combination extends back deep into the eighteenth century in many British industries, indicating a much more significant role in industrial relations for such institutions than some commentators have assumed. Early employers' organisations were shadowy, transient, unstable bodies, invariably formed in response to specific industrial relations crises, and usually fading away quickly thereafter. Such bodies rarely assumed permanent organisational form – even at the local level – before the middle decades of the nineteenth century. It remains highly significant, nevertheless, that at moments of crisis employers invariably combined to formulate a collective response towards external pressures, acting unequivocally in defence of economic and class interests.

Secondly, whilst the pace of collective organisation increased in the mid-Victorian period, a great deal of autonomy and power continued to reside in the local (town and environs) employers' associations. There were some concerted attempts to forge broader based alliances at the industry, or even parliamentary level (notably the NFAEL), but these appear to have had only limited influence before the 1890s.

Thirdly, if an extensive, though incomplete, network of employers' organisations emerged in Britain by the late nineteenth century, it needs to be stressed that such organisations varied considerably in form, structure, representativeness, cohesiveness and policies. Evidence suggests that highly industrialised regions, such as Lancashire, witnessed the earliest inception, longest tradition and most powerful of employer organisations. Here, local employers' associations formed the rump of a cluster of regional and national federations in building, engineering and cotton textiles formed in the third quarter of the nineteenth century. Whether this pattern was replicated in other industrialised regions, Clydeside and Tyneside for example, remains to be seen.

Fourthly, combinations of masters usually originated as coercive strikebreaking organisations, concerned above all else to root out and destroy trade unions. Unions were identified as the major threat to profit maximisation and a dangerous interference with employers' sacrosanct prerogative to manage and control their works as they saw fit. Thus the collective strength of capital was manifested through the lock-out and a plethora of blacklisting and strikebreaking weapons designed to neutralise the effectiveness of the rolling strike (strikebreaking tactics, c. 1880–1914, are investigated more systematically in chapter 4). In the course of the second half of the nineteenth century, the growth and resilience of trade unions, their ability to resist and use the strike weapon, combined with mass picketing – strategies systematically developed only from around 1870[64] – forced employers and their organisations to reformulate their labour relations strategies. Moreover, minimising time lost through industrial conflict became crucial as foreign competition intensified and employers faced the possibility of permanent loss of markets.

Therefore, and fifthly, the mid-Victorian period witnesses the halting and experimental origins of trade union recognition, joint negotiation and collective bargaining. In cotton, this was via the creation and administration of piece-rate wage lists and in engineering and building via the negotiation of joint local trade rules. Formal local disputes procedures developed sporadically, designed to contain militancy and de-escalate conflict. Such formalised systems of industrial relations were still in their infancy by the 1880s and had developed patchily across and even within industries. However, containment of militancy through the evolution of a sophisticated negotiating and procedural system was to become the predominant strategy of employers' organisations in the 1900s and 1910s when formal industry-wide bargaining was grafted on to the existing localised framework and informal structures. The evidence for north-west England suggests, moreover, that the initiative in developing such a system came as much from the employers and their associations as from the trade unions.

Sixthly, whilst not entirely reactive bodies, the very existence, representativeness and sustenance of employers' associations beyond a particular crisis period invariably depended upon a conjuncture of internally generated and externally imposed circumstances. Employers organised collectively when they felt unable to cope on an individual basis with growing pressures accumulating from a more hostile market environment, or when disgruntled with government intervention, or because they were concerned at the potential impact upon profitability arising from the establishment on their shop-floor of a significant trade union presence, or, perhaps, where an established union employed more radical tactics in defence of workers' interests. Keith Burgess has commented that growing overseas competition in the last quarter of the nineteenth century, combined with the legislation of 1871 and 1875 (which legitimised the position of the trade unions), provided the crucial stimulants encouraging the formation of permanent employers' organisations.[65]

---

[64] J. Cronin, 'Strikes, 1870–1914', in Wrigley (ed.), *A History of British Industrial Relations, 1875–1914*, pp. 74–98; J. Cronin, *Industrial Conflict in Modern Britain*, London: Croom Helm, 1979.   [65] Burgess, *Origins*, pp. viii–xi.

Finally, it is important to stress that prior to the 1890s there were severe limits upon the growth and power of employers' associations. Whilst there were pockets of very well-organised employers, the majority of British companies, at this point, undoubtedly remained outside any formal employers' organisation. Rarely did employer solidarity extend far beyond the immediate locality or outside the confines of a particular trade. Employers' confederations of trades (such as the NFAEL) and organisations which federated local associations remained either short-lived or failed to recruit widely and hence were not representative of the industry. The ITEA, the NAMB and the CSMA before 1890 all fall into this latter category. Employers were patently not a homogeneous group, and their attempts to forge powerful combinations against labour were undermined throughout the nineteenth century by competitive tensions, by disunity and fractured class consciousness. Conflicts of interest emerged between large and small firms, general contractors and subcontractors, private and limited liability companies, high and low wage payers and between employers specialising in particular product markets. The pressures on individual employers to combine were muted, moreover, by limited government intervention in industrial relations and by the limits to trade union growth and the 'labour threat' outside the crafts. As late as the mid-1880s, only around 5–10 per cent of British workers were trade union members. Even relatively well-organised industries such as building construction, metals, engineering, shipbuilding and cotton textiles rarely mustered more than 20 per cent unionisation of their respective labour forces by 1888.[66]

This scenario was to alter radically. The 1890s were a decade of rapid growth and consolidation in employers' organisation membership, and witnessed a significant extension of the employers' role in the formalisation of industrial relations, with strikebreaking by force being increasingly relegated to a second line of defence, utilised in many industries only if complex procedural mechanisms for containing industrial conflict failed. These developments are investigated in some detail in subsequent chapters, starting with an analysis of employers' association structure, membership and solidarity.

[66] Clegg, Fox and Thompson, *A History of British Trade Unions*, vol. I, p. 468. Pockets of workers within these industries, however, such as the spinners and boilermakers were *very* well organised. See also G. Bain and R. Price, *Profiles of Union Growth*, Oxford: Basil Blackwell, 1980, pp. 37–78.

Part 2

Forging employers' organisations, 1880–1920

3   Organisation, membership and solidarity

As noted in chapter 1, a significant strand of research upon employers' organisations emphasises the persistence of disunity, fragmentation, and fractured collective consciousness amongst British employers prior to the First World War. According to this interpretation, employer combinations in Britain before 1914 lacked centralised control and authority over their members, were unable to develop a consensus labour relations strategy, or significantly influence the existing division of labour.[1] Initiatives towards employer solidarity before the First World War thus generated weak, fragile alliances which were short-lived and episodic, the removal of the immediate threat leading inevitably to a rapid fracturing in cohesion, undermining employer organisation. Roy Bean's case study of Liverpool shipping provides one such example of a strong employer association critically weakened by breakaways after the threat from the dockers and seamen subsided. Indeed, the Employers' Labour Association in Liverpool haemorrhaged from covering fifty major shipping lines in 1890 to just thirteen in 1909.[2] But was this experience typical or exceptional in this period?

This chapter investigates the organisational structures which employers collectively constructed, evaluates membership trends and employer solidarity within associations and elaborates a little on the services offered by such institutions. How strong and cohesive were employers' associations before 1914? How were they organised? Who were members? What were the forces which stimulated collective organisation? It will be argued here that the interpretation presented above has important merits, especially in dispelling the myth of a monolithic employer class. However, on balance, this portrayal of British employer organisations is too negative and justifies some revision.

---

[1] See, in particular, the work of J. Zeitlin and references cited in chapter 1, nn. 29 and 30. Church also stresses disunity in his recent study of coalowners' associations: R. Church, *The History of the British Coal Industry*, vol. III: *1830–1913*, Oxford: Clarendon Press, 1986, pp. 651–74.   [2] Bean, 'Employers' associations', p. 369.

Table 3.1 *Employers' associations in Britain, June 1914*

Sectors/Industries	Number of associations (local, regional and national)	
Building	468	
Food, drink, tobacco	166	
Iron, steel, metals	144	
Paper, printing	116	
Newspapers		4
Textiles	99	
Cotton		35
Wool, worsted, shoddy		24
Finishing		18
Clothing	84	
Tailoring		54
Boot and shoe		23
Transport and communication	69	
Railways		1
Road		40
Water		28
Engineering	56	
Woodworking, furnishing	52	
Mining and quarrying	38	
Coal		24
Personal service	31	
Laundering, dyeing		29
Hairdressing		1
Undertaking		1
Shipbuilding	25	
Bricks, pottery, glass	25	
Agriculture and fishing	10	
Chemicals	2	
Commerce and distribution	68	
Other industries	34	
Total employers' associations	1,487	

Notes: The figures include only associations which are concerned with 'matters relating to the employment of labour' and hence exclude trade and technical associations, including Chambers of Commerce.
Source: Ministry of Labour, *Eighteenth Abstract of Labour Statistics*, 1926, p. 191.

The first question which needs to be addressed is just how representative and how powerful were British employers' organisations by the 1890–1914 period? This is a difficult question to answer with precision because we lack the kind of systematic, detailed membership data that exists for the trade unions. Few employers' associations registered under the Companies Acts or the Trade Union Acts and hence were not required to provide membership and financial data to the Board of Trade, the Registrar of Friendly Societies or any other government body.[3] However, the Labour Department of the Board of Trade did compile a directory of employers' associations (with the addresses of secretaries for reference) and this index suggests a more than fourfold growth in the number of employers' organisations (at the local and national level) in Britain from 336 in 1895 to 1,487 in 1914.[4] Unfortunately, constituent membership of such associations is not recorded, though the distribution across industries by 1914, as table 3.1 shows, is quite impressive. Such aggregated data suggest, at the very least, that employers' associations proliferated in the twenty years or so before the First World War and that many such institutions had made the transition from transient to permanent structures. By the First World War collective organisation had permeated many key sectors of the economy, including, significantly, some industries where trade unionism remained minimal – for example agriculture, personal service and clothing.

Clearly, by the First World War a comprehensive network of employers' associations had emerged in Britain, with individual companies organising at a local level and local associations federating at the regional and national level across a wide range of industries. A quite distinctive strand of specialist and overtly political organisations also emerged, including William Collison's National Free Labour Association and the Anti-Socialist Union.[5] An accumulation of economic, social and political pressures contributed to consolidation of class consciousness amongst British capitalists. For many employers it was the encroaching threat of a more militant organised labour movement, particularly at the peak of the trade cycle over 1888–90 and 1910–14, that provided the necessary cementing pressure. The 'new unionist' upsurge in the late 1880s, when trade union membership doubled, socialist involvement escalated and a major strike wave erupted, played a significant role in stimulating counter-organisation amongst employers, as the Royal Commission on Labour testified:

Employers' associations are of various degrees of solidarity and compactness in different trades, varying, perhaps, with the degree to which these qualities are found in the associations of workpeople in those trades . . . Just as in some trades many workmen remain outside the organisations, so many employers remain outside the employers' associations and it often seems to happen that non-associated employers employ non-associated men.[6]

---

[3] Royal Commission on Labour, *Rules of Associations*, 1892, c. 6795, p. xxii.

[4] Garside and Gospel, 'Employers and managers', p. 104.

[5] G. Alderman, 'The National Free Labour Association', *IRSH*, 21 (1976), pp. 309–36; K.D. Brown, 'The Anti-Socialist Union', in K.D. Brown (ed.), *Essays in Anti-Labour History*, London: Macmillan, 1974.

[6] Royal Commission on Labour, *Fifth and Final Report*, Part 1, June 1894, pp. 31–2.

Witness, for example, the formation in 1890 of the Shipping Federation, one of the most draconian of employers' associations in Britain before the First World War.

Increasing union density in the cotton textile industry, most notably the growing organisation of the semi-skilled, predominantly female, cardroom workers from the mid-1880s, altered the balance of power and precipitated a move to consolidate and strengthen employer organisation.[7] In 1886, the Oldham Master Cotton Spinners' Association articulated a growing concern: 'As from information received, the various branches of the operatives' trade unions are so combined that if the employers do not amalgamate in a similar way capital is certain to become, for a time at least, the servant and not the master of labour.'[8] Millowners' evidence to the Royal Commission on Depression of Trade and Industry in 1886 focused on the combined problems of escalating labour costs and the 'nanny' state which, through the Factory Acts and related legislation, had undermined competitiveness.[9] After several false starts, the Oldham association succeeded in creating the Federation of Master Cotton Spinners' Associations in 1891, combining around 40 per cent of the machine capacity in the Lancashire cotton spinning sector. Throughout the 1890s, cotton spinning employers' leaders and their trade journal *Textile Mercury* returned to the theme of trade union aggression. In June 1894 the Oldham MCSA chairman (J.B. Tattersall) referred to a trade union strategy designed to 'obtain a complete mastery... and to be able to dictate its own terms on any subject whatever connected with the work and wages of the hands'.[10] Later in the same year *Textile Mercury* lambasted the unions:

The policy of the leaders of the operatives is developing into one of universal harassment. Very soon no employer, either individual or corporate, will be permitted to turn around in their offices without asking the permission of Mr James Mawdsley or some one of his satellites ... Is it not high time that a resolute resistance were offered to such arrogant dictation?[11]

---

[7] *Textile Mercury*, 12 November 1892.
[8] Oldham MCSA, Minutes of the Annual General Meeting, 15 February 1886.
[9] See the evidence of S. Andrew, Oldham MCSA secretary, and the Manchester Chamber of Commerce to the Royal Commission on Depression of Trade and Industry, *Minutes of Evidence*, vol. 1, 1886, pp. 97–101; vol. 2, 1886, Q4365–70. One response, admitted by Andrew, was that work had been intensified through machinery speed-up. James Mawdsley, secretary of the cotton spinners' union (AAOCS), indicated that the 'large majority' of mills in Lancashire flouted the 1874 Factory Act by cribbing, on average, an additional 30 minutes' work a day over maximum working hours. See above, vol. 2, Q5053–4.   [10] Oldham MCSA, Minutes, 26 June 1894.
[11] *Textile Mercury*, 22 September 1894, pp. 244–5.

Table 3.2 *Cotton employers' federations, 1890–1914: proportion of machine capacity organised*

	Spinning percentage	Weaving percentage
1890	—	24.6
1892	39.2	32.8
1897	37.1	30.7
1900	—	43.8
1903	42.8	45.9
1905	60.0	46.0
1908	60.7	50.4
1914	64.2	61.0

Source: Percentages derived by comparing membership data in Federation of Master Cotton Spinners' Association, (FMCSA), *Yearbooks* and *Annual Reports*, 1892–1914 and Cotton Spinners' and Manufacturers' Association (CSMA), Minutes and Levy Book (1912–) with statistics for the entire Lancashire trade from *Worrall's Cotton Spinners' and Manufacturers' Directories*, 1890–1914.

Textile Mercury became an important vehicle, encouraging employer combination to combat the 'encroachments' of trade unionism: 'Employers in every industry need above all else to organise and confederate to prevent any further confiscation of their property and destruction of their civil rights.'[12]

Similarly, accumulating pressures from a more aggressive textile union movement helped to draw a cluster of independent local masters' associations in the weaving district of north Lancashire into the Cotton Spinners' and Manufacturers' Association[13] in the 1890s and finally to persuade the one remaining large independent master spinners' association in south Lancashire (Bolton) to join the FMCSA in 1905.[14] The net result was the consolidation of a network of local cotton associations (see map 3.1) and a marked rise in the proportion of the trade organised in the industry-wide federations. The percentage of total cotton weaving machine capacity organised by the Cotton Spinners' and Manufacturers' Association rose from 25 in 1890 to 44 in 1900 and to 61 by 1914. After a slight fall in the mid-1890s, the proportion of total cotton spinning machine capacity organised by the Federation of Master Cotton Spinners rose from around 40 per cent to 64 per cent by 1914 (table 3.2).

---

[12] Ibid., 31 October 1896, p. 346.

[13] Despite its title this was a federation of local associations.

[14] R.F. Dyson, 'The development of collective bargaining in the cotton spinning industry, 1893–1914' (Ph.D. thesis, University of Leeds, 1971), pp. 318–51, where the emergence and early growth of the FMCSA is charted in detail.

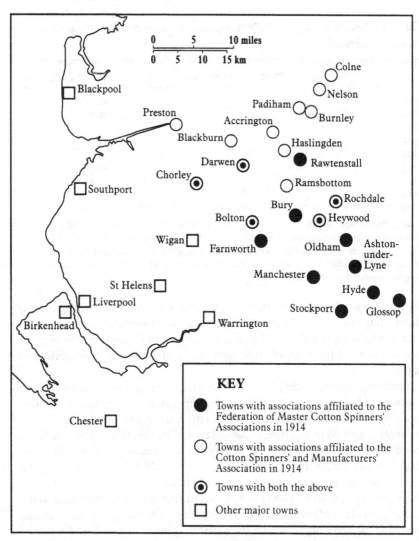

Map 3.1 Cotton employers' associations in Lancashire in 1914

The 1890s also marked a period of intensified collective organisation amongst British engineering employers. As Wigham and Zeitlin have shown, sustained trade union pressure during a revival of trade in the mid-1890s prompted the formation of the Employers' Federation of Engineering Employers' Associations (EEF) in the spring of 1896.[15]

---

[15] Zeitlin, 'Internal politics', pp. 54–5.

When addressing a group of engineering employers in Manchester the first president of the EEF graphically raised the spectre of union domination and the need for counter-combination:

The Amalgamated Society of Engineers intend making an organised attack on employers in England ... If the employer once yields to these demands he will be reduced to nothing more than a cashier in his own works ... The only solution in dealing with the present attitude of this most aggressive society is to have a complete and unified bond of union between the masters as exists with the men.[16]

Subsequently, vigorous campaigning from the newly formed EEF and the polarising impact of the 1897–8 engineering industry lock-out led to a marked upsurge in cohesion amongst engineering employers. In Lancashire, an engineering employers' association in Preston was resuscitated in 1896, the Manchester association formed in the spring of 1897 and the Rochdale and Burnley associations in 1898.[17] The successful prosecution of the 1897–8 engineering lock-out appears to have been an important catalyst for employer organisation growth, inside and outside the engineering sector.[18] Aggregate membership of the EEF rose from 7 local associations with 180 members at the beginning of the lock-out to 36 local associations and 702 firms at the end.[19] If industrial conflict helped cement worker solidarity and class consciousness, it often appears to have had similar effects upon employers. The success of the lock-out, as the FMCSA reported, was a great inspiration to employers, an unequivocal endorsement of the advantages of solidarity through formal combination over independent and maverick employer action.

One consequence was a tendency towards a greater degree of inter-association collaboration and the emergence of formal structures to co-ordinate regional policies. In the summer of 1899, when the Oldham Engineering Employers' Association appealed for support to resist a local strike of moulders for a wage rise, the neighbouring Manchester association readily provided assistance.[20] Similarly, the smaller engineering

[16] Manchester Engineering Employers' Association (EEA), Minutes, 29 March 1897.
[17] Local engineering employers' associations existed previously in many Lancashire towns in the early 1870s, including Manchester and Liverpool, and some north-west employers played an active role in the industry umbrella organisation, the Iron Trades Employers' Association in the 1870s and 1880s. Notably John Platt, Colonel R. Peacock, W. Hargreaves and B.A. Dobson.
[18] Federation of Master Cotton Spinners' Associations (FMCSA), *Annual Report*, June 1898, p. 10.
[19] Zeitlin, 'Internal politics', p. 56; Wigham, *The Power to Manage*, pp. 43–62. There was further steady growth to 55 local associations by 1914.
[20] Manchester EEA, Minutes, 6 June 1899. Oldham claimed that it could not resist the moulders' claims alone but would stand firm with the support of Manchester.

Table 3.3 *Engineering employers' associations: Lancashire membership, 1898*

Associations	No. of member firms	No. of men employed	Wage bill (in £s)	Representation on the EEF executive committee
Barrow	1	2,998	153,334	1
Liverpool	10	4,729	315,369	1
Manchester	60	20,494	1,023,449	3
Oldham	38	17,400	871,925	3
Bolton and Bury	35	9,400	463,600	1
Rochdale	8	700	47,194	—
Wigan	9	750	47,400	—
Preston	12	1,608	84,346	—
Blackburn	5	2,122	110,985	—
Burnley	7	950	60,000	—
Totals (Lancs.)	185	61,151	3,177,602	9
Totals (EEF)	671	194,843	10,279,630	35

Source: Engineering Employers' Federation, Levy Payments File, 1899.

employers' associations in north Lancashire began to co-ordinate their activities more closely over 1898–9 (table 3.3).[21] These emerging relationships were formalised towards the end of 1899 in the creation of a powerful regional employers' federation (the Mid-Lancashire Combination) which came to combine all the major engineering employers' associations in Lancashire and incorporate almost a third of the total EEF membership in Britain.[22] In 1908, H. Lawton, an Oldham EEA executive committee member, articulated the growing belief that in unity and organisation lay the power to resist trade union aggression, stating: 'It is a matter of mutual help . . . the next struggle may be in Oldham.'[23]

The 1890s also witnessed a marked growth in collective organisation amongst master builders in Britain. By 1905, Richard Price has commented, 'few employers of any consequence stood outside the master builders' associations'.[24] Moreover, the local master builders' associations (many of which had a very long independent existence) were moving towards more effective inter-association collaboration at the regional level during this period in an attempt to strengthen their position *vis-à-vis* labour. A crop of regional master builders' federations emerged

[21] Preston EEA, Minutes (General Meeting), 28 November 1898.
[22] Engineering Employers' Federation (EEF) Microfilm Archives, ref. F(5)5: Rules of the Mid-Lancashire Combination; Manchester EEA, Minutes, 1 May 1906.
[23] Oldham EEA, Minutes (General Meeting), 15 July 1908.   [24] Price, *Masters*, p. 197.

in the 1890s, in the south, the midlands, the north and north-west of England. The Lancashire and Cheshire Federation of Building Trade Employers was founded by the Bolton and Blackburn associations in 1894, with an initial membership of seven local groups.[25] An intensified strike wave brought the two major associations of Manchester and Liverpool into the regional federation in 1898, raising membership from some 661 firms in early 1897 to 1,400 firms by December 1898 in 20 affiliated associations.[26] The new organisation was open to all types of building firms, according to a Federation press release:

In consequence of what are considered the aggressive and unreasonable demands, notices of which have recently been received from the operatives by the employers in the building trades in the Manchester and Liverpool districts, the employers have felt compelled to federate for mutual protection . . . The object of this employers' federation is to form a powerful combination of employers to counter-act the trade unions, particularly in regard to interference with the management of works and freedom of employment.[27]

By 1914 there were 54 constituent local associations, with a total membership of some 2,943 building firms in the LCFBTE. At this point, this constituted around 30 per cent of the total membership of the National Federation of Building Trade Employers (table 3.4). Across the country, the membership of the NFBTE grew from around 1,300 firms in 1892 to peak at 7,000 firms in 1907. The subsequent recession in building construction took its toll and membership fell back sharply thereafter to 5,700 by 1913.[28]

Many other employers' organisations, including the Shipbuilding Employers' Federation, the British Federation of Master Printers and the regional coalowners' associations, also experienced significant growth over the 1890–1914 period.[29] The Shipping Federation claimed to organise lines representing over 90 per cent of British registered tonnage by 1905.[30] Evidence also suggests that strong employers' associations existed

---

[25] Lancashire and Cheshire Federation of Building Trade Employers (LCFBTE), Minutes of the First Annual General Meeting, 1 June 1895. See also H. Bullough, *The First Fifty*, Manchester: NWFBTE, 1945, pp. 9–10.

[26] McKenna and Rodger, 'Control by coercion', pp. 222–3.

[27] Unidentified press cutting in LCFBTE, Minutes, 1 June 1898.

[28] North-West Federation of Building Trade Employers (NWFBTE), Minutes of Administration Committee, 12 September 1912; NWFBTE, *Yearbook*, June 1914, p. 46; Burgess, *Origins*, p. 129.

[29] Church, *History of British Coal*, pp. 651–74; E. Howe, *The British Federation of Master Printers, 1900–1950*, London: British Federation of Master Printers, 1950, pp. 4–44; Lovell, 'Collective bargaining', pp. 64–6.

[30] Royal Commission on Trade Disputes and Trade Combinations, *Minutes of Evidence*, Cd 2826, p. 302. The actual figure was probably nearer to 70–75 per cent.

Table 3.4 *National Federation of Building Trade Employers: north-west England membership, May 1914*

Association	Member firms	Association	Member firms
Accrington	23	Leigh	74
Alderley	32	Liverpool	214
Altrincham	112	Llandudno	20
Ashton	44	Longridge	17
Bangor	15	Macclesfield	48
Barrow	61	Manchester	255
Birkenhead	56	Middleton	28
Blackburn	86	New Mills	40
Blackpool	92	Northwich	27
Bolton	134	Oldham	161
Burnley	125	Ormskirk	13
Bury	105	Preston	159
Buxton	25	Radcliffe	59
Caernarvon	10	Rhyl	20
Cheadle	14	Rochdale	78
Chester	55	Rossendale	24
Chorley	23	St Annes	32
Colne	35	St Helens	30
Colwyn Bay	27	Southport	63
Congleton	10	Stockport	33
Crewe	17	Todmorden	26
Darwen	16	Warrington	35
East Flintshire	16	Westhoughton	19
Fleetwood	26	Widnes	19
Frodsham	6	Wigan	110
Glossop	34	Winsford	13
Heywood	31	Wrexham	22
Knutsford	20		
Lancaster	54		
		Total	2,943

Source: NWFBTE, *Yearbook,* June 1914, p. 46.

in Scotland, especially on Clydeside, where Joe Melling discovered a 'sharp rise in membership of regional and national employers' associations' prior to the First World War.[31] A further indication of the growing professionalism and permanence of employers' associations was the trend towards employment of full-time salaried secretaries and officials. Nor

[31] J. Melling, 'Scottish industrialists and the changing nature of class relations in the Clyde region, 1880–1918', in T. Dickson (ed.), *Capital and Class in Scotland*, Edinburgh: John Donald, 1982, p. 88.

does formal organisation tell the whole story. George Askwith, the government's chief industrial relations conciliator and troubleshooter, noted how employers commonly forged collective responses to workers' demands between 1910 and 1914 even where no formal employers' associations existed.[32] Furthermore, in some cases the influence of the industry association extended beyond its numerical membership. There is evidence of compliance by non-member firms with the policy initiatives of the association in their trade, as, for example, in cotton spinning, where non-affiliated firms representing several million spindles supported an organised short-time movement and a threatened industry lock-out of ring-spinners in 1907 and 1908.[33]

The actual and perceived threat from organised labour, ebbing and flowing with trade conditions, though generally on an upward trajectory from c. 1880 to 1920, constituted a powerful inducement upon employers to combine. Changed labour market circumstances, tighter product markets and threats to profitability encouraged experimentation with different modes of control by management. In some cases this reaction by employers was internalised. The Singer Corporation's response to the emergence of mass unionisation of their Clydebank plant in 1910–11 would be an example.[34] However, an important factor increasing the capacity of employers to organise collectively over this period was that the structure of British industry facilitated externalisation of industrial relations – that is, delegation to an organisation – rather than internalisation. As Howard Gospel has shown, British firms before the First World War were generally smaller in scale, frequently family-owned and typically lacked a sophisticated managerial bureaucracy (in contrast to their German and American counterparts).[35] This constrained the ability of most British firms, acting independently, to counteract trade union growth and maintain managerial authority, thus providing a structural incentive towards collective organisation. One impact of this process of externalising industrial relations, however, was to retard further the development of internal management, with adverse implications for competitiveness.

Moreover, the existence of employer associations in industries where trade unionism was relatively insignificant suggests that unionisation was not the only factor cementing collective organisation amongst employers.

---

[32] G. Askwith, *Industrial Problems and Disputes*, new edition, Brighton: Harvester, 1974, pp. 347–55.   [33] FMCSA, *Annual Reports*, 1907 and 1908.

[34] Glasgow Labour History Workshop, *The Singer Strike, Clydebank, 1911*, Glasgow: Clydeside Press, 1989. Singer was, however, something of an exceptional company in the extent to which it experimented before 1914 with neo-Taylorite labour management methods.   [35] Gospel, *Markets*, pp. 16–17, 181–2.

The timing of the trade union upsurge and the context in which it occurred are of great importance. Significantly, the unions were becoming more powerful and aggressive during a period when many employers were pressurised by a profit squeeze as foreign competition intensified. The decline in profits was particularly sharp in the decade 1875–85, prompting a soul-searching debate on the roots of declining competitiveness amongst the British business community.[36] High labour costs were commonly regarded as the root cause. This crisis in profitability prompted a range of reactions by industrialists, including reorganisation of businesses to benefit from economies of scale and more streamlined management – epitomised in the limited liability company and in some, albeit limited, mergers and amalgamation movements. Re-equipment, modernisation, tightening discipline and supervisory structures (foremen replacing subcontractors), reorganisation and speed-up of work, and the extension of payments by results (tying wages more closely to effort) were all facets of this response to more hostile market conditions. Emphasis, however, was clearly laid upon cutting labour costs, rather than significantly raising capital investment in industry. This constituted in some industries (such as building) an attack upon what employers regarded as customary 'restrictive' trade practices and in others (such as textile manufacturing) a marked deterioration of 'welfarist' benefits and atrophying of traditional paternalist relationships between master and worker. At the same time, political developments, including the full legalisation of trade unions over the period 1871–5, provided a prerequisite for union expansion. Changing market forces sustained the momentum towards associational activity, creating the space for the implantation and growth of trades unionism and, in turn, the emergence of employers' organisation as a counterpoise.

Product market circumstances are thus vital in explaining the emergence of employers' organisations. What might be tolerated whilst profit margins were healthy became burdensome in harder times. Constraints on profitability due to a more hostile marketplace prompted employers to exercise more vigilance over their production costs and hence seek solace in collective organisations designed to contain trade unionism, regulate labour and product markets.[37] With growing competition, the costs of

---

[36] J. Saville, 'The British state, the business community and the trade unions', in W. Mommsen and H. Husung (eds.), *The Development of Trade Unionism in Great Britain and Germany*, London: Allen and Unwin, 1985, pp. 315–23. Blaming labour costs and a siege mentality characterise the employers' evidence to both the Royal Commission on Trade Depression of 1885–6 and the Royal Commission on Labour, 1892–4.

[37] See Garside and Gospel, 'Employers and managers', p. 104, where it is argued that employers' organisations were a product of the 'economic pressures of the time'.

industrial disputes were becoming increasingly unbearable. However, industrialists were induced to combine in such circumstances not just to address trade unions but also because association offered them the power to exert control over aspects of a more hostile and volatile product market.

Employers' organisations endeavoured to defend and promote the business interests of their members – to enhance profitability and protect managerial prerogative – in a number of ways. In the labour relations sphere, associations provided a critical bulwark against the main weapon of organised labour – the withdrawal of labour. Gradually, however, employer organisations came to accommodate trade unionism, making the transition to collective bargaining through the formulation of sub-stantive agreements and systematised procedures for the avoidance of disputes. This matrix of collectively bargained and arbitrarily imposed arrangements intimately influenced the organisation of work, the division of labour and workers' welfare across British industry. These pivotal labour relations activities will be analysed in more detail in subsequent chapters. Beyond strikebreaking and the formalisation of collective bar-gaining several additional areas of associational activity merit attention, not least because they impinged, albeit indirectly, upon industrial rela-tions and because such services clearly influenced affiliation and commit-ment to the association. Included here would be the organised regulation of the product market, political lobbying and the provision of mutual insurance covering employers' liability for injury, disease and death sus-tained at work.

Before the First World War, most British employers' associations engaged in modes of trade regulation, delving in distinctively non-com-petitive market behaviour, including price-fixing, regulating contract and tendering conditions and organising production curtailment. Indeed, this was often an important part of the package of services which came with membership and, arguably, a significant inducement to affiliate. The FMCSA, the CSMA and the NFBTE explicitly incorporated such ser-vices within their constitutions. The EEF was ostensibly involved only with labour relations, separate associations, such as the British Electrical and Allied Manufacturers' Association (formed in 1903), developing to regulate trade.[38] Nevertheless, evidence suggests that a number of the local associations of the EEF in Lancashire engaged directly in market regulation prior to the First World War and that the EEF was drawn inexorably into broader matters relating to product markets during the

---

[38] The 1947 *Directory of Trade Unions and Employers' Associations* lists over seventy registered trade associations covering sections of the engineering trade.

inter-war recession. This represented one strand of the wider movement towards collaborative business practices which characterised the years from around 1890, prompted by a more hostile product market and facilitated by a more flexible and liberal legal framework in Britain on restrictive business practices (compared, for example, to the USA).[39] Trustification and merger may well have been poorly developed in Britain compared to Germany and the USA. However, a variety of collaborative practices organised through industry employers' associations were common.

It was customary by the 1890s for local associations and the industry-wide federations in the cotton industry to organise systematic curtailment of production in periods of trade recession in an attempt to reduce over-stocking of the market and maintain yarn and cloth price levels. Such action undoubtedly worked to protect the more inefficient mills from the vagaries of the trade cycle, minimising company failures. The larger associations, such as the Oldham MCSA, organised short-time working across their industry as early as the 1860s. The secretary's notebook records twelve such extended periods of organised production curtailment over the period 1895–1914, the longest being the 4-day week in the American spinning sector from July 1909 to April 1910.[40] This regulation required an 80 per cent majority vote to implement and was backed up by fines as sanctions imposed upon those disloyal firms which attempted to gain a competitive advantage by exceeding production limits.[41] This policy also had the support of the trade unions and could have significant stabilising implications for industrial relations.[42] For example, by steadying the market through 1909–10 millowners were induced not to press for a further wage cut in 1910, accepting a five-year negotiated wage freeze in exchange.[43] Beyond production curtailment the organised millowners took two other important initiatives in an attempt to stabilise trading conditions. Both the CSMA and the FMCSA actively supported the British and the Empire Cotton Growing Associations which worked to develop new strains of raw cotton, better quality and a larger volume crop, thus

---

[39] 'British trade associations', *Planning*, 221 (May 1944), p. 2. For a detailed case study of the trade protection strategies of employers' organisations in one industry see Magrath, 'Wool textile employers' organisations'. Magrath develops a very persuasive critique of the artificial divisions within the literature between trade and employers' organisations.

[40] H. Cliff (Oldham MCSA secretary), *Notebook*.

[41] H. Booth, Solicitors, Legal Opinion No. 12, to Oldham MCSA, 17 July 1911.

[42] Turner, *Trade Union Growth*, pp. 339–40.

[43] Oldham MCSA, *Annual Report*, 1910, p. 4: 'There is no doubt . . . that this organised action had enabled the trade to pass through an unprecedented depression without a financial crash which would have more or less involved every firm, however well situated.'

reducing Lancashire's dependence upon US supplies. Secondly, the FMCSA was a major sponsor of the Manchester Cotton Association which worked to develop Manchester as a cotton importing entrepôt after the completion of the Manchester Ship Canal. Bales of cotton imported into the Manchester docks increased from 66,000 to 772,000 between 1895 and 1914 and this competition brought transport costs down significantly.[44]

In the building industry the employers' organisations intervened in the market more directly, including within their constitutions and objects the power to regulate tendering prices for both materials and labour. One example would be the Liverpool associations which specified schedules for daywork labour charges (labourers 6d–7d per hour; craftsmen 9–9½d) and prices for all building materials and cartage as early as the 1870s.[45] Such arrangements spread throughout the region, with Oldham and Manchester adopting tendering schedules by 1890.[46] However, it should be stressed that these were 'model' schemes, recommended to the trade rather than enforced. Complaints over non-compliance and of undercutting by neighbouring associations abounded, leading to a movement by the NWFBTE to formulate a regional schedule. Because of the diversity of local wage rates and internecine competition between associations this initiative floundered. However, a Regional Schedule of Prices for Measured Work was formulated in 1912, standardising tendering prices for such things as brickwork (by the yard), painting, graining, varnishing, and standardised joinery, such as door frames and sash windows.[47] Again, however, this was only a recommended list, lacking any formal sanctions against non-compliance. Such initiatives continued through the inter-war years, with local associations continuing to recommend compliance with their list and a number of regional and national initiatives geared towards controlling price competition.[48] Though it is difficult to assess the impact of these practices, undoubtedly such developments went some way to minimising the perennial problem of price undercutting through costing

[44] Oldham MCSA, *Annual Reports*, 1913, pp. 22–3; 1915, p. 27; 1920, p. 8. The FMCSA also lobbied the regional railway companies to obtain cheaper freight rates and the local authorities to secure reductions in mill rating assessments.

[45] Liverpool Master Masons, Minutes, 4 October 1870; 9 December 1873; Liverpool Master Bricklayers, Minutes, 8 and 15 December 1873; Liverpool Master Plasterers, Minutes, 10 December 1873. Tendering labour charges were around 20 per cent higher than actual wage rates.

[46] Oldham MBA, Minutes, July 1889; Liverpool MBA, *Yearbook*, 1909–10, pp. 63–6.

[47] LCFBTE, Minutes, 9 October 1912; 9 September 1914; 16 February 1915.

[48] Such as the National Standard Method of Measurement and the National Daywork Charges List (1932). These represented moves towards more sophisticated and scientific modes of quantity surveying and tendering. See NWFBTE, Minutes, 30 November 1933.

miscalculations and hence helped to stabilise what was an extremely volatile product market.[49]

Building employers' organisations also intervened to protect the interests of their members in relation to contracting conditions – indeed, one ex-secretary suggested this was one of the main objects of the NAMB.[50] What this amounted to was the drawing up of model contracts governing relations between client, contractor and architect by local associations and the promotion, from 1904, of the Standard Form of Contract drawn up by the Royal Institute of Building Architects (RIBA). Where evidence of objectional contracting conditions emerged, the employers' organisations co-ordinated resistance. This occurred on a number of occasions with local councils which insisted on restrictive profit limitation clauses, excessive financial penalties, fair wages and closed shop clauses.[51] Association action usually started with lobbying and could extend to membership boycotts of particular contracts. In September 1912, for example, the Bolton MBA obtained amendments to sixteen clauses in a corporation contract after a boycott. Later, the Liverpool association succeeded in getting an independent arbitrator clause inserted in local contracts. The Manchester association enforced such boycotts by heavy fines and expelling disloyal members.[52] The NWFBTE also provided its support, co-ordinating a campaign in 1914–15 which resulted in the abolition of council insistence on fully priced schedules of materials with tenders and almost universal acceptance across the north-west of the RIBA contract.[53] Such pressure group and watchdog functions continued through the war and inter-war years with association activity extended into negotiating discounts and preferential trading terms and opposing the expansion of local authorities' direct labour building departments.[54]

Despite the EEF being ostensibly a labour relations organisation, the local associations in north-west England provided wider services for their members. For example, the Manchester EEA organised boycotts of contracts which incorporated 'objectionable' clauses such as the closed shop and fair wages and conditions clauses. This policy was designed to roll back what one member, Sebastian de Ferranti, identified as 'obnoxious labour clauses which were more and more being included in Municipal

[49] This was the view of an editorial in *National Builder*, April 1935, p. 363.
[50] Royal Commission on Labour, *Minutes of Evidence* (Knox), Group C, Q18,443–6 (1892).
[51] Manchester BTEA, Minutes, 21 November 1905; 13 February 1906.
[52] Ibid., 12 November 1914.
[53] NWFBTE, Minutes, 7 August 1914, 9 and 20 June 1915.
[54] See, for example, NWFBTE, Minutes, 18 March 1918; 27 February 1923; 30 November 1931;14 May 1937; *National Builder*, November 1934, p. 188; April 1935, p. 363.

and County Council contracts'.[55] Of more significance is the evidence of formal price-fixing amoı ʒst the Lancashire engineering employers, though this service was con ꟷed to the associations dominated by textile engineering located in the nᴏrth of the county. The heterogeneity of the larger Manchester and Oldham industries militated against collaboration on price. Indeed, the only reference in the Minutes of the Manchester EEA between 1897 and 1939 was of a meeting of master boilermakers in 1904 which rejected a price-fixing scheme designed 'to prevent the disastrous quoting under cost price for the making of boilers'.[56] A similar situation prevailed in Oldham.[57]

Elsewhere price collaboration was a well-entrenched aspect of the services of local engineering employers' associations. The Burnley EEA formulated a minimum price list for weaving loom components (castings, forgings and beams) after an association survey of prices in 1906. This was a conscious effort to minimise competition between members and raise prices, preventing 'ruinous undercutting'.[58] Compliance was compulsory across the membership and the list was rigidly policed through a penalty clause, later incorporating a £200 forfeit.[59] The Blackburn association was reported to have a similar list. Moreover a cluster of EEAs developed 'model' lists for engineers' outworking jobbing charges, defining standard hourly labour charges for different grades of work to be charged to clients (often local millowners). Here competing areas, such as Burnley, Blackburn and Preston attempted to maintain a differential – slightly undercutting their competitors' list – in order to attract business.[60] Such activities extended into the inter-war period where there is some evidence of inter-association collaboration in the formulation of a standardised price list covering loom manufacturing in north Lancashire.[61]

Thus, product market regulation was an integral feature of employer organisation activity, though interventions differed depending upon the

---

[55] Manchester EEA, Minutes, 7 February 1899.   [56] Ibid., 15 November 1904.

[57] Oldham EEA, Minutes, 2 March 1921; 6 February 1923. On both these occasions the Oldham EEA responded to enquiries from the Oldham MCSA denying the existence of any price lists. However, whilst the associations do not appear to have been formally involved, this does not preclude the possibility that informal pricing arrangements existed in the Oldham and Manchester engineering industries.

[58] Burnley EEA, Minutes, 21 August 1906.

[59] Ibid., 17 July 1908, for an example of two local member firms being fined for selling beams below list prices. A new list, with a £200 bond, was formulated in 1914. See ibid., Minutes, 3 April 1914, 25 September 1914, 19 February 1915.

[60] For examples, see Rochdale EEA, Minutes, 11 July 1906, 4 July 1907; Burnley EEA, Minutes, 28 and 30 August 1906.

[61] Burnley EEA, Minutes, 23 October 1918, 19 January 1922, 7 January 1925.

nature of competition and demand. Direct price-fixing occurred where the product range was relatively narrow and product markets were restricted and domestic, as in the building industry or loom manufacture in north Lancashire. Where the industry was more heterogeneous and there was considerable external competition in product markets, collaboration on price was relatively rare. Here, other less direct modes of restrictive practices designed to regulate the product market – such as output restriction – were formulated. Similar diversity in product regulation tactics occurred elsewhere, for example amongst the wool textile employers' organisations in Yorkshire.[62]

There was one other important catalyst prompting more extensive employer organisation over the period from 1890 to 1914 – increasing government intervention in work conditions and industrial relations. In the aftermath of 'new unionism', the Royal Commission on Labour directly encouraged the regularisation of industrial relations via collective bargaining between groups representative of both capital and labour, and, as Davidson has shown, direct government involvement as mediator in industrial disputes increased considerably from c. 1908.[63] Moreover, social legislation passed by a progressively more democratic and liberal state cumulatively added to employers' costs just at a time when profits were under pressure (as, for example, the Workmen's Compensation Acts of 1897 and 1906; extensions in factory legislation, e.g. 1901; National Insurance, 1911). Other initiatives firmly legitimised the immunities and rights of trade unions (notably, the Trades Disputes Act of 1906) rolling back adverse judge-made precedents in the law courts which had undermined the legal position of the unions and, after Taff Vale, seriously circumscribed industrial action. These actions were interpreted by some employers as a challenge to proprietorial rights and by many others as impacting adversely upon profit margins as industrialists were besieged by additional direct costs, such as contributions to National Insurance and occupational injury and disease insurance premiums. These irritants were particularly acute within industries (such as coal-mining and the docks) where labour costs formed a high proportion of total costs and the risks of occupational injury and death were relatively high. Such developments led directly to an enhancement of the pressure group activities of employers' organisations vis-à-vis the state.

The cotton industry illustrates this point. The larger local cotton employers' associations performed a parliamentary pressure group

---

[62] Magrath, 'Wool textile employers' organisations', p. 379.
[63] R. Davidson, 'Government administration', in Wrigley (ed.), A History of British Industrial Relations, 1875–1914, pp. 159–79.

function from their origins in the mid-nineteenth century. This involved lobbying local MPs, government ministers and committees. Once formed, the industry federations such as the CSMA and the FMCSA largely took over such activities and work in this area was incrementally cranked up as state intervention in economic and social affairs intensified. In 1899, the main industry federations effectively combined (for the first time) to create the Cotton Employers' Parliamentary Association to integrate their views better with regard to legislation. This was partly stimulated by the passage of Workmen's Compensation legislation in 1897 and partly as a counterpoise to the very effective parliamentary activity of the cotton unions, co-ordinated through the United Textile Factory Workers' Association. The disillusionment of millowners with the recently formed Employers' Parliamentary Council (led by the Earl of Wemyss and a successor to the Liberty and Property Defence League) was also influential in the formation of the CEPA. Cotton employers were apparently dissatisfied with the extent of representation offered to the industry within the constitution of the EPC.[64]

During its twelve-year existence the CEPA performed a watchdog function for millowners, making the industry's case to the government and the legislature, attending at the lobby of the House of Commons and calling meetings of MPs from the textile regions. From c. 1903 to 1906, for example, the CEPA campaigned against David Shackleton's Trade Disputes Bill, designed to strengthen trade union legal immunity after the adverse judgement of Taff Vale in 1901. Similarly, the CEPA successfully opposed the Abolition of Fines Bill in 1909, arguing that fining for imperfections in work was a necessary quality control mechanism. Industry views were also articulated through the CEPA upon Factory Acts, Workmen's Compensation, 48 Hours Bills, the Cotton Cloth Factories Bill and the National Insurance Bill. There was also some co-ordination with the United Textile Factory Workers' Association on such issues as protectionism (opposing the Indian cotton duties) and the Machinery Rating Bill (1903). The arguments developed by the employers on all these issues were linked directly to their strategic aims – the enhancement of profitability and preservation of managerial prerogative (in turn considered essential for the maintenance of factory discipline and control). A common defence was to stress the adverse impact of the costs of such social legislation upon the competitiveness of the industry in international markets.[65]

---

[64] CEPA, Minutes, 10 March, 20 June 1899; FMCSA, *Annual Report*, 1899–1900. Subsequent approaches by the EPC were rebuffed. See CEPA, Minutes, 3 April 1906. The work of the Employers' Parliamentary Council awaits systematic research.

[65] CEPA, Minutes, 1899–1911.

Most of the literature dealing with the political activities of employers' organisations has emphasised their weakness and their patent failure to stem significantly the flow of 'progressive' legislation in the late Victorian and Edwardian periods which added significantly to employers' costs. Despite the existence of a network of industrial employer federations and the Employers' Parliamentary Council, statute after statute heaped additional burdens on to the shoulders of British capitalists, whilst extending state responsibility for workers' welfare in a number of key areas (such as injuries, sickness and unemployment at work). In cotton, the employers' activity helped to delay passage of legislation (e.g. Trades Disputes Act) and secured some amendments (such as Workmen's Compensation) but very few tangible successes were registered in preventing this significant growth of social legislation. Employer organisations evidently failed to develop an effective peak parliamentary pressure group with the clout of the Parliamentary Committee of the Trades Union Congress until during and immediately after the First World War when the Federation of British Industries (1916) and the National Confederation of Employers' Organisations (1919) emerged.[66]

These arguments appear persuasive, though more research is necessary to prove conclusively that employers' performance in the corridors of power prior to the First World War was barren of success.[67] Two points relating to this are worth making. First, industrial employers did not necessarily oppose social/welfare legislation; rather, a significant strand of larger and more progressive concerns welcomed legislation on the grounds that it enforced minimum standards across industry, hence undermining competition from what were regarded as 'unscrupulous' undercutting employers.[68] The broader commitment by employers to the

[66] See Price, *Labour in British Society*, pp. 210–11; Phelps-Brown, *Origins*, pp. 119–23; S. Blank, *Industry and Government in Britain: The Federation of British Industries in Politics, 1945–65*, Farnborough: Saxon House, 1973, pp. 11–21. See also Turner, *Businessmen and Politics*. Charles Macara, of the FMCSA, played a role in the formation of two other federations, the Employers' Parliamentary Association, established 1911, and the Central Association of Employers' Organisations, formed in 1915, both with their base in Manchester.

[67] In cotton textiles, for example, successful lobbying on the part of the industry employers' organisations played a crucial part in neutralising the campaign for a 48-hour week from the mid-1890s to the First World War. Important amendments were also secured to the Cotton Cloth Factories Act and the Workmen's Compensation Act of 1897. Nevertheless, Joe Melling's point that organised employers had little influence over the formulation of legislation c. 1880–1914 remains a valid one. See J. Melling, 'British employers and the development of industrial welfare' (Ph.D. thesis, University of Glasgow, 1982), vol. 2, pp. 214–16. For a detailed assessment of employers' political power in another region see R. Trainor, *Black Country Elites: The Exercise of Authority in an Industrialised Area, 1830–1900*, Oxford: Clarendon Press, 1993.

[68] J. Melling, 'British employers', vol. 2, pp. 168, 213–14.

concept of voluntarism could be significantly diluted by pragmatic considerations. Furthermore, many employers recognised the wider strategic benefits of welfarist legislation in containing industrial militancy, enhancing social stability and strengthening moderate trade unionism. Secondly, the critique of industrial capital in this respect ignores the evidence that a significant divergence existed between legislation and workshop practice and, indeed, that employers could evade liability and exploit loopholes in the law, aided by their associations. The cotton employers' associations, for example, regularly financed legal cases brought by member firms through local courts in order to establish precedents in judge-made law, gaining injunctions against picketing, for example, or organising cases against local factory inspectors to undermine their techniques (e.g. humidity measurement and air sampling methods) or prove that certain machinery need not be fenced, or fighting accident compensation cases under the Employers' Liability Act (1880) to the bitter end.[69] Doctors were employed by some employers' associations to legitimise such activities and to endorse a strategy of blaming the victim. Witness, for example, the medical representative of the West Scotland Engineering Employers' Association who claimed that Clyde boilermakers actually preferred to lose their hearing: 'He just stoically accepts it as being absolutely in some respects an advantage . . . I never heard a complaint from a boilermaker that his deafness in any way interferes with him either socially, or in his work.'[70]

The response to the passage of the Workmen's Compensation Acts of 1897 and 1906 provides a good example of effective collective intervention to protect the interests of employers. The 1897 Act provided automatic compensation to workers for injuries sustained in the workplace, with the onus for proving wilful negligence placed upon the employer (rather than, as under the Employers' Liability Act, 1880, the injured worker). Financial compensation was to be paid directly by the employer rather than through any state agency. The 1906 extension of the Workmen's Compensation Act improved payments and extended employer liability to a series of scheduled industrial diseases (initially six). This legislation has been hailed as revolutionary in its ameliorative effects on health at work.[71] However, Bartrip and Burman have persuasively demonstrated that the legislation failed markedly in adequately compensating either workers or their families for death and injuries at work, or in

[69] CSMA, Minutes, 15 October 1904; CEPA, Minutes, 28 September 1909.
[70] Departmental Committee on Compensation for Industrial Diseases, *Minutes of Evidence*, 1907, Cd 3496, Q5166–68, p. 163.
[71] See, for example, E. Hunt, *British Labour History, 1815–1914*, London: Weidenfeld and Nicolson, 1981, pp. 45–6.

raising safety standards in the workplace.[72] The expected improvement in occupational health standards was nullified partly because individual employers responded by insuring themselves against claims for accident or disease compensation with an annual premium. What is most significant from our point of view is that many established employers' organisations simply absorbed this insurance role within their services to members, or created a separate insurance company dealing specifically with such compensation in their trade. This occurred in cotton spinning, weaving and finishing in Lancashire and amongst a number of the major employers' organisations on Clydeside.[73] Some organisations, such as the FMCSA, supplemented the provision of mutual insurance with the formation of accident departments with a remit to investigate all claims and challenge employer liability, where appropriate, in the law courts. During 1898–9 the Federation refused compensation in around 15 per cent of cases, took a number of cases to court to prove 'wilful misconduct' and campaigned to prove that certain parts of their machinery were safe, even when unguarded, such as the mule carriage wheels and the faller stop of the mule.[74] The work of the FMCSA accident department was significantly enhanced with the appointment of George Chadderton, an ex-union official, as claims troubleshooter. By 1914 this was a major component of Federation business, not least because accident claims multiplied dramatically over this period.[75]

This policy cut down significantly on members' insurance costs, thus providing another powerful inducement to join the association.[76] This constituted a similar cementing force for employers to that which the administration of the National Insurance Act of 1911 provided for the unions. Employer policy also worked, however, to undermine somewhat the effectiveness of the legislation. This was so partly because the employers' associations delayed payments, refused to allow unions the right to inspect the locus of an accident (only miners had this right after the 1911 Mines Act) and negotiated one-off lump sums rather than weekly payments. Moreover, the Lancashire employers' organisations who

---

[72] Bartrip and Burman, *The Wounded Soldiers*, pp. 190–213; McIvor, 'Work and health', pp. 63–4.   [73] Melling, 'British employers', vol. 2, pp. 27–30, 48–50.

[74] FMCSA, *Annual Report*, 1898–9.

[75] Claims rose from an average of 90 per year in Oldham in 1898–1900 to 219 in 1904–6 and 850 in 1910–12. Figures from the Oldham Operative Spinners' Association, Handbook, 1913, p. 11.

[76] Oldham MCSA, Minutes, 31 March 1898, 14 April 1899. It was estimated by one Oldham official (John Brown Tattersall) that savings of up to 50 per cent on commercial insurance rates were secured by employers' organisations developing mutual insurance services.

performed such functions continued to impose levies on their members based on size of firm, with no rating system for firms with a higher than average accident or industrial disease propensity. Hence the sanctions operating to encourage welfare and safety measures, or medical services in the workplace were significantly diluted. As the Factory Inspector H.J. Wilson noted, this induced indifference to preventive safety because the financial burden was spread throughout the trade rather than falling solely on the individual enterprise.[77]

Employers' organisations also performed a vital educative function as disseminators of information relating to production, commercial and legal matters in their respective industries. For example, members of cotton and coal associations were kept informed of all the latest legal requirements regarding health and safety, including sanitation and ventilation. Data and advice were provided on the pros and cons of different dust extractors for the cardroom in an attempt to offset legal enforcement. In 1902 the CSMA sent a deputation to the USA to examine production methods and a subsequent report on the visit was circulated to members. In a less formal sense, associational activity undoubtedly stimulated interchange of ideas and discussion of innovations in working practices, wage payment, welfare provision and the like. Such activities supplemented and were occasionally dovetailed into initiatives taken by the Manchester Chamber of Commerce – which lobbied upon all the major legislative initiatives affecting trade and industry – and other trade and specialist associations.[78]

Once they were up and running, the role of employers' associations themselves should not be discounted in bolstering solidarity. Straightforward moral exhortations emphasising the need for loyalty, a united front against labour and the brotherhood of the association were common enough in annual reports, industry circulars and membership campaigns. In 1897 the Oldham MCSA urged non-members to weigh up 'the magnificent strength and organisation of the operatives' against 'the utter weakness of those employers acting independently of the association'. They continued: 'The uncombined employer . . . is not even a free agent, except to do mischief to himself and to his trade, or if he has the courage to resist an encroachment at the expense of a strike, his resistance generally proves fruitless or financially ruinous. This awkward predicament can only be escaped by combination.'[79] Trade journals were utilised to

---

[77] Departmental Committee on Accidents, *Minutes of Evidence*, Cd 5540, 1911 (evidence of H.J. Wilson).

[78] See Manchester Chamber of Commerce, *Monthly Record*, for a detailed survey. For comments on the role of the Glasgow Chamber of Commerce see J. Melling, 'British employers', vol. 2, pp. 181–4.   [79] Oldham MCSA, *Annual Report*, 1897.

advertise association activities and sympathetic editors often helped to drum up support. *Textile Mercury*, the millowners' trade and technical journal, was a relentless proponent of tighter employer solidarity throughout the 1890s. A typical editorial in 1896 scathingly castigated the unorganised masters: 'When a man has become purse-proud – too proud to join his fellows in the trade to protect its interests – it is quite time he retired from it. He has become a source of weakness to it and a danger to its welfare.'[80] Such pleas could be backed up with systematic canvassing and personal deputations by executive committee members to the largest, most embarrassing non-member companies and independent local associations. The Chorley MCSA, for example, was drawn into the orbit of the FMCSA in 1908 after its members received a deputation outlining the advantages of federation.

In his evidence to the Royal Commission on Labour, Joshua Rawlinson, secretary of the Cotton Spinners' and Manufacturers' Association, asserted that in cotton textile weaving no external pressure had been imposed on companies to become members of the organisation. Membership, Rawlinson postulated, was an entirely voluntary affair.[81] Other organisations were not so scrupulous, however, and the voluntary principle in membership affiliation was often breached. Following the advice of the EEF, the Burnley EEA discriminated powerfully against non-member firms by advising its existing membership to subcontract work only to fellow members where possible.[82] The use of the EEF crest on a firm's stationery was explicitly designed to facilitate such practices. However, it appears to have been in the building construction industry that such coercive methods were taken to the greatest lengths. In 1886, the Liverpool Master Builders' Association adopted a formal intertrading rule which barred members from providing work contracts with any non-organised building trade employer. Through the 1890s, similar intertrading rules were adopted by other building employers' associations in north-west England, including the largest association in Manchester:

That we, the members of the Manchester, Salford and District Building Trades Employers' Association hereby mutually agree not to give or take tenders to or from or otherwise employ or deal with regular employers in the building trades of this district who are not members of this association, or with a regular employer of any other district where there is a federated association, if he does not belong thereto.[83]

Eventually the LCFBTE made the intertrading rule compulsory across its entire membership in 1902.

[80] *Textile Mercury*, 22 February 1896, p. 145.
[81] Royal Commission on Labour, *Digest of Evidence*, Group C, vol. I, 1892, p. 88.
[82] Jefferys, *Story of the Engineers*, pp. 145–6.   [83] Manchester BTEA, Rules, 1901.

Just what influence this rule had on membership and employer solidarity in the building industry is difficult to gauge. Certainly the employers' associations themselves regarded their initiative as successful. The NWFBTE reported in 1914: 'The increase in membership in some of the local associations has been phenomenal, and shows what can be done by means of the intertrading rule, together with an energetic president and secretary.'[84] In an extensive analysis of the diffusion and impact of the intertrading rule in building before the First World War, McKenna and Rodger have argued that this rule led directly to a massive expansion in association membership, referring to 'the spectacular success of the intertrading rule in reinvigorating building employers' associations'.[85] This, however, may well be overstating the case. The membership of the Liverpool association, by McKenna and Rodger's own admission, only rose significantly from the mid-1890s, a decade after their intertrading rule was accepted. Moreover, the mere existence of such a clause in association rule books should not be taken as sufficient evidence that it was being consistently adhered to. Numerous complaints were made in the Minutes of the Manchester and District BTEA that despite punitive fines member firms were not adhering to the intertrading rule in the 1900s. Indeed, this disloyalty assumed such serious proportions that the association was forced to suspend the rule indefinitely at the end of 1909.[86]

Despite the considerable strides in employer organisation and collective consciousness over the period 1890–1914, wide differences existed in levels of organisation between different industries and many weaknesses and flaws in employer solidarity persisted. In some sectors employer cohesion was fractured by a number of separate organisations competing for membership, for example in shipping, building and textiles. In textiles, separate employers' organisations developed to represent employers in distinct product sectors – cotton, jute, wool, worsted, silk. Moreover, within the largest of these sectors employer organisation usually followed the predominantly specialised business structure. In cotton and wool, separate organisations developed to represent preparers and spinners, weavers and finishers, sometimes with further fragmentation by type of product, for example fine or coarse spinning, fancy or plain weaving. In cotton, attempts to amalgamate and rationalise such structures came to little prior to the 1960s, when the all-encompassing British Textile Employers' Association was formed. Trade union sectionalism and fragmentation had its parallel amongst employers' organisations. Indeed, the

[84] NWFBTE, *Annual Report*, in *Yearbook* (1914), pp. 29–30.
[85] McKenna and Rodger, 'Control by coercion', p. 226.
[86] Manchester BTEA, Minutes, 14 January 1909, 18 November 1909.

two are intimately interrelated. Internal differences could seriously fracture employer solidarity. The master builders' associations, for example, were divided internally between the dominant general contractors and the smaller subcontractors and by section (painting, plastering, masonry, plumbing, etc.). Such conflicts of interest created a serious rift within the Manchester building employers' association over 1911–12.[87] Product specialisms and competitive pressures within industries could, on occasions, completely undermine a concerted, consensus strategy to reduce wages, or sustain a lock-out. The cotton industry is a good case in point. Balancing the disparate interests of the two major local master cotton spinning associations – Oldham at the most competitive end of the market, spinning medium and coarse yarns and dominated by limited liability companies, and Bolton, insulated from the fiercest gusts of foreign competition spinning fine yarns in traditional family-owned firms – constituted a major preoccupation for the FMCSA leaders. These organisational weaknesses could work to undermine the power of capital *vis-à-vis* labour, as, for example, during the Brooklands lock-out of 1892–3 in the cotton industry.

Local autonomy, moreover, remained an important feature of employers' associations before the First World War and could work to frustrate expansionist and bureaucratic tendencies at the centre. *Textile Mercury* commented on the state of employer organisation in north Lancashire in 1896:

There are as yet too many loosely-compacted local associations, deficient in all the principal elements of a strong organisation. These, again, have only slight connection with any federation of employers' associations. They are quite as apt, and rather more so, to go their own way, if they can see the shadow of a local advantage by so doing.[88]

Local associations usually had complete financial and administrative independence and regional and national federations were typically required to consult their constituents directly, through referendums, before action such as a lock-out, or output restriction, or increase in subscriptions could be initiated.[89] Some local associations opposed the general drift towards centralisation through regional and national federations which characterised the 1890–1914 period. Frequently, for example, the local master builders' associations in Lancashire voted against levy increases to the National Federation, the Manchester BTEA voting to

---

[87] Manchester BTEA, Minutes, 16 January 1912.

[88] *Textile Mercury*, 22 February 1896, p. 144.

[89] For a discussion of the strength of local autonomy and the degree of independence in the cotton weaving sector see R. Smith, 'The history of the Lancashire cotton industry, 1873–96' (Ph.D. thesis, Birmingham University, 1954) pp. 304–5.

disaffiliate on at least two occasions between 1890 and 1914. Disagreement between the constituent local engineering employers' associations and concerns on behalf of the smaller north Lancashire associations related to the growing dominance of the Manchester Association led directly to the collapse of the Mid-Lancashire Combination in the engineering sector in 1912–13. Nevertheless, power was gradually and inexorably shifting from the localities to the central federations of employers over the twenty or so years prior to the First World War.

Wide variations continued to exist in the strength of employers' organisations in different industries, towns and regions, though the organised proportion of employers in the basic sectors of the economy was invariably high. The proportion of employers organised in the thirteen major cotton spinning towns in Lancashire averaged 76.5 per cent in 1914 (table 3.5). But this degree of aggregation obscures an organised density range from two towns with between 30–40 per cent organised (Stockport and Chorley) to the largest cotton spinning centres – Oldham, Bolton and Manchester – with 80 per cent and over. Moreover, there were still a few small, relatively isolated mill communities in Lancashire where the masters remained completely unorganised up to 1914, as at Earby and Barnoldswick. Similar differences existed amongst the regional coalowners' associations, as Roy Church has indicated, though the major regional associations had recruited between 50 per cent and 90 per cent of mineowners in their respective coalfields by the 1900s.[90]

It is perhaps important also to explore what type of firms affiliated to employer organisations, who held control and who the non-members were. Here size, extent of union penetration and location appear to have been significant determinants. In general, medium- to large-sized limited liability companies located in urban areas where trade union penetration was most marked were most likely to be attracted to collective organisation. On the other hand, the minnows of the trade and poorly unionised companies located in more remote, rural locations tended to remain independent. In the cotton industry, the average size of organised firms (measured by machine capacity) was more than double that of non-members. In Burnley, for example, all 7 of the biggest companies with over 1,500 looms were organised, 40 of the 52 firms with between 500 and 1,500 looms were organised, whilst only 15 of the 40 firms with less than 500 looms were members at the turn of the nineteenth century.[91] Most British employers' organisations (excepting those operating the

---

[90] Church, *History of the British Coal Industry*, pp. 651–74.
[91] Burnley CSMA, List of Members, 1899, compared with lists of all companies in the district in *Worrall's Cotton Spinners' and Manufacturers' Directory*, 1899.

Table 3.5 *Master cotton spinners'
associations: machine capacity organised
in major Lancashire towns, 1899 and 1914*

District	Percentage of total spindleage organised in local cotton spinning employers' associations	
	1899	1914
Ashton	70.2	78.8
Bolton	84.9	80.3
Bury	58.7	57.6
Chorley	?	36.8
Farnworth	?	65.1
Glossop and Hyde	66.7	72.3
Heywood	84.4	77.4
Manchester	58.4	80.0
Oldham	80.1	82.6
Rochdale	47.5	76.8
Stockport	9.5	32.6
Totals	71.6	76.5

Sources: Percentages are derived from
comparing the total number of spindles in all
the firms in these districts as ascertained from
*Worrall's Cotton Spinners' and Manufacturers'
Directories* for 1900 and 1914 with the spindleage
of member firms of the local master cotton
spinners' associations. Names of member firms
were obtained from the FMCSA Membership
Lists in the *Annual Reports* for 1899 and 1914
and the Bolton MCSA *Annual Report* for 1899.

intertrading rule) patently failed to develop the significant inducements
offered by some German and US organisations to attract and maintain
smaller firms with a largely non-union workforce. The Berlin
Metalworking Employers' Association, for example, had an innovative
rule exempting employers with over 40 per cent of their workforce non-
unionised from participating in employers' association lock-outs
and strikebreaking actions.[92] Tables 3.6 and 3.7 below provide further

[92] H. Homburg, 'The "human factor" and the limits of rationalisation', in Tolliday and
Zeitlin, *Power to Manage?*, p. 156.

Table 3.6 *Master cotton spinners' associations: size of firms in membership,*
c. *1900*

Size of firm (spindles)	Total no. of firms in the district	No. of firms organised in local associations	Percentage of firms organised
Up to 29,999	230	53	23.0
30,000–99,999	292	218	74.4
100,000–149,999	49	35	71.4
150,000 and over	27	22	81.5
Totals	598	328	54.8

Note: The above table does not cover the whole of Lancashire, only the major cotton
towns, namely: Bolton, Oldham, Ashton, Rochdale, Stockport, Bury, Darwen, Heywood,
Manchester and Glossop and Hyde. Catchment areas are those used in the Worrall's
directories.
Sources: For number of firms in the district: *Worrall's Cotton Spinners' and Manufacturers'
Directory*, 1900; number of firms organised: figures are from the membership list in the
FMCSA, *Annual Report*, year ending June 1899, and from a membership list of the
independent Bolton MCSA, 1900.

Table 3.7 *National Federation of Building Trade Employers: proportion of
local employers organised in Manchester, Preston and Bolton, 1914*

Trade section	Total no. of firms in these districts	No. of firms organised	Percentage of firms organised
General contractors Subcontracting master bricklayers, joiners, plasterers,	262	122	46.6
masons and slaters Subcontracting master plumbers	827	112	13.5
and painters	1,178	111	9.4
Totals	2,267	345	15.2

Note: This table assesses the proportion of local firms listed in trade directories that were
in membership of these three associations of the NWFBTE. Actual organised densities
are likely to be higher because of the possibility of membership of other organisations.
Sources: Figures for total numbers of firms are derived from the following: *Kelly's Trade
Directory for Manchester and Salford*, 1914; *Barrett's Directory of Preston and District*, 1913;
Tillotson's Directory for Bolton, 1916; figures for number of firms organised are derived
from the membership lists in the NWFBTE, *Yearbook*, June 1914.

evidence of the positive correlation between company size and association membership.

In 1908–9 the Bolton MCSA – which already incorporated firms
owning over 80 per cent of potential machine capacity in the area –
embarked on a major recruitment drive and recorded, in meticulous
detail, the results of a systematic canvas of the fifty-two mostly small,
family-owned, non-member firms in their region. This unique source
provides us with some useful insights into the range of attitudes and per-
ceptions of these smaller millowners and demonstrates just how difficult
it was to draw this particular group of capitalists into collective organisation. Sixteen companies simply refused to join, without offering any
reason, despite repeated deputations. The representatives of eleven non-
member firms argued that they had no need to associate because their
workers were not members of any trade unions (several commenting that
they would join only if and when their employees became union
members). Five declared the cost to be too high. Eighteen mills refused to
affiliate because their labour relations strategies deviated markedly from
that of the association. The latter consisted of both hawks and doves. The
doves were several paternalist employers who indicated that they paid
over standard list wages, had no trouble with their workers, sometimes
commenting that they disagreed fundamentally with the concept of combination. The hawks were more autocratic in labour relations, undercutting standard wage lists and insisting on total subordination of their
employees. Representative of the latter was the managing director of
William Gray and Sons of Darcy Lever, who commented that he would
lock out his workers on the first sign of any trouble. Similarly, Henry
Ashworth, of New Eagley Mills, Turton, accused the Bolton MCSA of
lacking 'vitality', being 'a weak-kneed lot' afraid of taking effective action
to slash workers' wages when circumstances permitted. Only two firms of
the fifty-two canvassed committed themselves and eventually joined the
Bolton association.[93]

Rather than courting membership, evidence suggests that some
employers' associations deliberately discouraged the affiliation of small
companies by setting very high entrance fees. More importantly, perhaps,
the internal decision-making procedures of many associations actively
discouraged the small firm from association. Like trade unions, employers' associations were financed by subscriptions levied on their constituent members. Whilst systems varied considerably, it was common
practice for bigger firms to pay more according to their stake in the industry. Certainly this was the case in engineering, building and cotton

[93] Bolton MCSA, secretary's report (manuscript) on the census of non-members, 1908–9.

textiles. Hence the level of a member firm's subscription was determined by the size of the company, measured by numbers employed (as in building), or wage roll (engineering) or machine capacity (textiles). This principle was also commonly applied to decision-making. Voting-power within most employers' associations was apportioned according to the size of a firm's subscription.[94] In cotton spinning, for example, member firms voted on issues such as organised short-time working in the trade or a lock-out through a system of one vote per 10,000 spindles owned. Other organisations which started with a one-firm-one-vote policy made the transition to proportionate voting by the 1900s. This happened, for example, with the Manchester MBA and the Manchester EEA. Inevitably, this led to associations being dominated by the larger companies, constituting a disincentive to the smaller employers, many of whom evidently opted to remain independent. In the mid-1900s, for example, seven companies out of a total membership of 71 controlled 50 per cent of the voting power of the Manchester EEA. Throughout the period from 1897 to 1914 a dozen major companies dominated the executive committee of the Manchester EEA, creating a virtual self-perpetuating oligarchy.

This did not mean, however, that the industry leaders were accepted into employers' organisations under any conditions, or that there were no large companies outside the local associations. Tables 3.6 and 3.7 indicate that a significant number of large companies did remain aloof from collective organisations in cotton and building before the First World War. This was also true of the engineering employers' associations. The Manchester Engineering Employers' Association, for example, managed to recruit only around 20 per cent of the limited liability companies in the district in the 1900–14 period.[95] Some of these unorganised companies undoubtedly disagreed with the industrial relations strategies of their industry association, preferring a personalised labour relations policy, perhaps more vigorously anti-unionist and coercive, or more openly welfarist and accommodating towards their workers. William Mather (Mather and Platt) and Hans Renold (Renold Chains), who, much to the annoyance of the organised employers, introduced the 48-hour working week into their plants, are good examples of the latter.[96] Another employer rebuffed the Manchester association, commenting: 'I cannot take part in any combination for the purpose of keeping down the wages of workmen, young or old,

---

[94] Royal Commission on Labour, *Rules of Associations*, 1892, pp. 308–16.

[95] Manchester EEA, Membership Journal, compared to *Kelly's Trade Directories for Manchester*, 1900, 1905, 1910, 1914.

[96] For a discussion of the shorter hours' experiment at Mather and Platt see A.J. McIvor, 'Employers, the government and industrial fatigue in Britain, 1890–1918', *British Journal of Industrial Medicine*, 44 (1987), pp. 724–32.

or of boycotting workmen who, in the absence of agreements to the contrary, have left their employers.'[97] Similarly, the General Electric Company withdrew from the Manchester Engineering Employers' Association in 1907, ostensibly because the association refused to sanction its adoption of the one break per day, 54-hour working week. Tweedale and Smalley, a major British textile machinery manufacturer based in Rochdale and employing 2,600 in 1913 also refused to join their association prior to the 1940s. This company was fervently anti-unionist and could not stomach the degree of union recognition implicit within the 1898 Terms of Settlement. Its directors were described by Lloyd George as being 'of that stubborn, autocratic type that was in its way at least as dangerous to industrial peace as the worst communist agitator'.[98]

Conclusion

The Board of Trade surveys of employers' organisations and internally generated membership data for a series of employers' associations suggest that the period c. 1890–1914 witnessed a quite remarkable surge in employer collectivism in Britain. In conclusion, four general points emerging from this chapter are worth reiterating: first, that a whole plethora of new organisations emerged during the period c. 1890–1914, extending the matrix of employer combination more broadly across the British economy. Secondly, that formerly independent local associations were increasingly merging their interests in broader regional and industry-wide employer federations, whilst at the same time collaboration between such bodies was increasing. Thirdly, that such employers' organisations were becoming more and more representative of their section of industry, sinking deeper roots within their constituency. In this period, c. 1890–1914, British employers' organisations in major sectors of the economy made the transition from transient, *ad hoc*, localised and relatively weak bodies to permanent, representative, centralised and, in many cases, relatively powerful institutions.

Fourthly, employers increasingly organised in response to intensifying pressures from three sources: the marketplace, the state and from trade unions. In particular, employers were bitterly resentful at trade union encroachments into the labour market (influencing labour costs and the wage-for-effort exchange) and what were regarded as property rights and sacrosanct managerial prerogatives to organise, control and manipulate their labour as they thought fit. Political challenges to property rights

---

[97] Manchester EEA, *Minutes*, 4 October 1898.
[98] David Lloyd George, *War Memoirs*, London: Odhams Press, 1938, p. 1149.

were also growing with the emergence of socialist politics and the electoral breakthrough of the Labour Party. Such shifts in the balance of power were the primary stimulants prompting employers to unite to present a solid and more effective front against the challenge of labour. However, state intervention and intensifying competition constituted other important threats to profitability and managerial prerogative, impinging upon individual companies and encouraging collective organisation. Magrath has made the point that employers' organisations exaggerated the 'labour threat' in their public profile and played down product market regulation in order to extract maximum support from their constituency.[99] What is evident is that a triumvirate of external pressures impacted upon the individual enterprise, raising capacities for collective organisation amongst employers.

However, pre-First World War capitalists were no monolithic group and their collective organisations varied greatly in strength, cohesion and orientation. The limits of employer organisation need to be recognised. To varying degrees, employers' associations, like most trade unions, were beset by internal divisions. They invariably constituted a heterogeneous collection of deeply individualistic, hard-headed, profit-orientated capitalists often with conflicting interests, competing against one another in product and labour markets. 'Employers frequently seem to combine rather unwillingly', the Royal Commission on Labour noted in 1894, 'and the trade competition between them often makes it difficult for them to hold together.'[100] However, this should not obscure the fundamental point that divisions and conflicts of interest between employers were increasingly being transcended in the common interest as the rules of the collective game were being incrementally absorbed between c. 1880 and 1914. As unions became more powerful, employers increasingly accepted the inevitable corollary of employer organisation and forged more cohesive, unified responses to the labour challenge. Though clearly not omnipotent, employers' associations were becoming more effective and evidence suggests that such institutions played a significant rather than a marginal role in regulating the labour market and structuring industrial relations in many industries prior to the First World War, developing innovative and flexible strategies to retain managerial autonomy, enhance profitability and constrain the power of the trade unions. Such matters are explored further in subsequent chapters, starting with an analysis of the pivotal role employers' organisations played in neutralising the key weapon of the trade unions – the withdrawal of labour.

---

[99] Magrath, 'Wool textile employers' organisations', p. 376.
[100] Royal Commission on Labour, *Fifth and Final Report*, Part I, June 1894, pp. 31–2.

4   Strikebreaking

'The rapid progress being made in the art of striking work', the employers' journal *Textile Mercury* noted in 1896, 'is a markedly distinctive feature of the closing years of the nineteenth century.'[1] James Cronin has argued that in this context 1870 was a significant watershed. Thereafter, the offensive strike became an integral feature of union policy, strike propensity incrementally increased, with most militancy being clustered at the peak of the trade cycle, notably in three phases, 1871–3, 1889–90 and 1911–13.[2] This process of escalating militancy had a salutary effect upon employers and their organisations. Such 'petty tyranny', *Textile Mercury* reported in 1892; 'has exhibited a tendency to become further and more strongly accentuated. The educational influence of this course of conduct upon the employers has been very considerable and has given a great impetus to organisation.'[3] As the ability of workers to sustain lengthy strikes increased, employers' strikebreaking mechanisms became more sophisticated, with employers' associations playing a key role in this process. Indeed, strikebreaking services lay at the heart of most employers' associations' functions in the late nineteenth century. This chapter examines this challenge–response relationship, focusing upon how employers' associations mobilised their resources to neutralise the strike weapon, discussing, in turn, the organisation of substitute labour for strikers, victimisation, legal action, strike indemnity and compensation schemes, and the utilisation of the lock-out. Collectively, this array of formidable weapons was aptly described by David Lloyd George as 'the steam roller'.[4]

Labour replacement in strikes

The Labour Department of the Board of Trade recognised that one of the most common features of British strikes in the late nineteenth century

[1] *Textile Mercury*, 31 October 1896, p. 345.
[2] See Cronin, 'Strikes, 1870–1914', pp. 74–98.   [3] *Textile Mercury*, 7 May 1892, p. 335.
[4] Cited in G. Alderman, *The Railway Interest*, Leicester: Leicester University Press, 1973, pp. 199–200.

was the tendency of employers to import substitute labour to fill the places vacated by strikers.[5] The objective here was not only to keep production running, but to administer a severe disciplinary lesson to workers who had the temerity to withdraw their labour and hence disrupt the production and profit flows of their masters. In this process of labour replacement employers had various options. They could organise resistance and obtain replacees independently, without recourse to external help. This was the procedure successfully pursued by Sebastian de Ferranti during the 1897–8 engineering lock-out.[6] Alternatively, employers delegated this task by drawing upon the support of their employers' organisation or recruiting the help of the plethora of specialist 'free labour' organisations and labour-registration schemes which emerged as part of the employers' counter-attack against 'new unionism' in the 1890s.

Even allowing for the rabid exaggerations within William Collison's fascinating autobiography, the National Free Labour Association, formed in 1893, was undoubtedly the most successful of these various specialist labour replacement agencies of the pre-First World War period in Britain. Like Allan Pinkerton, Jim Farley and Pearl Bergoff in the USA, Collison was utterly committed to his mission. Before he died he drew up a speech for judgement day:

I did the work that my soul and brain ached to do. I tried to do it manfully. I broke their strikes. I am a blackleg, my Lord God Almighty. I was called the king of the blacklegs. And if ever in Thy infinite wisdom it pleases Thee to thrust my soul into a human mould once more, I will rise up a blackleg and break their strikes again, so help me, God![7]

Other prominent 'free labour' organisations were the Free Labour Protection Association and the Association of Non-Unionists. Smaller organisations existed at the regional level. Between 1898 and 1914 both the Manchester EEA and Platt Brothers, textile machinery makers of Oldham (and the largest engineering company in Lancashire), provided annual donations to a Lancashire and Midland Non-Unionist Association.[8]

Such organisations, however, had severe limitations, particularly in breaking strikes of skilled craftsmen and in disputes in the well-unionised

[5] Board of Trade (Labour Department), *Annual Report on the Strikes and Lock-Outs of 1888*, c. 5809, p. 9.   [6] Manchester EEA, Minutes, 31 December 1897.
[7] W. Collison, *The Apostle of Free Labour*, London: Hurst and Blackett, 1913, p. 328.
[8] Manchester EEA, Ledger, 1898–1916, p. 286; Platt Brothers, Directors' Minutes, from 19 July 1900, *passim*. See also J.M. Ludlow, 'The Labour Protection Association', *Economic Review*, 9 (1899) and the evidence of F. Millar and J. Cardwell to the Royal Commission on Trade Disputes and Trade Combinations, *Minutes of Evidence* (hereafter referred to as RC on Trade Disputes, *Minutes*), Cd 2826, 1906, pp. 208, 245–6.

cotton and coal industries. Evidence suggests that only in trades where
the labour process involved little skill, and unions were weak, and the
employers were vehemently anti-unionist were the specialist 'free labour'
organisations utilised with any regularity and success.[9] The pro-'free
labour' journal *Textile Mercury* admitted that the 150,000 members
claimed by the NFLA were 'mainly drawn from the rougher classes of
industry'.[10] Even Collison conceded that a proportion of his members
were 'brandy moochers', who were only interested in the chance of good
wages, free booze, tobacco and other such 'perks', including the chance
of an occasional fight![11] In some strikes, foreign workers were used by
employers as blacklegs. Such workers were imported via a network of
charity organisations, contacts, emigration agents and workhouse
authorities, or heard of vacancies by word of mouth and letters from rela-
tives. As Kenneth Lunn has shown, however, the role of immigrants as
strikebreakers has been grossly exaggerated and their class-conscious-
ness and political awareness neglected. The stereotype of immigrants
typecast as strikebreakers is too simplistic an explanation for the diversity
of reactions which such labour exhibited to industrial conflict in
Britain.[12]

Employers' organisations played an important part in importing substitute labour during strikes, though different organisations placed
varying emphasis on the utilisation of this weapon. In some sectors –
notably shipping, railways and sections of the extractive industries in the
1890s and 1900s – this coercive and provocative option remained the first
line of defence against unionisation and strikes. Elsewhere, employers'
associations used labour replacement as a second line of defence, kept in
reserve and implemented when established collective bargaining machinery was exhausted or ignored by work groups and unions. The Shipping
Federation, founded in 1890, provides an archetypal example of the
former, confrontational type. The Shipping Federation was one of the
most militant of pre-1914 employers' organisations, established explicitly
as a 'permanent battle-axe' to protect shipowners against the strike
weapon.[13] It opened registry offices in all the main ports to engage labour
and forced workmen to sign the much resented registration 'ticket',

[9] G. Alderman, 'The National Free Labour Association', *IRSH*, 21 (1976), pp. 324–5;
   Clegg, Fox and Thompson, *A History of British Trade Unions*, vol. I, p. 172.
[10] *Textile Mercury*, 1 October 1896, p. 287. See also *Textile Mercury*, 3 November 1894, p. 355
   and 10 November 1894, p. 377.
[11] J.M. Ludlow, 'The National Free Labour Association', *Economic Review*, 5 (1895), p. 116.
[12] K. Lunn, 'Immigrants and strikes: some British case studies, 1870–1914', *Immigrants and
   Minorities*, 4, no. 2 (1985), pp. 30–42; K. Lunn (ed.), *Hosts, Immigrants and Minorities*,
   Folkestone: Dawson, 1980.
[13] L.H. Powell, *The Shipping Federation*, London: SF, 1950, pp. 1, 5.

pledging that they would work peacefully with non-unionists.[14] A special Federation Labour Department was responsible for importing labour to break strikes and ensuring that ships experienced minimum delays in 'turn-around' times during disputes, thus saving shipowners the enormous costs of having their capital lying idle. Strikes of seamen protesting against such draconian conditions were rapidly broken, and at a number of ports, including Aberdeen, Swansea and Cardiff, the employers protected their imported labour by housing them afloat on specially requisitioned ships.[15] The Federation maintained three such specially fitted-out depot ships for the housing of strikebreakers, and a store of bedding, cooking equipment and other necessities for the accommodation of up to 5,000 men within the docks.[16] Beer tokens and free tobacco were issued to strikebreakers as an added incentive and an artificial stimulant to morale. The smashing of the dockers' strike in Hull in 1893 (where 95 per cent of the men were in the union) was a clear indication of the power of the Shipping Federation's strikebreaking machinery. As a result, Hull rapidly made the switch from best to one of the worst organised ports in the country, and by 1900 had a reputation as a major supplier of blacklegs in shipping and other strikes throughout the United Kingdom.[17] A contingent was even sent from Hull to aid the Taff Vale Railway Company in South Wales in 1900.

The strategy of the Shipping Federation reflected the fiercely antiunionist commitment of most of its constituent member shipping companies. The customary casual system of employment at the docks and wharves, and the consequent over-supply of labour made the dockers particularly vulnerable to blacklegging.[18] However, the circumstances did not always remain so unequivocally in favour of the employers. Occasionally, as at Cardiff in 1910, the local labour market was peculiarly tight and the Federation found it impossible to obtain and retain even unskilled free labourers.[19] The attitude of tugmasters during strikes could also be of crucial importance, as they were often called upon to ferry free labour crews to ships, and Powell has shown that they did, on occasions, object to such a pivotal role in the strikebreaking operation.[20] Adequate

---

[14] Cuthbert Laws, testimony to RC on Trade Disputes, *Minutes*, p. 302.
[15] P. Leng, *The Welsh Dockers*, Ormskirk: Hesketh, 1981, pp. 24–6.
[16] 'The Shipping Federation: why it was formed and what it has done', *Fairplay*, 7 June 1895.
[17] R. Brown, *Waterfront Organisation in Hull, 1870–1900*, Hull: University of Hull, 1972, pp. 68, 74, 90–1.
[18] For a more detailed discussion of blacklegging on the waterfront see W. Kenefick, 'A social history of Clydeside dockers' (Ph.D. thesis, University of Strathclyde, forthcoming) and W. Kenefick, *Ardrossan, the Key to the Clyde: A Case Study of the Ardrossan Dock Strike, 1912–3*, Irvine: Cunninghame District Council, 1993.
[19] Leng, *Welsh Dockers*, p. 60.   [20] Powell, *Shipping Federation*, pp. 11–14.

protection was also of crucial importance. Usually the Federation could rely on generous state help to protect property and strikebreakers. However, by 1910–14 official attitudes were changing and the view was gaining ground that heavy picketing was justified where employers had provoked this response from labour by importing blacklegs. Consequently, the authorities became increasingly reluctant to provide military and police protection for substitute labour during strikes.[21]

Whilst it may have been somewhat less easy to replace skilled men, this was by no means impossible, particularly when the resources of the industry employers' associations were being drawn upon. Indeed, crude figures gleaned from the *Annual Reports on Strikes and Lock-Outs* suggest a surprisingly high replacement rate amongst skilled strikers, at least during the late 1880s and early 1890s.[22] The National Association of Master Builders organised the import of skilled blackleg labour from the European continent on a number of occasions. During the 1899 plasterers' dispute large sums of money were allocated by the local associations of the master builders' federation for advertisements and expenses, and agents were established in America, Scotland, Ireland and around England to engage non-unionist craftsmen to work on the employers' terms.[23] The Lancashire master builders' federation had a regional subcommittee in the 1890s which organised the import of blackleg labour to get strike-hit firms working again. In a strike of joiners (referred to the regional federation from the local employers' association) the committee first approached firms in the region who were known to be employing strikers and persuaded most of them to sack such workers. Then advertisements for labour were placed in newspapers in Newcastle, Carlisle, Lancaster and Kendal. Travelling expenses of replacees were defrayed by the Lancashire Federation. This soon had an effect. By the end of January 1897 the Chorley Master Builders' Association reported that they had recruited all the men they required and that the union had conceded defeat and had withdrawn their notices for a wage advance.[24] Elsewhere, in London, Collison's organisation had at least some limited success in recruiting skilled craftsmen to break strikes in the 1890s. Somewhat later, the London master builders claimed to have successfully replaced around half of the 20,000 operatives locked out in 1914, many of whom were craftsmen.[25]

[21] Hunt, *British Labour*, p. 331; Alderman, 'The National Free Labour Association', p. 326; Bean, 'Employers' associations', pp. 381–2.

[22] For more detail see McIvor, 'Employers' organisation and strikebreaking', table 3, pp. 16–17.

[23] Lancashire and Cheshire Federation of Building Trade Employers (LCFBTE), Minutes, 5 April 1899, 29 April 1899.   [24] LCFBTE, Minutes, 27 January 1897.

[25] LCFBTE, *Yearbook*, June 1914, p. 37. See also R. Postgate, *The Builders' History*, London: Scolar Press, 1923, pp. 367–8.

Similarly, many ironmasters, railway companies, engineering and ship-building employers' organisations undermined strikes by arranging to replace, fully or partially, a recalcitrant workforce. The Iron Trades Employers' Association (established in 1872) created its own Labour Registry Office for unemployed non-unionist workmen and used these men to break a number of strikes over the following twenty-five years, including the 1886–7 engineers' strike at Bolton and the strikes at the Taff Vale Railway Company in 1877 and 1895–6.[26] The employers' trade journal, *The Engineer*, attempted to justify these short, sharp, no-holds-barred methods: 'A short-lived war waged with the utmost vigour is in the end much more merciful in its effects than lingering campaigns fought with the greatest precaution to avoid inflicting injuries on the non-combatants. Nothing can be worse for the districts affected than a prolongation of the strike.'[27] Whilst there was negligible use of the National Free Labour Association during the 1897–8 engineering lock-out, evidence from north-west England indicates that local engineering employers' associations were organising advertisements for blackleg labour, working through agents in other regions, and were encouraging member firms to retain non-unionists and supervisory personnel and promote handymen, labourers and apprentices to skilled work. Such 'loyal servants' were also subsidised through a special reserve fund established by the Manchester EEA when circumstances forced employers to lay them off.[28] The Manchester Engineering Employers' Association also met the Lord Mayor and Chief Constable of the city to put pressure on them to increase police protection for imported labour.[29] These labour replacement tactics were evidently a limited success and the Engineering Employers' Federation claimed that 'in many cases from 20–50 per cent, more work of equal quality had been produced from machinery by comparatively inexperienced hands'.[30] Whilst this was probably an exaggeration, it was excellent propaganda for the employers' cause, capable of seriously sapping the morale of strikers.

Moreover, despite the firmer commitment of the engineering employers after 1898 to procedural forms of control, organised blackleg importation was still resorted to on numerous occasions up to 1914, usually when the formal disputes procedure was exhausted or ignored. For example, the United Machine Workers' Association strike at Brooks and Doxey (textile machinery manufacturers) in 1901, the smiths' strike at Vickers,

---

[26] ITEA, *Record*, pp. 25, 36, 84–5, 130.   [27] *The Engineer*, 8 April 1892, pp. 303–4.
[28] Manchester EEA, Minutes, 28 September 1897, 5 October 1897, 19 October 1897.
[29] Ibid.
[30] Cited in E.J. Hobsbawm (ed.), *Labour's Turning Point, 1880–1900*, new edition, Rutherford: Fairleigh Dickenson, 1974, p. 157.

Barrow, over 1905–6 and the ironmoulders' strike in Liverpool in 1907 were all completely crushed by labour importation aided by engineering employers' associations.[31]

Textile employers also increasingly delegated strikebreaking to their local and industry-wide associations. In 1889, for example, the Bolton Master Cotton Spinners' Association took over the administration of a strike of thirty-three union minders and their piecers (around 100 in total) at Joseph Crook's mill. Substitutes were imported from Preston and fed and lodged in the mill and in two rows of nearby cottages. Within three months, the secretary of the Bolton MCSA reported the spinning mules entirely filled, the mill transformed to a non-union shop and the matter closed.[32] Roughly the same series of events unfolded in strikes of overlookers in Radcliffe, and spinners at the Yew mill, Heywood, and the India mill, Darwen, in the early 1890s.[33] At the Stalybridge Mill Company in 1892 the operative spinners struck work in protest against heavier workloads associated with manipulating the poor-quality raw cotton mixings being used by the employers in an attempt to cut costs. The Ashton Master Cotton Spinners' Association took over the management of the dispute, imported outside labour, organised transportation, accommodation, food and protection and issued regular statements to the press defending their position and tactics. Unable to win a decisive victory, the Ashton association ultimately turned to the Federation of Master Cotton Spinners' Associations for assistance. The Federation stepped up the search for replacement labour and provided further protection against pickets. By May 1892, it was reported that the mill had resumed full-time working, employing a total of 360 substitute workers.[34]

Like the engineering employers' associations, the master cotton spinners' and weavers' federations continued after the adoption of formal stage-by-stage collective bargaining and disputes procedures to fall back on more coercive methods, including labour replacement when the formal conciliation machinery broke down. The inducement of promotion was utilised to persuade employees to blackleg. There was a marked tendency for piecers to be brought in to replace striking minders and for jobbers and weavers to replace striking overlookers. The strike of overlookers in

[31] Manchester EEA, Minutes, 3 December 1901; Correspondence, Vickers to the EEF, 14 November 1905 and 23 August 1906 – see EEF Microfilm Archive, ref. S(7)3; Collison, *The Apostle*, pp. 265–71.
[32] Bolton MCSA, Diary, 2 May 1889 to 7 August 1889; Bolton Operative Spinners' Association, *Tenth Annual Report*, 1889, pp. 8–9.
[33] *Textile Mercury*, 1 September 1894, p. 176; 6 October 1894, p. 276; 13 October 1894, p. 294; 27 October 1894, p. 324.
[34] FMCSA, Minutes, 6 May 1892 and 28 June 1892; Oldham MCSA, *Annual Report*, 1892, pp. 7–9; *Textile Mercury*, 12 March 1892 – 14 May 1892.

Radcliffe in 1894, for example, was undermined by weavers taking their places, forcing the overlookers' union to back down after twenty-one weeks on strike for a wage rise and to accept the old list of prices.[35]

Replacement of strikers by individual companies, employers' associations and 'free labour' agencies in the 1890–1914 period should not, however, be exaggerated. Analysis of the data contained within the *Annual Reports on Strikes and Lock-Outs* (*ARSLOs*) of the Board of Trade Labour Department (BTLD) helps to place the replacement tactic into perspective and to identify changing patterns over time.[36] From 1888 the BTLD collected information on strike activity in Britain, compiling material from employers' returns, union returns and newspaper reports. Clearly, the statistics generated through the *ARSLOs* have a tendency to underrepresent total strike activity. This was partly the result of the voluntary information-gathering procedure and partly because the BTLD opted to adopt more rigid inclusion criteria in 1897 which excluded one-day strikes and strikes involving less than ten workers. From 1900, moreover, the BTLD concentrates only upon what it terms 'principal industrial disputes'. Some evidence suggests that even some of the latter did not find their way into the official report.[37] Nevertheless, despite the deficiencies with this source, the *ARSLOs* provide a quite unique seam of comprehensive data on British strikes. Particularly pertinent for our purposes are the data compiled on employer policy in settling disputes.

Three general points emerge from tables 4.1 and 4.2. First, the propensity to utilise labour replacement as a weapon differed very substantially between sectors. Such variations have been discussed in more detail elsewhere, and can be largely explained by reference to differing patterns of technological change, unionisation, skills, employer attitudes and organisation.[38] Secondly, the vast majority of strikes were settled without recourse to labour replacement (less than one in forty strikers were replaced in the 1890s and 1900s). The importation of blackleg labour in cotton textiles, for example, occurred only at single-firm or sectional strikes involving relatively small numbers. Little or no attempt was made

[35] *Textile Mercury*, 1 September 1894, p. 176.
[36] I am indebted to Richard Devlin, who is currently compiling a sample database of strikes from the *ARSLOs*, for additional information on this source. See R. Devlin, 'Scottish trade unionism, 1885–1914: federal trade unionism, democracy and political development' (Ph.D. thesis, University of Paisley, forthcoming).
[37] For criticisms of the coverage of the *ARSLOs* see J.L. White, *The Limits of Trade Union Militancy*, New York: Greenwood, 1978, p. 184. White found thirty-six strikes in the cotton trade between 1910 and 1914 not included within the annual reports, despite being clearly within the Board's inclusion criteria. See also Glasgow Labour History Workshop, 'The labour unrest on Clydeside, 1910–14', in Duncan and McIvor (eds.), *Militant Workers*, pp. 84–6.
[38] McIvor, 'Employers' organisations and strikebreaking', pp. 13–18.

Table 4.1 *Labour replacement as a mode of strike settlement, 1891–1919*

	Total strikes	No. of strikes in which workers were partially or wholly replaced	Percentage of strikes in which workers were partially or wholly replaced	Workers involved in strikes	Workers replaced during strikes	Percentage of workers replaced during strikes
1891–9	7,135	1,059	14.8	2,581,319	80,271	3.1
1900–9	4,754	613	12.9	1,233,781	29,713	2.4
1910–19	9,109	440	4.8	7,800,000	23,000	0.3
Totals	20,998	2,112	10.1	11,615,100	132,984	1.1

Sources: Board of Trade, *Annual Reports on Strikes and Lock-Outs*, 1891–1913; *Abstracts of Labour Statistics*, 1898–1937.

Table 4.2 *Labour replacement in strikes by industry, 1888–99*

Industry	Total strikes	No. of strikes settled by partial/ complete labour replacement	Percentage of strikes settled by partial/ complete labour replacement
Mining and quarrying	1,735	59	3.4
Textiles	1,916	215	11.2
Metals	2,246	261	11.6
Building	1,864	261	14.0
Clothing	660	98	14.8
Transport	778	173	22.2
Cabinet and furniture making	244	63	25.8
Food and provisions	161	53	32.9
Printing	124	58	46.8
Miscellaneous trades[1]	556	178	32.0
Totals	10,284	1,419	13.8

[1] Miscellaneous trades include chemicals and explosives, brush making, cement manufacture, coach building, coopery, glass making, agriculture and general labour, leather, rubber, paper, pottery, saddle and harness making, and municipal employment.
Source: Board of Trade, *Annual Reports on Strikes and Lock-Outs*, 1888–99.

to replace cotton workers in the large-scale conflicts of the period: in 1891, 1893, 1908, 1910, and 1911–12. This pattern appears to have been typical of most industries after *c.* 1890. Thirdly, from the 1880s to the First World War the tendency of employers to replace labour during strikes in Britain was clearly declining.

Over this period employers and their associations were finding it more difficult to find substitute labour to replace strikers, and were increasingly choosing to eschew this tactic and pursue other, more subtle, strategies of conflict resolution. Why was this? The ability of employers to import blacklegs successfully had always been influenced by the prevailing, oscillating state of product and labour markets, and continued to be so. Labour replacement in British strikes peaked in the severe depression of the early 1890s, when it was considerably easier to obtain workers desperate enough to break strikes, and declined most rapidly in the prosperous trading years immediately before 1914. Short-term seasonal employment cycles (for example, in agriculture, building and printing) led to considerable fluctuation in the size of the 'reserve army' of unemployed, and hence influenced the ability of the employers to replace labour during strikes. However, several factors markedly altered over the period 1890–1920. These three decades saw an increasing number of employers shifting from coercive, anti-unionist, industrial-warfare policies towards a clearer, more unequivocal commitment to union recognition, conciliation and arbitration. The government also came to commit itself more openly in favour of voluntary conciliation. This was, as Davidson has demonstrated, a pivotal strategy of the newly created Board of Trade Department of Labour from 1893.[39] Consensus and common interests were increasingly emphasised by employers, and blackleg importation was increasingly regarded as too provocative an option, especially in periods of buoyant trade. During the immediate pre-war years, 1910–14, the strategy of many employers' associations was one of concession and flexibility in a rearguard attempt to prevent workers being taken in *en masse* by the growing socialist and syndicalist ideologies. Moreover, in a period of increasingly hostile product markets, employers perhaps came to appreciate more keenly the value of their regular workforce, especially when contrasted unfavourably to the lower productivity and shoddy work of inexperienced substitutes. Witness, for example, the Hull dock strike in 1893, when it was taking imported labour around twice the normal time to turn vessels around and less than 20 per cent of normal coal exports were leaving the port.[40]

Moreover, as unionisation and labour solidarity spread within industrial towns and even to some of the more remote agricultural districts of

---

[39] R. Davidson, *Whitehall and the Labour Problem in Late-Victorian and Edwardian Britain*, London: Croom Helm, 1985. Not only did the Department publicise conciliation and arbitration procedures, but it also openly deplored the costs of disputes and the impact these had upon competitiveness.

[40] Brown, *Waterfront Organisation*, pp. 81–2; RC on Trade Disputes, *Minutes*, p. 70. See also *ARSLO*s for 1889, p. 135; 1891, p. 309.

the country, the pool of easily available non-unionist labour shrank, thus further undermining the labour-importation weapon. The proportion of British workers in trade unions rose from around 10 per cent in 1890 to 18 per cent by 1910, 24 per cent by 1914 and around 45 per cent by 1920. This meant more effective picketing and more complete and demoralising social ostracism for the would-be strikebreaker. Furthermore, the development of a clearly defined legal right to picket in the Trades Disputes Act of 1906 may have substantially improved the ability of trade unionists to prevent the importation of outside labour during strikes.

Victimisation and intimidation

In the struggle to break strikes, to discourage industrial conflict and to penalise labour militants, employers and their associations also formulated and practised various forms of victimisation and intimidation. Indeed, the effectiveness of the labour-replacement weapon depended, at least in part, on the ability of employers to ensure that the replaced strikers would not find employment elsewhere. Blackleg importation and victimisation of strikers therefore often went hand in hand. Sophisticated methods were developed to keep militants permanently out of employment and to prevent strikers gaining work elsewhere whilst a strike was in progress. Such techniques changed significantly through time. In the first half of the nineteenth century, trade unionists were victimised through the non-unionist pledge, or 'document', whereas by the end of the nineteenth century it was predominantly strikers and labour militants (rather than union members *per se*) who were so singled out. The threshold of acceptance had significantly shifted. By the turn of the century, the 'document' was practically extinct in all but the most reactionary of industries (including agriculture, some sections of transport, shop and office work). The use of industrial spies, *agents provocateurs* and private investigation agencies, though not unknown, was much more characteristic of the USA than Britain. In the period 1890–1914, British employers resorted mainly to the character or discharge note, the enquiry, the blacklist, selective re-employment after a strike, legal prosecutions, and internal fining in an attempt to punish and deter actions which deviated from employer-formulated codes of acceptable industrial behaviour. Moreover, just as different industrial groupings exhibited varying commitments to the labour-replacement weapon, so too did each employers' organisation develop its own particular, favoured methods of victimising and intimidating strikers.

In the coal, shipping and railway industries, the employers' organisations enforced the character or discharge-note system before the First World War. This was a formal, written reference from a previous employer which an applicant for a job had to present in order to obtain work. Strikers and strike organisers were not provided with a note. The enquiry note performed a similar function, and was preferred and widely used by the engineering, shipbuilding, construction and cotton masters. The enquiry was a procedural rule, adopted by many employers' organisations, whereby all members agreed to make an enquiry to the previous employer about the position and credentials of each individual job applicant. Strikers could thus be identified and employment refused. These notes performed three major functions: they were evidence of a worker's competence; they aided general industrial discipline and strengthened managerial authority; and, most significantly, they prevented strikers from getting employment elsewhere and consequently prolonging strikes. A more idiosyncratic system was adopted in some Lancashire cotton towns, including Oldham, where employers retained operatives' birth certificates on recruitment and refused to return these to strikers, thus preventing them from getting work elsewhere.[41]

Such tactics might be backed up by the issuing of a blacklist of strikers, designed to prevent what *Textile Mercury* dubbed 'the mischief makers' from obtaining work elsewhere.[42] Attitudes towards the utility of blacklisting, however, differed considerably amongst employers. A number of employers' associations claimed never to have issued blacklists of strikers' names, including the master builders and the cotton employers.[43] Both these groups utilised the enquiry and on occasions only selectively re-employed hands after a strike, thus weeding out militants. The cotton employers' organisations feared the legal consequences of issuing blacklists, and usually contented themselves with the issue of a cautionary circular to member firms informing them of a local strike and reminding them of their 'duty' not to employ strikers.[44]

The use of the blacklist of strikers was particularly common in the coal, engineering and shipbuilding trades, in printing and in the boot and shoe trade, and the employers' organisations in these sectors played an important role in this process. The Leeds Boot Manufacturers' Association and the Yorkshire Master Printers' Association made the blacklisting of strikers a rule of membership and imposed penalties on any employer who gave work to strikers.[45] The Lanarkshire Coalmasters' Association

---

[41] H. Booth (Solicitors), Legal Opinion No. 34, to the Oldham MCSA, March 1909; see also Morris and Williams, 'The discharge note'.

[42] *Textile Mercury*, 14 May 1892, p. 340.

[43] Royal Commission on Labour, *Minutes of Evidence*, Group C, 1892, Q18,490–1, 18,526; RC on Trade Disputes, *Minutes*, p. 144.

[44] CSMA, Minutes, 21 February 1913 and Circular, 22 February 1913; RC on Trade Disputes, *Minutes*, pp. 126–7, 144, 148, 150, 288.

[45] Royal Commission on Labour, *Rules of Associations*, p. xxviii.

operated what they termed 'the block' on striking miners. 'The older miners', the Scottish socialist Bob Selkirk noted, 'had a real dread of victimisation.'[46] Selkirk and his whole section were sacked after initiating a strike at the Ormiston Coal Company when the manager refused to pay extra for sorting out small coal in 1909. The Iron Trades Employers' Association in the 1880s and the early 1890s, and the Engineering Employers' Federation (formed 1896) developed sophisticated procedures for the blacklisting of strikers. Lists of strikers were forwarded to the national federation, then printed in bulk and circulated to the secretaries of all the local engineering associations, and from them to all the member firms in the strikebound region.[47] The procedure was kept as secret as possible, despite the large scale of its operation. In Manchester, for example, 112 separate blacklists of strikers were circulated between 1898 and 1914, one of these alone including 560 names.[48]

This is not to suggest that such victimisation was monopolised by employers' associations. However, employers' organisations could significantly enhance the effectiveness of this strikebreaking weapon. Weeding out and vetting labour activists occurred at the whim of individual foremen and managers and through many informal channels, at least before the First World War and the arrival of the political blacklisting agency, the Economic League (see chapter 9). Clydeside provides much evidence of this. Commenting on the pre-war period, the Glasgow Marxist Harry McShane noted that during slack trade 'the socialists were always the first to be paid off' irrespective of skill or seniority.[49] John MacLean (a Marxist schoolteacher) and James MacDougall (a socialist bank clerk) were both dismissed from their jobs in Glasgow because of their political beliefs.[50] Similarly, J.P. Coats, the Paisley thread manufacturers, purged members of the Amalgamated Society of Dyers from their works in the summer of 1912.[51] Elsewhere, female workers attempting to form branches of the National Federation of Women Workers were sacked.[52] However, perhaps the most notorious single example of such victimisation before the First World War occurred at the multinational Singer Sewing Machine Company at Kilbowie, Clydebank.

---

[46] Bob Selkirk, *The Life of a Worker* (1967), pp. 7–9. For a more detailed analysis of such tactics on Clydeside see McIvor and Paterson, 'Combating the left'.

[47] EEF, Correspondence Files, 1898–1914, *passim*; RC on Trade Disputes, *Minutes*, pp. 164–5, 169.

[48] Manchester EEA, Circulars Index, 1898–1914; EEF, Circular Letter, 27 April 1905.

[49] H. McShane and J. Smith, *No Mean Fighter*, London: Pluto, 1978, pp. 19–20, 31.

[50] *Forward*, 13 March 1909, 20 March 1909, 27 March 1909. In MacDougall's case the bank was trying to prevent a branch of the Clerks' Union being formed. I am grateful to Irene Maver for this reference.   [51] *Forward*, 3 August 1912.

[52] *Glasgow Herald*, 6 September 1910; *Forward*, 20 August 1910, 4 February 1911.

After penetration by the Industrial Workers of Great Britain and a plant strike in the spring of 1911, Singer sacked between 400 and 1,000 activists, including all the 200-strong strike committee, 60 known Independent Labour Party members and 22 members of the Socialist Labour Party.[53]

Employers also resorted to the law courts and to private systems of fining workers in an attempt to punish and intimidate, and discourage future strike action and other behaviour regarded by management as 'deviant'. Amongst others, the cotton and coal employers' organisations encouraged their members to prosecute for breach of contract where workmen had gone on strike without giving notice. 'Wildcat' strikes were particularly resented by employers, partly because they provided no opportunity prior to the stoppage to organise replacement labour or to make other arrangements, such as maintenance and cleaning work.[54] Workers would also be prosecuted for their part in any violence on the picket lines. Fines mulcted from workers in the courts served both to reduce trade-union funds and to conserve employers' association finances.

Again, employers' organisations played a key role in this process, particularly by providing encouragement, moral support, and financial aid for legal action, especially cases which it was judged involved important principles deemed essential to win to establish precedent. The Oldham Master Cotton Spinners' Association, for example, noted in 1897 that it was 'an understood rule that if a firm considers they have a good defence and cares to go into court, that we pay one half of the legal expenses incurred'.[55] The employers' legal offensive in the 1890s and 1900s is well documented, particularly the impact of the Taff Vale decision on strike activity. There were many similar cases in the localities, all imposing constraints on effective strike action (e.g. Lancashire – Banister and Moore case). The employers were aided in their legal action by the biased, traditionally conservative, anti-labour attitudes of the bulk of the judiciary, and the drift of judge-made legal decisions in the 1890s and 1900s emphasised the partisan role of the courts as additional leverage for the masters. For example, whilst union blacklisting and boycotting of underpaying, 'unfair' employers was declared an illegal conspiracy (under the 1875 Act) to restrain trade, employer blacklisting of workers in a case taken against the Sheffield Master Tailors' Association in 1892 was declared legal on the grounds that this was done in order 'to defeat and

[53] Glasgow Labour History Workshop, *Singer Strike*, pp. 49–53.
[54] Oldham MCSA, *Annual Report*, 1892, pp. 28–9; *Annual Report*, 1899, p. 10; *Annual Report*, 1909, pp. 7–8; CSMA, Minutes, 27 June 1911.
[55] Oldham MCSA, Minutes, 29 January 1897. See also Minutes, 15 June 1894.

counter-act the purposes of the men's unions'.[56] The Scottish miners' leader, Robert Smillie, ruefully noted in 1898 in a letter to the Secretary of State for Home Affairs: 'In almost every case either of a strike or lock-out there are a number of prosecutions either for assault or intimidation and the sentences against the men have been very severe. An offence which under ordinary circumstances is met with 10–14 days imprisonment is at time of strike punished with six months without any option of a fine.'[57]

Accurately gauging the penetration and impact of coercive victimisation and intimidation tactics in the period 1880–1914 is difficult, not least because employers were extremely tactiturn about these activities. There is evidence of some successful evasion of victimisation by strikers giving false names, citing inaccurate previous employers for references and forging or stealing documents, discharge and character notes. In response, some employers' organisations jettisoned their blacklisting policies. Others developed sophisticated policing procedures, which included visiting member firms to examine their lists of employees, to neutralise any attempts at evasion and to ensure that employers were not illicitly employing strikers. Employers' associations, however, had no jurisdiction over non-member firms. Consequently, the effectiveness of victimisation policies was limited by the level of employers' organisation and solidarity within a trade or region. Undoubtedly, where employers' organisations were weak, victimisation was relatively ineffective in keeping strikers and activists out of employment within a particular trade or locality. The prevailing state of product and labour markets was also critical. In periods of sustained trade buoyancy, such as 1910–14, many employers tended to turn a blind eye to blacklists, the enquiry, character and discharge notes, and become considerably less sensitive to the status of job aspirants in their eagerness to exploit the enhanced possibilities for profit. A similar situation recurred during and immediately after the First World War, 1914–20, and again in the later 1930s.

In the final analysis, however, the weight of evidence suggests that the victimisation and intimidation policies of employers and their organisations were widespread over 1880–1914, and that they could be effective, especially when combined with blackleg importation, in breaking many existing strikes and discouraging future strike action. Already, the practice of not employing strikers had congealed into a fairly well-established custom amongst many groups of employers – organised and unorganised – by the 1890s. In engineering, there are numerous examples of strikers

[56] *Textile Mercury*, 12 March 1892. See also H. Booth (Solicitors), Legal Opinion No. 9 to the Oldham MCSA, 12 December 1907.
[57] Letter, R. Smillie to Secretary of State for Home Affairs, 29 November 1898, Home Office Files (Public Record Office), HO45 / 9930 / B25921.

being unable to obtain work elsewhere, and on returning to their employers being told that their places were filled and the matter closed. Many trade-union militants found it impossible to get work on the docks in the 1890s, and on the railways victimised strikers protested that even their chances of getting work abroad were prejudiced.[58] The provision of 'victim pay' by many unions, including the operative printers, and the experience of many of the more notorious union officials of this period also bear witness to the effectiveness of such victimisation. Moreover, whilst an employers' closed shop was rare before 1914, the increasing trend of organisation amongst employers and the accelerating representativeness of their associations and federations over the period 1890–1914 undoubtedly had the overall effect of consolidating and strengthening employers' victimisation and intimidation tactics.

Cementing employer solidarity in strikes

Successful strikebreaking depended not only on victimising and intimidating strikers and bringing in replacement labour, but also on retaining solidarity within the employers' ranks, and preventing any breakaways and defections by employers who were experiencing or threatened with a strike. Employers' organisations agitated to retain loyalty to the collective strategy, and encouraged employers to resist the temptation to grant embarrassing concessions 'in detail' or compromise managerial rights and prerogatives. This was achieved through formulating various internal disciplinary methods, including sophisticated strike indemnity schemes. These served further to strengthen individual employers' defences against strike action.

In the early and mid-Victorian periods, solidarity in strikes and lockouts was often maintained by employers' organisations imposing heavy financial fines on breakaway firms or by the system of the financial pledge or 'bond'. This was where combined employers fixed a certain sum of money as a financial penalty which they guaranteed to pay to the organisation if they conceded unilaterally to the demands of the men. Such tactics were occasionally backed up with threats of commercial embargoes and organised price undercutting directed against recalcitrant member firms.[59] By the 1880s and 1890s, however, such tactics, though not unknown, had declined considerably. Some organisations, including the cotton masters, continued with a formalised fining system until 1914 and beyond, where employers who had stepped out of line with federation policy were forced to pay a financial levy calculated on the number of

---

[58] RC on Trade Disputes, *Minutes*, p. 279.   [59] S. Chapman, 'A historical sketch', p. 74.

spindles or looms running during lock-outs per week. The ultimate sanction remained dismissal from the employers' organisation, and subsequent social ostracism amongst the local elite. Dismissal meant a loss of all the benefits of association, including strike insurance, participation in the disputes procedure and aid in strikebreaking, which, particularly for the well-unionised, medium- to large-sized companies, amounted to a very real deprivation. Furthermore, because of the intertrading and boycotting customs adopted by a number of employers' organisations, such disloyalty could adversely affect the business connections and prospects of a firm, especially in trades like construction, where there was a large subcontracting network.

Enhancing solidarity and giving employers an added incentive to resist during strikes were the financial compensation schemes developed by employers' organisations and funded by direct levies on members and the occasional windfall donation. Such schemes usually provided direct cash subsidies to strikebound employers to reimburse loss of profits and were designed to remove some of the pressure bearing upon employers to settle grievances by conceding wage rises above the norm or working conditions that were better than the standard ones. Strike compensation or insurance schemes had a long history, and were sometimes prompted into existence by the awareness that trade unions were themselves accumulating large reserve funds.[60] By the 1890s a great many employers' organisations, including those in shipping, coal, cotton, engineering, shipbuilding, clothing, furniture-making and building, had developed formal strike-indemnity schemes.[61] Alternatively, some employers' organisations developed work-sharing schemes during strikes, particularly when it was imperative to complete contracts and difficulties were experienced in quickly breaking a strike by blackleg importation and victimisation. Members of the Yorkshire Master Printers' and Allied Trades' Association, for example, were encouraged by their organisation to fulfil orders of strikebound firms 'at a profit not exceeding 10 per cent'.[62]

Employers' strike pay usually corresponded in some way to an estimate of the output lost because of the strike (e.g., tonnage, wages not paid, machinery idle) and, naturally, out-payments increased considerably in periods of intense strike activity (table 4.3). Some organisations paid compensation solely to cover fixed charges and defray overhead expenses, whilst others were more generous and provided compensation for losses on contracts, late delivery of products, and even for companies to pay a

[60] Bolton MCSA, Minutes, 5 August 1898; Darwen CSMA, Minutes, 24 January 1902.
[61] See the *ARSLOs*, 1888–95; K. G. Knowles, *Strikes*, Oxford: Basil Blackwell, 1952, p. 122.
[62] RC on Labour, *Rules of Associations*, p. xxvii. See also RC on Trade Disputes, *Minutes*, pp. 148, 170–1, 177, 278, 286.

Table 4.3 *Strike compensation paid by two employers' organisations, 1890–1914*[1]

	SWCA		CSMA	
	No. of firms compensated	Total indemnity payments (in £s)	No. of firms compensated	Total indemnity payments (in £s)
1890–4	Unknown	126,680	7	4,826
1895–9	45	254,609	35	5,562
1900–4	288	294,313	7	2,087
1905–9	289	230,597	48	9,703
1910–14	Unknown	676,067	7	11,197
Totals	622	1,582,266	104	33,375

[1] The South Wales Coalowners' Association (SWCA) and the Cotton Spinners' and
  Manufacturers' Association (CSMA).
Sources: Cotton Spinners' and Manufacturers' Association, Minutes, 1890–1914;
L.J. Williams, 'The Monmouthshire and South Wales Coalowners' Association,
1873–1914' (MA thesis, University of Wales, 1957), appendix.

dividend to shareholders.[63] The Shipping Federation, for example, indemnified members for all financial losses incurred in actions taken in pursuance of policy decisions made by local associations and the executive, compensating members for strikebound and boycotted ships at the rate of 2d per ton per day.[64] However, not all claims were paid automatically. The general rule was that claims would be rejected if the member involved had acted contrary to the advice or policy 'line' of the employers' association, or if a member had been responsible for provoking the stoppage by not paying standard wage rates or endeavouring to reduce wages or otherwise subvert well-established working conditions.[65] The associations were rarely prepared to subsidise individual employers to compete 'unfairly' by undercutting the labour costs of the majority of firms in the region.

Strike compensation was thus a further important weapon in the armoury of employers' strikebreaking tactics. Indeed, amongst some employers' organisations this was considered the single most important defence against strike action and sectional encroachments of the workmen.[66] Strike compensation played a particularly important role in

[63] Blackburn CSMA, Minutes, 9 September 1907, 18 February 1909; Ashton MCSA,
  Minutes, 29 December 1891, 3 March 1892, 9 May 1892.
[64] RC on Labour, *Rules of Associations*, p. xxvii.   [65] Ibid., p. xxvi.
[66] L.J. Williams, 'Monmouthshire and South Wales Coalowners' Association, 1873–1914'
  (MA thesis, University of Wales, 1957), p. 237.

periods of trade buoyancy by ensuring that strikes remained localised and isolated and, at the very least, by delaying, sometimes for very lengthy periods, the granting of pivotal precedents in wages and working conditions. The 'bad spinning' strikes in cotton between 1911 and 1913 are a case in point. In other trades, indemnity schemes were only symbolic of employers' solidarity. Clearly, most individual employers had a less crucial need for financial aid than did individual trade-union members, whose strike pay might reduce reliance on the pawnshop and keep a family from the indignity of the workhouse, or perhaps even starvation. Stoppage indemnity could also have a number of adverse effects and was not universally popular as a long-term strikebreaking weapon. Some employers found the cost of supporting such schemes prohibitive, whilst less strike-prone firms resented being forced to pay for the heavy-handed personnel policies of more unscrupulous companies.[67] Moreover, because the total resources of employers' organisations and trade unions could be drawn upon, strikes at individual firms could be maintained for very long periods, which could result in critical damage to the trading and business connections of individual companies. Partly as a consequence of this, an underlying commitment remained towards the ultimate strikebreaking weapon, the 'one-stop, all-stop' policy of the general lock-out.

The lock-out

The Labour Department of the Board of Trade defined a lock-out thus:

The lock-out is the action of an employer who notifies to his workpeople that on a certain date all existing contracts of service will terminate, and who lays down no definite proposal for the continuation of such contracts; or who closes his works to compel his men to cease to be members of a union, or to increase the difficulties of a strike organisation fighting with other employers by increasing the number of those it will have to support.[68]

Lock-outs occurred frequently in the later nineteenth century at individual companies, had the potential to spread across a local area and occasionally escalated into industry-wide confrontations. They can be divided crudely into two types, determined by which side took the initiative. First, there was what might be termed the 'offensive' lock-out, where a single employer or the combined employers in the locality or trade took the initiative to propose and force through (usually in periods of trade

---

[67] Membership of the EEF declined from 810 firms in 1913 to 744 firms in 1914, largely as the result of adopting a more costly strike 'Subsidy Scheme'. See Wigham, *Power to Manage*, pp. 82–3, 303.   [68] *ARSLO*, 1888, p. 5.

depression, as in 1892–3 and 1908) cost-saving changes in working conditions (on issues of manning and work hours, for example) and reductions in wages, and who locked out their workers in response to strike action opposing such changes. Here employers fought to retain the notion that the wages and other rewards of labour should rise and fall and be regulated solely by the market forces of supply and demand. The labourist argument that a wage determined by humanitarian considerations and common decency should be a first charge on industry was rejected by all but a thin strand of paternalist and welfarist employers before the First World War. The second group of stoppages might be labelled, though not entirely accurately, 'defensive' lock-outs. Such stoppages were an attempt by employers and their organisations to neutralise the trade-union policy of 'whipsawing' sectional strike action at single or several firms, which employers interpreted as an 'attack in detail', to establish unprecedented improvements in wage rates or improve working conditions, thus adding to total labour costs.

The main aims of the lock-out were to force the issue to a head, spread the dispute as widely as possible in order to take the pressure off individual companies and involve a broader cohort of employers in the trade or the district. Lock-outs served to drain trade-union funds rapidly, undermine workers' morale, and, if it came to it, starve the strikers into submission. In some cases, the employers supplemented the lock-out by exerting pressure on both Poor Law Guardians to refuse outdoor relief to strikers (aided by the Merthyr Tydfil legal case in 1900) and on local shopkeepers to withhold credit.[69] Where unions were poorly organised and no formal machinery to deal with disputes existed, lock-outs might be the immediate response of employers to a strike in the trade. Where employers were committed to a more incorporative labour-relations strategy, the lock-out would usually be a final sanction brought into action when disputes procedure was exhausted or ignored, often when all other strikebreaking methods had failed, and sometimes when (despite the payment of strike compensation and threats of disciplinary procedure) individual employers were wavering during strikes. *Textile Mercury* argued in 1892 that a lock-out of the cotton spinning trade was justified in response to strikes at three mills in Bury (to achieve a closed shop) because union picketing was preventing the successful importation of replacement labour.[70] The subsequent lock-out threat issued by the FMCSA proved sufficient to force the spinners' union to back down.

Quantitative evidence on lock-outs is practically non-existent, primarily because the BTLD failed to differentiate systematically between

---

[69] Knowles, *Strikes*, pp. 139–40.   [70] *Textile Mercury*, 12 March 1892, p. 184.

Table 4.4 *Lock-outs identified by the Board of Trade Labour Department in 1889*

Trade/ locality	Workers involved	Duration of lock-out	Notes
1 Boot/shoe, Bristol	4,000	5 weeks	Lock-out after strike in 1 firm
2 Brushmakers, East London	125	9 weeks	Lock-out of 7 firms after strikes at 2
3 Joiners, Londonderry	60	few days	Lock-out of 4 firms in support of 2 firms struck for 8 months
4 Plasterers, Glasgow	300	7 weeks	Lock-out of 32 firms vs. output restrictions
5 Coopers, Alloa	11	6 months	vs. closed shop
6 Smelters, Sheffield	—	—	vs. closed shop
7 Engineering, Glasgow	250	10 days	Lock-out of 9 firms in support of strikes at 5
8 Shipbuilding, Glasgow	900	2 weeks	Lock-out of several firms after 1 strike
9 Coal-miners, Kilmarnock	70	—	1 firm, to impose wage cut
10 Miners, Newcastle	24	3 days	1 firm
11 Cotton, Great Harwood	3,500	4 days	Lock-out of 10 firms after strikes at 2
12 Cotton, Chorley	400	1 week	1 firm
13 Linen, Forfar	1,950	6 weeks	Lock-out of 4 firms in support of strike at 1
14 Silk dyers, Leek	100	—	—
15 Wool, Honley	18	—	strikers replaced
16 Worsted, Leeds	20	—	1 firm

Source: Board of Trade, *Annual Report on Strikes and Lock-Outs*, 1889, pp. 113–16.

strikes and lock-outs in their *Annual Reports*. Table 4.4 nevertheless indicates something of the local scope of late nineteenth-century lock-outs and the tendency of employers to utilise the lock-out as a reaction to single firm and sectional strike action.

Where collective organisation amongst companies was weak, or non-existent, individual employers initiated lock-outs. One of the most notorious and longest lock-outs prior to the First World War occurred at the slate quarries owned by Lord Penrhyn in North Wales between 1900 and 1903. This was the 'Grunwick' of the day; a fight essentially for union recognition. The autocratic Lord Penrhyn and his manager E.A. Young saw themselves in the vanguard of a national employers' offensive to protect unilateral managerial authority against the encroachments of trade unionism and were determined to root out this cancer, whatever the cost. They attempted to bring in imported labour and induce the 'loyal' quarrymen to come back by using all the power and patronage at their disposal. Pressure was imposed to obtain police and military protection for those working and a blacklist drawn up (using information gathered from a network of spies and detectives) of strike organisers, sympathisers and 'disloyal' men (e.g., those involved in picketing incidents and prosecutions), who were never to be re-employed or given company tenancies or pensions. These draconian methods eventually broke the men's resistance. Out of the 2,800 who walked out of the Penrhyn quarries almost 1,000 were never to return. As Merfyn Jones has noted, it is a testimony to the power of community solidarity and the collective 'moral law' in face of intense deprivation in Bethesda that after two and a half years the quarries were still running at only around a third of their previous capacity.[71]

However, employers' associations often played a critical role in planning and organising lock-outs before the First World War. Indeed, the existence of some kind of employers' combination was an essential precondition for the initiation and prosecution of a lock-out beyond a single firm. The emergence of strong employers' organisations in the later nineteenth century potentially raised the conflict demarcation area from the domestic to the local, regional and national level, and, by raising the stakes, this in itself provided a powerful deterrent against strike action. The job of the employers' organisation during lock-outs was to ensure that the action was as solidly supported as possible on the employers' side. This could involve sending deputations to recalcitrant firms to encourage membership and solidarity and to urge sympathetic action (at the very least, short-time working), organising the formation of new local associations, preparing statements to the press to influence wider public opinion, and fining and sometimes expelling disloyal member firms. Directors of large member firms with interlocking directorships of other disloyal companies were persuaded by the employers' organisations to use their influence to turn such firms around. Member companies were also pressed by their associations to exert pressure on their clients, merchants and trading partners to boycott disloyal firms.[72]

As with labour substitution and victimisation, the effectiveness of the lock-out weapon depended, to a large extent, on the proportion of employers organised and on the dynamism of the organisation's executive

---

[71] This section is based on R. Merfyn Jones, *The North Wales Quarrymen, 1874–1922*, Cardiff: University of Wales Press, 1981, pp. 210–94.

[72] Bolton MCSA, Minutes, 26 October 1908.

in ensuring the widest possible support amongst the community of employers. Often, as in the 1895 boot and shoe lock-out and the 1897–8 engineering lock-out, the employers' organisation was successful in its efforts to induce more and more employers to join the lock-out and thus to widen the area of conflict and intensify pressure on labour. On other occasions, employers' organisations were crippled by the lack of cohesion and solidarity in their own ranks. Whilst the cotton masters had a good response in the south-east Lancashire coarse-spinning area during the Brooklands lock-out in 1892–3, both the north Lancashire 'mixed' master spinners and weavers, and the Bolton fine-cotton spinners refused all pleas for co-operation. Dyson has noted that conflicts and jealousies between the limited companies and private firms critically undermined the Brooklands lock-out.[73] *Textile Mercury* commented that, as a rule, the most recently established companies felt most pressure to continue working through lock-outs.[74] Such fragmentation proved instrumental in enabling the south-east Lancashire cotton operatives to resist for twenty weeks and ultimately score a significant moral victory in getting the proposed wage reduction decreased from 5 to 2.9 per cent. The Bolton Cotton Spinners' Union subsequently commented, rather hopefully, that 'reducing wages in the future is to be an undertaking so costly and hazardous that the game will not be worth the candle'.[75]

The propensity to lock out and the effectiveness of such action before 1914 was also influenced by prevailing public opinion, the government response, the anticipated and actual degree of labour resistance, and the state of product and labour markets. Evidence suggests that on occasions employers utilised the lock-out as a method to clear the market of excess production, and that firms were much more wary of escalating a sectional strike by voting for a general lock-out when product markets were particularly buoyant and when opportunities for a considerable profit were at risk (for example, over the period 1910–14). However, questions of wider principle and employers' prerogative could and did on occasions transcend such narrow, pragmatic self-interest and the short-term profit motive. The 1911 lock-out in cotton weaving to protect the 'open shop' is perhaps a case in point. A discernible pattern was emerging by the First World War. The utilisation of the lock-out weapon was declining and losing popularity, but, because of the rapid growth of employers' organisations, when lock-outs were called they tended to be more effective in throwing much larger swathes of workers out of employment.

[73] Dyson, *The Development of Collective Bargaining*, pp. 295–6.
[74] *Textile Mercury*, 5 November 1892, p. 335.
[75] *14th Annual Report of the Bolton Operative Spinners' Association*, 1893, pp. 4, 10.

Conclusion

Almost all employers' organisations in late nineteenth-century Britain provided a strikebreaking service, though tactics varied widely. Much continued to be done on the initiative of the individual firm – most employers, after all, remained unorganised prior to the First World War. However, the role of the employers' organisation should not be underestimated. Apart from the role employers' associations played in aiding employers to find blackleg labour, the existence of an employers' organisation was a precondition for the effective multi-employer victimisation of strikers, for the creation of a reserve fund to finance strike-compensation schemes, for the intensification of solidarity enforced by various internal disciplinary methods and for the successful organisation of a multi-employer lock-out.

Increasingly powerful employers' organisations, utilising an array of weapons, thus constituted a very significant bulwark against trade unionism and a protective buffer against the rising strike propensity of the later nineteenth and early twentieth centuries. Evidence suggests that strikebreaking tactics became more formalised and more sophisticated, evolving significantly over time, with labour substitution declining in incidence, whilst institutionalised victimisation was increasingly prioritised. Collective initiatives were replacing individual, single-company struggles against labour as more and more companies joined associations and tapped into this more formal strikebreaking system. Some employers' associations, including many of those in the transport sector, continued to refuse recognition of trade unions and utilised coercive strikebreaking tactics as a first line of defence against trade unionism and labour militancy. More common by the First World War, however, was the use of sophisticated strikebreaking procedures as a final deterrent forming a second line of defence, brought into action when established procedures to settle disputes without a stoppage of work were either exhausted or ignored. One of the major functions of employers' organisations was thus forcibly to break any strikes where they had failed, by incorporative and conciliatory methods, to prevent them from occurring. In turn, these coercive sanctions served to strengthen trades' union commitment to formal disputes and bargaining procedures.

There appear to have been marked regional and sectoral variations in employer strikebreaking policy. Clydeside employers, for example, may well have been more anti-union and less tolerant of strike activity, exhibiting a higher propensity to import replacement labour, at least during the period 1910–14, than elsewhere.[76] This had much to do with the heavily

---

[76] Glasgow Labour History Workshop, 'The labour unrest', p. 94.

labour-intensive nature of Clydeside industry and somewhat later development of strong trade unions north of the border.[77] By contrast, the response of the Lancashire millowners to strikes followed roughly the average pattern across the UK, only slightly skewed towards more authoritarian and hostile reactions.[78]

The propensity and success rate of employers' strikebreaking activities depended on a series of factors: on the degree of organisation and solidarity that existed amongst employers in the trade or locality; on the state of product and local labour markets; on the extent of worker organisation, resistance and community solidarity; on public opinion and the attitude of the government and local authorities; on the structure and nature of the business and the employment environment; and on the nature of the work process and the penetration of deskilling technology and the division of labour. The overall impact of collectivised strikebreaking before the First World War is difficult, if not impossible, to gauge. However, there were many clear successes for employers' associations which utilised such tactics. The Operative Society of Stonemasons lamented in 1905 what they perceived to be the neutralisation of the 'snowballing', sectional strike: 'It is clear that as a means of securing benefits for our trade, strikes have lost their ancient powers, no doubt largely due to the formation of powerful employers' associations throughout the country.'[79] The admittedly crude quantitative evidence collected by the BTLD lends some support to this view. The difficulty with these data is making allowance for changing economic circumstances – the state of trade and labour markets – which clearly influenced the outcome of strikes. Nevertheless, two points can be made. First, in the 1900s (in a period when formalised disputes procedures were extending in an attempt to prevent strikes) employers were responding to strike action in an increasingly hostile and autocratic way.[80] Secondly, what is clearly evident is the relative success of

---

[77] For a discussion of the nature of trade unionism and industrial relations on Clydeside pre-1914 see W. Knox, 'The political and workplace culture of the Scottish working class, 1832–1914', in W. Hamish Fraser and R.J. Morris (eds.), *People and Society in Scotland*, vol. II: *1830–1919*, Edinburgh: John Donald, 1990; Melling, 'Scottish industrialists'.

[78] I am indebted to Richard Devlin for this point. According to the *ARSLOs* in the four years 1889–90 and 1896–7, 56.5 per cent of strikes in the Lancashire cotton industry were settled by conciliation and arbitration; 36.3 per cent were settled by more hostile responses (submission of workers and replacement). The corresponding averages for the UK as a whole were 60 per cent and 29.8 per cent respectively. These figures are based on a 49.1 per cent sample of all reported disputes.   [79] Cited in Price, *Masters*, p. 193.

[80] Percentages of initial employer responses to strikes have been tabulated from the *ARSLOs* as follows: (1) 1889–90: authoritarian 27.4 per cent; conciliatory 49.7 per cent; workers replaced 10.1 per cent; arbitration 3.4 per cent. (2) 1901–13: authoritarian 39.5 per cent; conciliatory 39.5; hands replaced 3.8 per cent; arbitration 11.7. Again, I am indebted to Ricky Devlin for these data.

employers in dealing with strikes during the wave of militancy between 1911 and 1913 compared with the earlier strike wave associated with the origins of 'new unionism' during 1888–90. Both periods of labour unrest occurred at the peak of the trade cycle. Over the three years 1888–90, worker victories outstripped employer victories by a massive 69 per cent. From 1911 to 1913, worker victories were down 4 per cent below employer victories.[81] These figures are all the more impressive – looking from the perspective of the employer – when one considers the tightness of labour markets in the immediate pre-war years and that the proportion of the British workforce in membership of trade unions had more than doubled since the late 1880s. What this evidence indicates is that employers' ability to cope with withdrawals of labour improved between c. 1890 and 1914 and that the emergence of powerful employers' organisations, offering sophisticated strikebreaking services, played a pivotal role in this process. Strikebreaking was facilitated further by a more repressive legal framework, c. 1890–1905 and by sharp economic recessions in 1904–5 and 1908–9.

This partial success at neutralising the strike weapon was achieved, however, at a great cost. The challenge of trade unions and responses of employers' associations cranked up levels of industrial conflict, leading to the eruption of large-scale pitched battles, sustained for longer and longer periods by the growing resources of organised labour and organised capital. Once trade unions could sustain themselves through lean as well as good times employers found themselves in a very different situation. Increasingly, therefore, the labour relations strategy of employers' associations shifted and came to prioritise the prevention of disputes and strikes and the containment of industrial conflict through adopting and extending formalised disputes procedures, designed explicitly to minimise time lost through industrial strife. Emphasis moved towards finding mechanisms which would prevent strikes erupting in the first place. It is perhaps something of a paradox that the upsurge in employers' organisation which occurred from c. 1890 to 1914 provided the preconditions for both the accelerating commitment to institutionalised, procedural forms of control over labour, and the formalisation and strengthening of employers' coercive strikebreaking machinery. The next chapter explores the role played by employers' organisations in this transition towards a modern system of union recognition, formal collective bargaining and institutionalisation of industrial relations.

---

[81] Figures taken from J. Cronin, *Industrial Conflict in Modern Britain*, London: Croom Helm, 1979, pp. 222–3. This interpretation is supported by Devlin's sample data (nn. 78 and 80), showing a sharp fall in worker victories in strikes from 40.4 per cent (1889–90; 1896–7) to 26.2 per cent (1901–13).

5   Collective bargaining and procedural control

The conjuncture of rising worker organisation and militancy – an ability and will to sustain resistance – with intensifying competition and more hostile product markets encouraged many employers to seek alternative, less costly and provocative strategies to maintain labour discipline and stabilise industrial relations. Employers' associations played a key role in this process of formalising industrial relations, as this chapter will demonstrate. Not that this was a tidy, symmetrical or neat evolutionary process. Rather, union recognition and collective bargaining mechanisms spread slowly, sporadically and experimentally, in different shapes and forms, at different times and with differing consequences between and within British industries. Nevertheless, an increasing number of employers' organisations – indeed, probably the majority by 1914 – reorientated their labour relations policies towards acceptance of trade unions and towards prevention rather than the forcible breaking of strikes. Increasingly, the local, regional and national employer organisations were stressing the common interests and bonds between master and man, and seeking ways to reconstitute a stronger degree of consent towards capitalism, reversing the process of evaporating loyalty and indiscipline as strikes grew and became more bitter, as companies responded to growing competitive pressures by intensifying workloads and as traditional paternalist relationships fractured as firms grew larger. The secretary of the Oldham Master Builders' Association, Sam Smethurst, articulated a sense of this changing attitude in 1913:

Instead of having a series of struggles all over this vast area it would be better if we could thoroughly understand what is wanted, consider whether it is reasonable and whether we, as the heads of the building trade in this area, could make some recommendations for a settlement that would be friendly instead of antagonistic. There is too general a feeling that the masters are the enemy of the men and the men of the masters.[1]

The predominant route towards such corporatist restabilisation of industrial relations was through the formulation of increasingly sophisticated

---

[1] LCFBTE, Conference Minutes, 9 January 1913.

collective bargaining mechanisms – including substantive agreements and stage-by-stage disputes procedures.

Clegg, Fox and Thompson have charted the extension of collective bargaining in the 1890s and 1900s to cover a swathe of major industries, filtering down from craft workers to groups of intermediate, semi-skilled employees and even pockets of organised unskilled workers by the eve of the First World War.[2] Bargaining structures proliferated, usually from the local to the regional and national levels, prompted partly by government encouragement after the Royal Commission on Labour (1892–4), and, occasionally, as in the railways, by direct state intervention. Behind the scenes, as George Askwith has noted, there was much semi-official arm-twisting of recalcitrant employers.[3]

Interpretations of the meaning of this transition in industrial relations differ sharply. In the Marxist 'rank and filist' paradigm collective bargaining drove a wedge between a conciliatory union leadership, accepting the rules of the capitalist game, and the more radical mass of workers. Price argues that in the building industry conciliation agreements and no-strike clauses 'entrapped' the men, enabling employers to dismantle artisans' autonomous regulation of their craft and replace this with a system of joint regulation.[4] The alienation this strategy created burst forth in phases of spontaneous militancy – as during 1910–14 – but ultimately this was contained by judicious wage rises conceded on condition the formal industrial relations system remained in place. Zeitlin, on the other hand, has questioned the extent to which the imposition of a formalised industrial relations system actually undermined craft control and enhanced employers' authority in the engineering sector, stressing the ability of craftworkers to resist division of labour and the positive role played by their unions in defending customary craft rights and controls over work. There exists no stark dichotomy, Zeitlin suggests, between a radical 'rank and file' and a conservative, incorporated leadership – indeed the latter were as likely to be more militant than the membership, who could be apathetic, acquiescent and opposed to change.[5] To Clegg, Fox and Thompson, this formalisation of industrial relations represented a shift in attitude on the part of many employers and their organisations towards an acceptance of legitimate union rights and a pragmatic desire to work jointly with moderate unions to stabilise industrial relations.

But did the development of collective bargaining mean equal sacrifices for capital and labour? What was gained and lost by this accommodation

---

[2] Clegg, Fox and Thompson, *A History of British Trade Unions*, vol. I, pp. 326–3, 471–6. See also Clegg, *A History of British Trade Unions*, vol. II, pp. 75–96.

[3] See Askwith, *Industrial Problems*, pp. 134–241.   [4] Price, *Masters*, pp. 242, 249–51.

[5] J. Zeitlin, '"Rank and filism" in British labour history: a critique', *IRSH*, 34 (1989), p. 54.

with organised labour? Whilst trade unions undoubtedly gained in terms of prestige and membership from the recognition implicit in collective bargaining, employers also benefited considerably, and perhaps unequally, from this bureaucratisation of industrial relations. At the very least, as Trainor has argued in his case study of elites in the Black Country, formalised collective bargaining gave 'institutional effect to an underlying economic advantage'.[6] Bargaining procedures established in the 1890s and 1900s were invariably created on the employers' terms with the state of order books (rather than cost of living) commonly being the sole determinant of applications for wage rises and deductions.[7] Moreover, unions could be used to police unpopular joint decisions, wielding, as Price has emphasised, 'a power that was to be exercised over the men'.[8] Furthermore, employers could restrict the agenda, dictating the issues which might be subjected to a joint bargain, trading off joint regulation in some areas for unilateral managerial control in others, as for example in the 1898 Terms of Settlement in engineering.[9] Lovell has recently argued that in shipbuilding between 1889 and 1910 the scope of collective bargaining was not significantly extended and the procedure was utilised, in practice, to bolster employers' authority and control.[10]

What remains unclear is the role employer organisations played in this process; their contribution to the evolution of a formalised collective bargaining system. Were employers' associations innovators? How committed were employers to the agreed disputes procedure and why? Did employers gain disproportionately from such mechanisms? How were unions treated within disputes procedures? Did this switch in policy enable employers' organisations effectively to stabilise costs, limit craft control and autonomy and maintain managerial authority and control at the point of production? How did this formalised framework respond to changes in product and labour market circumstances? This chapter will address such questions, through a detailed analysis of the policies of local and regional employers' organisations in the cotton manufacturing and engineering industries in north-west England.

---

[6] Trainor, *Black Country Elites*, p. 165. Trainor also comments that there were advantages for the trade unions and that, significantly, the unions in the Black Country did not campaign to abrogate joint agreements and procedures prior to 1900.
[7] See Burgess, *Origins*, pp. 309–11; Lovell, 'Collective bargaining'; Phelps-Brown, *Origins*, p. 111; Porter, 'Wage bargaining', pp. 470–5.
[8] Price, *Masters*, p. 192; see also pp. 119–20.
[9] K. Sisson, *The Management of Collective Bargaining: An International Comparison*, Oxford: Basil Blackwell, 1987, p. 12; K. Sisson, 'Employers and the structure of collective bargaining: distinguishing cause and effect', in Tolliday and Zeitlin (eds.), *The Power to Manage?*, pp. 256–72.   [10] Lovell, 'Collective bargaining', pp. 59–91.

Cotton manufacturing: pioneering procedural control

In the cotton industry, collectively bargained local agreements on wage issues and working conditions usually came first, sometimes linked with, though more typically followed by, procedural arrangements to deal with industrial disputes. Howe has argued that the 1850s and 1860s witnessed the crucial shift from exclusion to recognition of trade unions in Lancashire textiles.[11] In reality, however, this was a much more complex and drawn-out affair. During the 1850s and 1860s uniform piecework wage lists were negotiated for spinners and weavers by the local employers' and operatives' associations and commonly these incorporated rudimentary disputes conciliation procedures, whereby grievances were to be discussed by the secretaries of the respective organisations prior to any stoppage of work.[12] The local disputes procedures were further extended in 1881 in weaving and in 1893 in spinning when the pioneering Brooklands Agreement established machinery creating formal domestic, local and national joint meetings to take place, prior to any strike or lock-out.[13] Meanwhile, wage standardisation was extended in weaving, through negotiation of the Uniform Wage List of 1892 (which amalgamated the Blackburn, Burnley and Preston lists), whilst in spinning, the majority of Lancashire workers were paid by either the Oldham (coarse) or Bolton (fine) lists. Recognition of lesser skilled (and more poorly organised) cardroom workers and female ring-spinners came only much later, with wage lists and rudimentary conciliation procedures being conceded in Oldham in 1891, Universal Lists negotiated over the period 1903–7 and a ring-spinning list in 1913.[14] Disputes procedure was tightened up on several occasions prior to 1914, often on the initiative of the employers.[15] On the weaving side, for example, streamlining took place in 1906 and 1909, including the incorporation of a compulsory local joint meeting four weeks after a strike or lock-out had been initiated. Perhaps the apogee of this process in spinning was the rather ambitious scheme proposed by Charles Macara, the FMCSA president, for a sliding scale to regulate automatically wage movements, which ultimately had to be abandoned, the Federation and the unions disagreeing on points of

---

[11] Howe, *Cotton Masters*, pp. 177–8.

[12] For a full discussion see Bullen, 'Pragmatism vs principle', pp. 27–43.

[13] For more detail of the events that led up to the Brooklands Agreement and the disputes procedure incorporated therein see A.J. McIvor, 'Employers' associations and industrial relations in Lancashire, 1890–1939' (Ph.D. thesis, University of Manchester, 1983), pp. 121–38.

[14] J.H. Porter, 'Industrial peace in the cotton trade, 1875–1913', *Yorkshire Bulletin of Economic and Social Research*, 19 (1967), pp. 49–50.

[15] Dyson, *The Development of Collective Bargaining*, pp. 445–7.

detail.[16] This abortive initiative is symbolic, however, of the degree of commitment on the part of the cotton employers' organisations by the early twentieth century to the procedural control strategy.

What were the factors that motivated this switch in labour relations policy? Undoubtedly, the increase in competition in product markets from the 1870s (prompting a 'speed-up' movement in the mills) encouraged employers to seek solace by controlling competition on labour costs through the uniform wage lists. However, the desire to contain and neutralise the growing power of the trade unions was a paramount consideration influencing employers to commit themselves to collective bargaining. Coercive control – via pitched battle trials of strength – proved increasingly costly in terms of production time lost as trade unions consolidated themselves. Significantly, the main developments in collective bargaining in cotton came after the experience of extended and damaging periods of intense industrial conflict in the 1850s and late 1870s in weaving and the early 1890s in cotton spinning. Five years after the event the FMCSA chairman, Charles Macara, reflected upon the lesson of the 1892–3 Brooklands lock-out:

> The chief of these was that severe suffering was inflicted both on the employers and the operatives and that large profits were made by employers who remained outside the Federation. That also was the case with our foreign competitors, who not only permanently secured part of the trade, but also, by the increase of their profits, had secured the means by which they had made further extensions.[17]

This threat to profitability provided a significant inducement for seeking alternative labour control mechanisms. To maintain competitiveness in a more hostile product market it was imperative that order be created out of chaos and instability.

Collective bargaining had important consequences for both capital and labour in cotton. Recognition encouraged wage rationalisation, increased union involvement in decision-making and raised union prestige and authority. Disputes procedures and agreements helped reduce industrial conflict, acting as a buffer against drastic movements in wages and conditions in periods of either extreme recession or trade 'boom'. Dyson has also argued that procedure in cotton worked to restrict technological advance by forestalling arbitrary managerial changes in work practices and processes, notably in the cardroom in the 1900–14 period.[18] Certainly, collective bargaining further encouraged unionisation and

---

[16] Oldham MCSA, *Annual Report*, 1906, pp. 6–7; 1911, p. 6.
[17] FMCSA, *Annual Report*, 1898, p. 33.
[18] Dyson, *The Development of Collective Bargaining*, pp. 534–8; *Textile Mercury*, 1 August 1896, p. 86; *Manchester Guardian*, 14 February 1901.

employers' organisation in order to meet the complicated administrative and mathematical requirements of joint negotiation. Public relations statements stressed, moreover, that collective bargaining meant a dispassionate and unbiased consideration of the merits of each case, thus providing equitable settlements acceptable to both sides without loss of production or wages.

The reality of the situation was, however, somewhat different. Both sides gained something in this trade-off, though in the cotton industry it was the millowners who benefited disproportionately from the transition to a more conciliatory labour relations strategy. The fall in time lost through industrial disputes after 1893 indicates that the formalised procedure in the spinning sector did succeed for many years in the primary objective of reducing the damaging effects of industrial conflict.[19] Few disputes in Oldham, previously the cockpit of industrial strife in Lancashire, reached the point of a stoppage between 1893 and 1908. The wage movements of 1894-5, 1897-8, 1899 and 1905-6 were all settled peacefully, a series of settlements unprecedented in cotton spinning. Significantly, it has been persuasively argued by J.H. Porter that wage rates may have become considerably less flexible in an upward direction as a result of the 5 per cent restriction clause of the Brooklands Agreement.[20] The procedure was very largely established on the employers' terms, with the 'state of trade' and wage rates paid by neighbouring competitors as the only criteria accepted by the employers in negotiating a wage change. This made procedure particularly restrictive to labour in the c. 1900-14 period of rising living costs and stagnating real wages. In joint bargaining, moreover, emphasis was laid on carefully collected and well-documented evidence, and here the employers had the considerable advantages of greater organisational and secretarial services to back up their cases.

Therefore, whilst the cotton unions may well have taken the initiative in demanding collective bargaining with employers, it was the employers' organisations which invariably exploited the opportunity provided by conciliation to impose new forms of procedural control over labour. Some far-sighted and shrewd employers – like Charles Macara – realised the potential advantages very early.[21] Despite some early criticism of the degree of 'class collaboration', most of the other employers in the trade became committed to conciliation through experience, with even the hawkish trade journal, *Textile Mercury*, championing collective bargaining

---

[19] Mitchell and Deane, *Abstract*, p. 72 for statistical evidence.
[20] Porter, 'Industrial peace', pp. 58-9.
[21] For more detail on Macara see A.J. McIvor, 'Charles Macara', in D. Jeremy (ed.), *Dictionary of Business Biography*, vol. IV, London: Butterworth, 1985, pp. 7-14.

from the mid-1890s.[22] Employers benefited because disappointing decisions of conciliation boards were endorsed by the workers' own officials,
who were given the responsibility of policing collective agreements. Rank
and file labour militancy could be contained and work stoppages fore-
stalled for a lengthy period of negotiation. Moreover, employers had the
advantage of being able to introduce changes and adjustments first, and
have them discussed through procedure thereafter.

Hardly surprising, therefore, to find that the cotton employers
remained firmly committed to working within the established collective
bargaining procedures from the early 1890s, whilst on the union side peri-
odic complaints accrued about the unjust working of the formal procedure, with James Crinion (cardroom) and Thomas Ashton (spinners)
amongst the most vociferous dissenters.[23] Criticism was particularly
directed against the Oldham Master Cotton Spinners' Association and
John Tattersall, for their delaying tactics and their all-encompassing interpretation of procedure. This especially applied (under clause 6) to
employers' refusal to discuss purely local issues, except under the formal
Brooklands procedure. Sectional union action was consequently stran-
gled as employers broadened the scope of procedural control. The
Oldham correspondent of the *Textile Mercury* dealt with the union complaints quite brusquely:

Usually these negotiations give time for reflection, and the consideration and
arranging of details which lead to settlements. The operatives, however, do not
seem to like these diplomatic movements; they believe in forcing matters on to a
quick issue, and not negotiating meeting after meeting. As they are parties to the
Brooklands Agreement, they will have to submit to the things that be.[24]

In the 1900s, the inability of the Brooklands procedure to solve bad material disputes rapidly was a major irritant, even after amendments in 1897
and 1906, ostensibly to reduce delays. This issue led to the Ashton operative spinners' association threatening to withdraw their district from
Brooklands:

What we want is a method of dealing with those firms who have habitual bad spinning and unless we have some improvement very soon in the quality of the spinning at these few firms we shall have to give a month's notice to terminate the
Brooklands Agreement as the spinners are getting out of hand. Then they can take
the matter in their own hands and leave work.[25]

[22] *Textile Mercury*, 3 March 1894, 6 June 1894.
[23] *Textile Mercury*, 6 January 1894, 15 June 1895 for some of the earliest critiques; Dyson,
The Development of Collective Bargaining, pp. 454–9; see also the *Cotton Factory Times*,
24 December 1908.   [24] *Textile Mercury*, 8 June 1895.
[25] Ashton MCSA, Minutes of Joint Meeting with the Ashton Operative Spinners'
Provincial Association, 11 October 1906.

A year or so later, Thomas Marsland, the Oldham operative spinners' secretary, articulated a vitriolic critique of the disputes procedure:

> On every occasion on which something takes place involving the conditions of the Brooklands Agreement you have arrogated to yourselves the right to construe its terms and conditions and I am afraid we have too often acquiesced . . . We have, in consequence, great difficulty in persuading our people of the need of the Brooklands Agreement. They tell us it may be true that the agreement has saved a lot of expense and trouble, but they feel this has all been done at the sacrifice of their interests and that they have not got all that they are entitled to.[26]

This situation prevailed until the economic boom and tight labour market conditions of 1910–14 cranked up mill workers' collective power. The Spinners' Amalgamation were forced by an explosion of rank-and-file dissent to abrogate the Brooklands Agreement finally in January 1913. The reaction of the cotton employers' organisations to the escalating pressure upon procedural control in the immediate pre-war years merits more detailed exploration. This will be returned to later.

Challenging craft control?

In the 1890s, as we have seen, employers in many of the staple sectors of the economy met the challenge of more militant trade unionism head on, by consolidating their employers' organisations and aggressively seeking confrontation, utilising replacement labour during strikes, sharpening methods of victimisation and initiating local and industry-wide lock-outs. This was the pattern in engineering, the boot and shoe industry, the railways, shipping and construction. Where employers were powerful enough, as in shipping and the railways, trade unionism was undermined and unilateral determination of wages and working conditions by employers and management usually prevailed. Elsewhere, these confrontations spawned more formalised collective bargaining procedures. Local master builders' associations in north-west England initiated an extension in customary *ad hoc* modes of local bargaining by establishing a formal second stage 'conciliation board' in 1905, and, from 1909, a regional court of appeal covering the northern counties. Price has detected parallel employer initiatives in the building industry in London.[27] A more centralised procedure, influenced by and similar to the Brooklands machinery in cotton spinning, developed in engineering with the Terms of Settlement in 1898. When grievances arose, the manager of an engineering firm was first to receive a deputation of operatives to discuss the issue. If no settlement could be arrived at then the trade

---

[26] FMCSA, *Annual Report*, 1907–8, pp. 21–2.   [27] Price, *Masters*, pp. 192–3.

union(s) could request that they be received as a deputation to the local engineering employers' association to state their case. If the two sides still disagreed, the dispute could be referred to a joint meeting of the Engineering Employers' Federation National Board and the union's national representatives, held at either London or York. No stoppage of work was allowed until the whole of this procedure was exhausted. Broader issues relating to wages and conditions could also be raised directly by any trade union with the local employers' association, or the EEF nationally, thus bypassing the domestic stages of procedure. Within local engineering employers' associations it was made a prerequisite of membership that impending disputes were to be immediately reported to the local association. Periodically, other unions were brought within the scope of this formalised procedure, including the labourers' unions between 1911 and 1913.[28]

What is important, however, is to determine the extent to which such labour management strategies, pursued at the multi-employer level, helped to promote the interests of their constituency, to protect or even advance the prerogatives of management. Here, Zeitlin has argued that employers' associations proved to be singularly ineffective because 'the proposals of aggressive employers to attack job controls and restructure payment systems were repeatedly blocked by other firms' reluctance to bear the costs of a long stoppage'.[29] Thus, engineering employers failed to capitalise fully upon the 1898 victory, partly because of sectoral and regional divisions within the Federation.[30] There is much evidence to substantiate this interpretation. However, on balance, this is too negative a view, which, in essence, applies too rigid criteria on which to assess the contribution employers' associations made to industrial relations. The evidence from a regional perspective suggests that local employers' associations in cotton, engineering and building in Lancashire did strengthen the resolve of individual employers and provide something of a bulwark against union encroachments. Financial grants from such organisations provided subsidies which bolstered resistance to union extensions of job control and damaging precedents in wages and working conditions, as for example in the Fern mill case in 1910. This was not always effective and much depended on the state of labour and product markets. However, where employer solidarity was maintained, inroads by trade unions into issues of work control could be severely limited. The building industry would be a classic example. In the late 1890s and the 1900s the National

---

[28] For the Terms of Settlement, signed 28 January 1898, see A. Shadwell, *The Engineering Industry and the Crisis of 1922*, London: Longmans, 1922, pp. 66–70.

[29] Zeitlin, 'From labour history', p. 176.   [30] Zeitlin, 'Internal politics', pp. 57–62.

Federation of Building Trade Employers indicated to its local and regional affiliates that they should prioritise the removal of craft restrictions on output rather than initiate wage reduction movements. In accordance with this directive the Lancashire master builders' associations took action on a number of issues – apprentice ratios, travelling time, worked stone, overtime, the employment of non-unionists – where it was deemed that the craft rules encroached too deeply into managerial terrain. Hence, by the mid-1900s many issues previously dictated to employers through unilaterally imposed craft rules were the subject of joint regulation. Here, the employers' organisation was an effective weapon in eroding craft control, within the parameters of the existing division of labour, and the North-West Federation of Building Trade Employers congratulated itself on this fact. Similarly in engineering, the success of the organised employers in 1897–8 enabled the encroachments into managerial terrain made by the ASE and other unions to be firmly resisted. Thereafter, employers jealously guarded their autonomy to man their machines as they thought fit, to work overtime and replace wage systems by time with payments by results and hence tie wages much more closely to effort. A close examination of industrial relations in engineering workshops in Lancashire between 1898 and 1910 illustrates this point.

Throughout this period, local engineering employers' associations in north-west England continued faithfully to uphold the rights and privileges of employers enshrined in the Terms of Settlement (1898) to the letter, dogmatically refusing to deviate in joint meetings with engineering trade unions. Platts of Oldham, a textile machinery manufacturer and the largest organised firm in Lancashire, was the exemplar of this uncompromising strategy.[31] Even the tactical flexibility of the national federation in the 1900s invariably fell upon stony ground in north-west England. A proposal by the EEF to introduce the 'one-break' slightly shorter working day, for example, was unanimously opposed by the Rochdale engineering employers, on the grounds that 'no amendment should be agreed to that would essentially restrict the privileges of employers as secured in 1898'.[32] The Lancashire EEAs staunchly defended the right of employers to work overtime, settling case after case in local joint conferences with the argument that the employer concerned had proved that the extra hours were necessitated by 'urgency and emergency'.[33] In the same vein, the right to employ either unionist or non-unionist labour without discrimination was fiercely contested and attempts made to wean supervisors away from

[31] See for example, Platt Brothers and Co., Oldham, Directors' Minutes, 25 April 1901.
[32] Rochdale Engineers' and Machine Makers' Association, Minutes, 4 July 1906.
[33] EEF, *Decisions of Central Conference, 1898–1925*, London: EEF, 1926, case 1654, p. 357.

union membership. The Manchester EEA, an enthusiastic proponent of the Foremen's Mutual Benefit Society, even went so far as to recommend to its members in 1908 that foremen be enticed to sign a non-unionist pledge, or that a clause to such effect be inserted in their contract of employment.[34]

Payments by results remained another contentious issue. The engineering employers' associations in north-west England continually refused to discuss disputes relating to this question, firmly adhering to the Terms which allowed for piecework rates to be fixed by mutual consent between only the individual employer and the worker or workers directly involved. The Lancashire employers' associations also played their part in promoting the premium bonus wage payment system – a crude method of work measurement incorporating an automatic piece price breaker. This issue flared up into open conflict in Manchester in 1902, when the system was introduced into a federated firm, Browett, Lindley and Co., steam engine manufacturers. The Manchester ASE rebelled against the conciliatory line of its national executive and authorised members to refuse to work the premium bonus system at any shop in the Manchester district. The Manchester EEA retaliated by recommending any member firm to sack any worker refusing to work under premium bonus.[35]

A similarly intransigent stance was taken by the Lancashire engineering employers' associations on the issue of apprenticeship. The requests of the ASE and other engineering unions to restrict apprentice numbers, or to speak on behalf of apprentices on wages and conditions, were continually refused. The principle of a paternalist mutual contract between employer and apprentice, unfettered by collective bargaining constraints, was rigidly upheld. The reaction of the employers to such attempts as that of the Manchester Ironmoulders' Society in late 1898, requesting a ratio of one apprentice to every four journeymen, was simply to reject the application as a breach of the Terms of Settlement. Apprentices who occasionally took matters into their own hands were dealt with severely. Lads who left work in Manchester during the 1897–8 lock-out were discharged by many employers, or required to work out the lost time before receiving any wage and before they could be regarded as having formally completed their apprenticeship. Recourse was also had to the enquiry note, suspensions and deferring of annual rises as deterrents.[36]

A major issue was the staffing of machinery. Engineering employers' associations in the north-west persistently protected the prerogative of

---

[34] Manchester EEA, Minutes, 3 June 1908.
[35] See EEF, *Decisions*, case 1244, pp. 258–9; Manchester EEA, Minutes, 1902, *passim*.
[36] See, for example, the Manchester EEA, Minutes, 25 January 1898, 7 February 1898.

employers to employ whoever they chose on their machinery. Numerous local joint conferences were held at which the employers' officials adamantly refused to accept the argument of the unions that specific wage rates should be set for specific machines.[37] Wages aside, by far the most numerous cases being brought through the Lancashire disputes machinery, however, were those which concerned the placing of unskilled or semi-skilled labour on machinery which the craft unions felt should be only worked by skilled men who had completed a full formal apprenticeship. The Lancashire engineering employers' associations were literally inundated with domestic and local conferences on such issues, and at least seventeen such cases went the whole way through procedure to central conference. Significantly, none of these Lancashire cases prior to 1910 was won by the unions. Such skilled labour dilution included the growing employment of women for certain classes of engineering work in Lancashire. In 1905, for example, the local branch of the Electrical Trades Union in Manchester complained of the employment of women as armature winders, claiming this to be a skilled man's job. The retort of the Manchester EEA was a predictable one. A conference to discuss the issue was refused and it was stated that as it was the prerogative of employers to utilise women where they thought fit and that other firms used women on these processes, the association was not prepared to establish an adverse precedent by removing the women from the job.[38]

Employers' associations in engineering, building and cotton textiles thus played a significant role in the multi-faceted counter-attack against labour in the 1890s and 1900s. However, the limitations of this process need to be clearly delineated. If one is measuring the success of employers' associations by the degree to which they promoted rationalisation of work and radically altered labour processes then their achievements appear, indeed, quite meagre. Jonathan Zeitlin has persuasively argued that the victory of the engineering employers' associations in 1898 did not lead to a thoroughgoing transformation of the division of labour.[39] With some caveats, this interpretation holds good for Lancashire. Most employers' associations appear to have adopted a backward-looking, conservative, even archaic attitude to labour management. Perhaps this is a reflection of their attracting the older 'statesmen' of their respective industries to their leadership and executive positions? No evidence has been unearthed of the Lancashire employers' organisations promoting

---

[37] Several such Lancashire cases were taken through to central conference. See EEF, *Decisions*, case numbers 95, p. 26; 296–7, p. 67; and 304, p. 68.

[38] Manchester EEA, Minutes, 3 October 1905, 7 November 1905.

[39] Zeitlin, 'Labour strategies'. McKinlay has also developed this argument with reference to Clydeside metalworking. See McKinlay, *Employers and Skilled Workers*, pp. 39–43.

Taylorism, the main protagonists of pseudo-scientific managerial ideology being maverick employers like Mather, Renold, Ford and British Westinghouse who were non-members or who disassociated themselves from their industry associations.[40] Experimentation with working hours and conditions, in an attempt to increase efficiency by reducing worker fatigue, was firmly denounced by the Iron Trades Employers' Association and the Engineering Employers' Federation and, for a time at least, membership of such organisations was refused to any company not conforming to the standard two-break 54–5-hour working week.[41] Fear of a backlash from trade unions, the precarious industrial peace being breached, and, perhaps, one group of employers gaining a competitive edge, prevented the master spinners' associations from attempting radically to transform the division of labour by replacing the traditional minder, big and little piecer work team with a two-man joiner-piecer team. Likewise, the master weavers failed to press forward with a campaign to spread the system of higher loom complements per weaver (common in the USA), or encourage a more radical shift to the automatic loom, despite precedents in utilising such techniques abroad and in non-member firms, most notably Ashton Brothers in Hyde.[42] This earned the cotton employers' associations the scorn of more innovative, rationalising employers and the trade journal, the *Textile Mercury*. The evidence consequently tempts speculation as to whether the delegation of aspects of labour regulation to a collective organisation inculcated a degree of complacency amongst internal management regarding the development of more efficient modes of work organisation and more detailed division of labour. Whether, in other words, the maintenance of peaceful industrial relations was prioritised over any attempt to alter radically traditional modes of work organisation.

Nevertheless, the achievement of many employers' organisations in holding the line, rather than initiating change, was significant in itself. In many industries before the First World War powerful employers' organisations served to bolster the authority and control of internal management and undermine the influence of organised work groups. Certainly this appears to be the case within the engineering, construction, cotton

---

[40] On Clydeside, the same argument would apply to the giant Singer Corporation (sewing machines) based at Clydebank, which remained outside the employers' association but was amongst the most innovative firms in the region before 1914, grafting alien American-inspired scientific management techniques on to their Scottish labour force. See Glasgow Labour History Workshop, *The Singer Strike*.

[41] McIvor, 'Employers, the government and industrial fatigue in Britain, 1890–1918', *British Journal of Industrial Medicine*, 44 (1987), pp. 727–8.

[42] A. Fowler, 'Trade unions and technical change: the automatic loom strike, 1908', *North West Labour History Society Bulletin*, 6 (1979–80), pp. 43–55.

spinning and weaving sectors in north-west England. In cotton spinning, attempts by the cotton unions to spread the use of more favourable wages lists determined by weight rather than speed (indicators) were firmly resisted, as was the campaign to raise wage payment for spinning fine counts in the Oldham area.[43] Union campaigns in spinning and weaving to have the powers of supervisors curbed, excessive 'driving' brought under control and overlookers paid by time rather than by the set poundage were also stymied. The cotton employers' organisations interpreted this latter move as a direct threat to the rights of management and the maintenance of productivity levels in the weaving shed. Similarly, cotton associations refused to sanction a removal of the fining system for indiscipline and poor workmanship, or the slate system where individual production levels were publicly displayed. Whilst the more radical transformation of the division of labour linked with the joiner minding system and with the automatic and more looms systems was eschewed, as Lazonick and Fowler have shown, it is significant that the cotton spinning employers' organisations took the initiative to create a somewhat more detailed, if limited, division of labour in the Lancashire mule spinning room by creating a separate class of mule cleaners.[44] The cotton employers' federations also indicated – in the most forcible way possible – on a number of occasions that they would not tolerate encroachments into sacrosanct areas of managerial terrain. In 1910, the refusal of one stripper and grinder in the Fern mill to undertake certain duties which were claimed to be not customary without additional payment prompted a two-week lock-out of the entire federated cotton spinning sector, which brought the cardroom workers' union (CWA) to heel. A year later, significantly during a period of buoyant product markets, the CSMA initiated a successful lock-out of the organised weaving masters to reject forcibly a union rolling strike campaign to impose a closed shop. These issues will be explored in rather more detail in the next section. Suffice it to say at this juncture that in cotton spinning and weaving, at least, the strength of industry employers' associations enabled millowners to reassert a degree of discipline on the shop-floor. Crucially, the sanctions of the associations encouraged employers to cut labour costs by intensifying work, albeit invariably within the parameters of the existing technology and traditional division of labour.

On the other hand, managerial control over labour costs, work organisation and craft restrictions could be muted where employer solidarity

---

[43] On fine counts see Oldham MCSA, Minutes, 5 January 1894, 5, 12, 17 and 22 June 1896.
[44] On continuities in the division of labour in cotton manufacture see W. Lazonick, 'Industrial relations and technical change: the case of the self-acting mule', *Cambridge Journal of Economics*, 3 (1979), pp. 248–9; Fowler, 'Trade unions and technical change'.

was weak and, conversely, trade unionism was deep rooted. One example would be the cotton printing sector – based predominantly in Lancashire and Scotland – where there was no tradition of effective employer organisation prior to the formation of the Society of Master Calico Printers (SMCP) in 1905. In this section of the industry well-unionised craftsmen like the engravers and calico printers retained a privileged position, a closed shop, high earnings and firm control over the labour process right up to 1914 even after business rationalisation and considerable labour shedding over the period 1899–1901. This was largely because the dominant combination in the trade, the Calico Printers' Association, adopted a conciliatory line and shirked a radical challenge to unilateral craft regulation, leaving the smaller firms in the SMCP mortified by such lack of resolve.[45]

Tactical flexibility: pragmatism over principle?

The particular mixture of conciliatory and coercive policies prosecuted by employers' organisations was influenced by trade union pressure, wider public opinion, state intervention, the passage of labour laws and by the idiosyncrasies and political orientations of leading association officials. However, policy was largely determined by relative organisational strengths and weaknesses and the strategies adopted by trade unions, which in turn were critically influenced by the fluctuating state of product and labour markets. Strategies were massaged in line with prevailing market conditions. The official pronouncements of employers' organisations in defence of managerial prerogatives proved, in practice, to be subject to much pragmatic flexibility when market circumstances empowered labour. Often, however, it took some time for the altered market situation to impress itself upon employers and workers, and for changing power relationships to be fully absorbed. The cotton industry over the period 1908–14 provides a good example of this process of adjustment and change as market conditions radically altered.

The Brooklands lock-out of 1892–3 demonstrated not only the tenacity and resilience of the cotton unions, but also the lack of cohesion amongst the millowners. The dearth of support from the north Lancashire mills and, more critically, the fine-spinning mills of the Bolton region, critically undermined the lock-out prosecuted by the Federation of Master Cotton Spinners' Association mills, centred on Oldham.

---

[45] For a more extensive discussion see A.J. McIvor, 'Work, wages and industrial relations in cotton finishing, 1880–1914', in Jowitt and McIvor (eds.), *Employers and Labour*, pp. 131–4.

Organisational weakness encouraged the Federation to tread cautiously until the fine spinners threw in their lot with the Federation. Persistent pressure from their unions induced the employers' associations covering fine spinners in Bolton, Manchester and Chorley to join the FMCSA between 1905 and 1908. This provided the necessary precondition for a renewed employer offensive, whilst the sharp economic recession which set in during 1908 provided the igniting agent. The period 1908–10 witnessed two industry-wide lock-outs (both successful for the employers), one threatened industry-wide lock-out (averted by the cardroom union backing down), the imposition of a 5 per cent wage cut and a major coup for the employers – a negotiated five-year wage freeze agreement, covering 1910–15.

One of these lock-outs illustrates the strength of feeling amongst employers on the broader issue of employers' authority to manage their concerns without interference. On the instruction of his union, a grinder employed in the cardroom of a Federation firm (the Fern mill) refused to undertake certain duties (extracting matted fibres from the flats of the carding engine, utilising a tool called an awl) which the employers claimed were customary at the mill. As a consequence the man was discharged. The CWA refused to accept that the work was customary, declined to visit the mill for a joint inspection, ignored procedure and brought their members out on strike after a week's notice on 14 June 1910. At this point the FMCSA took over the management of the dispute. After informal talks on 5–6 August, negotiations broke down, deadlock ensued, with the Federation supporting the mill with generous financial compensation. The dispute looked set to remain localised and unresolved for some time.

However, the position changed when the CWA opened up another front on this same issue at the Rutland mill in mid-August 1910. This sharpened the resolve of the Oldham masters: 'There is no doubt that this action aggravated the real point at issue in the Fern case and made it clear that the cardroom operatives' association had adopted a new policy, and had decided without consultation with employers that many duties which have existed for years at different mills were not the duties of grinders.'[46] By mid-September, millowners were united in opposition to what they now interpreted as a concerted and systematic attack on sacrosanct principles:

The strike is not on the merits of picking flats. That has not been discussed. The questions at issue are the assured right of the local cardroom officials to settle, without reference to the management of the firm, what method of performing their duties shall be adopted by the grinders, and their refusal to hold a joint enquiry into the case before the mill was put on strike.[47]

[46] Oldham MCSA, *Annual Report*, 1910, p. 14.   [47] Ibid.

In other words this was interpreted as an attempt to extend workers' control into managerial terrain. In a very well-attended mass meeting of Federation members the millowners reiterated their unilateral authority to determine workers' duties, demanded that the established disputes procedure be utilised and agreed to initiate an industry-wide lock-out (discharging all employees – not just the cardroom workers) from 1 October. After a week's stoppage the CWA climbed down and agreed to the reopening of the Fern mill without the sacked grinder. A face-saving formula was also concocted whereby George Askwith (troubleshooter with the Board of Trade Labour Department) was asked to arbitrate on the respective rights of the unions and employers under clauses 6 and 7 of the Brooklands Agreement. In giving his opinion Askwith criticised Brooklands as a poorly drafted agreement and noted in his summing up that there was every chance of a recurrence of conflict on the issue of changes in work practices because no mutual understanding had been achieved.[48] The bitterness left by this clash, and the autocratic line pursued by the Federation, contributed to a growing disillusionment amongst spinning and cardroom workers as to the utility of the Brooklands collective bargaining structures.

On the weaving side, it was the issue of the closed shop which precipitated a similar stand on the basis of employers' rights and authority to manage. In response to a series of threatened mill strikes in breach of procedure, the master weavers' federation, the CSMA, initiated an industry-wide lock-out, supported by 95 per cent of its members, which threw 160,000 out of employment and a further 100,000 on to short-time. The CSMA line was to stress that they did not oppose trade unionism *per se*, but that they could not deviate from the principle of an open shop and sanction unionisation, either explicitly or tacitly. The two-week stoppage was resolved, again, through the arbitration of George Askwith.[49] The settlement allowed for a return to work for six months, after which Askwith was to give his considered views on the issue. At least another six months was to elapse before any industrial action could be constitutionally taken by either side. Meanwhile, the CSMA drew up a new, aggressive policy plan to deal with non-unionist strikes, incorporating the blacklisting of strikers, generous financial strike compensation, a local association lock-out to be initiated three weeks after any individual strike, and an industry-wide lock-out two weeks thereafter.[50]

What is most revealing is the way in which the very firm stances

[48] Ibid., 1911, p. 5.
[49] Askwith, *Industrial Problems*, pp. 188–9. For a full discussion of this dispute see White, *Limits*, pp. 126–45.   [50] CSMA, Minutes, 2 February 1912.

adopted by the FMCSA and the CSMA began to wobble and eventually crumble as buoyant product and labour markets throughout 1912 until 1914 weakened employers' resolve. In the process, sectional interests, pragmatism and perhaps individual greed fractured employer solidarity and undermined the pursuit of supposedly sacrosanct principles, forcing their organisations to pursue a rearguard action pivoting around the localisation of disputes and de-escalation of the rising tide of worker militancy.

In the cotton weaving industry the closed shop issue revived and became a running sore, centred on the Nelson area, through 1913 and 1914. The Nelson masters' association agreed to implement the hard-line strategy agreed in February 1912, and earned the support of the CSMA Executive for an escalating lock-out supported by high strike compensation. However, the other local associations registered, at best, lukewarm support for such procedure. A majority could not be obtained to sanction the proposed 6-shilling per week per loom compensation. Also, of the three largest associations, Burnley agreed to a general lock-out only after Nelson had been locked out for four (rather than the planned two) weeks, whilst Blackburn and Preston suggested that Nelson fight alone, the latter arguing: 'We believe delay is all in favour of settlement, whereas we are of opinion that a threatened general lock-out would most probably enlist the sympathy of the local unions of the other districts and increase our difficulties.'[51] This effectively paralysed decisive action by the CSMA, which left the two Nelson firms affected to struggle on alone, with reduced financial backing until a settlement almost four months later.[52] Though disgruntled, the Nelson mills held firm. However, it is significant that a lack of solidarity and evident unwillingness amongst most of its constituent members to face a long stoppage in a period of buoyant trade forced the CSMA to abdicate a struggle that it had taken up in earnest less that two years previously.

A similar series of events unfolded within the cotton spinning sector. After the grinders' duties lock-out in 1910, the predominant strategy of the FMCSA pivoted around the localisation and de-escalation of conflict, milking procedure for all that it was worth in an attempt to keep the growing tide of industrial militancy within bounds. Joseph White has charted the breadth of cotton union militancy during 1910–14.[53] However, White failed to analyse adequately the role employers' played during this phase of intense conflict. In short, tactical flexibility on the part of their organisations minimised the loss of production time for cotton millowners, particularly from the spring of 1912. The following two examples help to substantiate this argument.

---

[51] Ibid., 3 June 1913.   [52] Ibid., 1 August and 29 August 1913.   [53] White, *Limits*.

First, in the Bolton fine spinning area a forward movement in 1913 by the cardroom union to control changing work practices as a consequence of technological renewal was met by the Bolton MCSA proposing the creation of a new uniform wage list. The association thereafter delayed matters for as long as possible, holding eighteen joint meetings between March and December 1913. The eventual settlement, operative from March 1914, provided for substantial wage rises for most cardroom workers. However, sectional strikes and snowballing concessions had been averted, hence, the Bolton masters' president asserted: 'The Committee had saved the trade no end of trouble by agreeing to draw up a list, as there is no doubt that individual attacks would have been made upon the members.'[54]

Secondly, frustrated by delays in procedure over 'bad spinning' cases, the spinners' union withdrew from the Brooklands Agreement in January 1913.[55] Between February and August 1913 there were strikes at fifteen Federation mills, with the spinners alleging gross inferiority in the raw material supplied.[56] What is most surprising, given the initiatives pursued between 1908 and 1910, is that in the face of what amounted to the most widespread sectional attack on the Federation in its history, the employers' organisation did not retaliate and escalate the conflict by a general lock-out. Tactical flexibility governed employer policy whilst product markets were buoyant and labour shortages most evident. Millowners bided their time until more favourable circumstances arrived. In the event, after over six months of deadlock, both sides agreed to settle by adopting a faster and more streamlined disputes procedure, incorporating both local and central joint meetings held within seven days. At the company level, the altered market circumstances were reflected in growing wage drift, bonuses on wage lists and additional *ad hoc* payments, especially granted to piecers.[57]

More buoyant market conditions in the engineering sector from 1910 to 1914 also encouraged pragmatic, tactical flexibility on the part of the employers and undermined the intransigent pursuit of managerial prerogative, as enshrined in the Terms of Settlement of 1898. At least this is what the experience of local joint conferences in Lancashire from the summer of 1910 suggests – in marked contrast to the preceding decade or

---

[54] Bolton MCSA, general meeting, Minutes, 21 January 1914.
[55] 'Bad spinning' disputes occurred when operatives alleged that the quality of raw material being spun was so poor that this eroded piecework earnings, hence they claimed some financial compensation.
[56] FMCSA, *Annual Report*, 1913–14, pp. 12–21; Rochdale MCSA, *Annual Report*, 1912–13, pp. 4–5.
[57] Oldham MCSA, General Committee Minutes, 12 September 1913, 7 November 1913, 5 December 1913, 6 February 1914, 13 February 1914.

so. The changed environment was particularly discernible on the machinery staffing question.

In May/June 1910 the boilermakers' society in Manchester threatened to strike at an EEF firm, Daniel Adamson and Co., Dukinfield, because they objected to a particular job on water tube boilers being undertaken by handymen. The response of the employers is significant. The firm made it very clear that they regarded this as a breach of the Terms and an encroachment into employers' prerogative. They claimed that the work did not necessitate the employment of skilled boilermakers, that they were aware of unskilled workers being used elsewhere and that to compete successfully they too had to utilise cheap labour. The Manchester EEA, however, refused to square up to the challenge. Instead of the usual bald assertion of the employers' right to employ whom they thought fit under the Terms, the association initiated an investigation of precedent and local practice. The subsequent survey of various federated districts found that skilled workers were, in fact, generally used for tube expansion processes. A strategic decision was made at this point. Rather than spearheading an offensive to cheapen labour costs, the Manchester EEA counselled the firm to return to standard practice and not compete unfairly with other employers in the trade. 'Under the circumstances,' the Manchester association concluded, 'in view of the attitude taken up by the union, there was no alternative other than the firm giving way.'[58]

At the textile machinery making firms of H. Livesey and Co., Blackburn, in 1911–12 and at Dobson and Barlow, Bolton, in 1914, the unions also scored significant points in struggles over machine staffing. At Livesey's, a dispute arose over the employment of unskilled handymen on lathes. Procedure was completely exhausted, with the employers having the full benefit of the cheaper labour for fifteen months between May 1911 and August 1912. The ASE struck at the firm on 9 August 1912. A settlement was reached some twelve weeks later which incorporated some key concessions to the ASE, including the retention of skilled turners on two capstan lathes in the shop, and the employment of apprentices on certain work formerly undertaken by handymen (bush lathes and lathes fitted with expanding chucks).[59] At Dobson and Barlow, a dispute occurred over the displacement of skilled men by handymen in the process of erecting ring frames. The result at central conference was a significant victory for the union. The employer agreed in May 1914 to revert to workshop practice existing prior to the dispute, to reintroduce skilled

[58] Manchester EEA, Minutes of a local joint conference with the Boilermakers' Society, 10 June 1910.   [59] EEF, *Decisions*, case 232, pp. 50–1.

men to complete certain processes in the erection of ring frames, and to concede a wage rise to the remaining handymen working on ring frame erection, thus recognising the increased status of the job.[60] The line in the sand drawn and enshrined in the Terms of 1898 was most definitely being breached in the immediate pre-war years.

The attitude of employers' organisations in north-west England towards the recognition of labourers' trade unions also mellowed in the period directly preceding the First World War. Recognition of labourers' unions for collective bargaining purposes was almost totally rejected before 1911 – at least by the master builders' and engineering employers' associations. Individual member firms were left to establish wage rates with their labourers as they thought fit.[61] However, tightening labour markets and the passage of the 1911 National Insurance Act precipitated a surge in trade unions catering for unskilled and semi-skilled workers.[62] Inevitably, such unions pressed for official recognition and a guaranteed minimum wage. In Lancashire, almost all of the major local engineering and building employers' associations received simultaneous requests from J.R. Clynes (MP and president of the National Union of Gas Workers and General Labourers' Union) for improvements in the rates of pay and working conditions of labourers, including a minimum wage of 20 to 22 shillings and time-and-a-quarter overtime pay.[63] The responses of the local associations in Lancashire reflect something of the heterogeneity in orientation and labour relations policy that characterised industry before the First World War.

In building, Manchester was the pivotal district in the north-west pressed by the labourers for union recognition. Initially, backed up by the regional federation, the Manchester building masters refused to concede.[64] In response, the labourers stepped up their industrial action from boycotting firms to sporadic strikes, culminating in an all-out strike in the Manchester building trade by July 1912.[65] The degree of solidarity achieved by the labourers shocked the Manchester employers, whose intransigent, exclusionist strategy clearly backfired. In the event the organisation had little stomach for a long-drawn-out conflict, admitted its miscalculation and settled by agreeing a minimum wage and a signed

[60] Ibid., case 306, p. 68.
[61] Manchester MBA, Minutes, 26 September 1911. The only exceptions were the Oldham and Wigan MBAs, where a degree of recognition had been granted previously to the labourers' unions.   [62] Askwith, Industrial Problems, p. 355.
[63] EEF, Wage Movements 1897–1925, London: EEF, 1926, pp. 571, 836–7. This was a movement replicated in most major engineering areas, including Clydeside. See Glasgow Herald, 13 September, 16 September and 21 October 1912.
[64] Manchester MBA, Minutes, 4 October, 10 October, 21 December 1911; LCFBTE, Minutes, 4 December 1911.   [65] LCFBTE, Minutes, 10 May, 23 July, 26 July 1912.

code of working rules.[66] After Manchester collapsed, the Liverpool masters peacefully granted the same concessions to their labourers, and recognition rapidly spread during 1912–13 to all the other major towns in the region.

In engineering, three of the smaller local associations, Blackburn, Preston and Wigan, rejected the labourers' applications in 1911, but agreed a 20-shilling minimum wage in 1912 or early 1913.[67] The Bolton employers proved to be the most intransigent, leaving the 1911 application to be dealt with by individual firms and not formally recognising a minimum wage until mid-1914, and then only on the condition that the labourers' unions accept a four-year wage freeze.[68] These districts, however, accounted for less than 25 per cent of the employing capacity of the Lancashire engineering industry. Most of the other local associations approached conceded recognition and a minimum wage to the labourers' societies in 1911. Barrow, Rochdale, Burnley and Oldham agreed to recognise, settle collectively and established minimum wage rates of 20 shillings. According to the *Rochdale Observer* this meant a wage rise of up to 3 shillings to many labourers, or between 15 and 20 per cent.[69] In 1912–13, the Burnley and Oldham associations had their first official joint conferences with representatives of the labourers' unions – the initial claims having been undertaken completely by correspondence.

When the Manchester master engineers were faced with the original labourers' wage application in 1911 they conducted an association vote on whether to settle the claim collectively or individually. In a low poll, 18 voted in favour of collective bargaining, 9 against. The association chairman favoured the minority line, arguing that if the association negotiated collectively it would mean 'practically the recognition of a minimum wage'.[70] Lack of unanimity persuaded the Executive of the association to leave members to settle the best terms possible on an individual basis, within maximum guidelines laid down by the organisation. However, the Executive Committee were disappointed with the results of this exercise when they reviewed the settlements, concluding, significantly, that a better deal could have been achieved through collective bargaining.[71] Again, the employers had indicated their vulnerability to sectional attack. This lesson precipitated a volte-face. From 1912 Manchester reversed

[66] Ibid., 16 August 1912, Joint Minutes, 20 August, 10 September 1912. This pivotal agreement included allowances for overtime, travelling expenses and nightworking, together with a conciliation clause preventing any stoppage of work until after a local joint meeting and a hearing of the local conciliation board.

[67] EEF, *Wage Movements*, pp. 128, 795–6, 941.   [68] Ibid., pp. 151–3.

[69] Ibid., pp. 23–4, 210–12, 749, 816–17; *Rochdale Observer*, 23 August 1911; Rochdale EEA, Minutes, 16 August 1911.   [70] Manchester EEA, Minutes, 8 August 1911.

[71] Ibid., 6 September 1911.

their policy, granted formal recognition, overtime concessions and a minimum wage, and henceforth embraced collective bargaining with the unskilled labourers' unions.[72] This policy reorientation undoubtedly owed much to the growing industrial and political muscle of unskilled and semi-skilled workers over the preceding period. Thus, this concession represented an example of tactical flexibility on the part of the employers – the success, perhaps, of pragmatism over dogmatic principle. However, it is equally conceivable that conceding collective bargaining rights to such workers was at least facilitated by the relatively smooth working of the disputes procedure since 1898 and the undoubted advantages that accrued to engineering employers from this process. By 1914, minimum wage rates of 20–22 shillings were recognised by all the large Lancashire engineering employers' associations and collective bargaining with the labourers' unions was clearly and firmly established on a local basis.

Stabilising labour costs

It was argued in chapter 3 that employers were attracted to combine together partly because of the incentive which organisation offered to control competition within the trade and to stabilise volatile product and labour markets. Indeed, stabilising costs may well have been a more significant service to employers than pioneering managerial prerogatives and controlling work. Employers' associations performed such regulatory functions in a variety of ways. Where they were successful, such multi-employer price-stabilising techniques could have a direct impact on industrial relations, allowing wage costs to be passed on to the customer, or perhaps reducing pressure to cut wages. It was this latter inducement which encouraged the cotton unions to support directly, on occasions, the short-time work movements initiated by the millowners in the 1890s and 1900s.

Most employers' organisations, however, controlled competition within the trade in a rather more oblique manner, through exerting their influence to determine, regulate and control wages and other labour costs. The evidence for Lancashire suggests that such influence increased incrementally throughout the 1890s and 1900s, partly to deter wage escalation through sectional trade union action and partly to equalise wage costs between employers, hence creating conditions conducive to 'fair' competition, eliminating both the 'unscrupulous' undercutting employer and the embarrassment of the overpayer. One implication was that employers' associations performed an important function in reducing

[72] EEF, *Wage Movements*, pp. 625–6.

wage differentials at the local, regional and national level, thus removing conflict-creating anomalies. Historians investigating the erosion in spatial wage differentials over this period have underestimated the role played by employers' organisations in this process.[73] G.H. Wood, secretary of the Huddersfield and District Manufacturers' and Woollen Spinners' Association, argued in 1910 that the higher level of wage standardisation in cotton than in wool was the direct consequence of more powerful and effective employers' organisation in Lancashire than in Yorkshire.[74] The uniform piecework wage lists in cotton weaving, spinning, and, rather later, the cardroom performed such a standardising function. Even where formal wage lists did not exist, for example amongst peripheral workers like the cop packers in the 1890s, local cotton employers' associations frequently determined wage levels on the basis of the average wage of neighbouring mills employing such workers.[75] The commitment to uniformity in labour costs in cotton manufacture is indicated by the extent to which weaving employers openly supported the efforts of the Amalgamated Weavers' Association to spread union membership and the payment of list wages to poorly organised 'outlying areas' (like Earby and Barnoldswick). To galvanise such action, the Cotton Spinners' and Manufacturers' Association even threatened the union with cuts on the wage lists, pleading inability to compete with the handful of independent 'undercutting' masters. On its part, the cotton unions targeted non-member firms and publicly declared a preference for associated millowners paying collectively agreed list prices.

But were employers' organisations strong enough to sustain such a policy and significantly influence wage levels and working conditions within a region? In this respect, Zeitlin's assertion that discipline within employers' organisations was minimal and ineffective is an overgeneralisation.[76] Perhaps this is the way it looked from the centre, but trawling through the minute books of the local and regional employers' associations in Lancashire provides quite a different impression. Employers' associations in north-west England, as we have seen, invariably refused to allow membership or support member firms or other associations where deviation from the standard rate and/or association working conditions was evident. The twelve engineering employers' associations in Lancashire all met in joint regional conference from 1906 to discuss proposed wage alterations at the local level, and the pivotal area, Manchester,

[73] See, for example, Hunt, *British Labour History*, p. 102; E. Hunt, *Regional Wage Variations in Britain 1850–1914*, Oxford: Clarendon Press, 1973, pp. 352–4.
[74] *Textile Mercury*, 12 February 1910, p. 117.
[75] Oldham MCSA, Committee Minutes, 27 August 1895.
[76] Zeitlin, 'From labour history', pp. 175–6; Zeitlin, 'Internal politics', pp. 52–3.

refused to support any local association deviating more than one shilling per hour from the Manchester standard wage list. Similarly, the North-West Federation of Building Trade Employers centralised the consideration of wage movements within its fifty-four affiliated local associations and drew up 'model codes' of working rules covering working hours, overtime rates, apprenticeship ratios, etc.[77] This was designed to head off an unprecedented barrage of sectional claims by building trade unions through 1911–12, as the Manchester association noted: 'to prevent any decision being arrived at which would in practice act detrimental to the interests of the adjoining district'.[78] The benefits of standardising labour costs between heterogeneous affiliated members were clearly spelt out: this would minimise cut-throat competition and underselling amongst building employers and, if all stood firm, enable the additional costs to be added to prices.[79]

These policies served to reduce competitive pressures between employers – hence removing one further disincentive to collective organisation – and also critically circumscribed the ability of the trade unions to drive wages up by selectively targeting industrial action and 'snowballing' concessions made throughout a region. Recalcitrant firms would be treated not only with opprobrium but could also be formally disciplined by fines (e.g. in cotton when not complying with lock-out notices) and the stripping of membership. Dismissal was a very real sanction where the intertrading rule applied, or where employers' associations provided insurance functions or ran complex disputes procedures. With employers' organisation, in other words, went tighter discipline and control – a closing of ranks and a tightening of loyalty to protect the common interest. This brought an unprecedented degree of stability and standardisation in labour costs, as increasingly organised employers sought to minimise unfair, undercutting competition from their fellow capitalists. By mobilising the support of the industry, wage reductions during downswings in the trade could be more effectively and painlessly obtained. Contrast the problems of the Oldham cotton spinning masters fighting alone in the 1880s, with organised wage movement campaigns through the FMCSA in the 1890s and 1900s. The same could be said of the Manchester engineering sector. Moreover, strong employers' organisations could utilise their bargaining strength to achieve long-term agreements stabilising wages. For example, the FMCSA traded a proposed wage reduction in the spring of 1910 for a five-year wage freeze.[80]

[77] LCFBTE, Minutes, 5 December 1912, 6 January 1913, 9 January 1913, 13 February 1913, 17 February 1913.   [78] Manchester MBA, Minutes, 27 April 1911.

[79] LCFBTE, Minutes, 9 January 1913.   [80] FMCSA, *Annual Report*, 1910–11, pp. 11–14.

Similarly, in August 1909, the Manchester EEA traded off a proposed wage cut for an agreement with the ASE for a three-year wage freeze.[81] This was followed by agreements with other trade unions in 1910–11, including the moulders, coremakers, boilermakers and iron and steel dressers, for wage freezes of between two to five years. And, in 1912, on the termination of the first three-year wage freeze, a further agreement was signed with the ASE conceding a 2-shilling wage rise and a further three-year moratorium on wage movements.[82] Such agreements were widely copied by other smaller engineering employers' associations in the north-west.[83] It is tempting to speculate that here lies at least part of the explanation for stagnating real wage levels in the immediate pre-First World War period.

Conclusion

The growing network of employers' organisations which developed in Britain prior to the First World War assumed diverse forms and pursued a wide range of strategies which defy generalisation, but were designed to protect class interests. Much more empirical research is necessary to illuminate the rich mosaic of experience across industries and regions. However, the evidence from north-west England suggests that the prevailing revisionist view of employers' organisations prior to the First World War as weak, ephemeral, disunited and ineffective institutions needs, perhaps, to be modified. The argument developed here has been that employers' organisations at the local and regional level performed an important, positive and increasingly innovative role in industrial relations, not least in helping to neutralise the sectional strike weapon, minimising the cost of labour legislation and in promoting uniformity in unit wage and other costs throughout the region, hence taking wages out of competition and removing many conflict-inducing anomalies. However, perhaps the most significant role of associations of employers lay in the initiatives they took to create and extend a more formalised industrial relations system based on joint regulation of wages and hours and increasingly complex disputes procedures. In some industries, such as cotton textiles, such a system of procedural control came to replace coercion and the strategic use of mill paternalism in the late nineteenth century as the dominant mechanism of labour control.

[81] Manchester EEA, Minutes of local joint conference, 18 August 1909.
[82] EEF, *Wage Movements*, pp. 624–6.
[83] Ibid.: see pp. 749–50 and pp. 151–3 for examples of such agreements in Oldham and Bolton.

Despite occasional aberrations, the leaders of British employers' organisations were, in the main, perceptive enough to recognise that quite different circumstances existed in Britain to those prevailing in the USA and over much of the European continent and hence developed a more subtle, though perhaps no less effective, response to the escalating challenge of labour prior to the First World War. Procedural control, backed up by coercive sanctions – what Lloyd George referred to cryptically as 'conciliation at first, but, failing that, the steam roller'[84] – brought a degree of stability, order and discipline to industrial relations which, in the final analysis, was perhaps the most pervasive and significant of employers' associations' successes before 1914. This ironed out wage fluctuations and increased wage standardisation across industries, bolstered workshop discipline and constrained industrial militancy, taking many aspects of industrial relations off the shop-floor and outside the individual determination of industrialists. At the same time, heightened collective organisation and bargaining raised the stakes, increasing the possibility of all-out confrontation, supported by powerful institutions of capital and labour on both sides of industry.

To argue that employers' organisations played an increasingly significant role in British industrial relations prior to the First World War is not to suggest, however, that they were monolithic or omnipotent. Clearly, the power of employers' associations, and indeed trade unions, was in a constant state of flux, fluctuating markedly with alterations in product and labour markets and influenced by the wider political, social and cultural environment. At the workshop level, craftworkers, whose skills remained much in demand, retained much of their autonomy and power, successfully resisting, in the metal trades at least, a thoroughgoing transformation of the division of labour. In the face of residual craft resistance, employers adapted general agreements, such as the 1898 Terms of Settlement in engineering, in a flexible and pragmatic fashion. Unions were active agencies and, depending upon the circumstances, could provide significant institutional defences, negating employer attempts to extend control through procedural or autocratic means. This was the case in metalworking, though in building and cotton textiles employers' organisations appear to have had more success in exploiting procedure to their own ends. What is clear is that workers and their trade unions responded positively to the erosion in their bargaining position that the formation and strengthening of employers' associations implied. Effective employer organisation and the imposition of forms of procedural control could generate stronger union organisation and rank-and-file alienation which incubated more

[84] Cited in Alderman, *Railway Interest*, pp. 199–200.

radical tactics – mass picketing, the sympathy strike, 'wildcat' actions, and the growth of syndicalist and industrial unionist strategies.

The tightening of labour markets during the period 1910–14, in particular, saw a marked alteration in the balance of power between capital and labour which created something of a crisis for employers' organisations, whose reflex action was predominantly defensive. In the cotton industry, lock-outs and lock-out threats were eschewed as associations adopted de-escalatory tactics in an effort to contain wage drift, isolate sectional strikes and minimise production time lost across the industry. The bad-spinning and non-unionist crises in cotton from 1912 to 1914 are examples of this process. The years 1910–14 witness a marked wave of employer-initiated deviations from the sacrosanct Terms of Settlement in the engineering industry in Lancashire – concessions being made to a resurgent craft unionism, particularly on the machinery staffing issue. The extension of welfare services was another response to escalating industrial militancy – a strategic reaction to retain worker loyalty and maintain managerial prerogative.[85] However, collective bargaining was clearly failing to contain disputes; indeed, procedural controls were increasingly being questioned, blatantly bypassed (as in building) and, in some cases, the constraints were thrown over – the 1898 engineering Terms of Settlement and the 1893 Brooklands Agreement, for example, both being abrogated by the operative spinners and engineers' union in the immediate pre-war period.

On the eve of the First World War, many employers' organisations were struggling to maintain the existence of the formal industrial relations system which had so effectively facilitated the maintenance of workshop discipline and protection of managerial prerogative. In some regions, such as Clydeside, some employers were prophesying a concerted labour offensive against the bastions of managerial prerogative.[86] In the event, the war intervened and proved to be a catalyst for the consolidation and further extension of the collective bargaining system. The war emergency stimulated collective organisation on both sides of industry, providing employer organisations and trade unions with sufficient leverage to reassert the validity of formalised disputes procedures. This drew trade unions further into a corporatist compromise which accepted rather than fundamentally challenged the proprietorial rights of industrialists.

---

[85] See Melling, 'British employers', vol. 2, pp. 53–4 and J. Melling, 'Employers, industrial welfare and the struggle for workplace control in British industry, 1880–1920', in Gospel and Littler (eds.), *Managerial Strategies*, pp. 55–81.

[86] See, for example, the comment of the works manager (Richmond) at Weir's engineering factory, Glasgow, cited in T. Dickson (ed.), *Scottish Capitalism*, London: Lawrence and Wishart, p. 273.

6   The impact of the First World War

The war emergency dislocated product and labour markets, radically altering the social and political environment in which employers' organisations operated. This produced conflicting and paradoxical results. The volatility of product and labour markets increased intra-class competition, undermining solidarity as competition intensified for scarce labour, for raw materials and for government contracts. Labour was directed into the armed forces and into war-related work, producing radical changes in the employment profiles of British industries (see table 6.1). The effects of war upon product and labour markets were perhaps the main destabilising agents, setting in train forces which fractured internal discipline, undermined central control over wages and conditions, making consensus collective action more problematic. This was particularly marked, as one might expect, in the engineering sector, where, McKinlay, Wigham and Zeitlin have argued, employer cohesion waned and central authority atrophied between 1914 and 1920, resulting in a diminution of managerial rights and the adoption of a flexible, conciliatory, rearguard defensive policy by the EEF.[1]

On the other hand, unprecedented government intervention in industry, combined with a quite remarkable surge in trade union growth and shop-floor labour militancy during the period 1914–20 placed great pressure upon individual employers, raising the capacity for collective action amongst industrialists. Hence, these years witnessed a counter-surge in the number, representativeness and stability of British employers' organisations, at all levels, peaking in the early 1920s. Moreover, many employers' organisations acted, often quite aggressively, though with varying degrees of success, to bring the destabilising influences, especially of the period 1914–17, under some control. Howard Gospel has outlined the dimensions of this growth phase and persuasively argued that many British employers' organisations played a key role during the period

[1] Zeitlin, 'Internal politics', pp. 62–7; McKinlay and Zeitlin, 'The meanings of managerial prerogative', pp. 38–41; Wigham, *Power to Manage*, pp. 86–109.

Table 6.1 *Employment in the UK: selected industries, 1914–20 (thousands)*

	July 1914		July 1918		July 1920	
	male	female	male	female	male	female
Building	920	7	440	29	796	10
Cotton	274	415	146	359	219	396
Engineering/Shipbuilding	928	45	1141	349	1256	117
Metals	1634	170	1824	594	2104	303

Source: C.J. Wrigley (ed.), *A History of British Industrial Relations*, vol. II: *1914–1939*, pp. 62–3.

1914–20 in reorganising and consolidating their industrial relations systems, extending still further the scope of national wage bargaining and formalised stage-by-stage disputes procedural systems.[2]

The wider repercussions of the war heightened class awareness, and, indeed, class polarisation. Significantly, the war and immediate post-war years witnessed the formation of powerful and permanent peak employers' confederations – the Federation of British Industries and the National Confederation of Employers' Organisations. These bodies, whilst wracked by internal dissension and politically impotent before 1920, as John Turner has shown, were nevertheless symbolic of a tightening of class identities.[3] Similarly, the various anti-labour propaganda, strikebreaking and blacklisting agencies which appeared between the Bolshevik Revolution in Russia and the early 1920s provide further tangible expressions of class consciousness amongst employers and collective initiatives to protect capitalist interests. Moreover, these developments were also manifested at the local/regional level.[4] The war brought new levels of employer co-operation and a considerable extension of union recognition and collective bargaining. It also embroiled industrial employers in a closer relationship with the state.

The war drew the state inexorably into industrial relations, accelerating the trend of 1910–14, and this influenced organisational structures and

[2] Gospel, 'Employers and managers', pp. 160–3.
[3] J. Turner (ed.), *Businessmen and Politics: Studies in Business Activity in British Politics, 1900–1945*, London: Heinemann, 1984, pp. 33–49.
[4] In a detailed examination of the Clydeside region, Joe Melling has argued that the war emergency exposed employers to their own weaknesses, divisions and lack of political clout, and, as a result, by 1920 'employers became much better organised under a coherent industrial leadership at regional and national levels' (Melling, 'Scottish industrialists', p. 104). See also McIvor and Paterson, 'Combating the left', pp. 137–40; McIvor, 'Crusade for capitalism', pp. 631–4.

collectivist behaviour, attitudes and labour relations policies in many significant ways. By the end of the war around 5 million workers were directly employed by the state within 'controlled establishments', and major industries – such as coal and railways – were effectively nationalised. Industrial relations during wartime has generated much interest, particularly in relation to the meaning and implications of this growth of state intervention. To Keith Middlemas the war witnessed a major extension of corporatism – a process whereby the state intervened as a broker between the conflicting interests of capital and labour, drawing the organisations of both sides more closely into the process of government to ensure social harmony, hence maximising production for the war effort.[5] Corporatism as an industrial relations strategy was premised on the notion that class conflict was counter-productive, that capital and labour had common interests and mutual obligations and that the national interest would be served by institutionalising this relationship at all levels. This enhanced the prestige of such institutions, raising their status, Middlemas posits, to 'governing institutions'. However, did government policy during the First World War favour one side or the other within this cosy relationship? More than twenty years ago James Hinton hypothesised that state labour policy during the First World War reflected the dominant interests of the industrial business community and that labour during the war found itself subject to tight legal controls: disciplined and muzzled within a 'servile state'.[6] Here the Munitions Act of 1915 and the Ministry of Munitions were the primary mechanisms of social control; both tangible expressions of the dominance of business interests over labour in state policy. This perspective was refined and developed in the work of Burgess and Melling.[7]

Recently, however, these interpretations have been subjected to serious revision.[8] It has been argued that Middlemas exaggerated the power of both trade unions and employers' organisations, that state strategy was more diffuse due to conflicts between government departments and

---

[5] Middlemas, *Politics*, pp. 120–51. See also L. Panitch, 'The development of corporatism in liberal democracies', *Comparative Political Studies*, 10 (1977), pp. 61–70.

[6] See J. Hinton, *The First Shop Stewards' Movement*, London: Allen and Unwin, 1973, pp. 23–55.

[7] Burgess, *Challenge of Labour*, pp. 153–94; J. Melling, 'The servile state revisited', *Scottish Labour History Society Journal*, 24 (1989), pp. 68–85.

[8] A. Reid, 'Dilution, trade unionism and the state in Britain during the First World War', in S. Tolliday and J. Zeitlin (eds.), *Shop Floor Bargaining and the State*, Cambridge: Cambridge University Press, 1985; I. McLean, *The Legend of Red Clydeside*, Edinburgh: John Donald, 1983; C. Wrigley, 'The First World War and state intervention in industrial relations', in Wrigley (ed.), *A History of British Industrial Relations*, vol. II; G.R. Rubin, *War, Law and Labour: The Munitions Acts, State Regulation and the Unions, 1915–1921*, Oxford: Clarendon Press, 1987.

that the corporatist tendency clearly failed to prevent the explosion of militancy after the First World War. In this reappraisal state policy emerges as more *ad hoc* in conception, even-handed and neutral, and employers as more defensive, frustrated and embattled. subjected to greater pressures and constraints. The state-directed wartime regime was aimed more at achieving stability in industrial relations, thus facilitating maximum productivity (vital for the war effort), than nakedly pursuing employers' class interests in a repressive conspiracy against labour. Rubin has recently argued that the Munitions Act had a 'double-edged' nature, that its key purpose was 'conflict management' and that wartime corporatism did not operate solely in the interests of capital, but rather in the 'national interest', cutting indiscriminately across class boundaries.[9]

This chapter is not directly concerned with the formulation of state labour policy during the First World War but provides an analysis of the reaction of employers in three industries – engineering, cotton and building – to the dislocation caused by war, and to the heightened role of the state in industrial relations. The focus is upon organisational developments and collectively formulated labour strategies: how, in other words, industrialists responded to a radically altered environment and attempted to maintain managerial prerogative and profitability in the face of new demands and pressures. This allows an opportunity to engage with some of the issues raised in the ongoing historiography, relating these to an important industrial region neglected in the literature, thus providing a different perspective on a debate which has pivoted around the Clydeside region and the metalworking trades. The focus here is not the munitions tribunals but the day-to-day relationships between organised employers, their members and the trade unions in north-west England between 1914 and 1920. How did employers and their associations in these three quite different sectors react to war conditions? Was the experience in engineering (heavy product demand) similar to or different from that of other sectors where war demand was less significant, for example cotton and building? To what degree were employers thrown on to the defensive and powerless to prevent serious erosion in managerial prerogative as well as escalation in labour costs? To what extent did employers' organisations actively intervene to recast industrial relations systems? And, how damaging were divisions within and between the local associations, as well as between the regional and the central federations during the crisis years of 1914–20?

[9] Rubin, *War, Law and Labour*, pp. 242–56.

Engineering, 1914–20

From the outbreak of war a new spirit of co-operation between capital
and labour became apparent within the engineering factories and workshops in north-west England. The tightening labour market radically
increased workers' capacity to organise and enhanced their bargaining
power. A flexible policy of strategic withdrawal upon points of principle
became evident as both masters and men accepted a temporary moratorium to co-ordinate their efforts against a common external enemy. An
important dispute on the crucial manning issue at Joseph Adamson and
Co. (Manchester boilermakers), for example, was settled in December
1914, both sides agreeing to postpone the issue until after the war: 'It is
agreed that the policy of the federation and of your society during hostilities is that neither side will introduce new conditions of labour but both
parties will allow conditions of labour to remain as they are without prejudice to the rights of either party in any discussion which may take place
after the war.'[10] Similar points of conflict tended to dissolve with the
initial surge in patriotism and consolidation of a corporatist spirit. In stark
contrast to Clydeside, the introduction of wartime dilution and the
removal of restrictive practices provoked little trouble over 1915–16 in
north-west England. Dilution strikes, for example at Smith and Coventry
in Manchester, were relatively short and isolated affairs.[11] A more openly
co-operative relationship prevailed.

State labour policy was enshrined within the Shells and Fuses
Agreement, the Treasury Agreement and the Munitions Act of 1915,
which introduced various practices to ensure that the armed forces and
the munitions industries were adequately staffed and that maximum production possible was achieved. The code included the outlawing of strikes
and lock-outs, with compulsory arbitration; legalised wage regulation; the
banning of 'restrictive practices', including constraints on the dilution of
labour through the importation of unskilled workers; tightening of
factory discipline; and prevention of labour mobility through enforcement of a leaving certificate. Munitions tribunals, staffed by a labour and
employer assessor and a neutral chair (usually a lawyer), policed the
system, adjudicating on grievances and determining penalties. This went
some way towards neutralising the enhanced bargaining power conferred
on labour by wartime market circumstances. However, there were limits
set upon this process by public opinion and there were also some, albeit
less rigid, restraints upon employers. Profits were to be controlled

[10] Manchester EEA, Minutes, 2 December 1914.
[11] Manchester EEA, Minutes, 3 November 1915; Rochdale EEA, Minutes, 17 June 1915.

through imposition of an excess profits tax, and wages effectively became subject to central regulation, through awards of the Committee of Production. The state also directly promoted collective bargaining. Employers became alarmed as the war progressed at the spread of joint committees and the erosion of managerial prerogative this entailed. Further external constraints on engineering employers' freedom of action followed when the majority of engineering firms were brought under direct control to ensure prioritisation of war production over commercial production. Throughout 1915 and 1916 the majority of engineering firms in Lancashire converted a growing proportion of their machine capacity over to munitions production and other related war work. In response to these developments, the engineering employers in Lancashire formed a district association of controlled establishments which in mid-1917 claimed to represent 278 out of 348 controlled engineering establishments in the region.[12] This body campaigned on a number of issues, including excess profits tax.

The distribution of government contracts, general tightness of the labour market – especially for skilled workers – and rampant inflation over the war years combined to pose serious threats to employer solidarity. The minutes and records of the engineering employers' associations in the north-west bear graphic testimony to the loss of power and authority of the organisations, which manifested itself particularly in a reduction of control over the actual wages and conditions of work in constituent member firms. Unregulated recruitment to the armed forces proceeded at a rapid pace and by January 1915 there was a serious skilled labour shortage in many of the munitions-producing areas in Lancashire. The Manchester, Rochdale and Oldham engineering employers' associations first recognised the problem of firms offering extra unofficial wage bonuses and other inducements to attract scarce labour as early as the winter of 1914–15.[13] The Rochdale master engineers, for example, reported extreme difficulty in obtaining and keeping men and requested permission from the EEF to act independently in dealing with a scheme proposed for 'a distribution of profits from time to time' from a member firm making rifles and shells.[14] Workers on munitions production and other war work were quick to apply for sectional wage rises in Manchester

---

[12] Lancashire Association of Controlled Firms, Minutes, Annual Meeting, 31 July 1917. This association combined members and non-members of the EEF and confined its functions to matters relating to the institution of government control working through 1918–19 with the Controlled Firms Committee of the Federation of British Industries.

[13] See the Manchester EEA, Minutes, 2 December 1914; Rochdale EEA, *Minutes*, 20 January 1915; Oldham EEA, Minutes, 20 January 1915.

[14] Rochdale EEA, Minutes, 20 January 1915.

and other districts in Lancashire to keep pace with wartime inflation.[15] Between December 1914 and March 1915, the Manchester Engineering Employers' Association was forced to concede wartime wage 'bonuses' to a cluster of engineering unions.[16]

Quite apart from such official wage escalation, the position of the local engineering employers' associations was compromised by many member firms complying with the workers' demands and granting wage bonuses without informing the association. Many complaints were made to the associations of firms enticing workers – especially apprentices and juveniles – by paying excessive rates above the standard rates of the district. Rumours were rife and some firms conceded extra unauthorised war bonuses simply on the word of the unions that other establishments in the district were paying a higher rate. In 1916, the Churchill Machine Tool Co., Manchester, paid their fitters who were supervising dilutee women 48 shillings per week in line with a trade union assertion, later found to be incorrect, that this sum was received for such work at Armstrong-Whitworth's.[17] Such extra unofficial payments were subsequently 'snowballed' throughout the region by the unions. Nasmyth Wilson (Manchester locomotive builders) were censured in the Manchester engineering employers' association for conceding an extra 1 shilling per week to their hand drillers. This had seriously prejudiced the position of other members, several of whom had duly received requests from their hand drillers and semi-skilled labourers to be paid the extra rate. In another case, Kendall and Gent (Manchester machine tools) initiated an unofficial scheme conceding a penny an hour bonus (around 4s 6d per week and this forced the neighbouring and competing firm of Hulse and Co. Ltd (machine tools) to consider paying the same in December 1916. Similarly, to cite just one more example, J. Petrie Junior and Co. Ltd tendered their resignation from the Rochdale master engineers' association so that they could be free to compete with a disloyal firm, D. Bridge and Co. Ltd, who had conceded an unofficial 15 shillings bonus to their moulders.[18]

Whilst the influx of large numbers of female dilutees into the engineering industry may have eased some of the strain on the labour market, the government orders on minimum wage payments for such labour helped to escalate further unofficial wage payments, not least amongst similarly low-paid labour (e.g. apprentices, labourers and the semi-skilled). In April 1916, J. Holroyd and Co. Ltd (one of the largest firms in the

[15] Clegg, *A History of British Trade Unions*, vol.II, pp. 141–2: cost of living rose by around 25 per cent during the first year of war.   [16] EEF, *Wage Movements*, pp. 627–8.
[17] Manchester EEA, Minutes, 3 February 1916.
[18] Rochdale EEA, Minutes, 25 May 1920.

Rochdale district) were enticing apprentices from other firms by their scheme for paying such lads 10 per cent above the standard rate. Their representative at the association explained: 'Matters have been made extremely difficult for us owing to a large number of apprentices working piecework and others working daywork, and also through the dilution of labour by women workers, the apprentices in many cases having to show the women rated at twenty shillings how to do the work.'[19] Holroyd's later argued that they had not overstepped the rules of the association out of any sort of hostility towards the organisation:

What we would like you to take into consideration when judging our firm is that we have been under the impression that during the period of the war, both federation and union rules have been suspended, perhaps not so much by the federation, as by the Ministry . . . The rules that have been transgressed by us have been solely transgressed with the object of increasing our output to the Ministry of Munitions.[20]

The serious erosion of employer organisation control over wage payments during the war was clearly confirmed by a Manchester Engineering Employers' Association survey of member firms in January 1917. Out of 71 firms which replied, 34 alleged that they adhered strictly to the standard rate, whilst 37 admitted to paying some extra bonus or emolument in addition to the standard rates.[21] The problem was even more serious because other firms cloaked enticements within overly generous payments by results schemes.[22]

Upward wage drift from association rates was just one manifestation of a general corrosion of employer cohesion and loyalty over the war period. The time-honoured disciplinary mechanisms pioneered by the engineering employers' associations fractured in the face of wartime pressures. A key tool of labour market regulation – the enquiry note – became subject to long delays and fell into disuse as employers scrambled to obtain workers in any way that they could.[23] The legally enforced leaving certificate provided some relief – but this was abandoned in the autumn of

---

[19] Ibid., 8 April 1916.

[20] Letter, J. Holroyd and Co. Ltd, to the Rochdale EEA, 2 March 1917.

[21] Manchester EEA, Minutes, 1 February 1917.

[22] Joint Standing Committee of Lancashire Engineering Employers' Associations (hereafter referred to as Lancashire Engineering JSC), Minutes, 1 June 1920.

[23] Oldham EEA, Minutes, 20 January 1915; Manchester EEA, Minutes, 28 September 1916, 1 February 1917; Lancashire Engineering JSC, Minutes, 20 October 1920. A similar situation prevailed on the Clyde where Sir James Lithgow suggested that the employers introduce a discharge note to compensate for the collapse of the enquiry system. However, this did not meet with much support. See McKinlay, *Employers and Skilled Workers*, pp. 309–10.

1917. Forms of organised victimisation, such as the blacklist and character note, were also widely ignored, strike hands invariably being employed
by member firms without scruples. Some associations, such as Rochdale,
abandoned the pre-war practice of circulating blacklists of sacked or
striking workers around member firms.[24] In one case striking coremakers
and moulders at one Wigan firm were quickly snapped up by neighbouring firms, including two member companies.[25]

Part of the problem, as far as engineering employers in the north-west
were concerned, lay with what they regarded as the vacillating and pusil-
lanimous actions of the government. The legalised wartime labour code
provided employers with some leverage, but, as far as they were concerned, this did not go far enough. Initially, the EEF attempted to introduce its own more draconian set of disciplinary rules (including fining for
absenteeism and bad work, and freedom to introduce unrestricted piecework) but was prevented by a series of strikes and forced to accept the
rather more liberal Ministry of Munitions code.[26] Though strikes were
illegal, employers complained bitterly that sanctions were invariably not
applied to discourage such action.[27] In two strikes of ASE members in
Manchester between December 1916 and May 1917 the Manchester EEA
urged the government to initiate instant prosecutions and refuse the
recalcitrants exemption from call-up under the schedule of protected
occupations. In both cases no such initiatives were taken.[28] The attempts
of employers' organisations to regulate the labour market after the leaving
certificate was abandoned were also compromised by government action.
The Manchester EEA scheme formulated in the summer of 1917 forced
all member firms to pledge not to engage workers unless formally
released by their previous employer, or sent under the dilution scheme.
However, the Ministry of Munitions declared this to be a deliberate
attempt to nullify the abolition of the leaving certificate and forced the
association to abandon the project.[29] At the central level, national wage
bargaining became a permanent feature of industrial relations, with the
unions and employers agreeing from February 1917 that wages should be
settled every four months by the Committee on Production. However,
this drew sharp criticisms from employers thereafter, with complaints of
overly favourable awards to the unions and lack of consultation with
employers. Moreover, as Rubin has shown, the munitions tribunals
restricted employer activities in a number of ways, declaring employer

---

[24] Rochdale EEA, Minutes, 27 August 1919.
[25] Lancashire Engineering JSC, Minutes, 5 October 1920, 2 November 1920.
[26] Wrigley, 'The First World War', p. 33.   [27] Manchester EEA, Minutes, 5 July 1917.
[28] Ibid., 4 December 1916, 3 May 1917, 10 May 1917.
[29] Ibid., 5 October 1917, 19 October 1917.

suspensions of workers illegal, supporting the right of workers to join unions and fining employers for labour poaching.[30] From this evidence the war years produced accumulating frustrations for engineering employers and a marked erosion in collective control over the labour market.

Serious attempts were made to re-establish the undermined authority of engineering employers' organisations towards the end of the war. At the regional level, at the suggestion of the EEF, six Joint Standing Committees were created throughout Britain in the early part of 1919 in order to promote a closer community of interest between the local associations and close ranks to stem wage drift and the erosion of workplace discipline. Through 1919 and 1920, the Lancashire Engineering Joint Standing Committee, embracing all eleven local engineering employers' associations, became a key co-ordinating forum through which some vestiges of control were reimposed over local labour markets and some traditional defences re-erected against union encroachments into areas of managerial prerogative. The pivotal rule of the JSC was that all union-initiated wage claims made upon the eleven constituent local associations had to be submitted to the JSC for approval. Those who ignored this injunction were to be refused the support of all the other local associations.[31] The effective overseeing of wage movements throughout the Lancashire region by the JSC restored some order into wage bargaining and, it appears, closed the gap between negotiated wage rates and actual payments. Wage standardisation was also successfully promoted. By the end of 1920 pre-war differentials between Manchester and the neighbouring towns had disappeared, and all skilled workers in member firms in north-west England were reported to be receiving the Manchester rate.[32]

The Lancashire JSC also co-ordinated the resistance of the region's engineering employers to the post-war strike wave and deterioration of workshop discipline. In 1919–20 the engineering employers were faced with a concerted offensive by the ASE, pressing to extend their control over work conditions. Failing to be placated by the concession of a 47-hour working week immediately after the war, the Manchester ASE banned overtime working, refused to supervise and set up for dilutees, demanded apprenticeships for all classes of machine operations and the skilled wage rate for machine minders. Strikes and sit-ins were initiated at a number of large member firms – including the Lancashire Dynamo and

---

[30] Rubin, *War, Law and Labour*, pp. 21, 262.
[31] Lancashire Engineering JSC, Minutes, 5 December 1919.
[32] Lancashire Engineering JSC, Minutes, 11 May 1920, 2 November 1920.

Motor Co., Ferranti's, British Westinghouse and Crossley Motors – to press this radical programme forward.[33]

The rapidly growing electrical engineering sector emerged as the cockpit of industrial strife on the critical staffing of machinery issue in the north-west. Throughout 1918, the issue of minimum wage rates and skilled status for armature and transformer winders and assemblers in the Manchester region was discussed, without settlement, in the Committee on Production on two occasions and through Central Conference on four occasions. In July 1918, the Electrical Trades Union (ETU) and the EEF agreed a mutual recommendation, allowing a differential of 2–3 shillings a week above the labourers' rate for this work.[34] However, this led to a rank-and-file revolt, with shop stewards leading unofficial strikes at two of the largest electrical engineering companies in Manchester – Ferranti and Westinghouse. Tension had existed at Westinghouse (the largest company within the Manchester EEA) before the war, workers complaining of rigorous supervision, selection and dismissal procedures and detailed division of labour aimed, they believed, at 'Americanising' the workforce.[35] Discontent smouldered throughout the winter of 1918–19, with strikes again erupting at Ferranti and Westinghouse in February 1919.

The engineering employers' associations addressed this and other challenges to their prerogatives during 1918–20 with a remarkable degree of resolve. The determination of the Manchester employers not to concede on the principle of machine staffing was clearly articulated in a letter to Allan Smith at the EEF in February 1919:

The electrical engineering undertaking at the present time is one which has every appearance of rapid expansion, and in order that this expansion can take place it will be necessary to recruit from the adult unskilled labour rendered available, either by demobilisation or from other sources of supply. Secondly, it has been the practice in this area from the beginning to divide the building of transformers as well as other electrical machinery of a similar type into operations, some of them being skilled, semi-skilled and others practically not necessitating any degree of skill, and if we have to continue in the future to compete in the markets of the world for this apparatus it will be necessary to continue this practice.

The association continued by stressing the wider repercussions of conceding the principle of skilled status for such work: 'If the ETU were able

---

[33] Manchester EEA, Minutes, 3 February 1919, 27 May 1919; EEF, *Central Conferences*, cases 1290/1, pp. 268–9.

[34] EEF, *Central Conferences*, cases 1280, 1281, 1283, 1285, pp. 265–6.

[35] Court of Arbitration between the Manchester EEA and the Electrical Trades Union, Minutes of Proceedings, 29 November 1918, pp. 8–10, 22. For workers' memories see Manchester Studies, *Trafford Park, 1896–1939*, Manchester: Manchester Studies, 1979. The firm earned the nickname 'the twisting house' amongst Trafford Park residents.

to establish the principle they are at the present time attempting to negotiate, we shall immediately have the United Machine Workers'
Association and other semi-skilled unions establishing the same principle.'[36] The Ferranti and Westinghouse strikes were thus fiercely resisted
by the Manchester EEA, with the full support of the Lancashire JSC and
tacit approval of the EEF. The strikers were blacklisted, foremen induced
to stay on and replacement labour actively sought.[37] This firm action cor-
roded the commitment of the strikers, who returned to work on 6 March
1919, after a four-week stoppage. The agreement conceded minimum
starting wage rates for the disputed work at 3 or 4 shillings above the
labourers' rates. However, the critical principle of skilled status and commensurate wage rate was dropped and the firm retained the right to place
unskilled labourers on the work.[38]

Similarly, in mid-1919, a challenge by the Manchester branch of the
Iron and Steel Dressers' Society was met head on by the Manchester
EEA. In breach of the national agreement, the dressers struck work in
Manchester for a wage rise, and, more menacingly, to abolish piecework
and overtime working. In response, the Manchester EEA instructed
members to replace strikers with labourers and to ensure no strikers
gained work elsewhere. This was followed up by posting notice of a
general lock-out of the Manchester EEA. This had the desired effect: the
dressers returned to work under pre-existing conditions, gaining only a
promise that no victimisation would be practised.[39] Nor was this an isolated resort to the coercive option by the engineering employers in the
north-west. When sheet-metal and foundry workers banned overtime
working in fifty-eight Lancashire firms, the Lancashire JSC immediately
threatened a lock-out of all sheet-metal workers (within seven days), to be
followed by a general lock-out of all trade unionists in Lancashire federated firms (after a further fourteen days).[40] Faced with this evident determination to escalate this dispute the unions settled, agreeing
unconditionally to remove all embargoes on overtime working in January
1920.

Here, then, in microcosm in north-west England in 1919–20, the
pattern of events played out on the national scene in 1922 was already

[36] Letter, Manchester EEA to Sir Allan Smith at the EEF, 13 February 1919.
[37] See the Manchester EEA, Circulars, 1261 (3 February 1919) and 1276 (19 February
1919) to all members, with lists of stikers annexed. Also the EEF, Letters, 12 February
and 26 February 1919, to all secretaries of local employers' associations, with lists of strikers.
[38] Local conference, Minutes, Manchester EEA and the Electrical Trades Union, 6 March
1919.   [39] Manchester EEA, Minutes, 1 July 1919, 21 August 1919.
[40] Lancashire Engineering JSC, Minutes, 5 December 1919; Wigham, *Power to Manage*,
p. 115.

unfolding. The Lancashire evidence suggests that, after a period of frag-mentation, destabilisation and loss of control, employers' organisations reasserted their authority and, in the event, proved capable of solidly and successfully defending managerial prerogatives, notably in the key areas of machine staffing, overtime and piecework. Undoubtedly, the scaling down of munitions and war-related demand from 1918 provided some-thing of an opportunity for employers. James Hinton has shown, for example, how victimisation of militant shop stewards started soon after hostilities ceased.[41] However, critically important in bolstering employers against the challenge of labour was the consolidation and growth of their collective organisations, which kept pace with trade union growth. From 1914 to 1920 membership of the eleven Lancashire EEAs almost doubled, from employing around 70,000 workers to around 130,000.[42] From 79 firms with a total wage bill of £2.9m in 1914 the Manchester association had grown to represent 201 firms in 1920, with a combined wages bill of over £12m.[43] Indicative of strengthened employer solidarity and inter-association cohesion was the Lancashire Engineering JSC, combining effectively for the first time the eleven independent local asso-ciations in the county and, perhaps more significantly, the fact that con-stituent associations financed the appointment, from May 1920, of the region's first full-time organiser, Major Challen.[44] At the national level employer cohesion was strengthened as closer links were forged with the Shipbuilding Employers' Federation and the EEF was a prime mover in the creation of the NCEO in 1919.[45] Here lay the employers' organisa-tions' most tangible response to dislocated markets, state intervention in industrial relations which compromised their interests and union attempts to snowball wage concessions and extend control over work. Such developments provided the necessary preconditions for a rigorous rearguard defence of managerial prerogatives between 1918 and 1920 and a platform for a more aggressive offensive against labour when economic circumstances changed markedly in 1921-2.

Building, 1914-20

The outbreak of war brought immediate and deep retrenchment to the construction industry and, in its train, a series of stresses which seriously affected the organisation and policies of the network of master builders'

[41] Hinton, *First Shop Stewards' Movement*, pp. 270-1.
[42] EEF, Levy Register 1914 and 1920, Numbers Employed File, 1914 and 1920.
[43] Manchester EEA, membership reports, in Minutes of annual general meetings, 1914-20.
[44] Lancashire Engineering JSC, Minutes, 19 July 1921.
[45] Zeitlin, 'Internal politics', pp. 66-7.

associations. Building employers were faced with two major economic
difficulties: first, the rapid escalation of building material prices, resulting
in a curtailment of new commercial work and a squeeze on profit margins
on existing contracts;[46] secondly, a sharp reduction in local authority
capital expenditure, combined with a curtailment of local authority bor-
rowing (cheap credit) for building schemes. Consequently, few new
building contracts were entered into in 1915 and by the end of 1916 the
volume of building work had been reduced to half its 1914 level.[47] In the
north-west, the estimated value of plans submitted to the local authorities
for building work in the first nine months of each year declined from
£12.2 million in 1914 to £7.8 million in 1915 and £5.9 million in 1916.[48]
Of the contracts agreed in 1916, a little over half were for factories and
workshops on war work. This led initially to a rise in unemployment and,
subsequently, absorption of much of this displaced labour by the armed
forces and the munitions factories. In 1915 alone, over 35,000 building
operatives, or nearly 30 per cent of the total, left the building trade in
north-west England.[49] By the end of the war, the building industry labour
force in Britain had fallen to half its pre-war level (see table 6.1).

In common with other industries, the building trade also suffered from
severe wage drift during the war period. The Lancashire building employers' associations gradually lost a great deal of the control over wage payments at members' firms that they had previously (and sometimes
painfully) built up. Under the encouragement of the NWFBTE many
local master builders' associations in Lancashire over the twenty years or
so before the war had collectively agreed local working codes of rules,
incorporating uniform wages and working conditions. Often these
included a relatively inflexible annual wage regulation process by which a
union claim (if one was made) had to be submitted by November in any
year, considered over the next few months, and settlements enforced from
the following May. This rigidly regulated process benefited the employers
as it guaranteed them a period of stabilisation from fluctuations in labour
costs, a precondition for effective estimating on long-term contracts for
building work. A very large proportion of a builder's total costs went in
wages, and employers could not normally recoup the costs of higher

[46] According to the NWFBTE estimates, by mid-September 1914 timber prices had risen
by almost 20 per cent, glass by 10 per cent and lead by 33 per cent over pre-war prices. See
NWFBTE, Minutes, 23 September 1914.   [47] Bullough, *First Fifty*, p. 56.
[48] NWFBTE, *Half-Yearly Report*, December 1916; Minutes, 20 December 1916.
[49] Ministry of Labour, *Gazette*, January 1915, p. 20 and January 1916, pp. 22–3. The shortage of apprentices was particularly acute in the north-west. A survey of thirty-five building employers' associations in March 1916 indicated that member firms had lost 43 per
cent of their apprentices since the the start of hostilities. See NWFBTE, Minutes,
22 March 1916.

wages (or material costs for that matter) by higher charges once a contract had been drawn up.

The evidence for north-west England suggests that, in the face of the wartime conditions of full employment, rampant inflation in the cost of living and rapid wage escalation in the munitions and related industries, orderly wage regulation in the building trade collapsed. During January and February 1915, the local master builders' associations were bombarded by irregular applications for immediate war bonuses from the trade unions in Lancashire, based on the criterion of the accelerating cost of living. The formal disputes machinery became stretched to its limits: the Northern Counties' Conciliation Board alone had to deal with over 300 appeals in a period of six months.[50] Understandably, most building unions did not anticipate the scale of the increases in the cost of living or the acute labour shortage that gathered momentum through the winter and spring of 1915 and consequently had not put in a claim by November 1914 to be settled for May 1915. This meant that under existing working rules many operatives were faced with being unable to receive any kind of war bonus until at least May 1916, despite accelerating inflation. Frustration boiled over into a series of wildcat strikes for wage concessions.

The employers, however, were suffering from difficulties in obtaining raw materials and by an erosion of profit margins on pre-war contracts due to the rapid increase in the price of building materials and the shortage of skilled personnel. In the first instance, some relief was sought through Parliament. The National Federation of Building Trade Employers (NFBTE) and the Employers' Parliamentary Association were approached to pressure the government to pass a bill to allow building employers to concede war bonuses and recoup their losses from clients. However, the Employers' Parliamentary Association failed to press the matter and nothing was achieved by way of compensation for increased costs on pre-war contracts until the passing of the Courts (Emergency Powers) Act in 1917. Given the prevailing economic situation, the NWFBTE and its constituent local associations did not feel obliged to add to their rapidly increasing costs and liabilities by conceding the war bonuses demanded by the unions in the early part of 1915. The Manchester MBA, determined to resist any wage escalation, argued: 'if one association conceded these demands it will prejudice the position for all other associations throughout the country'.[51] Under pressure from Manchester, the NWFBTE initially counselled resistance, resolving in February 1915 that irregular notices that had not expired on 1 May after six months' notice should be ignored.[52]

---

[50] Bullough, *First Fifty*, p. 39.   [51] NWFBTE, Minutes, 24 February 1915.
[52] Ibid.

The stand taken by the master builders' associations was soon compromised, however, by escalating wage drift as building firms responded to growing competition for labour, especially in the areas where there were large munitions plants, including Warrington and Barrow-in-Furness.[53] Labour shortages were also acute where large government building contractors had gone into an area to build aerodromes, erect billets or extend munitions factories and were paying war bonuses. By the spring of 1915 some member firms had felt obliged to concede war bonuses unofficially in an attempt to retain a viable labour force.[54] Faced with an alarming growth in the number of such 'disloyal delinquents', the NWFBTE accepted the inevitable in September 1915, arguing:

Although . . . the conditions prevailing in the building trade do not justify generally any payment of war bonus, it be a recommendation to the local associations at their option, that they may, in the present abnormal circumstances relax the conditions now obtaining as to giving notice for alteration of rules, and in the event of applications for increases of wages they are to decide, after hearing evidence, whether such an increase is justified or practicable.[55]

This was an implicit admission that the cost of living was to be considered as of more importance in the regulation of wage rates over the war period than the usual criterion of the 'state of the trade'. This effectively opened the floodgates and wage stabilisation rapidly broke down in the building industry in north-west England.

What emerged, as central regulation was abandoned, was an opening up of wage differentials and a quite chaotic lack of standardisation between different localities. The local associations in north Lancashire (Blackburn, Accrington, Colne, Darwen and Rossendale, for example), in areas where commercial trade was very poor and there was very little competition for labour from nearby munitions factories or contractors on government work, continued to hold out throughout 1915 against any irregular war advances. The employers here argued that, had 'the operatives' wages been governed by a sliding scale, as in some industries, wages in the building trades today would be considerably less'.[56] The competitive position of the employers in such north Lancashire towns was also compromised by the low rates being paid for building labour in the surrounding country areas. On the other hand, inducements and extra bonuses proliferated within firms benefiting from government contracts for war work. Typically, such firms paid extra travel and lodging expenses,

[53] Ibid., 9 June 1915. The Vickers munitions plant at Barrow was reported as one of the most aggressive labour 'poachers'.   [54] NWFBTE, Minutes, 23 June 1915.
[55] Ibid., 8 September 1915.   [56] Ibid., 7 April 1916.

worked ten or eleven hours a day, paid overtime rates for all Saturday afternoon at time and a half and Sundays at double time and introduced automatic bonus schemes that were not necessarily related to production. One Bolton slater in 1918 was reported to have been offered 87 hours' work per week at 1s 3d per hour, with 7s 6d per week bonus and 5s lodging money by a contractor with a job in Shrewsbury.[57] Similarly, the government building contractors at the Lilac and Gorse mills at Middleton and Shaw – north of Manchester (which were being adapted and fitted out for aeroplane manufacture) – were offering 1s 3d per hour to joiners, and an additional bonus of either 12½ per cent or a flat-rate 9 shillings.[58] Such large payments were easily financed by the contractors, working on a fixed percentage profit on cost (often more than 5 per cent). The objections of the building employers' associations to the government that such a payment scheme was extravagant and wasteful of scarce labour supplies fell upon deaf ears.[59]

The chaos that developed in wage payments in the Lancashire building industry over the war years was thus exacerbated by the existence of, on the one hand, pockets of employers and local associations who were not benefiting from wartime contracts, whose industries were relatively depressed and who opposed wage advances because the state of their order books did not warrant them, and, on the other hand, numbers of large building firms and local associations in the urban areas who were heavily involved in government wartime building work, were seriously affected by labour shortages and the high wage payments of neighbouring munitions firms, and who consequently conceded large war bonuses. There was probably never a time when the economic fortunes of building firms varied so much as during the war. In such a situation, the regional master builders' federations found it very difficult to reconcile the conflicting interests of different segments of employers and formulate a successful and popular consensus strategy. Such pressures led directly to an erosion in authority, a disintegration in employer solidarity and a notable collapse in collective regulation of labour markets and earnings.

One manifestation of this decline in loyalty and discipline amongst the Lancashire building masters was a falling off in the implementation of the coercive strikebreaking rules, regulations and customs of the organised masters. Evidence suggests that the trend in building paralleled that in engineering in so far as the enquiry, blacklisting, the non-employment of strikers and other covert forms of victimisation were widely ignored by member firms and local associations in the north-west. The Manchester MBA refused to enforce the enquiry rule throughout the war period and,

[57] Ibid., 6 March 1918.   [58] Ibid., 13 March 1918.   [59] Ibid., 20 March 1918.

on occasions, vetoed proposals from more hawkish member firms to blacklist strikers, arguing that in the circumstances such action was overly provocative.[60] Several local master builders' associations, including Preston and Oldham, were reprimanded by the NWFBTE for persistently breaking rule 23A – employing strike hands and refusing to discharge them. In many of these cases, the existence of large government contractors in the district indiscriminately taking on strikers seriously compromised the position of the organised masters.[61]

The attitudes and policies of the government over the war period further undermined the position of the north-west building masters. The NFBTE and the NWFBTE persistently complained that the views of capital were being ignored by a government whose sole policy seemed to be to conciliate the operatives at any cost. In a circular from the War Office in 1915 it was stated that:

Whatever may be the rights of the parties in normal times and whatever may be the methods considered necessary for the maintenance and enforcement of those rights, we think there can be no justification whatever for the resort to strikes or lock-outs under present conditions ... when the resulting cessation of work would prevent the production of ships, guns, equipment, stores, and other commodities required by the government for the purpose of the war.[62]

In particular, the Lancashire building employers felt frustrated by the government's lack of real effort to control wage escalation. Whenever their organisations attempted to hold the line, they felt their position weakened by government policy. In the middle of 1918, for example, the NWFBTE determined to make a stand, refusing to allow wages in any of its districts to rise above £1 over pre-war weekly rates. The resistance rapidly broke down, however, after the government (despite previous assurances) refused to co-operate by forcing building contractors on war work not to take on strike hands.[63]

Weaknesses within employers' organisations were also exposed and exacerbated by the pressure of wartime. The local master builders' associations were far more seriously undermined than the employers' associations in engineering and cotton by the existence of independent sectional masters' associations. In 1916, there were at least twenty-seven local master painters' associations and eleven local master plumbers' associations in Lancashire.[64] The local associations of the NWFBTE had made a relatively good job of combining all the other sub-trades with the general

[60] Manchester BTEA, Minutes, 23 August 1917, 4 August 1920, 30 September 1920.
[61] NWFBTE, Minutes, 24 July 1918.
[62] Ibid., 24 March 1915 (citing War Office circular, 11 March 1915).
[63] Ibid., 22 July 1918.   [64] Ibid., 25 October 1916.

contractors, but the painters and plumbers refused either to amalgamate or consistently to co-ordinate their policies and wage movements with the NWFBTE. This lack of co-ordination created quite serious problems, as the regional federation lamented in mid-1916:

How the want of this in some districts has brought trouble in its train is shown by the separate branch trade associations negotiating with the men, giving new conditions and advances in wages, which has immediately brought about demands for similar concessions to other trades not consulted. If all of these trades had met – as they would have done had they all been members of the Builders' Trades' Association of the district – and come to a common understanding, they would have been in a stronger position locally, as well as having the right to call on the rest of the federated members not to employ strike hands.[65]

During the war the NWFBTE found itself being forced to follow precedents established by the master painters and plumbers. Relations deteriorated further when many local master painters' and plumbers' associations in Lancashire negotiated agreements with their respective operatives' societies during the period 1917–20, promising to employ only union labour, in return for the union agreeing only to work for employers who were members of the master painters' or master plumbers' associations.[66] The NWFBTE remained opposed in principle to this tacit acceptance of the closed shop and the advanced form of recognition this offered to the trade unions. The acceptance of the Associated Shop and Union Labour Rule by many master painters' and master plumbers' associations also had the effect of putting pressure on the master painters and plumbers in the NWFBTE to leave the organisation and join the local master craft associations. The penalty for not doing so was the withdrawal of all unionist painters and plumbers.

Fragmenting market pressures, erosion in traditional modes of labour market and payment regulation, growing union organisation and militancy – manifested particularly in the influence of syndicalist ideas and growing co-ordination between local craft branches[67] – encouraged the

---

[65] NWFBTE, *Year Book and Directory*, June 1916, p. 36.
[66] The Manchester Master Plumbers' Association negotiated such an agreement in 1917. See the Manchester BTEA, Minutes, 19 September 1917. The Manchester Area Painters' and Decorators' Joint Council accepted a closed shop in 1920. See the NWFBTE, Minutes, 22 June 1920. The NWFBTE rejected the inclusion of such a rule under the Area Arrangement negotiated in 1919.
[67] For example, the Manchester building operatives' Joint Management Committee was established towards the end of 1917 and covered the whole of the building trades in a 15-mile radius, with the exception of the painters and plumbers who retained their own separate regional committees. The formation of the National Federation of Building Trades Operatives in the spring of 1918 aided such developments. See Postgate, *Builders' History*, pp. 431–7; Denver, *Fifty Years*, pp. 40–2.

formulation of more conciliatory and corporatist labour relations strategies by the master builders. Samuel Smethurst, president of the Oldham BTEA and past president of the National Federation, was one of the earliest advocates of a reorientation in labour relations strategy. In a paper delivered to the NWFBTE, Smethurst argued that the employers should grasp the opportunity that the war offered to encourage 'a new relationship' between masters and men based on trust and co-operation rather than suspicion and conflict.[68] Operatives should reject going slow and increase productivity, whilst employers should be willing to reward extra effort with extra money. To Smethurst, a flexible form of capitalism, based on trust, conciliation and a high wage strategy, was the only way to avert a slide into socialism. As a precondition for good industrial relations, he argued that the pre-war initiatives should be extended: that there should be uniform working rules and times of giving notice and that operatives throughout the Lancashire region should be given an equal real wage as far as possible.

Smethurst's ideas struck a chord and were enthusiastically taken up by the local associations, who pressed increasingly through 1917 and 1918 for more centralised bargaining, including the creation of a formal zonal wage scheme aimed at re-establishing some central control over labour costs and bringing to task both undercutters and overpayers.[69] The North-West Area Arrangement Scheme came into effect on 1 January 1919. It represented the most ambitious effort to date by the master builders to regulate their labour markets and extend centralised authority over the localities, thus creating order out of wartime chaos. Under it, the seventy or so local employers' associations in north-west England were amalgamated into ten wage areas or zones, each of which was governed by one of four rates of wages established for the region. The process of joint regulation was formalised through the creation of ten District Joint Standing Committees (DJSC) and a regional forum.[70] The result, in

---

[68] S. Smethurst, 'The relations of employers and employed in the future: what they should be'. Paper printed in NWFBTE, Minutes, 20 December 1916.
[69] NWFBTE, Minutes, 24 July 1918.
[70] NWFBTE, North-West Area Joint Meeting, Minutes, 14 January 1919.

Wage Rates in the North-West Area Scheme (Building), 1 May 1919 (per hour)

Regional rating	Craftsmen	Labourers
A	1s 8d	1s 4d to 1s 4½d
B	1s 7d	1s 3d to 1s 3½d
C	1s 6d	1s 2d to 1s 2½d
D	1s 5d	1s 1d to 1s 1½d

some country districts, was a considerable wage rise of as much as 6d or 7d per hour, or 40–60 per cent on previous wage rates.[71] Under the scheme, hours of working were made uniform at 46½ hours in the summer and 44 in the winter and each of the ten DJSCs were empowered to negotiate and settle a uniform set of working rules for the district and re-establish annual bargaining. A parallel new procedure for the settlement of disputes was also created which included the District Joint Standing Committee and the North-West Central Area Joint Standing Committee in an extended and more sophisticated stage-by-stage procedure.

The Area Arrangement was thus a far-reaching innovation in the industrial relations system of the Lancashire builders. In this reformulation the local and regional building employers' organisations played a key role in what amounted to an attempt to recast both the established substantive and disputes bargaining machinery of the industry in north-west England. In the event, however, the scheme ultimately foundered in the face of local sectionalism and self-interest, critically undermined by the weakness of employers during the post-war replacement boom and the prevalence of marked local variations in product and labour markets. Initially, the scheme encountered severe teething troubles over the grading of towns into areas. The major problems, however, came with the master painters and plumbers in the region, and with the Liverpool master builders. The master painters' and plumbers' associations in Lancashire remained autonomous, operated their own more generous area schemes and refused to co-operate with the NWFBTE and its constituent local associations.[72] This was a serious problem because of the large number of firms in these sectors that remained outside the NWFBTE.[73] Thus, many Federation-affiliated master plumbers and painters felt obliged to concede higher rates in contravention of the NWFBTE Area Arrangement.

Whilst the autonomy of the master painters and plumbers seriously compromised the working of the Area Arrangement, relations with the Liverpool master builders created intractable problems which completely undermined attempts to stabilise wages in the region and ultimately led

---

[71] Bullough, *First Fifty*, p. 39; NWFBTE, Minutes, 20 October 1918, 27 October 1918.

[72] NWFBTE, Minutes, 12 February 1919. The master painters' scheme allowed for a flat rate of 1s 8d per hour to painters throughout the 15-mile radius from Manchester city centre.

[73] Ibid., 25 April 1919. In a survey of thirty-six local master builders' associations, it was found that, whilst there were 342 master plumbing firms and 123 building firms employing plumbers in membership of the Federation (employing 1,042 operative plumbers), there were also a further 664 master plumbing firms in these districts which were non-members.

to the estrangement of the Liverpool and Birkenhead associations from the NWFBTE throughout the 1920s and 1930s. The roots of these problems lay in the destabilisation of local labour markets that resulted from the war. Competition for labour became particularly intense, with the Merseyside building trade competing with outside government building contractors, large engineering and munitions establishments and, probably most important of all, with the shipbuilding and repairing trade based in the Mersey docks.[74] Sharp wage rises in the latter trades, regulated directly by the government through the Committee on Production, led inevitably to a draining away of personnel from the Liverpool building industry and a commensurate erosion in bargaining power amongst the employers.

Given the prevailing local labour market situation combined with high wage precedents (Liverpool led the regional wage league table during and preceding the war) it was inevitable that the wage levelling of 1919 under the Area Arrangement Scheme would create trouble. A mass meeting of Liverpool building operatives repudiated the Area Scheme on 7 June 1919, and an unofficial strike wave gathered momentum within the building trade on Merseyside.[75] This fits a pattern of industrial relations volatility in the Merseyside region which contrasted sharply with traditions of formalised and more orderly collective bargaining elsewhere in Lancashire. The NFBTO admitted that they had lost all control over the rebel Liverpool branch and refused to grant any strike pay. With their coercive strikebreaking tactics undermined by the tightness of labour markets and the rampant disloyalty of member firms, the NWFBTE opted to play a waiting game, aware that concessions to Liverpool would disrupt wages in the whole region. For their part, however, the Liverpool masters became increasingly exasperated by the lack of positive action by the Federation, arguing that Merseyside was being unfairly expected to shoulder the lion's share of worker opposition to the Area Wage Scheme. Bitter recriminations were also directed at other local associations for poaching Liverpool workers during the dispute, contrary to the tradition of not employing strikers. After sustaining the strike for two months, the Liverpool masters' association capitulated, reaching a unilateral local settlement in mid-August which raised wage rates from 1s 8d to 2s per hour for craftsmen (with commensurate rises for labourers).[76] The result of this 20 per cent rise in the wages of craftsmen in Liverpool was, first, a drain of Lancashire building operatives westwards, and, secondly, a growing agitation by the unions in the other north-west districts for

---

[74] NWFBTE, Minutes, 23 May 1917.   [75] Ibid., 17 June 1919.
[76] Ibid., 15 August 1919.

comparable rises of 4d or 5d per hour. Given the *fait accompli* in Liverpool, the regional federation counselled for compromise and phased increases to bring 'A'-rated districts up to the new Liverpool rates of 2s an hour were agreed in October 1919.[77]

With this settlement the NWFBTE anticipated that by May 1920, the wage rates of the Area Arrangement would again be in line with those of the recalcitrant Liverpool masters' association. However, 1920 saw almost an exact repeat of the developments of 1919. A further round of wage rises occurred in shipbuilding and engineering. The cost of living escalated.[78] Competition for labour tightened.[79] The building trade was also experiencing its greatest period of prosperity for a generation as the local authorities' post-war housing schemes rapidly got under way. The vast profits made in these two years and the greatly increased demand for operatives were not the sort of economic circumstances that favoured the establishment of a long-term inflexible wage scheme such as the North-West Area Arrangement. In face of growing demands from their operatives, the Liverpool employers agreed to raise the Liverpool wage rates by another 4d per hour from 1 May 1920. The result paralleled 1919, with agitation and comparability strikes in the other Lancashire districts forcing the NWFBTE to match Liverpool's initiative, conceding uniform wage increases of 4d per hour. This time, however, the NWFBTE felt unable to tolerate the disloyalty and sectional selfishness of the Liverpool master builders' association and the latter was expelled from the Federation at the end of April 1920, ostensibly for 'defiance of federal obligations'.[80] Terminally weakened by the loss of Liverpool, the abortive experiment with regionally negotiated and tightly regulated wages and conditions collapsed. The Area Arrangement scheme was formally terminated with six months' notice from 30 October 1920.

For the building trade employers in north-west England, therefore, the First World War proved to have a markedly fragmenting and dislocating impact. Widening differences between prevailing product and labour market circumstances within the region, especially between Merseyside, the Greater Manchester area, and outlying towns in north Lancashire,

[77] Ibid., 24 October, 1919.
[78] The period 1919–20 was a time when the cost of living was soaring, with the official index rising from 205 in June 1919 to a peak of 276 in November 1920. See Department of Employment, *British Labour Statistics: Historical Abstract, 1886–1968*, London: HMSO, 1971, table 89, p. 167.
[79] NWFBTE, Minutes, 21 April 1920. Joiners in shipbuilding and engineering works received a rise to 2s 4½d per hour, to be in force from 1 May 1920. The Liverpool master builders claimed that, with bonuses, the ship joiners on the Mersey were in some cases receiving as much as £5 15s 0d per week.   [80] NWFBTE, Minutes, 28 April 1920.

reversed the pre-war centripetal tendencies, eroding the authority of the regional masters' federation and threatening the pre-existing system of disputes settlement and wage regulation. Independent subsections of the trade, notably the master plumbers and painters, critically undermined the position of the NWFBTE. The war thus fractured employers' association control over local labour markets, wage rates and working conditions. Traditional methods of regulation, such as the use of the intertrading rule, victimisation of strikers, the enquiry and use of the lock-out atrophied in the face of employer apathy and disloyalty. The Area Arrangement Scheme of 1918–20 represented the most serious attempt to recast industrial relations and extend control over labour costs by the regional federation. However, this foundered in the face of sectional and local employer disloyalty, combined with strident and aggressive rank-and-file worker opposition to the imposition of bureaucratic constraints on their freedom of action. In the event, the growth in union membership in the industry (especially amongst the unskilled), combined with a marked increase in co-ordination between previously independent craft branches, could not be matched by the employers. Indeed, between 1914 and 1920 building employers' organisation membership in the north-west stagnated and fell.[81] The corrosion in employers' bargaining power over this period is evident in their failure to stem upward wage escalation, and also in the cuts in working hours, more generous working conditions and, notably, in the closed shop agreements conceded between 1918 and 1920. The evidence thus suggests that, in contrast to the master engineers, where strong local and regional employers' organisations proved to be a significant bulwark against the aspirations of labour from 1914 to 1920, the master builders' organisations in the north-west failed to defend managerial prerogatives effectively, control labour costs or regulate the labour market over these crisis years.

Cotton, 1914–20

Wartime conditions and the immediate post-war replacement boom created a similar package of pressures upon employers' organisations within the cotton textile sector. Labour shortages and the issue of wage drift were significant, though certainly not as acute as in building or engineering. This was partly due to the gender composition of the cotton labour force. Cotton textile employers also had to grapple with a sharp expansion in trade unionism, especially in 1918 to 1920, combined with a revival of industrial militancy, notably amongst the spinners, as Alan

[81] NWFBTE, *Yearbooks*, June 1914, p. 46; October 1921, p. 28.

Fowler has demonstrated.[82] Cotton millowners also faced direct government intervention in industrial relations, and, through the Cotton Control Board, in production allocation and trade regulation. This section explores the responses of cotton employers' organisations to such external pressures. It will be argued that, whilst initially placing great strains upon associational activities and employer solidarity, ultimately this crisis period witnessed, as in engineering, greater, indeed unprecedented, levels of cohesion and co-ordination forged between cotton millowners.

The onset of the war caused a great deal of dislocation in the cotton trade. An initial loss of demand and underemployment gave way, after the first few months of unregulated recruitment to the armed forces and the munitions factories, to a critical shortage of labour in certain all-male occupations, particularly amongst mule spinning firms. Here, minders were facing unemployment because of an inability to find piecers to help tend the mules.[83] In 1915, many master cotton spinners' associations in Lancashire (including Ashton and Oldham) introduced 'dilution' of their mule spinning labour force, agreeing 'relaxation schemes' with their respective unions, permitting the limited employment of women on mules as creelers or piecers. Such relaxation of existing customs became the means whereby more men could be released for the forces. In the process, however, the employers collaborated in the underpayment of women replacees – allowing male minders to retain a larger proportion of the team piecework wage on each pair of mules.[84] This helped somewhat to neutralise real wage erosion for many of the pivotal, skilled labour aristocrats within cotton spinning during the war. However, such action had important repercussions at the end of the war, because the re-establishment of the traditional division of labour (a minder and two male piecers to each pair of mules) necessitated commensurate wage cuts for minders.

Between 1914 and 1920, the FMCSA and the CSMA experienced severe loss of control over labour markets. The escalating costs of living and the improved bargaining position of the operatives and their trade unions militated against sustaining the pre-war strategies of the cotton employers' organisations: orderly collective bargaining and inflexible and binding long-term wage agreements. Despite employer entreaties for restraint, the operative spinners and cardroom unions refused to be bound by any long-term wage 'freezes' over the war period. The attitude of the cardroom officials was summed up by Crinion in 1917 when the CWA violated the Askwith Award of June 1916: 'You will tell us there has

---

[82] Fowler and Wyke, *Barefoot Aristocrats*, pp. 146–64.
[83] Oldham MCSA, *Annual Report*, 1915, pp. 17–18.   [84] Ibid., 1916, p. 11.

been an award given which is binding on us. Under the present circumstances, I have no hesitation in saying that I would be willing to break agreements every day.'[85] In the event, however, cotton workers' wages clearly failed to keep up with rampant wartime inflation.[86] This created another potentially explosive issue which erupted during the volatile period immediately following the war.

Wartime economic circumstances tended initially to fragment further the interest groups which coexisted within the cotton industry into two camps: those with lucrative government contracts (particularly those firms working the coarse counts) who were relatively prosperous, and those who suffered severely from the market disruptions of the war years (particularly fine spinning firms) and whose order books did not include government contracts. In essence, this reversed the pre-war product market situation. The FMCSA commented in June 1915:

There was probably never a time in the history of the trade when the conditions and results of firms engaged on the same class of work varied so much as they do at the present time. The shortage of workpeople and the consequently lessened production alone are factors which make it impossible to lay down one common rule as applying to all firms.[87]

Areas of common interest between firms and local associations were thus severely undermined. The experience of the CSMA in October 1915 illustrates something of the dilemma facing textile employers. Some districts of the masters' federation threatened to withdraw from the association if weavers' union demands for a 5 per cent war bonus were granted. On the other hand, the Blackburn association believed that 'there is no doubt that if a few mills [where government contracts were being worked] were notified that unless the 5 per cent war bonus was immediately granted the hands would cease work, the employers would accede to their demand'.[88] The FMCSA proved to be rather more flexible in its attitude to overpaying than did the CSMA. In late 1915, the FMCSA accepted the inevitable, allowing member firms to grant wage bonuses, restricted to the period of the specific government contract.[89] Despite the growing evidence of wage drift, the CSMA, however, refused to sanction any deviation from uniform lists.[90]

CSMA stonewalling had only a very limited effect, however, and the

[85] FMCSA, *Annual Report*, June 1917, p. 19; see also ibid., June 1916, pp. 30–1.
[86] Clegg, *A History of British Trade Unions*, vol. II, pp. 141–2.
[87] FMCSA, *Annual Report*, June 1915, pp. 52–3.
[88] Blackburn CSMA, Minutes, 28 October 1915.
[89] FMCSA, *Annual Report*, June 1915, p. 46.
[90] CSMA, Minutes, 10 October 1916, 19 December 1916, 26 February 1916.

overpaying trend continued throughout the 1915–20 period. In 1919, the Blackburn CSMA lamented that when they met the operatives with regard to wage applications their position was invariably compromised by the fact that several federated firms in the region had already unofficially paid what the trade unions were asking for.[91] Clearly, despite the association's entreaties to members that all 'applications for increases from any section of the operatives should be brought before this association, so that they can be dealt with in a proper manner, and all the members could act together',[92] ability to control sectional wage drift eroded significantly over the period 1914–20.

In the Oldham cotton spinning sector (most heavily affected by government contracts) the enticement of operatives and the loss of control over firms' wage payments became particularly serious in 1916–17. The shortage of operatives and disruption in trade through lack of raw material was very unevenly distributed. Whilst some mills had all their machinery manned and running, others had as much as 40–50 per cent stopped. In the struggle to maintain and increase the amount of machinery running, competition for labour became so keen that it led to conflicts and much ill-feeling and loss of solidarity between employers in the trade. One response of the Oldham MCSA was to create several 'watchdog' committees, covering districts within the association, which met and kept the management of every mill in the district informed about local abuses in attracting and recruiting operatives.[93] The FMCSA pressed this initiative further and campaigned in 1917 for the government to intervene and enforce a scheme for more equitable distribution of labour in the trade. The Federation accepted the burden of releasing labour for the army and munitions works but claimed:

It is unfair that any mill should relieve itself of this burden by taking the operatives of another, and thus doubling the burden of another . . . Such process would eventually lead to the collapse of a large number of firms which would be a national calamity. It is essential to maintain all the individual firms possible in the trade, so that the nation as a whole can obtain the fullest advantage of all their activities in the world's commerce when the war comes to an end. This can best be done by equalising as far as possible the burden.[94]

1917 was characterised by violent fluctuations in cotton product markets caused by wartime disruptions in trading. Stocks of raw cotton at Liverpool and in the mills were very low and there were increasing difficulties in securing freight for importing cotton from America (and, to a

---

[91] Blackburn CSMA, Minutes, 25 August 1919, 8 September 1919, 17 November 1919.
[92] Ibid., 2 December 1919.   [93] Oldham MCSA, *Annual Report*, 1917, pp. 6–8.
[94] Ibid., p. 9.

lesser degree, Egypt) during the approaching season. The intensification of the sea blockade around Britain provoked a crisis in the cotton trade, with the government ultimately stepping in to place the trade under direct control. This was to ensure priority of production on textile war work.

The employers' organisations saw in the industry regulation scheme of the Cotton Control Board (CCB) a method of controlling wage inducements and enticements and consequently gave it their full support. Deputations from the principal employers' federations, operatives' amalgamations and trading interests persuaded the government to allow the CCB to consist of representatives of the main workers' and employers' organisations, presided over by A.H. Dixon, managing director of the Fine Cotton Spinners' and Doublers' Association Ltd. An assessment of the immediate trade situation resulted in the CCB curtailing the working of American cotton, no spinner of these grades being allowed to run more than 60 per cent of his or her spindles without paying a levy on spindles running in excess of this amount. In any case, no American spinners were allowed to run more than 70 per cent of capacity unless they were on government contracts, for which the restrictions did not apply.[95] Firms which had previously managed to keep a high percentage of machinery working on commercial contracts were consequently most affected by the scheme. Many single piecers at such firms were thus displaced and redirected to mills with government contracts or made available to make up the full complement of two piecers on the 60–70 per cent of machinery that was working. The scheme also provided for levies to be made by running mills into an unemployment fund through which workers were compensated for loss of work. Wildcat strikes, particularly by piecers suffering wage erosion under the control scheme, were contained by retaining wages due and issuing summonses to enforce damages.[96] Thus the CCB represented an example of corporatism in action. In effect, the scheme provided a range of vital benefits for the cotton millowners – stabilising the market, regulating industrial relations and controlling costs with few real sacrifices in terms of loss of managerial prerogative because trade union influence in the CCB was negligible. Private ownership was retained and the existing authority relations in the industry left intact.[97]

In cotton weaving, the CSMA attempted to alleviate wage drift and reimpose central authority by initiating closer co-ordination with both the FMCSA and the operative weavers' amalgamation, and pursuing the possibility of legalising the Uniform Wage List. In weaving, however, the

[95] Ibid., pp. 3–4; Blackburn CSMA, Minutes, 29 October 1917, 18 December 1919.
[96] Oldham MCSA, *Annual Report*, 1917, pp. 11–14.
[97] Wrigley, 'The First World War', pp. 40–3; Burgess, *Challenge of Labour*, p. 183.

problem was as much one of undercutting as of overpaying. When the Burnley association first suggested that the CSMA should investigate the question of getting the Uniform List legalised in 1915, their argument was that this would reduce 'unfair' undercutting competition from employers in such non-federated areas as Earby, Barnoldswick and Harle Syke. In July 1915, the CSMA duly initiated a survey of the opinions of all local associations for their views on legalisation. The objective was to remove 'the disadvantage under which members of this association are placed by the reason of unfair competition by those firms in various districts whose weaving prices are considerably less than those which have to be paid under the Uniform List and the Colne Coloured Goods List'.[98] Although around 65–70 per cent of the total looms in Lancashire were organised in either the CSMA or the FMCSA, the master weavers' federation lamented that it could not completely control wages and prices in the industry:

During periods of depression, when the total volume of trade is not adequate to keep the looms fully employed, the employers in outside districts, who do not pay wages by the standard list, set the prices for cloth, and these prices are invariably so low that manufacturers who recognise and pay by the list cannot compete except at a serious loss.[99]

Despite a majority of local associations being in favour of pursuing legalisation in the 1915 ballot, the CSMA opted to eschew this strategy, instead applying pressure upon the Amalgamated Weavers' Association to extend trade unionism, thus forcing the recalcitrant employers to pay by the Uniform List. Applying some leverage, the CSMA threatened a general reduction in wages if wages in outside districts were not brought up by union efforts or legalisation of the List. In the autumn of 1915, the AWA brought their members out on strike at the non-member firms at Harle Syke to enforce the payment of the wage list. The union also agreed, when every war bonus was conceded by the CSMA, to do all they could to enforce the additional wage costs on members and non-members alike.[100] The successes of this policy were, however, strictly limited. Significantly, in May 1919, the Burnley CSMA again complained of the disadvantages which associated firms suffered in competition with non-members, which, they asserted, paid even lower wages than ever before in comparison to the federated establishments in 1919. Whilst the CSMA conceded large wage bonuses, especially during 1917–19, non-members had not made comparable concessions. The wage gap between organised and unorganised mills appeared to have grown rather than narrowed.[101]

[98] CSMA, Minutes, 30 July 1915.   [99] Ibid., 17 May 1915.
[100] Ibid., 8 October 1915.   [101] Ibid., 2 May 1919.

Wages and conditions in the two largest sectors of the cotton trade –
spinning and weaving – had always been enmeshed to some degree, but
over the period 1917–20 the policies of the two dominant employers'
organisations were further interrelated and, from the end of 1917, wage
rises were made of uniform application throughout the industry. In the
early years of the war, the cotton spinning sector tended to be relatively
more profitable than the weaving sector and consequently war bonuses in
the spinning sector prior to December 1917 preceded similar bonuses in
the weaving sector by several months. Towards the end of 1917, two
factors encouraged the integration of wage agreements within the spinning and weaving sectors. First, the formation of the CCB: the Board was
staffed by representatives of the CSMA, the FMCSA and the cotton trade
unions and the co-ordination that developed in trade regulation also
encouraged joint action in the negotiation of wages and conditions.
Indeed, the CCB often got all the parties together to discuss jointly
respective wage claims. Secondly, from November 1917, the cardroom,
spinners' and weavers' amalgamations all co-ordinated and submitted
their notices for wage increases at the same time and consequently (so as
not to prejudice the position of one another by arbitrary rises) the CSMA
and the FMCSA had joint meetings in order to discuss and come to some
agreement on the percentage war bonus to be conceded. From this, a
formal agreement emerged for joint negotiations between the two
employers' federations in relation to wage claims by cardroom and spinning workers.[102] Joint bargaining over the subsequent period was not
entirely unproblematic for the cotton employers, though this did become
a permanent feature of the cotton industry industrial relations system
thereafter.[103]

Quite astute tactical flexibility appears to have characterised the strategies of the cotton employers' organisations during the brief post-war
replacement boom. Through 1919 and 1920 reductions in the working
week from 55½ to 48 hours were negotiated and compensatory wage rises
conceded which at last brought cotton workers' earnings in line with price
inflation.[104] The employers continued to oppose the concession of a
closed shop in theory, though in practice, with rapid expansion in union
membership, more and more mills were unionised by 1920. Centrally
negotiated agreements also legitimised additional financial allowances for
cleaning time during normal working hours in the spinning room and, in
weaving, some key groups of workers were conceded a guaranteed wage.

[102] Ibid., 1 November 1918.
[103] CSMA, Minutes of Joint Meetings, 20 March 1919; FMCSA, *Annual Report*, 1920,
pp. 40–1; Oldham MCSA, *Annual Report*, 1919, p. 7.
[104] Fowler and Wyke, *Barefoot Aristocrats*, pp. 160–1.

The weakened position of the employers was clearly illustrated on the latter question, which appears to have started in Blackburn, with a strike by overlookers at forty mills in December 1918. The local employers' association, keen to resist this important precedent, found its freedom of action crippled by fourteen firms arbitrarily conceding the union's demands and an inconclusive lock-out ballot in which less than half the association members supported an unconditional lock-out on the issue. Impotent under such circumstances, the association had little choice but to back down and concede fully the claims for a guaranteed minimum wage to the overlookers.[105]

The war and immediate post-war years were thus characterised by growing government intervention in the cotton industry, serious disruption in product and labour markets and, especially between 1918 and 1920, sustained trade union expansion and a revival in militancy. In 1919, more working days were lost through industrial action in cotton textiles than in any other year since recorded statistics were systematically kept (from 1891). Cotton employers' solidarity was eroded somewhat by the wide variations in demand, especially between 1915 and 1918, and serious problems of labour poaching and wage drift plagued the industry through to the early 1920s. In the main, employers and their organisations were thrown on to the defensive, relatively powerless, in the circumstances, to resist effectively union campaigns to raise wages and improve work conditions. The 70 per cent increase on the wage list forced on employers by the intervention of Sir David Shackleton (on behalf of the government) in the spring of 1920 particularly disturbed millowners.

However, it would be quite wrong to overstate the fragmenting tendencies of wartime. Whilst constrained by circumstances largely outside their control, the cotton employers' organisations continued to play an active role during these years and, significantly, conceded little of fundamental importance on issues of work control and managerial prerogative. Moreover, large post-war wage advances could be justified by reference to the fact that cotton workers' wages had failed to keep pace with inflation during 1914–18 and to the unprecedented profiteering during the speculation years of 1919 and 1920. Most significantly, perhaps, the cotton employers' organisations forged new and lasting levels of co-ordination from 1914 to 1920 between the two major sectional federations, thus removing a pivotal weakness which had undermined cotton employers' collective labour relations policies on a number of occasions before the First World War. By 1920, more cotton textile employers were members of their local employers' organisations and industry-wide federations than at

[105] Blackburn CSMA, Minutes, 2, 6 and 9 December 1918.

any previous time in their history and a centralised bargaining system, under threat just prior to the outbreak of war, was firmly entrenched.[106] The collective organisations of cotton employers were thus well placed to move on to the offensive against labour when markedly changed economic circumstances offered the opportunity from the winter of 1920–1.

Conclusion

The experience of employers' organisations in north-west England brings into very sharp relief the dislocating impact of the First World War and the immediate post-war product replacement boom. These were years when an accumulation of external pressures, primarily from the market, unions and central government, impacted upon established networks of employers' organisations, having initially a fragmenting and, ultimately, a cohesive effect upon industrialists. On the one hand, the disruption to markets and patchy diffusion of war-related demand exacerbated local and sectional divisions of interest between employers, raising intra-capitalist competition and undermining the formulation of strong consensus strategies at the collective level. Specifically, association controls over labour markets sharply atrophied. The evidence for north-west England demonstrates that more representative and internally coherent organisations – such as those in cotton textiles and engineering – responded in a more positive and effective fashion to these pressures than did other organisations, including the master builders, weakened to a greater extent by internal fragmentation. Moreover, engineering employers and cotton millowners had their ability to limit the wartime empowerment of labour enhanced by state intervention. Whilst the impact of such intervention should not be exaggerated and was clearly double-edged, the Munitions Act and the Cotton Control Board worked, in practice, to enhance employers' profitability and control, not least because such intervention explicitly accepted the capitalist mode of production and employers' right to manage as prerequisites for maximising production for the war effort.[107] These fundamental cornerstones of capitalist enterprise were not challenged by the state and in this respect such intervention operated unequivocally in the interests of capital.

Prevailing circumstances during wartime tended to throw employers on to the defensive in their labour relations policies and intensified pressures which incubated associational activity. A broader matrix of

---

[106] The proportion of Lancashire loomage organised in the CSMA rose from 61 to 66 per cent over the period 1914–20, whilst the proportion of Lancashire spindleage organised in the FMCSA rose from 64 to 76 per cent over these years.
[107] Melling, 'Servile state revisited', pp. 68–85.

organisations appeared and existing employers' organisations emerged from the 1914–20 period as more representative and powerful bodies. Despite internal fractures, the general expansion in employers' organisation at all levels – local, regional, industry-wide, inter-industry, political, specialist-propaganda – bears testimony to intensifying loyalties and a sharpening of class consciousness. Sir Vincent Caillard commented in 1919:

In the sphere of manufacture and production the day of unadulterated individualism is over, and a new spirit of cooperation is being born to meet the new problems of the future . . . It is now scarcely an exaggeration to say that there is no trade which is not represented by a body to protect its corporate interests and to express its corporate opinions.[108]

This was exemplified at the highest level with the emergence of the Federation of British Industries in 1916 and the National Confederation of Employers' Organisations in 1919. Within north-west England, the trend towards greater co-ordination between localities and product specialisms in engineering, cotton and building is also significant in this context.

By 1920, more employers than ever before delegated key aspects of labour relations to their industry employers' associations, which, in turn, played an increasingly active role in industrial relations. This was necessitated in part by the heightened intervention of the state in industrial relations and trade regulation and in part by the tightening of labour markets, strengthening of trade unions and the formulation of more radical demands by the labour movement. The wartime emergency facilitated two pivotal changes. It undermined controls over labour markets and led to an escalation in wage rates, fracturing employer opposition to the notion of cost of living as a variable in wage negotiations. More fundamentally, perhaps, the period 1914–20 saw radical ideas of worker control gain currency which challenged the sacrosanct concepts of proprietorial control and managerial prerogative. The enhanced bargaining power of labour during this period meant that some ground had to be conceded on such issues, which resulted in an erosion of industrial discipline in the workplace. Employers were faced in 1919–20 with an escalating strike wave, widespread support for nationalisation, shop stewards extending the 'frontier of control' in many engineering workshops and an alarmingly wide and growing sympathy for socialist ideas and syndicalist tactics. However, the pill was sweetened during this period by the opportunity wartime and post-war demand offered for gross profiteering. The

[108] Cited in Wrigley, 'The First World War', p. 55.

organisations in engineering, cotton and building in north-west England operated in this context, attempting to adapt to changed circumstances and forge policies which would protect the interests of their members. All played a pivotal role in consolidating, and, in some cases, recasting the industrial relations systems of their industries, promoting more cen-tralised disputes machinery and substantive bargaining mechanisms over the period 1914–20. In the face of eroded coercive control mechanisms (victimisation and forcible strikebreaking) – a product of the market, enhanced unionisation and public and government disapproval of coer-cive strategies during wartime – employers' organisations turned towards an extension of bureaucratic control. This was crucially facilitated over the war years by a corporatist government industrial relations strategy which saw orderly collective bargaining as the key to social harmony and to maximising productivity for the war effort. Employers' organisations had to wait until a radically different political and economic climate in the 1920s provided the necessary leverage to sustain a counter-attack, claw back union and workplace encroachments into sacrosanct managerial terrain and reimpose a degree of central control over labour markets and labour costs. That process will be analysed in some detail in the next three chapters.

Part 3

Reacting to the economic slump, 1920–1939

7 The millowners' counter-attack

Pre-war and wartime co-operation and incorporation strategies proved to be short-lived and with the onset of a deep economic recession from the autumn of 1920 employers moved on to the offensive against trade unions.[1] Evidence suggests that the markedly altered economic circumstances and onset of mass unemployment empowered employers and precipitated a concerted counter-attack, spearheaded by their collective organisations. This was designed primarily to roll back the concessions labour had won over the 'radical decade' of 1910–20. The nature of this movement differed markedly between industries, with significant divergences in the strategies promulgated by the worst hit, export-orientated sectors – including cotton and sections of engineering – and those industries – including building – with more sheltered markets. The export sector witnessed a dual offensive, on the one hand to reassert managerial authority on the shop-floor and on the other to reduce labour costs substantially. Utilisation of the range of coercive weapons at the disposal of employers' associations (discussed in chapter 4) revived, including the lock-out, whilst employers also benefited from an anti-labour propaganda campaign and the emergence of more centralised and clandestine blacklisting mechanisms, designed to identify labour militants and ensure their removal from the shop-floor.[2] Decontrol and the drawing back from active intervention in industrial relations by the state were also welcomed by most employers' associations. In cotton, engineering and other hard-pressed export trades the battle was fought upon the principle of management's right to organise production and employ whom they thought fit under conditions determined unilaterally by the employers. The initial priority was to curtail wartime aspirations of 'encroaching' workers' control.

There were, however, limits to the depth and success of the employers'

---

[1] Garside, 'Management and men', pp. 259–62; Clegg, *A History of British Trade Unions*, vol. II, pp. 312–52; Middlemas, *Politics*, p. 128.

[2] McIvor, 'A crusade for capitalism', pp. 647–9; McIvor and Paterson, 'Combating the Reds', pp. 137–52.

inter-war counter-attack. The Lancashire evidence suggests that this strategy achieved only limited success in the face of sustained worker resistance and divisions within employers' ranks. In the staple industries, intensification of work within the parameters of the existing technology and traditional division of labour remained more important than automation, rationalisation and any extensive deskilling right up to the Second World War. This represented an employers' victory of sorts, albeit a short-term and rather prescribed one. Moreover, at the multi-employer level this offensive against labour rarely constituted an attack upon trade unionism *per se*. By the 1920s collective bargaining lay at the very heart of the activities of employers' organisations and it is significant that it survived intact through a challenge or even, in a number of staple sectors, a crisis, of unprecedented proportions between the wars. Employers' organisations may have been shunted by pressure imposed by their more radical constituents into a more assertive industrial relations stance. However, the deep-rooted commitment within employers' associations for the maintenance of working relationships with trade unions proved to be a significant constraining agency upon more hawkish capitalists.

Centrifugal tendencies also characterised these years. In the event, whilst the role played by employers' organisations in industrial relations remained important between the wars, the intensified competitive environment, combined with the rolling back of state intervention and erosion in union membership – crucial cementing agents – set in motion fragmenting pressures which proved difficult to contain. Already, prior to the Second World War, it is possible to discern a decline in solidarity amongst employers and a growing tendency for the initiative in labour market regulation to pass back to the individual firm.[3]

Many of these developments are clearly identifiable within the cotton textile industry, one of the most export-orientated of British industries and one of a cluster of staple sectors that experienced sharp decline in profitability between the wars. Raw cotton consumption in the UK peaked at 2,178 million lb (980 m kg) in 1913, fell to 1,726 m lb (770 m kg) in 1920 and sharply to 1,066 m lb (480 m kg) in 1921. The key profitability indicator in the industry – margins between the prices of raw cotton and spun yarn – slumped sharply. After a margin of 38½d in May 1920 between the price of middling American raw cotton per lb and a lb of 32's (coarse quality) twist yarn there was a collapse to a margin of just

---

[3] In coal, for example, national bargaining collapsed and in wool there was a return to individual plant bargaining, culminating in the abolition of the wool industry Joint Industrial Council in 1929.

4½d by September 1921. Consumption recovered somewhat to average 1,400–1,500 m lbs (630–75 m kg) from over 1922 to 1929, though margins remained desperately low, stretching only a little to average around 6d. Thereafter, consumption and margins slumped again to a low point between 1930 and 1933, reaching a nadir of 985 m lbs (443 m kg) in 1931 and margins as low as 3d–5d. From 1933, some recovery is discernible, fuelled primarily by domestic demand. By 1939, margins had stretched to 9½d. The collapse in export markets was, however, the dominant trend of this period. In 1939, despite some recovery, cotton cloth exports remained at 20 per cent of their 1913 volume.[4]

This produced a sharp contraction in the industry, which took place within the context of changes in business structure. Machine capacity declined by 38 per cent in spinning and by 43 per cent in weaving between the wars, whilst employment in the industry had dropped by 1939 to about 330,000, just half that of 1914.[5] The industry was influenced by the merger movement of the 1920s and witnessed some consolidation in the scale of the enterprise, notably in the coarse spinning sector with the formation of the Lancashire Cotton Corporation in 1929. However, these changes were limited and the industry remained characterised between the wars, as before 1914, by a large number of competing firms specialising in particular types of yarns and cloths, and invariably operating in only one segment of the textile production process, usually either spinning, weaving, or finishing. Cotton textile manufacturing in Britain remained fragmented, relatively small in scale and lacking in vertical integration.

Compared to engineering, the industry's product was relatively homogeneous. Nevertheless, there were quite fundamental local product specialisms (see chapter 1) and some marked variation in demand between the wars. Product markets for the fine and fancy end of the trade centred in Bolton and Preston remained relatively buoyant compared to the crisis in demand (particularly in the India and China markets) witnessed within the coarse and plain sectors concentrated in the Oldham, Burnley and Blackburn districts.[6] The problems of the latter group were compounded, moreover, by the fact that it was predominantly these millowners who had recapitalised during the year or so of booming profits after the First World

---

[4] Mitchell and Deane, *Abstract*, pp. 179–82. Margin figures are taken from the Bolton Operative Spinners' Association, *Annual Reports* (Trade Review section), 1920–39.
[5] J.H. Porter, 'Cotton and wool textiles', in N.K. Buxton and D.H. Aldcroft (eds.), *British Industry between the Wars*, London: Scolar Press, 1979, pp. 38, 44.
[6] Porter, 'Cotton and wool textiles', pp. 28–30, 39; Oldham MCSA, *Annual Report*, 1939, pp 6–7; M.W. Kirby, 'The Lancashire cotton industry in the inter-war years: a study in organisational change', *Business History*, 16, no. 2 (1974), pp. 147, 152.

War, thus burdening themselves with massive debts at relatively high interest rates. Writing in 1920, the Nelson Weavers' Association official Zeph Hutchinson prophesied that under the new conditions fierce competition and cut-throat driving for profits were inevitable.[7] Divisions which existed within the industry prior to the First World War became irreconcilable chasms between the fine spinning firms and the hard-pressed, recapitalised coarse spinners. Intensified, cut-throat competition, variations in product markets and differences in structure thus critically combined to undermine solidarity amongst millowners and this, in turn, had important implications for the pursuance of multi-employer industrial relations strategies in the industry.

The cotton employers responded to the sharp recession in the winter of 1920–1 with a quite remarkable degree of unanimity. Initially, the FMCSA organised short-time work across the industry in an attempt to restrict production and raise margins. Only after this tactical regulation of trade failed to improve profitability did the spinning and weaving employers' federations attack labour costs, combining to enforce wage reductions in 1921 and 1922.[8] Whilst these cuts were not quite of the magnitude of those imposed in iron and steel, shipbuilding or mining, they nevertheless represented cuts in money wages of over 40 per cent and in real wages of over 10 per cent for cotton workers.[9] The costs reduction drive continued thereafter on a domestic, local and national level up to the mid-1930s, further industry-wide wage reductions being imposed in 1929 and 1932, and in the weaving sector in 1935.

The millowners' associations pressed further, eager to exploit their enhanced bargaining power resulting from overstocked labour markets. The opportunity was seized to rid themselves of what was regarded as overly generous labour agreements conceded in moments of weakness. One of the first to be singled out was the overlookers' minimum or fall-back wage agreement of August 1917. After a CSMA campaign this was cut from 85 per cent of normal piecework earnings down to 70 per cent in August 1921.[10] The tapers' guaranteed weekly wage was similarly

---

[7] Z. Hutchinson, *The Trusts Grip Cotton*, Independent Labour Party Pamphlets, new series, 28 (1920). Firms owning 46 per cent of the spindles and 14 per cent of the looms in the industry recapitalised in 1919–20 (i.e. reissuing shares; refloating with new share issue; transferring to a new company in name only). Few were fine spinners. See also G.W. Daniels and J. Jewkes, 'The post-war depression in the Lancashire cotton industry', *Royal Statistical Society Proceedings* (January 1928).

[8] FMCSA, *Annual Report*, June 1921, pp. 59–64, 67; June 1922, pp. 52–9.

[9] Clegg, *A History of British Trade Unions*, vol. II, p. 335.

[10] CSMA, Minutes, 21 January 1921; Joint Minutes, 5 August 1921. See also the General Union of Associations of Loom Overlookers, *Jubilee History*, Manchester: The Union, 1935, p. 44.

curtailed in 1921, and later abolished completely in 1936.[11] Wage induce-ments above the Uniform Lists, common between 1915 and 1920, disap-peared and the trend was reversed to one of wage cribbing and unofficial undercutting, usually on the grounds of competitiveness. Other relatively cheap cost-cutting methods were also increasingly exploited, including downward regrading of jobs to facilitate the employment of less expensive labour (e.g. jobbers for overlookers) and resorting to the time-honoured palliative of utilising cheaper inferior quality raw cotton.

The changed market circumstances stimulated the millowners' associ-ations to bolster managerial authority and tighten discipline at the point of production. This element of the counter-attack incorporated a number of dimensions. First, the employers' organisations shifted from a defen-sive to an offensive posture in relation to individual mill disputes and the 'strike in detail'. In 1921, the Oldham MCSA articulated the signs of a firmer line: 'For a long time it has become evident that some change was required in the method of dealing with disputes at individual mills, which are pushed to the extremity of a strike . . . It cannot in the future be allowed to be carried on until a firm is practically forced to cease busi-ness.'[12] The Rochdale masters also indicated the same hardening of resolve three years later: 'We are in agreement with the policy of taking strong measures against one mill being stopped indefinitely in order to enforce upon it an unreasonable condition, which, if conceded, would ultimately apply to the whole trade.'[13] In response to such pressure from below, the propensity to invoke the lock-out revived. In a phase of direct brinkmanship in the 1920s, the FMCSA threatened a general industry-wide lock-out on five separate occasions in response to individual mill disputes. Each time the trade unions involved felt obliged to back down.

Secondly, the employers' organisations supported the utilisation of replacement labour and the victimisation of union activists. The number of dismissal cases brought through the official disputes procedure rose sharply.[14] Moreover, the network of employers' associations supported member firms where disputes arose over dismissals. In 1928 such a case arising at the Mather Brothers' mill in Nelson led to a five-week local lock-out of the Nelson and Colne association, generously supported by £28,000 in financial compensation paid out by the CSMA. In the worst single year, 1932, the cotton unions claimed that around 5,000 of their

---

[11] CSMA, Minutes, 7 February 1921 and 28 June 1921; Blackburn CSMA, Minutes, 29 June 1936.   [12] Oldham MCSA, *Annual Report*, 1921, p. 8.

[13] Rochdale MCSA, *Annual Report*, 1924, p. 13.

[14] Bolton MCSA, Minutes, 6 March 1923 and 12 April 1932; Rochdale MCSA, *Annual Report*, 1930, p. 7.

members had been victimised by replacement.[15] Significantly, in the Midland Hotel Agreement which settled the 1932 disputes, the organised employers refused formally to forgo their privilege to victimise strikers selectively.

Thirdly, the Lancashire cotton employers' associations also successfully defended the fining system as an essential element of mill discipline and control. The cotton unions had campaigned vigorously to abolish the fining of employees for poor-quality work and other misdemeanours, regarding it as a form of 'tyranny' and claiming it to be a potent source of victimisation. Over the decade 1910–20 a number of mills had been pressurised to drop fining formally, whilst many others had apparently found it politic to allow the system to fall into disuse. In the 1920s, however, millowners resurrected fining and, when challenged by the unions, the CSMA defended the legality of fining in the law courts. In both the 1926–7 and the 1929–30 cases, the suit was won on appeal by the employers (after losing locally), custom proved and the legitimacy of fining firmly established.[16]

Such actions underwrote and energised a resurgence of unilateral managerial control in the mill, which, in turn, bolstered the capacity of individual millowners to intensify workloads, allowing more to be squeezed out of the wage-for-effort exchange. The Blackburn CSMA articulated a sense of such changed power relationships in January 1927: 'We claim the right as employers to employ whom we think fit, and also the right to make a change without being compelled to give a reason.'[17] The overstocked labour market, short-time working and lay-offs had their own salutary effect, inspiring greater work intensity and enhancing managerial discipline. The use of cheaper raw cotton, subject to more breakages in the mule and loom, inevitably increased workloads, as did the speeding-up of machinery and the manipulation of traditional staffing levels, especially in the weaving shed. Not only were the weavers being pressed to supervise more traditional Lancashire looms (a key issue which will be returned to later), but so were the overlookers as well. The earnings of overlookers were also tied more directly to performance, standard weekly wages giving way to payment strictly by poundage produced by the set of looms they were supervising.[18] This change placed pressure on overlookers to drive their subordinates to maximise productivity.

---

[15] CSMA, Joint Minutes, 9 August 1932; Blackburn CSMA, Minutes, 28 October 1932, 25 November 1932.
[16] CSMA, Minutes, 26 April 1927, 22 October 1929, 12 December 1930.
[17] Blackburn CSMA, Minutes, 17 January 1927.
[18] Ibid., 18 March 1932. At the Parkside mill, Blackburn, for example, overlookers were reduced from ten to eight, sections increased from 88 to 110 looms per supervisor and poundage cut from 1s 9d to 1s 7½d.

Whilst the cotton employers' organisations successfully spearheaded a cost reduction drive and bolstered managerial authority, the intensity of the industry's problems and the variable impact of the recession exacerbated divisions within the ranks of the millowners. This had two major effects. First, it diminished the regulatory authority of the employers' associations over their constituent members. The FMCSA recognised this, appealing to members in 1927: 'It would appear to your committee that general observance of their recommendations has become sharply imperilled during recent years by the increasing disparity of competing power between one firm and another, in consequence of the widening difference in financial status.'[19] Secondly, it became increasingly hard, as the depression deepened, for the employers' federations in the industry to form any kind of consensus strategy. The centrifugal, fragmenting tendencies resulted in a bureaucratic inertia at the multi-employer level. Disloyalty and breakaways grew. Clearly the initiative in industrial relations and labour contract determination was passing back to individual firms.

The unanimity achieved in the early 1920s on wage cuts and short-time working dissolved in bickering and fundamental disagreements within the industry over trade regulation and labour strategies. On the one hand, the employers' federations did not go far enough in slashing labour costs to satisfy the 'hawks' whose market position had deteriorated considerably. The most trenchant criticisms, however, in the 1920s were directed at the 'inefficient and short-sighted leadership' of the millowners' federation in trade policy.[20] Some members felt dissatisfied that their organisations failed to stabilise product markets through tighter central controls, including compulsory price-fixing. This view was articulated in particular by the Provisional Emergency Committee (PEC) – a loose organisation representing the particularly hard-pressed coarse yarn spinners established in the early 1920s. Led by a past president of the FMCSA, Sir Charles Macara, the PEC was particularly critical of the lack of executive action by the FMCSA and campaigned for a more active policy to contain capital depletion, including the creation of a Joint Cotton Control Board along the lines of the Board established during the First World War.

For their part, the cotton employers' federations were unwilling to initiate any crisis recovery package without the democratic mandate of their membership. Throughout the 1920s, the FMCSA balloted its members on a range of ameliorative measures, including price-fixing, sectionalisation of the industry and a Cotton Control Board. On each occasion the vote was inconclusive and no action was taken. However, a clear indication that the peak federations were taking the lead in cutting labour costs

---

[19] FMCSA, *Annual Report*, 1927, p. 18.   [20] Ibid., pp. 16–17.

came in 1928, when the executive committees of both the FMCSA and the CSMA agreed to recommend further industry-wide cuts in wage rates to their members. Again, however, the ballot in that year failed to produce the necessary consensus for action. Significantly, the vote was neatly split along product specialisms in the spinning sector, with 76 per cent of the spindleage in the American yarn sector against 35 per cent of the Egyptian sector supporting the recommended wage cuts.[21]

The 1928 ballot exemplified a traditional division of interest based on product specialism within the spinning sector which was exacerbated significantly by the desperate circumstances of the recession. The Bolton fine spinning employers tended to subscribe to a low-key federation trade strategy, characterised by a continuation of unfettered free and open competition. This was diametrically opposed to the interventionist strategies of the Oldham-based coarse spinners and their mouthpiece, the Provisional Emergency Committee (PEC). William Howarth, the Bolton MCSA president, regarded legalised price-fixing as anathema, trenchantly criticised the idea of joint control as 'one of the worst forms of socialism' and openly courted unpopularity amongst the coarse spinners by publicly declaring that they only had themselves to blame for rashly recapitalising during 1919–20.[22] His Bolton MCSA campaigned for maximum autonomy for member mills in the formulation of commercial policy, in accordance with the state of order books and the views of the boardroom.[23] On the other side, the 'traditionalists' in Bolton were lambasted by the Oldham/PEC 'interventionists' for failing to innovate to save the industry. In 1931, the Bolton group were accused of having given 'no serious consideration to the question of reducing the costs of production'.[24] The accusations of labour and trade poaching made relations worse. A number of Oldham firms in the inter-war period switched to working the more profitable Bolton counts, whilst some Oldham coarse spinners migrated to Bolton seeking the more steady employment prospects of fine spinning.[25]

Given such internal conflicts, it became increasingly difficult to work out a common strategy at the multi-employer level. A pincer movement was operating here, working to undermine the regulatory power of the employer federations in the industry. On the one hand, loyalty to multi-employer labour market regulation atrophied, particularly through undercutting of wage lists and blatant flouting of other 'constraining'

[21] FMCSA, Annual Report, 1928, pp. 14–15.
[22] Bolton MCSA, Minutes, 24 July 1923; Bolton Evening News, 24 July 1923. Howarth was also vice-president of the FMCSA.
[23] Bolton MCSA, Minutes, 27 July 1925 and 16 March 1926.
[24] Ibid., 1 September 1931.   [25] Ibid., 11 November 1924.

Table 7.1 *Cotton employers' federations:*
proportion of machine capacity organised,
1920–39

	Spinning percentage	Weaving percentage
1920	76.2	65.5
1922	80.3	64.8
1925	75.7	63.6
1929	75.9	59.3
1933	65.9	53.1
1935	66.5	58.0
1939	70.9	61.4

Sources: Membership data in the FMCSA, *Yearbooks*
and *Annual Reports*, and the CSMA, Minutes and Levy
Book, 1920–1939; compared with statistics for the
entire Lancashire trade from *Worrall's Cotton Spinners'*
and Manufacturers' Directories, 1920–39.

collective agreements (including the 48-hour week).[26] On the other hand, maverick, disgruntled member firms disaffiliated from their employers' organisations, to give themselves a free hand to formulate their own labour relations policies. Whilst the majority remained organised, a sizeable minority resigned, taking the organised proportion in weaving down from 66 per cent to 53 per cent of the machine capacity in the trade and the organised proportion in spinning down from 80 per cent to 66 per cent of total machine capacity between the early 1920s and 1933 (see table 7.1). Attendance at annual general meetings, another barometer of employers' solidarity, also declined in a number of local associations in the inter-war years.[27]

It was the most hard-pressed companies, in plain weaving and coarse spinning, where the product market collapse was most acute, who were haemorrhaging from the associations. Figures for the spinning sector – see table 7.2 below – clearly show a disproportionate fall in the proportion of active millowners in membership in the lower counts (coarse spinning) areas of Oldham, Heywood, Rochdale and Ashton, compared to the fine spinning region. By contrast, Bolton's membership held up reasonably well, whilst two predominantly fine-spinning towns, Chorley and

[26] Bolton Operative Spinners' Association, *Annual Report*, 1928, p. 5. The Livingstone Mill Co., Oldham, for example, was expelled from the master spinners' federation in 1928 after increasing working hours from 48 to 55½ and running double shifts.
[27] Blackburn CSMA, Minutes of General Meetings, 1905–29.

Table 7.2 *Master cotton spinners' associations:*
machine capacity organised in major
Lancashire towns, 1920 and 1935

District	Percentage of total spindleage organised in local cotton spinning employers' associations	
	1920	1935
Ashton	82.5	60.2
Bolton	87.2	84.1
Bury	69.4	66.6
Chorley	67.5	96.9
Farnworth	68.7	99.3
Heywood	83.3	56.1
Manchester	92.1	84.4
Oldham	91.5	75.0
Rochdale	80.6	60.7
Stockport	68.1	61.4

Sources: Membership data in the FMCSA, *Yearbooks*
and *Annual Reports*; *Worrall's Cotton Spinners' and*
Manufacturers' Directories, 1920–39.

Farnworth, managed to buck the trend, registering significant improvements in employer solidarity during 1920–35. A similar scenario unfolded in north Lancashire, where the major master weavers' associations experienced serious decline in membership between 1920 and the mid-1930s (see table 7.3). A critical body blow to the FMCSA came in 1929 with the formation of the Lancashire Cotton Corporation, which refused from the outset to affiliate or associate itself with the Federation. The Lancashire Cotton Corporation absorbed 106 mills by 1931, incorporating almost 10 million spindles and 20,000 looms. The constituent firms included around 15–16 per cent of the FMCSA's active membership, thus significantly undermining the collective strength of the Federation and creating a minor crisis in the FMCSA finances at a critical juncture when the organisation was facing a resurgence of labour militancy.[28]

These organisational changes form the backcloth to an industrial relations crisis of unprecedented proportions in the early 1930s which seriously threatened the very foundations of collective bargaining and,

[28] Oldham MCSA, Lancashire Cotton Corporation (LCC) File; *Daily Dispatch*, 23–4 October 1930; FMCSA, *Annual Report*, 1930, pp. 23–4; 1933, p. 40; Preston CSMA, Minutes, 4 February 1931. Frustratingly little is known about the labour relations strategies of the LCC.

Table 7.3 *Cotton Spinners' and Manufacturers' Association: machine capacity organised in various towns, 1920, 1935 and 1939*

District	Percentage of total loomage organised in local cotton weaving employers' associations:		
	1920	1935	1939
Blackburn	97.5	81.4	88.2
Burnley	77.1	57.1	67.9
Nelson and Colne	88.3	67.9	69.8

Sources: Membership data in the Blackburn, Burnley and Nelson and Colne CSMA, Minutes, 1920–39; *Worrall's Cotton Spinners' and Manufacturers' Directories*, 1920–39.

hence, the representative institutions of both capital and labour in the cotton industry. The period 1929–32 witnessed three major lock-outs in cotton manufacturing and, in all, around 20 million working days were lost in industrial disputes, making this a period of unparalleled industrial conflict not surpassed in the whole turbulent history of this sector.[29] This crisis in cotton occurred, moreover, at a time when unemployment peaked and industrial relations in Britain were relatively peaceful. This merits extensive treatment, not least because the employers' role in these events has been neglected and is vital to an adequate understanding of such developments.

Whilst deep divisions of interest remained beneath the surface, the second sharp slump in 1929 provided the basis for a brief phase of unified action and agreement upon a further round of industry-wide wage cuts. What cemented solidarity and strengthened millowners' resolve for cost reductions was the crushing universality of the recession from 1929. As the FMCSA noted:

Its seriousness is all the more alarming since it has extended to almost every branch of the industry. Hitherto, financially strong and well managed combinations and individual units in industry have had faith in their ultimate ability to escape the more serious consequences of the depression. Trading results for the past year, however, in almost all of these cases, show either actual losses or seriously diminished profits.[30]

[29] Mitchell and Deane, *Abstract*, p. 72.   [30] FMCSA, *Annual Report*, 1930, p. 12.

Such product market circumstances produced a fair degree of unanimity in the 1929 ballots on industry-wide wage cuts, 93 per cent voting in favour within the FMCSA and 80 per cent within the CSMA.[31] What was perhaps surprising, given the defeats of the 1920s and the labour market situation, was the resolve of the unions to resist the proposed 13 per cent wage reduction.[32] In the event, the millowners locked out the entire workforce and the dispute drifted into deadlock. After three weeks the conflict was settled by direct government intervention, Sir Horace Wilson, Permanent Secretary to the Minister of Labour, persuading both sides to submit the claim to arbitration, which conceded a 6.4 per cent wage reduction. Not in itself very significant perhaps, but an early symbolic indication of the failure of the voluntary bargaining system in the industry.

As the recession deepened during 1930 the FMCSA gathered its resources for a further campaign to slash wages and to attack one of the sacred cows of the post-war labour insurgency – the 48-hour working week. Concurrently, the master weavers became embroiled in what has become known as the 'more looms crisis'. The details of the more looms dispute are well known, though the role employers played requires some further elaboration.[33] Essentially, the more looms scheme was a management-inspired initiative (couched in much pseudo-scientific jargon) designed to break the mould of traditional working arrangements in cotton weaving. By the First World War it had long been customary for Lancashire weavers operating the ordinary (non-automatic) loom to have a maximum complement of four machines. Whilst the idea of more loom working was not new to the inter-war period, the recession revived interest in a range of cost-cutting production methods, leading some weaving employers into experimentation with six and eight ordinary looms per weaver.[34]

Burnley became the centre for such initiatives, with the Burnley CSMA playing a key role. In 1928 the Burnley association approached the Amalgamated Weavers' Association seeking joint agreement for a collectively monitored experiment in more loom working.[35] With union

---

[31] CSMA, Minutes, 16 July 1929; FMCSA, *Annual Report*, 1929, pp. 12–13.

[32] Ibid., 12 July 1929.

[33] See, in particular, A. Bullen, *Lancashire Weavers' Union*, pp. 50–63; J.H. Riley, 'The more looms system' (MA thesis, Manchester University, 1981); A. and L. Fowler, *The Nelson Weavers*, Manchester: Amalgamated Textile Workers' Union, 1984, chs. 4–6; Turner, *Trade Union Growth*, pp. 327–31.

[34] The earliest reference of millowners attempting to introduce more than four-loom (as distinct from automatic loom) working occurred at Burnley in 1908. I am indebted to Andrew Bullen for this reference.

[35] Burnley CSMA, Minutes, 29 November 1928, 20 December 1928. In 1929, the Burnley association organised a deputation to Holland and Germany to examine machinery and working methods.

co-operation a twelve-month trial was initiated, entailing thirteen local mills running 4 per cent of their machinery on the more looms basis.[36] Each worker was paid a standing wage of 50 shillings per week to work eight looms, set on plain cloths and running at slightly lower speeds. Ancillary labour was provided for the cleaning, carrying and oiling processes. From the union side, the tests were considered far from satisfactory. First, there were bitter complaints that the employers were choosing their most efficient workers for the test – hence producing results that were not representative of the productivity of average operatives. Secondly, alarming evidence of worker fatigue accumulated as the year progressed. Thirdly, the extent of labour displacement that a widespread adoption of the scheme would bring became increasingly evident. The union adopted a stonewalling attitude, failing to agree collectively with the employers a piece price list that would govern more loom working.[37] In the second half of the nineteenth century cotton workers had embraced the inner incentive concept of the piecework wage payment system, benefiting from the flat rate basis of the Uniform List. In Lancashire, this was equivalent to an implicit commitment to a high-intensity mode of production.[38] However, the 1920s recession and the employers' attack on labour costs embittered industrial relations, creating a markedly different atmosphere in Lancashire, inducing a protective stance and eroding millworkers' customary acceptance of increases in workload and machinery speed.

For their part, the employers expressed satisfaction with the experiments and enthusiasm for the more looms system, which resulted in a direct saving of around 20 per cent in wages and up to 7 per cent in total production costs.[39] Critically, however, such savings could be achieved with negligible capital expense. In their general meeting in March 1930, 41 Burnley firms indicated plans to adopt the system (pending negotiations), 28 of which were willing to sanction force if necessary. Only 4 firms voted against the proposal.[40] Lines were clearly hardening. When the experimental year terminated, the AWA refused to sanction the more looms system, instructing members to return to four-loom complements. This drew a barbed censure from the FMCSA against 'insensate, obstructionist tactics'.[41] The response of the employers' organisations

---

[36] Burnley CSMA, Minutes, 4 and 26 April, 1929; CSMA, Minutes, 14 January 1930.
[37] CSMA, Minutes, 5 March 1929, 5 February 1930, 23 October 1930; Board of Trade, *Industrial Survey*, pp. 137–47.
[38] P. Bolin-Hort has recently drawn attention to the wide differences between the Lancashire and Scottish cotton industries in this respect. See P. Bolin-Hort, 'Managerial strategies', pp. 63–83.   [39] Board of Trade, *Industrial Survey*, p. 17.
[40] Burnley CSMA, Minutes, 12 March 1930.   [41] FMCSA, *Annual Report*, 1930, p. 33.

was to decline to force the more looms firms to return to four-loom working and the Uniform List.

Although an increasing number of firms introduced the system, little progress was made in joint negotiations, which ground into deadlock. This impasse was broken in December 1930 when the CSMA gave one month's notice to all their local associations that they would be free to introduce the more looms system, at the piece rates unilaterally decided by the employers' side in the joint negotiations. The weavers' union reacted by bringing the Burnley weavers in the more loom firms out on strike in January 1931. The employers posited that the unions had a distinct tactical advantage in such a sectional strike, insofar as they had the resources to support action indefinitely at a dozen or so firms. In line with the more aggressive policy developed in the 1920s on individual mill disputes, the employers immediately widened the area of dispute. First, the remaining sixty or so firms in Burnley locked out in sympathy with the stopped firms, followed by an industry-wide lock-out of 110,000 weavers initiated by the CSMA.[42] At this juncture, the employers quite consciously reinterpreted the breakdown in relations as an arbitrary union challenge to managerial prerogative and authority. This was clearly articulated by John H. Grey, chairman of the CSMA, in a statement on 7 January 1931: 'The question has resolved itself into whether or not an employer should be allowed to use his machinery in the manner in which he thinks best, or whether he must be governed by the Operatives' Association.'[43] Emphasising such a principle was most likely to solicit the widest possible support amongst millowners.

In essence then, the 1931 more looms lock-out in weaving was very similar to the pivotal 1922 lock-out in engineering. Both actions were located within the context of a concerted employers' offensive, co-ordinated by industry employers' organisations, designed to cut labour costs and reassert managerial authority on the factory floor. In both the stakes were extremely high and the resolution likely to influence fundamentally the character of industrial relations in their respective industries. However, their immediate (as distinct from long-term) outcomes could not have been more different – the one a complete and unequivocal employer success, the other an abject and unqualified failure. After a four-week stoppage, in a period when unemployment in weaving topped 40 per cent, the employers' federation backed down, calling off the lock-out and instructing members to end all more looms experiments pending further negotiations. How can this failure be explained? Part of the

[42] CSMA, Minutes, 30 December 1930, 6 January 1931, 23 January 1931.
[43] Burnley CSMA, Minutes, 7 January 1931.

explanation lies in the determination of the weavers – bolstered by long traditions of unionisation and embittered by a decade of recession – to resist a fundamental alteration in their working arrangements liable to result in massive labour shedding. For labour, the other key issue at stake was the removal of the principle of joint determination of wages and work conditions.[44] For their part, the employers undoubtedly under-estimated worker resistance and anticipated a short, sharp and successful lock-out. However, the records of the employers' associations indicate that a crucial factor in the failure of the lock-out was the lack of cohesion amongst the masters. This latter point, neglected in the literature, is worth emphasising.

From the outset, support for the lock-out was never as comprehensive as the 'hawks' in the CSMA would have liked. Despite the attempts to broaden the basis of the conflict to one of principle, in the CSMA ballot in January 1931 only firms owning 68 per cent of organised machine capacity unequivocally sanctioned the lock-out option. In certain districts, the lack of solidarity was alarmingly high. In Blackburn only 55 per cent agreed to stop, in Accrington only 32 per cent, and in Burnley – the cockpit of this particular struggle – only 68 per cent. More alarming, in a survey only six days before the lock-out was scheduled to start, the CSMA discovered that out of 524 firms, only 297 (57 per cent) had definitely posted up notices to stop production.[45] In the event, a significant number of mills, particularly in the Preston, Accrington, Nelson and Colne fancy and coloured goods districts, refused to support the lock-out.[46] Here product markets were much more buoyant than in the plain weaving sector, which had been disrupted by the Indian boycott. The critical factor, however, was that only a minority of mills working the plainest cloths were liable to benefit from the more looms system. The majority, involved in more intricate weaving work, had little, if any, stake in the struggle.[47] The pressure imposed by the long recession in trade encouraged many firms to exploit the opportunity for competitive advantage. Such disloyalty was actively nurtured by some cloth buyers who refused to grant extensions on cloth delivery contracts and offered enticements to firms tempted to exploit the temporary increased demand for cloth stimulated by the stoppage.

Some room for compromise existed at the executive level, indicated in the London talks, arranged through the intervention of the Ministry of Labour. Here both sides agreed on the need for a further period of

[44] CSMA, Minutes, 9 February 1931, 28 February 1931.   [45] Ibid., 9 January 1931.
[46] Ibid., 23 January 1931.
[47] Blackburn CSMA, Minutes, 20 October 1930 – 11 February 1931.

experimentation, but could not agree on the basis for this. In the event, the union officials had offered more than they could deliver. On 7 February the General Council of the AWA rejected any settlement involving a continuation of more looms experiments along the lines of the London negotiations. Whilst the operative weavers' stand hardened, splits became more evident amongst the millowners. The Bolton association admitted that its members in the Westhoughton district had not closed down. Accrington reported that two members had restarted work.[48] Consequently, the CSMA circularised members for views. The Colne and Bolton associations supported an immediate end to the lock-out. The Blackburn, Nelson and Chorley districts reported further erosions in solidarity and indicated that a number of firms had intimated that they would reopen the following weekend. Other districts expressed loyalty to the Federation and a willingness to abide by their decisions. Interpreting this survey as a significant expression of dissatisfaction with the stoppage, the CSMA called off the lock-out unconditionally and instructed all members to end more looms experiments. In a forthright statement the pragmatic employers' leader John Grey admitted that the 'will to win' was far greater amongst the unions than the employers. Curtailing the lock-out, he argued, would earn the employers respect and create the basis for goodwill and stability in industrial relations.[49]

In reality, Grey was only thinly concealing the impotence of his own organisation, wracked as it was by internecine divisions of interest and undermined by a growing non-organised segment of the industry. In the aftermath, employer cohesion waned further and the traditional function of the cotton employers' organisations – to regulate labour markets – virtually collapsed. Many more looms firms refused to end their experiments and others arbitrarily established the system in 1931 and 1932. This set in train a domino effect, with an increasing number of traditional four-loom complement mills cutting wage rates below the collectively agreed Uniform List, ostensibly to compete with the more loom companies.[50] The employers' organisations turned a blind eye to such developments, patently unable to control the actions of their members. Meanwhile, joint negotiations on the more looms system were revived, though agreement remained persistently elusive.

At this juncture, towards the end of 1931, the FMCSA approached the CSMA with a proposal for joint action to impose further wage cuts across the industry and terminate the 1919 48-hour week agreement.[51] Initially,

[48] CSMA, Minutes, 27 January 1931.   [49] CSMA, Minutes, 13 February 1931.
[50] Ibid., Minutes, 20 November 1931.
[51] FMCSA, *Annual Report*, 1931, pp. 30–1; Oldham MCSA, *Annual Report*, 1931, p. 11.

this overture was rebuffed, despite the unanimous support of the hard-pressed plain weaving firms. The CSMA executive argued that such precipitate action would prejudice any chances of achieving joint agreement on more looms.[52] The FMCSA went ahead alone. Following the refusal of the unions to accept any wage cuts the FMCSA suspended all collective agreements in their section in January 1932, leaving member firms free to exploit the situation as they saw fit. After further abortive negotiations on more looms the CSMA duplicated the action of the Federation, terminating joint agreements on 11 June 1932.[53] Significantly, support amongst the weaving employers for this atomisation of industrial relations was extraordinarily high, the ballot achieving a vote of 98.5 per cent in support. Unable to impose their will on the unions at industry level, unable to control their own members and unable to regulate the market effectively through joint collective bargaining, the employers' organisations abdicated responsibility entirely. Quite rightly the Bolton operative spinners interpreted this strategy as a green light to millowners to 'have a go' at the unions and challenge 'practically the whole of the concessions gained during the past fifty years of strenuous trade union effort'.[54]

The disintegration of the industrial relations system and collapse of any vestiges of central control over labour markets in cotton textiles ensued. Within a couple of weeks 69 member firms had intimated to the CSMA that they had diverged from the wages and conditions agreements prevailing prior to 11 June 1932.[55] In Preston, Bury and Haslingden negotiations were in progress in July to reduce wages. Padiham negotiated an interim wage cut applicable for three months. In Blackburn, the association reported that the circumstances within the local industry varied more widely than at any other time in their history: 21 Blackburn firms were closed; 19 had reduced Uniform List wages by 22 per cent; 16 reduced wages by 12 per cent; 3 were working the more looms system; at 7 the wages and conditions varied so much that it was impossible to generalise. Only at the remaining 20 or so firms was the Uniform List still in force.[56] On their side, the unions organised resistance to this strategy in the summer of 1932 with almost as much tenacity as during 1931. A crop of individual mill strikes snowballed into an all-out strike in Burnley.[57] The employers met strikes with company lock-outs, concerted attempts to recruit replacement labour and widespread victimisation of strikers. Negotiations were resurrected, only to break down over the size of the wage cut and the refusal of employers' organisations to guarantee

---

[52] CSMA, Minutes, 19 November, 4 December 1931.   [53] Ibid., 3 May, 7 June 1932.
[54] Bolton Operative Spinners' Association, *Annual Report*, 1931, p. 4.
[55] CSMA, Minutes, 21 June 1932.   [56] Ibid., 5 July 1932.   [57] Ibid., 22 July 1932.

reinstatement of strikers.[58] Incensed by the determination of the mill-owners to purge strikers, the Northern Counties Textile Trades Federation declared an industry-wide strike, bringing out around 150,000 workers. An NCTTF spokesperson indignantly declared: 'There can be no virtue in collective bargaining if workpeople are to be victimised when they endeavour to uphold agreements arrived at.'[59] The strike lasted a month.

Settlement of the summer 1932 crisis was achieved only through direct government intervention. According to the analysis of F.W. Leggett, the Chief Conciliation Officer of the Ministry of Labour, the system of industrial relations in cotton had been virtually inoperative since 1929. Market conditions had precipitated a price war and a desperate cost-cutting employers' offensive, setting in motion centrifugal tendencies which had completely undermined the authority of the established employers' organisations in the industry. The upshot was a return to a mid-nineteenth-century-style experiment in unregulated class warfare and a complete collapse in the traditional employer organisation functions of collective bargaining and market regulation. Thus, recreating the authority of the industry employer organisations and the viability of the collective bargaining system were seen as the main objectives of any lasting settlement.[60] After an intensive phase of tripartite negotiation these aims were embodied in the Midland Hotel Agreement, signed on 27 September 1932. Abrogated agreements, including the 48-hour week, were restored. A wage cut of 15½ per cent from the list was agreed, to apply to all weavers except those working the more looms system. Collective bargaining was accepted explicitly on both sides and an important innovation made in procedure with the inclusion of a final body of appeal – the Conciliation Committee. The latter incorporated, moreover, voluntary independent arbitration, thus institutionalising the *ad hoc* and informal tripartite system which had operated since the war. The more looms system was referred for settlement under the new conciliation machinery, whilst the possibility of legalisation of the Uniform List and other collective agreements was mooted as an effective mechanism to ensure a degree of labour cost standardisation. Subsequently, the spinning employers settled for a similar wage cut (14 per cent on list) and joined the Conciliation Committee.[61]

The year 1932 marked an important watershed in cotton industrial relations in a number of respects. In a very real sense, the industry was at

[58] CSMA, Joint Minutes, 9 August 1932.   [59] Ibid., 25 August 1932.
[60] CSMA, Minutes, 7 September, 23 September 1932; Joint Minutes, 13–16 September 1932.
[61] CSMA, Joint Minutes, 24 September 1932; FMCSA, *Annual Report*, 1932, pp. 14–16.

a crossroads, facing a choice between a future of atomised, mill-level industrial relations reminiscent of the mid-Victorian period or one char-acterised by orderly collective bargaining, procedural controls constrain-ing both sides, and effective regulation of labour markets. In the event, employers' organisations, cotton unions and their constituents recoiled from the edge of the abyss. Points of conflict emerged thereafter – on alleged victimisation, more looms, wage undercutting and the Uniform List – but, generally speaking, these were all satisfactorily resolved within the improved collective bargaining procedure. Indeed, if the lock-outs of 1931 and 1932 mark the culmination of an aggressive employers' counter-attack against cotton trade unions, the strategy thereafter is markedly more conciliatory. Consciously, escalation of points of principle or pre-rogative were avoided after 1932. Both sides submitted to procedural control and a much closer working relationship between the two sides emerged. Time lost through industrial disputes in cotton textiles totalled only 716,000 days in the seven years 1933–9 in contrast to the astronomi-cal 20 million work days lost in 1929–32.[62] Employer organisation mem-bership also reached a nadir in 1932 and recovered thereafter. The precondition for restabilising industrial relations in the industry, however, was direct government intervention. The regulatory function of employers' organisations and the policing role of trade unions – both crit-ically and permanently undermined by the deep economic crisis in the industry – were shored up by legal sanctions. This in itself was a radical departure for an industry that had placed great store upon the autonomous operation of its voluntary collective bargaining system.

The main threats to industrial relations in the aftermath of the Midland Agreement were the instability in wage payments across the industry, exacerbated by endemic undercutting and the problems associated with more looms. The employers' organisations made vigorous efforts to address these issues and regain some semblance of control over the indus-try. After several months of contentious negotiation, under the watchful chairmanship of F. W. Leggett, a more looms agreement was reached. The agreement, enforced from January 1933, was extremely complicated, but basically allowed for weavers to work six looms, paid by piecework at a lower rate than the Uniform (four-loom) List on the basis that a weaver of average ability working standard cloths should earn 41 shillings for a 48-hour week. Loom speeds were reduced by 7½–10 per cent, ancillary labour provided for cleaning, oiling and heavy cloth carrying, and provi-sion made for a guaranteed minimum wage of 28 shillings, or 66 per cent of six-loom earnings, when four looms or fewer were running out of six

[62] Mitchell and Deane, *Abstract*, p. 72; Knowles, *Strikes*, pp. 307–10.

because of lack of work. The agreement covered only standard cloths, though a clause allowed other weaving firms to experiment with not more than 6 per cent of their machine capacity on the more looms system. In effect, weavers' earnings under the system could be around 15–20 per cent higher than the four-loom complement weavers' (and the more looms weavers won the concession of a minimum wage), whilst millowners potentially benefited from a reduction in their total wage bill of around the same order of magnitude.[63]

On the surface, this appeared to remove a significant and long-standing point of conflict in the industry. However, stabilisation was dependent upon the collective organisations in the industry enforcing the agreement upon their members and this proved difficult, particularly for the employers. A fresh round of cut-throat wage undercutting broke out in 1933.[64] Some millowners attempted to enhance their competitiveness simply by paying the lower more looms piece rate for traditional four-loom working. Elsewhere, the Uniform List was undercut with impunity. Some more looms firms also ignored the minimum wage agreement. The worst offenders were non-federated firms, though a number of disloyal federated mills were also involved. Whilst both the trade unions and the employers' organisations publicly deplored such practices, neither had the power nor the inclination to control their constituents. Weavers invariably acquiesced – fearing unemployment and possible victimisation – whilst owners were locked into a price-cutting war in which they either engaged or went under.[65] With their membership down to just over half of the industry, the CSMA could do little but tacitly ignore such disloyalty.[66] It was this impotency, however, which finally convinced the organisation that it should pursue legalisation of the industry's wage lists. This, the CSMA posited, was a vital prerequisite for the stabilisation of dramatically fluctuating cloth prices.[67]

The proposals for a legalised wage list drawn up by the CSMA in 1933 flew in the face of opposition from within and outside the industry. The National Confederation of Employers' Organisations debated the issue and voted by a big majority against the principle, ostensibly on the grounds that this would set a precedent which could substantially add to industry's labour costs.[68] The initial response of the Minister of Labour – baffled by the complexity of wage calculations in the industry – was a negative one. In Lancashire, the more looms firms expressed dissatisfaction that the narrowing of the wage basis between themselves and the Uniform List would provide a further disincentive to shift from the four-

[63] CSMA, Joint Minutes, 6 December, 28 December 1932.
[64] CSMA, Minutes, 15 February, 10 May, 30 May, 29 August 1933, 13 March 1934.
[65] Ibid., 21 February 1933.   [66] Ibid., 10 August 1933.   [67] Ibid., 12 December 1933.
[68] Ibid., 30 May 1933.

to the six-loom complement. The CSMA pressed on regardless, backed up by the majority of cotton manufacturing employers, and the most powerful local association in Blackburn. In an area little affected by more looms, Blackburn millowners were increasingly voicing the opinion that the dual wage-list system was unworkable, destabilising and unfair, providing the more looms firms with an unnecessary competitive advantage.[69]

By the spring of 1934 the Minister of Labour was persuaded of the utility of legalising wage lists by means of an Enabling Act. The legalised list, the product of many months of hard negotiations, included a final wage cut of 5.7 per cent and made separate provision for six-loom working at the relatively high standing wage of 48 shillings (plus a performance related bonus).[70] The wage list was trenchantly criticised by the more looms protagonists as too generous, eliminating the incentive to switch from the traditional four-loom to the six-loom complement. Nevertheless, given the legal sanctions, the industry had little option but to resign itself to the new list. At a stroke, the wage cutting and cut-throat competition which had characterised the industry since the early 1920s was effectively contained.

Wage list legalisation was a necessary precondition for the stabilisation of industrial relations in cotton manufacturing. However, this was not the only factor. The flattening out of the recession and some limited though marked improvement in product markets in cotton textiles between 1935 and 1939 eased the pressure upon millowners, containing undercutting propensities somewhat. After the débâcle of 1929–32, cotton millowners were also reconciled to developing a closer working relationship with their trade unions. This involved more joint determination of commercial policies and more openly co-operative, conciliatory labour relations strategies. The scope of collective bargaining widened, to incorporate, for example, occupational health and safety issues (with mediation by the factory inspectors).[71] Despite their apparent weakness, the cotton employers' organisations played a significant role in bringing about this *rapprochement*, which was exemplified by two new organisations, the Conciliation Committee and the Joint Committee of Cotton Trade Organisations (JCCTO). The stabilisation of industrial relations enabled the employers' associations to regain some standing within the community of Lancashire millowners, which was reflected in a significant strengthening in their membership between 1933 and 1939.[72]

---

[69] Ibid., 8 November, 14 November 1933.   [70] FMCSA, *Annual Report*, 1934, pp. 35–6.

[71] Helen Jones, 'An inspector calls', in P. Weindling (ed.), *The Social History of Occupational Health*, London: Croom Helm, 1985, p. 230.

[72] See table 7.1. CSMA membership was further boosted by the affiliation, for the first time, of local associations in Wigan, Todmorden, Earby, Skipton and Radcliffe from 1934 to 1939.

The Conciliation Committee became a permanent feature of the cotton weaving disputes procedure, lasting beyond the Second World War, to the satisfaction of both sides. The situation was rather different, however, in cotton spinning, where this higher tribunal appeared to operate clearly in the employers' favour. In four cases heard at the Conciliation Committee and one case of independent arbitration (by the Lord Mayor of Manchester) the employers' position was upheld. Two cases of alleged unjustifiable dismissal were thrown out. Two cases made for sectional wage advances to twiner piecers were rejected, whilst one case of a wage reduction (to ring-spinners, following some alteration in work methods) was upheld.[73] This catalogue of failures confirmed the suspicions of the spinning and cardroom workers' unions that the procedural extension could not be divorced from class bias and they duly abrogated the Conciliation Committee agreement and withdrew at the end of the three-year trial period in 1935.[74] Nevertheless, the evidence suggests that the attitude of the spinning employers' organisations towards their trade unions was mellowing rather than hardening. This was particularly evident on the closed shop question. Here, the FMCSA registered a volte-face from its pre-war stance, indicating quite categorically in 1935 a preference for trade union employees: 'On behalf of the federation it is stated that they prefer that employees in cotton spinning mills should be members of a trade union. Further, to remove any doubt that might exist on this point, they agree to circularise the members of the federation to this effect.'[75] A similar softening of attitude on the closed shop can be perceived within the weaving sector, though the CSMA drew the line at going as far as their sister federation in publicly declaring a preference for trade unionists.[76]

Underpinning a markedly more conciliatory and more openly co-operative labour relations strategy by the cotton employers' organisations was the stabilisation of product markets. Mirroring the legalisation of wage lists in weaving were the multi-employer initiatives (with the FMCSA playing the dominant role) in spinning to legalise price maintenance schemes. Unlike abortive attempts in the 1920s, these later price-fixing arrangements – such as the American Ring Spinners' Agreement, the Coarse Counts Agreement, the Egyptian Type Mule Yarn Scheme and the 42s and 56s Weft Agreement – were all effective in maintaining price levels. Indeed, by 1936 it was estimated that firms owning more than half

[73] FMCSA, *Annual Report*, 1933, p. 19; 1934, pp. 50–1.   [74] Ibid., 1935, pp. 38–9.
[75] Ibid. Some of the rank-and-file employers were opposed to conceding such a principle. For one dissenting voice, see Rochdale MCSA, *Annual Report*, 1936, pp. 5–6.
[76] CSMA, Minutes, 8 September, 15 September, 6 October, 3 November 1936; Joint Minutes, 11 August 1937, 18 January 1938.

of the spinning capacity of the industry were covered by such schemes.[77] Some employers' associations also attempted to address the problem of inefficient costing – the CSMA drawing up and circularising a comprehensive model cloth costing system.[78] Market stabilisation was further aided by the passage of the Cotton Spinning Industry Act, providing subsidies for the scrapping of excess spinning machinery. By September 1939, the Spindles Board had acquired and scrapped some 6.2 million spindles, representing around 15 per cent of total capacity.[79]

By 1936–7 the cotton employers' organisations were operating in a changed economic situation and having to adapt accordingly. Domestic demand rose, prompted by rising employment, the national rearmament programme (particularly uniforms and other coarse cloth) and preparations for the coronation festivities of 1937. From May to December 1936, vacancies at mills in Oldham increased threefold from 939 to 2,722, and cotton workers registered at the local employment exchange declined from 2,517 to 1,502.[80] By the autumn of 1937, 92 per cent of the machine capacity in Oldham was running full-time and millowners reported an acute labour shortage, particularly of young workers – piecers, creelers, doffers and back tenters.[81] Part of the labour supply problem was the outflow of young labour from the cotton mills, attracted by the expansion of the armaments and allied industries from 1935. Cotton manufacturing was characterised in the late 1930s by an experienced though ageing workforce.

Tangible signs of an alteration in the balance of power came with a spate of unauthorised 'wildcat' strikes (many by juvenile workers) and union applications for wage rises across the board in 1936: the first was headed off by widespread, intimidatory use of legal action, mulcting absentee workers of damages for leaving work without notice;[82] the latter were settled by conceding the first wage advances (of between 5 and 7 per cent) in the industry since 1920. Further concessions followed. In weaving, buoyant sections won additional wage rises and a pivotal precedent was set in 1938 when the CSMA bowed to AWA pressure and conceded a minimum wage to weavers.[83] The latter decision, arrived at

[77] FMCSA, *Annual Report*, 1936, pp. 17–19; 1937, p. 94.
[78] CSMA, *Annual Report*, 1936, p. 20; FMCSA, *Annual Report*, 1937, p. 127. This was designed to prevent undercosting, a common problem during the recession as millowners desperate for orders took on unfamiliar work outside their normal range of production.
[79] FMCSA, *Annual Report*, 1937, p. 14; 1938, p. 14; Oldham MCSA, *Annual Report*, 1940, p. 14.   [80] Oldham MCSA, *Annual Report*, 1936, p. 8.
[81] Ibid., 1937, pp. 8, 24–5. A FMCSA survey indicated that members were almost 20 per cent understaffed. See FMCSA, *Annual Report*, 1937, pp. 134–5.
[82] Rochdale MCSA, *Annual Report*, 1937, pp. 9–10; Oldham MCSA, *Annual Report*, 1936, p. 19.
[83] CSMA, Joint Minutes, 16 September 1937, 5 May 1938; Minutes, 14 December 1937, 22 June 1938, 21 October 1938.

through the Conciliation Committee and in the face of much opposition from the local associations, emphasises the co-operative/corporatist strategy of the CSMA.[84] In spinning the story was much the same. In mid-1938, in response to union complaints, the FMCSA improved their disputes procedure to cope more speedily with recurring bad spinning complaints. The principle of financial compensation for production time lost by millworkers during mill limewashing was also conceded.[85] Moreover, in line with other industries, the FMCSA and the CSMA combined to draw up a scheme providing one week's annual holiday with pay.[86] By 1939, the shortage of labour had become so acute in a number of regions in Lancashire that unofficial wage inducements above list wages were being offered by millowners, raising the spectre again of rampant wage escalation.[87] Clearly, changed market circumstances from the mid-1930s stalled the inter-war costs reduction offensive and prompted reversion to a defensive and conciliatory posture by the cotton employers' organisations. Evidence suggests, moreover, that the central employers' federations were playing a pivotal role in this process of adaptation, even riding roughshod on occasions over residual pockets of employer conservatism in the localities in order to sustain industrial peace.

Conclusion

Taking the inter-war period as a whole, a pertinent question to address is: to what degree had cotton millowners exploited market circumstances and a changed political environment which significantly eroded the power of trade unions to initiate fundamental changes in work organisation and the division of labour? And, linked to this, what role did the employers' organisations in the industry play in this process? Does Jonathan Zeitlin's hypothesis that engineering employers failed to take advantage of the 1922 lock-out victory and the recession to push through a thoroughgoing transformation in the division of labour have any resonance in the cotton industry? Were millowners, like engineering companies, reliant upon skilled labour and inhibited by the weakness and vacillation of their employers' associations? Despite internal divisions and centrifugal tendencies, the evidence does suggest that the cotton employers' organisations performed a central role in producing an environment

[84] Ibid. The Blackburn, Darwen, Nelson, Ramsbottom and Earby local associations, comprising 38 per cent of the loomage of the CSMA, unequivocally opposed conceding the principle of a minimum wage.   [85] FMCSA, *Annual Report*, 1939, p. 35.
[86] FMCSA, *Annual Report*, 1938, pp. 30–1; CSMA, Minutes, 23 December 1938, 23 May 1939. The scheme was not actually operative until the end of the Second World War.
[87] Oldham MCSA, *Annual Report*, 1939, p. 11.

conducive to work intensification and, to a lesser extent, innovation. Though there was no single industry-wide lock-out on the issue of control, as in engineering, the whole period from 1920 to the mid-1930s was punctuated by multi-employer campaigns to redress the balance of power in the cotton industry. A cluster of hard-won collective agreements sanctioned some quite significant changes in working practices in the industry. In spinning, the division of labour was extended with the removal of cleaning and oiling duties. The Cleaning Time Agreement of 1919 (giving spinners a specified time to clean and oil their machinery) was abrogated by the FMCSA in 1929. This required mule spinners to spin for a fully productive 48-hour week, whilst teams of labourers were employed as cleaning and oiling squads. More fundamentally, the traditional spinning work team of two piecers and one minder was challenged by the joiner-minder system.[88] Moreover, collective agreements undermined the overlookers' job. Savage has shown how a more strident, direct form of mill management emerged between the wars which curtailed the traditional craft controls, independence and range of activities of weaving overlookers.[89] Overlooking became significantly more specialised and functionalised, and diluted with the recruitment of less skilled labour. The abrogation of the gaiting-up agreement by the Blackburn master weavers' association in 1931 accelerated this trend, providing member firms with 'liberty of action' to employ cheaper 'jobbers' for this task, traditionally part of the duties of the overlookers.[90] Finally, the more looms agreement critically broke down traditional machine staffing arrangements in the weaving shed, opening the way for quite drastic labour shedding.

The pace and scope of these changes were, however, quite limited. Rather than initiating a radical transformation in the division of labour, the majority of cotton millowners had narrower horizons. They utilised their opportunities in the 1920s and 1930s to speed up and intensify work within the parameters of the existing technology, and, to a large extent, within the orbit of traditional modes of work organisation. For most cotton mill workers the pace of work was very much faster by the late 1930s than in 1920. However, their work tasks would have been familiar in

[88] This was where two workers of equal status replaced the traditional spinning work team of one minder, one big piecer and one little piecer. Both joiner-minders earned about as much as adult male weavers, thus eliminating the spinners' craft level wage.

[89] M. Savage, 'Capitalist and patriarchal relations at work: Preston cotton weaving, 1890–1940', in L. Murgatroyd et al. (eds.), Localities, Class and Gender, London: Pion, 1985, pp. 188–93.

[90] CSMA, Minutes, 12 October 1931. For examples of overlookers being replaced by cheaper labour see CSMA, Minutes, 12 January, 30 November 1926, 29 August 1927, 6 January 1928.

almost every respect to their parents and grandparents. By 1930, only around 12 per cent of Lancashire spinners were joiner-minders.[91] The ring frame – worked by female labour – was growing in popularity, though still, on the eve of the Second World War, over 70 per cent of Lancashire spinners manipulated the mule frame. Similarly, high draft winding in the cardroom and the new vacuum card stripping apparatus diffused only very slowly.[92] In weaving, where perhaps the most fundamental challenge to traditional modes of organising work had taken place, change was also extremely slow. By 1939, only around 20 per cent of Lancashire weavers were operating either automatic looms or more than the customary complement of four looms per weaver.[93]

But does this represent a failure on the part of the industry's employers' organisations? To a degree, the answer must be affirmative. They may well have spearheaded a costs reduction offensive, and, by bolstering managerial authority, the cotton employers' organisations facilitated work intensification. However, there is little evidence of organisations campaigning vigorously for scientific management, work rationalisation (for example on the Bedaux model) or, for that matter, technological renewal. Such matters were regarded as the prerogative of internal management. The records of the employers' associations are remarkably silent on automatic looms and ring spindles. Nor, until after the Second World War, did the cotton employers' federations promote work study, though there were occasional association visits abroad to study production methods. There were signs, moreover, that during the long struggle over the more looms system, the CSMA sacrificed the interests of the minority of more innovative millowners. Initially, the employers lacked the power to impose this innovation unilaterally in working practice because of staunch worker resistance combined with critical divisions within the millowners' ranks. However, the final settlement in 1935 was so restrictive and the wage basis established was so high for more loom weavers that the incentive to transfer from four- to six-loom weaving was minimised. This reflected, above all else, the internal politics of the CSMA and the dominance of the traditionalist lobby over the rationalisers. The interests of the latter were sacrificed to create the basis for stability in industrial relations.

The evidence suggests, therefore, that the cotton employers' associations were, in essence, fairly conservative organisations between the wars, most concerned to cut labour costs in time-honoured fashion and to

[91] Lazonick, 'Industrial relations', pp. 248–9.
[92] Bolton MCSA, Special Committee Minute Book, 6 May 1931, 11 August 1931, 19 August 1931. Millowners believed the vacuum stripping job could be performed by women and could halve the numbers of strippers and grinders needed.
[93] CSMA, Wage Census Files, table 3, 'systems of weaving'.

regulate labour and product markets in order to control competition and stabilise industrial relations. The latter were, however, no mean achievements in themselves, given the fragmenting pressures of the inter-war recession. The employers' associations remained at the vanguard of an offensive against labour which succeeded in slashing labour costs and reviving managerial discipline on the mill floor. Above all, the employers' associations in cotton struggled to maintain fair competition through industry-wide regulation of the labour market. When divisions in their own ranks precipitated by the economic crisis of 1929–32, threatened this, the employers' organisations proved willing to support radical and innovative measures to restore stability, categorically rejecting the vagaries of the market for the certainty of legalised wages and the lottery of arbitration. This transformed collective bargaining in the industry from a voluntary 'common law' model to one based on legal compulsion, or a 'statute law' mode.[94] In this the CSMA at least was flying in the face of opposition from the broader capitalist fraternity. Moreover, it is also of significance that the employers' organisations in the industry did not disintegrate during the crisis of 1929–32. Clearly, multi-employer bargaining was still important in the industry at the end of the 1930s. The threatened atomisation of industrial relations had been contained and, with wage list legalisation, a much larger slice of the industry was now effectively regulated by rates jointly determined by the employers' associations and unions. Legalisation did not remove the regulatory functions of these institutions; rather it provided them with the power to enforce joint decisions across the industry.

In the final analysis, cotton employers' organisations survived the roller-coaster years of the 1920s and 1930s and the particular industrial relations crisis of 1929–32 by prioritising effective control over labour and product markets above any concerted campaign to reorganise production methods radically. Given the circumstances, this was quite understandable and rational behaviour. Employers' associations were caught between a resilient labour movement unwilling to condone radical labour-shedding changes in working methods and their member firms, many suffering acute capital starvation and unable to afford extensive re-equipment. The recession seriously exacerbated divisions within millowners' ranks and made the formulation of a consistent consensus strategy at the multi-employer level extremely difficult. As a consequence, short-term crisis management characterised cotton employer organisation policies between the wars. Such policies, however,

---

[94] These distinctions are used by Hugh Clegg. See Sisson, 'Employers and the structure of collective bargaining', p. 259.

contributed significantly to the shape of industrial relations in the industry during these turbulent years. Whilst their authority was dented by the centrifugal forces unleashed by the recession, the cotton employers' associations at the local and central levels remained primary 'shakers and movers' within the industry in the inter-war years. The evidence also suggests that organised capital in the cotton industry absorbed one crucially important lesson from the years of crisis in 1929–32 – that the survival of the industry depended not upon authoritarian opposition to trade unionism but upon flexible accommodation, working in co-operation with the trade unions rather than against them.

8   Stabilising labour markets: building

During and immediately after the First World War, the master builders had experienced a serious erosion of their authority and bargaining power. This was reflected in their failure to prevent upward wage escalation via sectional and local claims, the concession of generous working conditions and, perhaps most significantly, in the proliferation of closed shop agreements. The local employers' associations, regional federations and the NFBTE made concerted efforts to control this situation, but with little evident success. It was argued in chapter 6 that the building employers were critically weakened by the structure of their industry and the nature of their product markets. In particular, a large non-organised sector of predominantly small firms and disagreements over strategy within the organisation weakened the building employers in their relations with construction trade unions.

Market circumstances altered markedly in the following two decades. This chapter analyses the responses of building employers and their collective organisations to the inter-war economic crisis, focusing on their evolving relationships with their trade unions. The evidence suggests that the employers' associations managed to exploit changes in labour markets to regain authority and control at the point of production, though this stopped far short of any open attack upon building trade unionism. Quite the contrary. The building employers took the initiative to widen union recognition by extending collective bargaining procedures in the 1920s. The scope of substantive norms was also widened, notably through the formulation of a national wage grading scheme for the industry. This lends support to Gospel's hypothesis that employers' organisations were operating in a dynamic fashion between the wars, playing a pivotal role in structuring industrial relations in their respective industries.[1] The building employers' organisations, in common with other industries where labour costs were the major component of final product price, had a

---

[1] Gospel, 'Employers and managers', p. 181; Gospel, 'Employers' organisations', pp. 30–3, 368.

Table 8.1 *Unemployment in the UK building trade, as a percentage of those insured, 1921 and 1924*

	October 1921	October 1924
Plasterers	1.6	1.6
Bricklayers	4.9	1.2
Carpenters	5.3	2.3
Masons	8.8	2.5
Plumbers	6.3	4.7
Painters	15.9	16.6
Slaters	—	3.6
Other skilled	19.9	—
Navvies	11.5	—
Labourers	19.9	10.1
All trades (UK)	13.8	10.3
All trades (north-west)	13.0	11.3

Source: NWFBTE, *Half-Yearly Report*, December 1921, December 1924.

major interest in stabilising wages. This was a recurrent, indeed a dominant, theme within the records of the associations in north-west England throughout these years. Before examining these developments, however, it is necessary to outline market experience from 1920 to 1939 and how this affected the organisational framework within the construction industry.

Market experience and employer organisation

The immediate post-war building boom was followed by a sharp and deep recession in 1921–2. Housebuilding schemes were cut back by local authorities starved of subsidies by central government spending cuts.[2] Commercial work was also curtailed, especially in the heavily industrialised regions, as companies cut back on plans for repairs, extensions and new buildings. Unemployment in the industry increased commensurately, peaking in north-west England at 24 per cent of building workers in April 1922.[3] Significantly, however, not all sectors were affected equally, as table 8.1 indicates. Unemployment was highest where labour markets were most overstocked during the 1914–20 period (especially

[2] NWFBTE, *Annual Report*, June 1921.   [3] NWFBTE, Minutes, 28 June 1922

painting and labouring). Conversely, there were markedly lower unemployment rates amongst the trowel trades – plasterers and bricklayers – where acute labour shortages in 1919–20 had held up housebuilding programmes.[4] These labour market differentials were to have an important impact upon industrial relations in the industry in the 1920s.

New government housing schemes precipitated a revival in orders between 1923 and 1927, though the commercial sector remained relatively depressed. The slashing of the housing subsidy in October 1927 heralded a further slump in building activity, exacerbated by the economic recession in 1929 and the National Government's 'Economy Campaign' in the autumn of 1931. Activity thereafter remained at a low ebb until 1934. This second slump also affected the trowel trades – unemployment in plastering, for example, rising from 1.8 per cent in August 1927 to over 20 per cent in March 1928.[5] From 1933, some recovery in the industry is discernible, led by a surge in speculative housebuilding. However, in areas like north-west England this had a negligible impact. Complaints continued through 1934–5 of cut-throat price cutting and taking contracts at uneconomic prices.[6] Only in 1936–7 did the majority of construction firms achieve full order books, notably through commercial contracts under the Government Defence Programme for aerodromes, depots, factories, camps and air raid shelters.[7] Serious shortages of key building craftsmen were again being reported in the late 1930s.[8]

As in cotton spinning and weaving, the economic recession undermined employer solidarity in the construction industry. Membership of the NWFBTE fell from 3,048 firms in 1921 to 1,794 firms in 1939. It is difficult to gauge what this actually meant in terms of the proportion of the trade that was organised because the trend was towards amalgamations and mergers which reduced the number of competing units and pushed the average company size upwards. However, the wage roll of the NWFBTE fell from £7.11 million in 1921 to just £3.01 million in 1933. This reduction was significantly greater than the proportionate fall in both employment and money wage rates, suggesting at least a stagnation and probably a reduction in the proportion of employers organised over these years. Such averages however, mask, a quite considerable degree of diversity across the region. Some associations, including those which continued to operate the intertrading rule rigidly, experienced growth – including Bolton, Blackpool and Lancaster. Elsewhere, the majority of

[4] NWFBTE, *Half-Yearly Report*, 13 December 1922. For example, the Manchester area housing schemes were delayed because of shortages of plasterers in 1920–1.
[5] NWFBTE, Minutes, 12 March 1928.   [6] Ibid., 6 November 1935.
[7] Ibid., 2 December 1936; *Annual Report*, June 1936.   [8] Ibid., Minutes, 19 May 1936.

Table 8.2 *NFBTE membership in three*
Lancashire towns (Manchester, Bolton and
Preston), 1921, 1930, 1939

	1921	1930	1939
General contractors			
Total	265	283	260
Percentage organised	45.7	40.6	45.0
Subcontractors			
Total	1,861	1,877	1,699
Percentage organised	10.3	14.8	13.7

Sources: NWFBTE, *Yearbooks*, 1921, 1930, 1939 (for
Membership Lists). *Kelly's Trade Directories for Manchester*
and Salford, 1921, 1930, 1939; *Tillotson's Directories for*
Bolton and District, 1921, 1930, 1939; *Cope's Bolton and*
District Directory and Buyers' Guide, 1930; *Barrett's*
Directories of Preston and District, 1921, 1930, 1939; *Aubrey*
and Co., Directory of Lancashire, 1938.

local associations registered sharp declines in membership.[9]
Rationalisation through mergers somewhat streamlined the structure of
employers' associations in the industry. Twenty-nine local associations
went out of existence in the north-west region alone between the wars.

We lack the kind of detailed data on company size and structure in
building that exist for cotton textiles. However, some comparative analysis, cross-referencing membership lists of three of the larger local associations against local trade directories provides a profile of the coverage of
the NFBTE.

Two points might be highlighted from table 8.2. First, whilst some marginal improvement occurred in their representation of the smaller subcontractors in the industry, the Federation patently failed to extend its
influence significantly beyond the general contractors. More than 80 per
cent of the subcontractors remained outside the Federation between the
wars. Many of them were organised in separate sectional associations. In
north-west England the master painters had 40 local associations, incorporating more than 1,200 members. The Manchester region master
plumbers' association alone boasted 650 individual members in 1926.[10]
Secondly, the Federation's recruitment of the largest employers failed to

[9] Including Manchester and Burnley. Membership of Burnley MBA fell from 190 in 1921 to
just 35 members in 1930.   [10] NWFBTE, Minutes, 29 September 1926.

improve significantly over these years. Indeed, the Federation represented less than half of all the general contractors in these towns throughout this period.

Three other factors weakened the NFBTE between the wars. First, the speculative housebuilders were rarely organised.[11] Secondly, public works and direct labour departments of local authorities were taking an increasing slice of the market. Thirdly, the Federation was plagued by local associations going their own way. The major problem in this respect in the north-west was again Liverpool (the second largest local association in the region), which remained outside the Federation for all but a few years between the wars (1923–6).

Regulating industrial relations

The immediate post-war period witnessed a major innovation in industrial relations in construction with the creation of a formal procedure for national collective bargaining on substantive issues. This replaced local and sectional bargaining. An essential precondition for this had been fulfilled in 1918 with the reorganisation of the craft-based building unions into the industrial union, the National Federation of Building Trade Operatives (NFBTO). For the employers, the National Wage and Conditions Council (operative from April 1921) offered the opportunity to standardise labour costs across the industry and utilise the policing authority of the NFBTO to ensure that nationally negotiated agreements were accepted by members. The substantive norms initially agreed were comprehensive, with a 44-hour working week all year round and the creation of eleven wage gradings, with differentials dependent upon prevailing living costs within local areas. The aim here was to achieve equal real wages across the industry. Most of the large Lancashire towns, for example, were graded A (at the top of the range) by the Council, with a weekly wage of 2s 4d. Future movement of wages was to be governed not by the respective bargaining power of the parties but through a sliding scale agreement tying wage movements up or down to the official cost of living index. The employers stressed that this would remove potential sources of conflict and enable them to make more accurate forecasts and costings on tenders.[12]

How did this institutionalisation of industrial relations in the industry survive the pressures of the inter-war economic recession? As market

[11] Ibid., 14 May 1924, 3 November 1926. A separate National Housebuilders' Association existed.
[12] NFBTE, *44th Annual Report*, 31 December 1921, pp. 1–2; NWFBTE, Minutes, 30 March, 21 April 1921; Bullough, *First Fifty*, p. 43.

conditions altered and construction contracts sharply declined, building employers moved on to a cautious offensive. Craftsmen's wages were slashed by 3½d per hour in 1921 and by an additional ½d per hour in February 1922 under the sliding scale.[13] By 1922, the building employers in the most hard-pressed districts – including north-west England – were agitating for deeper wage cuts and an increase in working hours. The North-West Federation was in the vanguard of this movement, articulating a sense of dissatisfaction with the National Wages Council, and arguing that advantage should be taken of prevailing conditions to impose heavier wage cuts irrespective of the sliding scale.[14] In the localities, loyalty to the national agreement proved transitory. Evidence of undercutting swamped the NWFBTE, which was also inundated with official claims for wage downgrading from local associations.[15] Wage rates were arbitrarily cut, especially in the more remote country districts, and some firms returned to a longer working week in 1922–3.[16] A key problem was the unorganised sector, as the NWFBTE argued:

The general unrest, unemployment, break-up of trade and fall in prices are common to all, yet supplementing these matters . . . we find that it is difficult to sustain business as federated firms paying National and graded standard rates against the unfederated companies, public works contractors and direct labour schemes . . . So all along the line there comes the plea to press for a clear cut to operate and supplement the present unsatisfactory arrangement of the sliding scale.

We are told that our policy is too hesitant and timid, and our people threaten that rather than stand by and see their businesses completely ruined, they will be compelled to leave our federation.[17]

The NFBTE responded to this percolating pressure from their more militant constituents, opening negotiations with the NFBTO for further wage cuts. Reductions totalling an additional 4d per hour were agreed in the Wages Council (operative in two stages in April and June 1922), despite the fact that the cost of living index did not justify such cuts.[18] The National Federation pressed further in the winter of 1922–3, initiating a campaign for an increase in summer working hours to 47 per week and a further wage cut of 2d.[19] Opposition by the unions led the industry to the brink of a lock-out in the spring of 1923.[20] This was averted when both sides agreed to arbitration. The award imposed wage cuts of 1d per hour

[13] NFBTE, 44th Annual Report, 1921, p. 22.
[14] NWFBTE, Minutes, 25 January 1922, 22 February 1922.
[15] Ibid., 7 September 1921, 1 March 1922.   [16] Ibid, 11 July 1923.
[17] Ibid., 2 March 1922.   [18] Ibid., 13 December 1922.   [19] Ibid., 27 February 1923.
[20] NFBTE, 46th Annual Report, 31 December 1923, p. 2; NWFBTE, Minutes, 26 March 1923, 11 April 1923.

to A and B graded men, cuts of ½d per hour to C graded men and an increase in summer working hours to 46½. This brought grade A craftsmen's wages down to 1s 7d per hour. Within a couple of years, therefore, the employers had reneged on two of the original premises of the 1921 national agreement: the 44-hour week and the concept of wage movements tied to the cost of living index.

In other respects, it is evident that the changed market circumstances facilitated a revival of employers' authority and a reimposition of work discipline in construction. As in cotton textiles, this resulted in an intensification of work, largely within the parameters of the existing technology. According to the NFBTE president, productivity in the industry almost doubled between 1920 and summer 1923.[21] Evidently, building workers were grafting longer and harder for a lower real wage. Some time-honoured craft controls were also sucessfully challenged. In 1923, the NFBTE threatened a national lock-out to end the operative joiners' refusal to work with imported joinery. The NFBTE president, A.G. White, argued that the Federation was 'supporting the principle that the builders in this country have the right to purchase their goods and carry on their business without any dictation from the operatives'.[22] In the subsequent national agreement the Amalgamated Society of Woodworkers agreed to install imported joinery that had been manufactured under 'fair' conditions. The employers' strategy also incorporated an attempt to create and maintain a labour surplus in the industry. Against union opposition, the NFBTE initiated a government-sponsored scheme for the employment of ex-servicemen in 1921. Up to 50,000 ex-servicemen were given places in the building trade on a two-year special training scheme, with wages starting at 60 per cent of the skilled rate, reaching the full rate on completion. Again, the Federation indicated its willingness to lock out if union opposition was encountered.[23] Similarly, it spearheaded an attack on the craft control of the operative painters. In 1921 member firms were encouraged by the Federation to introduce an intermediate grade of semi-skilled 'brush-hands' who were not required to have any specific apprenticeship training and were to be paid at 12 per cent below the standard craft rate after three years.[24] At the same time, the building employers' organisations exhorted members to ignore union attempts to restrict apprentice numbers and to take on more youths, aiming at a ratio of one apprentice to four craftsmen.[25] The evidence suggests, then, that the employers' aims were to deskill craftwork – starting with the most

---

[21] NWFBTE, Minutes, 18 July 1923.   [22] Ibid., 10 August 1921.
[23] Ibid., 3 March, 10 March 1921.   [24] Ibid., 13 December 1921.
[25] Ibid., 11 October 1922, 13 February 1923.

vulnerable groups – and to maintain an overstocked labour market, thus benefiting from the downward pressure on wages that this produced.

Just how far such initiatives were taken up in the industry is unclear. On the building sites, the situation was more complex, with the evidence suggesting a considerable amount of regional and sectional variation in the employers' offensive. Within the National Federation there were fundamental divisions of interest between the hard-pressed and most militant northern builders and those in London and the south whose markets – especially on the commercial side – held up better. The latter employers were markedly more conciliatory and patently failed to breach union apprenticeship restrictions and maintain recruitment levels.[26] Whilst the northern employers pressed hardest for labour cost reductions, it was reported that many federated building employers in the south deemed it expedient not to enforce the 1923 wage cuts.[27]

A great deal of diversity also existed within regions, which worked to break down employer solidarity and constrain the cost-cutting labour relations strategies of the employers' organisations in the trade. In north-west England, building activity remained buoyant in Blackpool and along the Fylde coast during 1921–3. Federated firms there opposed national wage cuts and loyal firms found themselves losing labour to speculative builders paying higher wage rates. The NWFBTE exhorted Blackpool members to stand firm 'shoulder to shoulder'.[28] Some firms got over the problem by working excessive overtime. Others unofficially paid over the odds, or resigned from the Federation.

The situation in Liverpool, however, proved to be even more serious. Because Liverpool had been expelled from the Federation, they were not included within the scope of the National Wages and Working Conditions Agreement. Liverpool BTEA made a separate and more generous local agreement, providing an hourly wage differential of around 2d over the Manchester grade A rates.[29] With the recession, however, the Liverpool masters resolved to regain control over wage rates and negotiated re-entry to the Federation and the national wage agreement in 1923. This was conditional upon bringing wages and conditions on Merseyside in line with NFBTE grade A rates.[30] Whilst the NFBTO publicly supported the Liverpool employers in this initiative, the Liverpool unions determined to resist, striking on Merseyside from 1 June 1924.[31] The NWFBTE declared full support for the Liverpool masters and campaigned for the

---

[26] NWFBTE, *Annual Report*, June 1925; *Half-Yearly Report*, 30 November 1936. These reports included a survey of apprentices with returns from 1,151 firms in the north-west.
[27] NFBTE, *46th Annual Report* 1923, p. 2.   [28] NWFBTE, Minutes, 18 July, 27 July 1923.
[29] NWFBTE, Annual General Meeting, Minutes, 18 June 1924.
[30] NWFBTE, Minutes, 19 April, 21 July 1923.   [31] Ibid., 22 May, 4 June 1924.

declaration of a national lock-out to neutralise what was interpreted as an attack on the sanctity of national agreements. Meanwhile, the NFBTO declared a national strike from 5 July 1924 in support of their claim for 2d per hour wage rise, over and above the sliding scale adjustments. This example of residual militancy amongst the building workers was interpreted by the NFBTE Executive Committee chairman, J.H. Nicholls, as evidence that the unions were still intent on removing employers' right to manage: 'it is not a struggle for wages, but for the control of industry'.[32]

Initially, the National Federation was unwilling to escalate the dispute by declaring a national lock-out. The latter strategy was opposed by regional associations in south and east England. Official policy was to allow workers to retain employment or return to work, provided they observed the National Wages Agreement and pledged not to support strikers financially.[33] However, the NWFBTE and the Northern Federation (covering north-east England) overrode these instructions, imposing a lock-out of union workers in their respective regions and prophesying 'the destruction of the National Federation' if a national lock-out was not initiated.[34] The NFBTE responded belatedly to this groundswell of pressure, declaring a national lock-out from 26 July 1924.

Solidarity was high in the north-west, with the Liverpool employers, the master plumbers and the master painters adhering to the Federation lock-out. However, there were some significant weaknesses. The lock-out was least effective on the Fylde coast.[35] Municipal authorities, speculative housebuilders, the Co-op and a number of large non-member general contractors continued their construction work across Lancashire, many providing a ½d wage rise and working a 44-hour week.[36] Some took advantage of the conflict and employed strikers. The employers' organisations worked vigorously to ensure the effectiveness of the lock-out, reintroducing the intertrading rule, fining and expelling disloyal firms and attempting, with some success, to prevent the supply of building materials to working firms. 'Stop-supply' lists were circulated to all regional brickmakers and building suppliers and a number of brickyards and suppliers closed down, including all but one in Bolton and Oldham.[37]

In the event, the National Federation negotiated a compromise settlement with the NFBTO three weeks or so into the national lock-out. The settlement allowed for wages to rise by ½d per hour, with an eighteen-

[32] Ibid., 4 July 1924.   [33] Ibid., 16 July 1924.   [34] Ibid., 21 July 1924.
[35] Oldham BTEA, Minutes, 22 July 1924; NWFBTE, Minutes, 6 August 1924.
[36] Manchester BTEA, Minutes, 30 July 1924; Oldham BTEA, Minutes, 28 July 1924; NWFBTE, Minutes, 16 July, 18 July, 25 July, 31 July 1924.
[37] Manchester BTEA, Minutes, 30 July 1924; Oldham BTEA, Minutes, 7 July, 14 July 1924; NWFBTE, Minutes, 31 July, 6 August 1924.

month wage freeze thereafter. However, the stand made by the Liverpool employers was seriously prejudiced by an agreement to allow the exceptional rates on Merseyside to remain for a further year and a half. This was simply postponing an intractable problem and was deeply resented by the Liverpool employers.[38] In the spring of 1926, the issue arose again, when the Liverpool building unions threatened a strike over the loss of their wage differentials. This time the NFBTE took a firm stand, refusing to open joint discussions. The Liverpool employers trenchantly criticised this vacillating strategy by the Federation over 1924–6, acquiesced in the strikers' demands, arbitrarily negotiating wage rises which created an even wider wage differential (2d–3d) between Merseyside wage rates and those elsewhere.[39] This had repercussions across the north-west, drawing labour to Merseyside from adjoining areas like St Helens and Wigan and prompting copycat claims across the region, including Manchester.[40] Facing a barrage of calls for expulsion, Liverpool resigned from the Federation, claiming gross neglect by both the national and regional Federations.[41] The Liverpool association thereafter remained an independent organisation, outside the orbit of the NFBTE until 1942.

Two other challenges to national collective wage bargaining emerged in the mid-1920s, from the National Association of Operative Plasterers (NAOP) and the Amalgamated Union of Building Trade Workers (AUBW: bricklayers and masons). Markets for such labour were particularly tight from 1923 through to the autumn of 1927, encouraging both unions to give notice to secede from the National Wages and Conditions Council in April 1925. Both organisations expressed disgust at the cautious policy of their federation, the NFBTO, and particular dissatisfaction with the 'betrayal' of the 1924 agreement (settling the lock-out) which tied them to an eighteen-month wage freeze.[42] For their part, the organised building employers indicated a firm commitment to preserving the industry-wide wage system: 'The NFBTE will resist to the utmost of its power any action having for its object the substitution of sectional methods of negotiations, either nationally, regionally or locally for the national, industrial method of negotiation at present in force.'[43] This lays bare the intrinsic advantages of the national wage bargaining agreement for the employers' side. It effectively contained the traditional union

---

[38] NWFBTE, Minutes, 4 November 1926.   [39] Ibid., 27 April, 4 November 1926.

[40] Ibid., 19 May, 25 May 1926.

[41] Ibid., 4 November 1926. The Liverpool association went on to try to claw back £500 from the NFBTE of its 1926 subscriptions on the grounds of gross negligence of its interests.

[42] NFBTE, 48th Annual Report, 31 December 1925, p. 2; NWFBTE, Minutes, 21 January, 18 February 1925.   [43] NWFBTE, Minutes, 18 February 1925.

tactic of attacking in detail – using sections where labour markets were most buoyant – then 'snowballing' concessions won throughout the trade. In the 1920s and 1930s, any attempts made by sectional groups such as the plasterers and bricklayers to force more favourable conditions for their sections were firmly resisted by the National Federation, which placed an embargo on any negotiations with particular trade groups.[44]

Again, however, there were divergent views within the Federation on how such threats should be addressed. For bricklayers, a key demand in the 1920s was for 'wet time' compensation.[45] The temperate climate further south made this a non-issue as far as the employers were concerned and National Federation discussions on this question produced a failure to agree in 1925.[46] Conversely, the northern regional federations treated the claims of the AUBW for wet time compensation with much sympathy.[47] This extended to the point of ignoring the National Federation ban on negotiations with the AUBW, opening joint discussions and fleshing out an agreed scheme of compensation over the winter of 1925–6.[48] The proposed insurance scheme was to be jointly financed and administered, providing half pay during inclement weather. Significantly, however, employers retained the sole power to determine when work was to be suspended and all workers were obliged to stay 'within call', or on the site, until the usual finishing time.[49] Even with such provisos, the north-west scheme failed to obtain National Federation approval and was rejected decisively by a Federation national ballot in February 1927.[50] In response, a number of local AUBW branches – including Manchester – threatened strike action in support of the wet time scheme, wage rises and a return to the 44-hour week. The National Federation headed off this agitation by offering an olive branch, agreeing to open joint meetings with the AUBW on wet time if the union reaffiliated to the National Wages and Conditions Council.[51] The union prevaricated, then, with their bargaining position rapidly ebbing with the collapse of the building boom in the autumn of 1927, agreed to these conditions, rejoining the NFBTO and the National Wages and Conditions Council (NWCC).[52] The opportunity for effective industrial action on

---

[44] NWFBTE, *Annual Report*, June 1925; Minutes, 18 March 1925.
[45] The custom in north-west England was for building employers to lay off workers during bad weather, without pay, whilst expecting them to stay either on site or 'within call' – which often meant a predesignated local pub. The bricklayers' claim was effectively for a guaranteed minimum wage during inclement weather.
[46] NFBTE, *48th Annual Report*, 31 December 1925, p. 2.
[47] NWFBTE, Minutes, 21 October, 30 October 1925, 6 January 1926.
[48] Ibid., 3 February 1926.   [49] Ibid., 5 March, 31 March 1926.
[50] Ibid., 7 February 1927.   [51] Ibid., 13 April, 20 April, 11 May 1927.
[52] NWFBTE, *Half-Yearly Report*, 14 December 1927.

wet time had now passed. In the event, wet time was shelved by the Council after several inconclusive joint meetings in 1928 and 1929. The evidence suggests, therefore, that this particular challenge to the 1921 bargaining system in the building industry was most effectively neutralised by a combination of regional flexibility, national intransigence and tactical concession at the critical point in the spring of 1927.

The building employers were also faced in the mid-1920s with a more serious challenge to national, industry-wide bargaining from the operative plasterers. The NAOP were similarly embittered by the conclusion of the 1924 campaign and pursued a strategy thereafter of sectional action, resigning from the NFBTO and the NWCC in 1925. This was in response to rank-and-file dissatisfaction and escalating militancy in the localities. In Manchester, T. Lane, the NAOP secretary, instructed members to work only a 44-hour week, advised them to seek employment at non-federated firms and informed the local employers' association frankly that they would not observe the 1924 agreement under any circumstances.[53] By spring 1925 a number of branches across Lancashire were refusing to work the 46½-hour week and it was reported that some master plasterers had formally accepted such terms.[54] Throughout 1925 the local associations in the north-west were inundated with requests for local joint meetings to establish new joint codes of working conditions for plastering. The official line adopted by the employers was to refuse to recognise the NAOP and ignore such requests.[55] The NWFBTE, however, campaigned within the National Federation for a more conciliatory approach, advocating a greater degree of flexibility within the national framework and more allowance for local circumstances.[56] This bore fruit in the spring of 1926 with the National Federation formulating a new constitution for the NWCC which proposed more decentralisation. Under the proposals regions could submit 'variations' on the national substantive norms for approval, including differential wage rates between building craftsmen.[57]

In the spring of 1926 these proposed reforms patently failed to contain discontent. The NFBTO rejected the differential wage rate. The AUBW wanted inclusion of wet time compensation in principle. The NAOP advocated complete local autonomy, a 44-hour week and an immediate wage rise, threatening strike action in support of such claims.[58] At this point the Liverpool employers conceded wage rises and withdrew from

[53] Manchester BTEA, Minutes, 2 September, 16 September, 27 October 1924.
[54] NWFBTE, Minutes, 17 December 1924, 18 March, 21 April, 13 May 1925.
[55] NWFBTE, *Annual Report*, June 1925, and see the Manchester BTEA, Minutes, 3 May 1926.
[56] NWFBTE, Minutes, 14 October 1925; *Half-Yearly Report*, 22 December 1925.
[57] NWFBTE, Minutes, 10 February, 17 March 1926.   [58] Ibid., 14 April 1926.

the national procedural agreement. In effect, the national, industry-wide
bargaining system was in disarray. The federated employers galvanised
themselves, however, to resist sectional action, reconstitute industry bargaining and retain control over labour costs. In the north-west, employers
voted by a massive majority (2,189 votes to 266) to lock out all building
workers in response to any sectional claim. The focal point swung towards
Manchester, where the NAOP declared a strike in June 1926 to achieve
similar conditions to those conceded in Liverpool.[59]

Whilst it involved only 200 or so workers, the 1926 Manchester plasterers' strike was immediately recognised by the NFBTE to be a pivotal
dispute, over which the system of national industry bargaining hung in
the balance. Their strategy in this instance, however, was to reject
regional pleas for escalation to a lock-out (as in 1924). The National
Federation kept the dispute localised, throwing the full weight of the
organisation behind the attempt to break the plasterers' strike. This
included the formulation of a financial compensation scheme – an
innovation in the industry – through a levy of 6d per £100 wages
exacted upon all National Federation members. At the local level, the
Manchester BTEA and the NWFBTE co-ordinated the task of strikebreaking. They had two basic aims: first, to prevent the strikers getting
work elsewhere, and secondly to find replacement labour. Blacklists of
strikers were circulated widely throughout the region and deputations
organised to non-members, local authorities and member firms sus-
pected of employing strikers.[60] To attract substitute labour, the NFBTE
authorised the Manchester association to advertise and offer wages up
to 5d per hour more than the standard rate. When this failed to
produce a significant response the National Federation broadened
the net, financing advertisements in the national press, appointing
regional agents to find suitable labour and channel it to Manchester
and authorising the granting of other material inducements –
generous travelling and lodging expenses, guaranteed overtime and
two months' guaranteed employment. A local volunteer team of
employers, family members, non-unionist foremen and apprentices
was also formed to tackle contracts of particular urgency, whilst
efforts were made where possible to find alternative materials.[61]
Such efforts were co-ordinated by the specially formed Vigilance
Committee of the Manchester BTEA, operating under the utmost

[59] Manchester BTEA, Minutes, 14 June, 16 June 1926; NWFBTE, Minutes, 17 June, 21 June 1926.
[60] Manchester BTEA, Minutes, 29 June 1926; NWFBTE, Minutes, 16 August 1926.
[61] Manchester BTEA, Minutes, 30 July 1926.

secrecy.[62] This soon had an appreciable impact, with large contingents of blackleg labour regularly arriving in Manchester from early August, despite heavy picketing. Faced with this *fait accompli*, and lacking support within the industry, the NAOP called off the strike, returning to work after nine weeks on the conditions which prevailed before the stoppage.

This sealed, temporarily at least, another significant fissure in the 1921 settlement. The Manchester branch of the NAOP was forced to accept the principle that 'no local agreement is possible except under a national agreement' and that pending a national agreement a truce be declared.[63] The dispute was also important in another sense. The building employers absorbed the tactical lesson that localising this dispute and providing generous financial support to Manchester had achieved a significant victory. Subsequently, moves were made to formalise a strike indemnity scheme by the NFBTE, 'aimed at restricting the area disturbed . . . to avoid the cumbersome and costly method of a lock-out'.[64] The 6d per £100 levy exacted on members in 1926 became an annual levy into what became known as the National Defence Fund. This marked a significant transition in building employers' strikebreaking methods from escalation towards localisation of disputes. The Fund was to serve an important function in subsequent disputes, including in 1928 when confrontation again flared up with the plasterers.

By the end of 1926, the NFBTE were congratulating themselves that they had neutralised the sectional demands of the plasterers and bricklayers and that changed economic circumstances upon the horizon would enable control over labour to be consolidated: 'The time is approaching when the demand for the services of the last two classes of operatives will fall to a point such that they will not be able to uphold their present attitudes and that when that time arrives they will have to fall in line with the wishes of the employers and accept the National Agreement.'[65] This transition was by no means as smooth as the employers anticipated, nor was the 1926 defeat of the plasterers as complete as the employers had hoped. With the onset of the building recession from the autumn of 1927,

[62] Ibid., 5, 9, 10 August. The clandestine nature of the association's strikebreaking activities was tightened after an embarrassing incident during the first week in August. Representatives of the Manchester BTEA turned up at Manchester Victoria railway station to meet a contingent of replacees only to be cut off by T. Lane (the Manchester NAOP secretary) and a group of pickets. A heated argument ensued, during which Lane threatened to throw the employers' secretary, John Denver, on to the rails. The employers concluded that the union must have been 'tipped off' by a 'traitor' in their own ranks who knew of the secret rendezvous at the station.

[63] NWFBTE, Minutes, 19 August 1926; Manchester BTEA, Minutes, 23 August 1926.

[64] NWFBTE, *Half-Yearly Report*, 15 December 1926.

[65] NWFBTE, Minutes, 8 December 1926.

building industry wages were cut under the sliding scale agreement in February 1928 by ½d per hour to 1s 7½d.[66] Whilst the NFBTO accepted such cuts peacefully, the NAOP resisted, the Manchester branch countering with claims for a rise to 2 shillings per hour and a five-day working week.[67] The situation was most critical in Lancashire, where employers in most districts had unofficially been paying their plasterers 2d per hour above standard wage rates since the 1926 settlement. The Manchester BTEA and the NWFBTE were determined that the time was opportune to bring plasterers' wages back into line with those of other building craftsmen and were acutely aware of the dangers of setting another regional overpaying precedent after Liverpool.[68] The situation across the region was, however, more complicated. The independent National Association of Master Plasterers refused to co-operate with the NFBTE and continued to sanction a 1s 10d hourly rate. Citing this as an excuse, some local employers' associations, including relatively large ones in Southport and Accrington, concluded unofficial local agreements to pay 1s 9d or 1s 10d per hour to their plasterers. Elsewhere, in Bolton and Bury for example, the wage cuts were peacefully accepted, whilst strikes in opposition to employer notices to cut wages to 1s 7½d erupted in Wigan, Altrincham, Blackburn and Manchester. In all these instances the employers held firm, their resistance bolstered by generous financial support through the recently established National Defence Fund.[69]

Manchester, where around 400 plasterers, labourers and apprentices went on strike from 1 May 1928, was again the focal point. The state of labour markets in 1928 should have helped the employers to find replacement labour. In practice, however, the task of finding substitutes for striking plasterers was even more difficult in 1928 than in 1926. This was partly because the NAOP addressed significant weaknesses in their 1926 campaign. Moreover, the intractable problem of the inefficiency of the substitute labour plagued the employers. In the first phase of the strike-breaking campaign a little over 300 replacees were found. Of these, 160 had to be rejected as 'incompetent'.[70] But 140 or so were employed, although within a week (by mid-June) only 62 remained. Picketing was reported to be particularly effective, with sabotage, predominantly through theft of tools, much in evidence. In the event, it took the local association and NWFBTE fully three months to obtain something approaching a full complement of workers (336 semi-permanent replacees).[71] The problems with quality of work, however, remained.

[66] Ibid., 1 February 1927, 20 January 1928.
[67] Ibid., 6 November 1927, 22 February 1928.   [68] Ibid., 16 November 1927.
[69] Ibid., 15 February, 9 May, 22 May 1928.   [70] Ibid., 22 May, 13 June 1928.
[71] Manchester BTEA, Minutes, 1 August, 15 August 1928.

Output was significantly lower, complaints proliferated and some jobs had to be replastered and repaired.[72] In one case, the Clerk of Works ordered the substitute labour off the site on the grounds of unsatisfactory workmanship.[73] Other contracts involving particularly skilled work (such as fibrous plastering) were seriously delayed. Attempts to import outside contractors to complete such work failed when the NAOP threatened to extend the strike to all such companies' work.[74] Nor was the victimisation of strikers particularly effective in 1928. It was reported that the most skilled of the Manchester plasterers had experienced little trouble in getting work within the region.[75] The NFBTE position in this respect was compromised by a large non-federated segment (reported to be employing around 120 plasterers) and by Manchester Corporation, who employed around 100 plasterers (at the 1s 10d rate).[76]

This experience left the Manchester employers embittered and, by September 1928, convinced that a national lock-out was necessary to defeat the union. Other local associations were castigated for their lack of tangible support and the National Federation for apathy and inaction. Clearly, the loyalty of the Manchester association was being severely strained by the longevity of the strike: 'If the Federation are not sufficiently strong to enforce their will upon the small group of operatives who remain out on strike then it would become a question for the Association to consider as to whether it would not do better acting on its own and effecting local agreements with the operatives.'[77] The NWFBTE also supported escalation of the dispute by resort to a lock-out. However, the National Federation could not obtain a mandate from the other regions, which clearly favoured localising the dispute in Manchester.[78] As in 1926, the situation was stabilised with direct intervention from the National Federation, which dispatched a deputation of representatives to Manchester to inject new vigour into strikebreaking operations. By mid-December the situation was reported to be firmly under control, with a full complement of reasonably skilled replacees and satisfactory progress on all contracts.[79] The plasterers, however, held out for a further two months before obtaining a formal settlement, through Ministry of Labour mediation.

The terms of settlement were harsh indeed, reflecting the dominant

---

[72] Ibid., 4 July, 27 August, 1 October 1928; NWFBTE, Minutes, 13 June, 10 July, 19 July, 15 August 1928.   [73] NWFBTE, Minutes, 10 July 1928.   [74] Ibid., 21 June 1928.
[75] Manchester BTEA, Minutes, 1 October 1928.
[76] NWFBTE, Minutes, 15 August 1928.
[77] Manchester BTEA, Minutes, 1 October 1928; NWFBTE, Minutes, 10 September, 3 October 1928.   [78] NWFBTE, Minutes, 14 November 1928.
[79] Ibid., 12 December 1928, 11 February 1929; Manchester BTEA, Minutes, 11 February 1929.

position of the building employers in the late 1920s. The NFBTE, negotiating with the NAOP for the Manchester employers, agreed only that
strikers would be re-engaged 'when practicable' on the wages, conditions
and hours laid down by the National Joint Council for the industry.[80]
When pressed by the Manchester NAOP secretary (T. Lane) the
Manchester employers refused to commit themselves to dismissing
replacees, who were retained where they were willing to accept Joint
Council conditions, including the industry wage rate of 1s 7½d.[81] The
Manchester strike was the final point of resistance for the NAOP, which
had supported strikes across a broad front, including Birmingham and
the north-east, all of which had collapsed by August 1928. Thereafter the
union remained defeated and demoralised, eventually reafiliating to the
National Joint Council on a formal basis in 1933.[82]

Preservation of industry-wide bargaining involved, therefore, tactical
procrastination (AUBW) and forcible strikebreaking (NAOP) by the
employers. However, use of the stick was tempered by concessions
designed to strengthen the position of the moderate building union federation, the NFBTO, and enhance its commitment to the National Wages
and Conditions Council. In return for the suspension of the differential
wages clause, the NFBTO formally accepted a new, more decentralised
and flexible constitution for the NWCC. The 1926 reforms retained a
national framework of substantive norms – wages, hours and other
working conditions such as overtime and travelling time – but provided
for regional and area joint committees which could formulate variations
reflecting local circumstances. This included the creation of exceptional
wage rates for a limited period to address peculiar permutations in local
labour markets.[83] This was followed in 1927 with some significant streamlining of the national disputes procedure (through the adoption of the so-
called 'Green Book'), which added a local emergency joint disputes
committee and formalised arrangements to meet regularly through the
duration of a stoppage in an attempt to find an amicable settlement.[84]

Significantly, it was this formula, combined with the decisive action of
the employers' organisations in the construction sector when faced with
sectional action over the period 1924–8, which ensured the survival of the
industrial relations system set up in 1921, albeit in a somewhat less centralised and bureaucratic mode. The key objectives of wage standardisation, control over labour costs and reassertion of managerial discipline

---

[80] NWFBTE, *Annual Report*, June 1929; Minutes, 21 February, 28 February 1929.
[81] NWFBTE, Minutes, 13 March 1929.   [82] Ibid., 22 May 1933.
[83] Ibid., 28 July, 15 September 1926.
[84] *National Builder*, August 1934, pp. 4–5, September 1934, p. 39; Bullough, *First Fifty*,
pp. 59–60; NWFBTE, *Annual Report*, June 1927; *Half-Yearly Report*, 27 November 1929.

had been achieved and local and sectional challenges – with the sole exception of Liverpool – were effectively neutralised by 1929. However, the struggles of the 1920s had clearly indicated the weaknesses, fragmentation and divisions of interest within the industry. The NFBTE was a significant power bloc, but by no means an omnipotent one. In 1929, organised capital in construction faced a strategic choice. Employers could exploit overstocked labour markets to press their advantage further, eroding craft controls and attacking trade unionism. Alternatively, they could pursue a less confrontational and more co-operative policy with organised labour. Organisational weaknesses and divergent market experience constrained choices, helping to persuade building employers' organisations to opt for the latter.

Wage cuts in pace with deflation were imposed over this period under the sliding scale and accepted without opposition by the unions, including the NAOP. However, in contrast to the early 1920s (and to the engineering and cotton industries), the building employers made no concerted attempt to cut real wages during 1929–33. The organised employers firmly resisted claims from the union side which would have increased labour costs, such as 'wet time' compensation, tool allowances and a wage freeze.[85] On the other hand, there were no serious initiatives by the building employers' organisations to force reorganisation of work or attack existing work regulations. If anything, the employers' federations appear to have been acting as a constraining force upon some of the more militant and aggressive local associations. In the spring of 1930, responding to pressure from members, the NFBTE did propose to the National Joint Council a modest package of cost-cutting proposals, including more flexible working hours and overtime rules, an alteration in the sliding scale basis (effectively leading to a wage cut) and reductions in labourers' and painters' wage differentials *vis-à-vis* craftsmen.[86] Significantly, however, these claims were dropped when the NFBTO countered with proposals to suspend the sliding scale wage regulator and threatened their resignation from the National Joint Council when negotiations broke down.[87] In another case, a campaign began amongst several local associations to scrap what was regarded as a generous scheme providing travelling expenses to bricklayers in Manchester. Action in this instance was vetoed by the NWFBTE, who argued that it was hardly worth while being dogmatic and provoking a conflict when relations between capital and labour were so good.[88] Later, in 1932, the

---

[85] NWFBTE, Minutes, 11 December 1929, 11 November 1931.   [86] Ibid., 6 March 1930.
[87] Ibid., 1 October 1930; *Annual Report*, June 1931.
[88] NWFBTE, Minutes, 7 January 1930, 12 February 1930.

existence of the Manchester expenses scheme was formally accepted by the National Federation. Evidently, above all else, the building employers valued the maintenance of wage standardisation and the preservation of orderly industrial relations, particularly with the NFBTO. Sustaining the status quo was deemed more important than provoking conflict.

Market circumstances altered from the mid-1930s, with a revival first in housebuilding, followed by sustained activity in the commercial sector, stimulated by rearmament. This increase in building activity had a significant impact upon industrial relations, resuscitating workers' bargaining power and creating a fresh round of challenges for the employers' organisations in the trade. Three related issues predominated: wages policy, 'peripheral' costs, and control over labour markets.

As labour markets tightened, the NFBTE intensified attempts to maintain a labour surplus, thus enhancing employers' bargaining power with the trade unions. This was achieved by pressuring members to prioritise recruitment of new labour rather than unemployed craftsmen. The aim was to increase the ratio of apprentices to craftsmen employed, and, where possible, to make use of intermediate labour, such as the 'brush-hands' who had not been through a formal apprenticeship. The Federation's internally generated statistics on recruitment suggest some limited success in the application of this strategy of labour market manipulation, though there were marked regional and sectional variations in experience.[89] Particularly heavy recruitment – more than three times the national average – of apprentice plumbers and plasterers took place in the early/mid-1930s. Perhaps significantly, neither group figured within the more militant sections of the trade over the period 1935–9. The employers who were most successful in achieving high apprentice-to-journeymen ratios were those in Scotland and the north of England; apprentice numbers were particularly low in London and the south. This pattern reflected the quite different labour market circumstances under which building employers operated – in short, the greater availability of alternative work adversely affected building contractors in London and the south, whilst the opposite was the case in the depressed, heavy industrial heartlands of the north.

Inevitably, given the improved market circumstances, building employers faced pressure from organised labour to improve wages and working conditions. In response to an NFBTO claim for an improvement in real wages (irrespective of changes under the sliding scale) the NFBTE conceded a 1d per hour rise (given over two stages, in July 1935 and January 1936). However, there were important strings attached to this concession:

[89] NWFBTE, *Annual Report*, June 1935; *Half-Yearly Report*, 30 November 1936.

namely a joint agreement for a five-year moratorium on applications for wage increases beyond the sliding scale and upon claims for regrading districts for three years.[90] This provided contractors with the opportunity to stabilise labour costs, aiding more accurate tendering in the later 1930s.

However, individual building contractors found it increasingly difficult, in practice, to maintain basic wage rates. Upward wage drift re-emerged as a significant problem in the later 1930s, despite concerted Federation attempts to retain control over industry wage rates.[91] In the north-west the position of federated employers was compromised by high wages paid by speculative housebuilders and by the Liverpool wage settlement in 1938, which provided for staged wage rises (irrespective of living costs) in 1938, 1939 and 1940.[92] Moreover, the constraints imposed by the wage freeze encouraged unions to seek material compensation by other routes. Regional federations were inundated with claims for the establishment of differential payments and exceptional rates, particularly where government defence contracts were being worked.[93] Claims also flooded in during 1938–9 to upgrade areas, thus securing indirect wage rises.

The building employers' organisations responded in a positive fashion to this escalating labour offensive from the mid-1930s, as often as not meeting demands with joint negotiations and concessions. Significant improvement in work regulations appears to have been accepted by employers as a quid pro quo for industrial relations stability. Hence, in considering possible resistance to regional joiners' claims for a tool allowance (½d per hour) in 1938 the NWFBTE argued: 'a strike would be difficult to meet under present conditions and the demands of the government programme. It might be sound policy to appease the joiners by meeting their claim for tool money.'[94] A scheme was subsequently fleshed out providing 2d a day tool allowance, incorporated in the National Joint Council Wages and Conditions Agreement. The North-West Regional Joint Council conceded additional wage rates to masons fixing worked stone, to labourers working with pneumatic picks and for 'dirty' work in 1938.[95] Two more fundamental concessions were granted at the national level. In 1937, the employers' side of the National Joint Council accepted the principle of some financial compensation for time lost during wet

[90] NWFBTE, *Annual Report*, June 1935.
[91] Ibid., June 1937; NWFBTE, Minutes, 22 April 1936, 10 June 1936.
[92] NWFBTE, Minutes, 18 October 1938.
[93] Ibid., Minutes, 23 June 1938; *Annual Reports*, 31 December 1937, 31 December 1938; *Half-Yearly Report*, June 1939.   [94] NWFBTE, Minutes, 11 May 1938.
[95] Ibid., 21 September 1938.

weather in the trade. An agreement emerged which legalised wet time payments within the industry under the 1935 Unemployment Act.[96] Secondly, a scheme providing holidays with pay, drawn up by the London Master Builders' Association, was also accepted by the National Federation, though, as with the wet time scheme, war intervened before this could be implemented.[97]

Conclusion

Does all this imply that the building employers' organisations were failing to protect members' interests in the later 1930s? Probably not. The evidence suggests that these organisations were flowing with the tide of members' views rather than diverging from constituent opinion. Membership figures for the NWFBTE, at least, suggest that the proportion of the trade organised improved – albeit marginally – in the later 1930s. Moreover, on the eve of the Second World War the building employers' associations could legitimately congratulate themselves on a number of grounds. First, stability had been maintained in industrial relations, with working days lost through industrial disputes remaining at negligible levels through the 1930s. This contrasted sharply with the industrial relations experience during a similar phase of quite intense building activity during the years immediately before the First World War. Secondly, labour costs, particularly basic wages, had remained under control, with industry-wide wage rate standardisation intact, though there had been some noticeable drift in earnings and in non-wage labour costs. Both these outcomes – wage standardisation and industrial relations stabilisation – were manufactured by the employers' organisations in the industry. They were a product of a mature disputes procedure, which the employers' organisations struggled hard to sustain, and a policy of active support for the more moderate NFBTO, firm acceptance and prosecution of joint bargaining in the industry, the negotiation of a wage and regrading freeze in 1935 and a substantive system pivoting around a cost of living sliding scale which effectively took basic wages out of contention. Nor were the building employers' associations active and provocative champions of managerial prerogative, in the mould of the EEF. In the event, the strategic choice of flexible appeasement – via a series of concessions on working conditions and wages – successfully deflected building unions from pursuing sectional action outside the

[96] NWFBTE, *Annual Report*, June 1937 (though this was not operative until after the Second World War).
[97] NWFBTE, Minutes, 18 October 1938.

established collective bargaining system. National, industry-wide collective bargaining, on a range of substantive issues, had been defended by the building industry employers' associations in the 1920s and the system was consolidated in the 1930s. In the circumstances, given the relative organisational weaknesses of the building employers' associations and events in other less sheltered industries, this, in itself, was of no small significance.

9   Defending managerial prerogative: engineering

This chapter examines the industrial relations policies of engineering employers' associations during the inter-war economic recession. A key issue taken up is how the industry responded to economic change – first the sharp and sustained economic recession and later the rapid recovery which came with rearmament from the mid-1930s. Previous published studies have tended to concentrate upon the national, industry-wide perspective, with the debate pivoting on the question of employers' collective authority and power during the slump.[1] One interpretation stresses the altered balance of power in the employers' favour during the 1920–35 period. Gospel posits that, despite serious divisions within engineering employers' ranks, their organisations exploited the enhanced bargaining power conferred by market developments and the collapse of trade unionism to play a primary role in structuring industrial relations during these years.[2] Zeitlin argues, conversely, that engineering employers' organisations between the wars were weakened by internal strife and patently failed to influence industrial relations at all levels – within the workplace, the local labour market and at the national/political level.[3] According to Zeitlin, engineering employers were unable to exploit the success of the 1922 national lock-out to 'Americanise' industrial relations and achieve a transformation in the division of labour in the industry. Hence, the industry's long-term competitiveness was fundamentally compromised.

The aim here is to examine such interpretations critically in the light of detailed evidence from a single region. Thus developments within engineering factories and within local labour markets are brought more sharply into focus, whilst internal divisions within the engineering

---

[1] For a regional study of Clydeside engineering see Alan McKinlay's Ph.D. thesis, 'Employers and skilled workers'.

[2] See Gospel, 'Employers and managers', pp. 170–1; Gospel, 'Employers' organisations', pp. 156–9, 267–73.

[3] Zeitlin, 'Internal politics'; see also McKinlay and Zeitlin, 'The meanings of managerial prerogative', pp. 32–47.

employers' power bloc will be identified. My argument is that the revisionist perspective has unduly narrowed the benchmark for evaluation of employers' organisation behaviour, overly sanitised their activities during this period and that engineering employers' associations did indeed play a significant role in structuring industrial relations, protecting business interests and championing anti-socialist ideas between the wars. The evidence for north-west England suggests that there was a unifying, proactive employers' movement in this period, and that the engineering employers' associations were within the vanguard of an offensive designed to cut labour costs and reassert managerial authority which proceeded in tandem with an ideological crusade to disseminate the virtues of private, free-enterprise capitalism.

The economic and organisational context

Tight labour markets, the challenge of labour during the First World War and the increasingly interventionist policies of the government, whilst undermining employers' bargaining power, ultimately strengthened their cohesion in engineering over the decade 1910–20. This was reflected at a number of levels. First, association membership increased rapidly during wartime. The number of affiliated firms in the EEF rose from 744 in 1914 to 2,440 in 1920, representing more than a doubling of employing capacity.[4] Secondly, the integration of local associations was strengthened through the creation of a network of regional federations. Thirdly, the representation of employer organisations within the corridors of political power was considerably enhanced by the creation of the Federation of British Industries and the National Confederation of Employers' Organisations. The EEF was a prime mover in the formation of the NCEO and a key player within the Confederation in its early years. A crop of other new organisations was spawned during this critical period of destabilisation in industrial relations, providing specialist anti-labour services, such as the Economic League, with which the engineering employers' organisations maintained a quite intimate relationship between the wars. This point will be returned to later.

The growth spurt in employer organisations peaked in 1920–1 and stagnation set in thereafter as trading conditions in engineering worsened. As order books contracted, unemployment of AEU members nationally rose from 4.3 per cent in December 1921, to 15 per cent by March 1921, and 31 per cent by June 1921, fluctuating thereafter between 20 and 25 per cent through 1921 and 1922, significantly above the

---

[4] Figures for EEF membership are derived from Wigham, *Power to Manage*, pp. 303–4.

Table 9.1 *Engineering workers on short-time (percentages), 1924–35*

	1924	1928	1931	1935
Marine engineering	2.6	1.1	33.7	22.4
Agricultural engineering	18.0	7.7	45.0	47.1
Textile engineering	52.5	37.0	64.6	54.9
Structural engineering	3.2	5.4	18.8	9.2
Larger motor and cycle	4.6	3.3	18.6	24.2
Smaller motor/cycle	2.5	2.7	6.6	2.7
General engineering	6.4	3.9	26.7	15.1
Total engineering	7.7	4.9	22.4	18.1

Source: *Ministry of Labour Gazette*, cited in Gospel, 'Employers' organisations', p. 50.

national average. There was some improvement in trade thereafter, with the proportion out of work declining to between 11 and 15 per cent during 1924–6 and to around 8–10 per cent (around 80,000 in engineering) during 1927–9.[5] These aggregated figures obscure, however, a great deal of variation in experience within what was an extremely diverse sector. Product markets for the capital goods, export-orientated segments of the engineering industry – including textile machine making, locomotives, agricultural machinery, engines and machine tools – were worst affected, whilst the consumer goods, home-market-orientated sector – including electrical engineering, cycles and motor vehicles – fared much better. Few engineering employers, however, escaped the deleterious impact of the 1929–32 slump.

With the slump, trade union membership in engineering atrophied. By 1933, AEU membership had shrunk to a low of 168,000, just 40 per cent of its 1920 membership of 423,000.[6]

Such conditions worked initially to enhance employers' authority and bargaining power significantly, whilst proving somewhat corrosive of employer solidarity within the heterogeneous engineering sector by the later 1920s. The latter might be expected, given the diminution of the vital cementing pressures of trade unionism and state intervention. Variation in the impact of the recession on different sectors of the trade made the formulation of a consensus policy increasingly difficult. Witness, for example, the wide differences in unemployment levels in mechanical engineering compared to the motor vehicles, cycles and aircraft sectors.[7]

[5] EEF, *Realities*, p. 3.
[6] Clegg, *A History of British Trade Unions*, vol. II, p. 570; Jefferys, *Story of the Engineers*, p. 292.
[7] EEF, *Realities*, pp. 41–5.

The intensity of the recession forced some firms to seek short-term economic advantage outside the organisation, with breakaways coming from both more militant and more progressive employers who felt alienated from the 'Federation line'.[8] From the mid-1920s, disloyalty within the Federation was also much in evidence, with member firms ignoring agreements and turning a blind eye to local standard wage rates and working conditions.[9]

However, what is most striking, given the circumstances, is the degree to which employer organisation membership in engineering was sustained during the recession. Membership of the EEF, which had peaked at 2,690 companies in 1922, fell back to 1,806 members by 1935. Undoubtedly, however, much of this shortfall can be accounted for by liquidations, company mergers and the haemorrhaging of relatively small member firms. It is difficult to be definite about whether this represented any real fall in the proportion of the industry organised. The EEF statements on density recruited are prone to exaggeration and notoriously unreliable. It appears, however, that even at the nadir of the recession the EEF-organised firms employed around two-thirds of those working in the industry.[10] In Manchester, the decline in the number of engineering companies functioning between 1920 and 1939 (from 357 to 156) far outstripped the fall in association membership (from 201 to 164). At the very least, evidence suggests that the coverage and viability of the EEF was sustained during the slump far more effectively than the engineering trade unions. Moreover, as union membership revived from 1933 to 1934, so too did employer organisation membership. EEF national membership increased to 2,023 companies by 1939, with numbers employed more than doubling between 1933 and 1939 to 861,200.[11] This relative organisational success served further to enhance employers' collective power (bolstered by labour market and political developments) between the wars in relation to organised labour.

Employer organisation in engineering was, however, changing significantly in character over this period and, if anything, internal divisions were sharpening. On the one hand, the EEF was becoming more professionalised, with a cadre of full-time officials. The old guard of employers who had forged the 1898 settlement were passing out of the frame. Power

---

[8] Fifty-one firms were expelled from the EEF for not posting notices to lock out in 1922 and 1926.

[9] For examples see Lancashire JSC, *Minutes*, 1 September 1925, 3 November 1925, 5 April 1927, 1 November 1927, 4 September 1928, 6 November 1928.

[10] Gospel, 'Employers' organisations', p. 100. Gospel estimates the degree of exaggeration in the region of +25 per cent. The EEF claimed to represent around 90 per cent of the productive capacity of the industry.   [11] Wigham, *Power to Manage*, pp. 303–4.

Table 9.2 *Engineering employers' associations: Lancashire membership 1920, 1930, 1939*

	1920[1]		1930[1]		1939[1]	
Barrow	1	8,706	1	5,783	1	11,600
Birkenhead	3	2,060	1	1,382	2	2,596
Blackburn	29	8,084	18	6,548	22	5,957
Bolton	66	10,874	60	4,187	61	8,343
Burnley	28	1,848	15	602	16	1,063
Liverpool	28	4,762	23	5,120	21	14,129
Manchester	207	67,630	170	47,252	164	75,884
Oldham	32	13,035	21	9,769	18	6,427
Preston	35	7,601	26	7,811	31	10,065
Rochdale	33	4,281	28	2,157	32	3,099
St Helens	9	312	5	233	5	492
Wigan	14	1,743	12	599	11	928
Total (Lancs.)	485	130,936	380	91,443	384	140,583
Total (EEF)	2,440	698,746	2,024	466,415	2,023	809,923

[1] In each case the first column represents the number of member firms; the second represents number of employees in member firms.

Sources: EEF, Levy Registers, Numbers Employed Files, Annual Subscription Files, May 1920, September 1930 and October 1939.[12]

within the organisation, once dominated by the heavy capital goods companies concentrated in the older industrial regions of the north, was drifting inexorably towards the newer, more prosperous consumer goods producers located predominantly in the midlands and the south. In north-west England the stranglehold of the mechanical engineers over association policy atrophied. By 1939, eight of the largest ten member firms in the Manchester EEA were involved in the arms, electrical, motor and aeronautical sectors.[13]

Moreover, the recession threw up marked differentials in product market experience, exacerbated in the late 1930s by the maldistribution of government rearmament orders. Such marked disparities in experience strained loyalty to the organisation and to collective policies. Indeed, it became increasingly difficult for the EEF to develop a consensus labour relations strategy which would satisfy the disparate interests of all its members. Whilst the regulatory power of the engineering employers'

[12] Note: these figures are slight underestimates of actual numbers employed by the EEF based upon incomplete membership surveys. For example, in 1930 returns came in from member firms representing only 92.5 per cent of total Federation employing capacity. In 1939, the figure was 94.2 per cent.   [13] Manchester EEA, *Journal*, 1897–1953.

organisations remained significant in the 1920s and 1930s and should not be underestimated, it is possible, even before the Second World War, to detect an increasing devolution of initiative in industrial relations from the EEF to the local associations, and from the organisations to the constituent companies. National agreements, the EEF discovered in a survey in the mid-1930s, were routinely flouted.[14] Interest in the work of the employers' organisation declined, reflected in the later 1930s, when the twenty-strong executive committee of the Manchester EEA had to be left permanently understaffed because of lack of interest amongst directors and principals of member firms.[15]

The employers' counter-attack

Even prior to the economic slump that began in the winter of 1920 there is evidence that engineering employers' associations were galvanising their membership to resist what they regarded as further encroachments into managerial terrain. At the national level in 1919–20, the Federation remained conciliatory, pursuing, as a primary strategy, the creation of an all-embracing national agreement covering a range of substantive issues.[16] Elements of such a policy include the 1919 piecework agreement, the 1920 overtime and nightshift agreement and the incorporation of engineering shop stewards into the formal disputes procedure in 1919. A number of local employers' associations, however, including West Scotland and Manchester, pursued a more militant line.[17] Strikes to achieve skilled status and wage rates for armature and transformer winders and assemblers at British Westinghouse and Ferranti were successfully broken by the Manchester EEA, which organised replacement labour and the blacklisting of strikers. Significantly, in this instance the employers retained the right to employ labourers on this class of work. A resolute stand was also taken against the Iron and Steel Dressers' Society in the summer of 1919. Their claim for the abolition of piecework and overtime, and for a wage rise, was dropped after the Manchester EEA threatened a retaliatory lock-out. The stakes were raised even higher during a dispute with the sheet-metal and foundry workers towards the

---

[14] Zeitlin, 'Internal politics', p. 72.
[15] Manchester EEA, Minutes, 10 January, 7 February 1938. Gospel notes a similar decline in participation in the 1930s; see Gospel, 'Employers' organisations', p. 127.
[16] Zeitlin, 'Internal politics', pp. 67–8.
[17] For more detailed analysis of Clydeside see McKinlay, 'Employers and skilled workers', pp. 82–111. McKinlay argues that the relative homogeneity of Clydeside engineering – dominated by marine engineering and shipbuilding – facilitated a strong collective identity and that the Clyde employers were amongst the most aggressive in the post-war years.

end of 1919. These unions had banned overtime at fifty-eight Lancashire firms, unless it was paid at double rates. The employers responded with the threat of a Lancashire-wide lock-out of engineering firms, which was supported by the EEF with the threat of subsequent escalation to a national lock-out. The union's reaction was to settle in January 1920, unconditionally agreeing to remove all overtime and piecework embargoes.

As trade slumped and unemployment escalated, the engineering employers' offensive intensified and coalesced into a three-pronged attack: to cut labour costs, to revive managerial authority and to re-establish ideological commitment to free-market capitalist enterprise. At the national level, the moderate tone of Allan Smith (EEF president) and the conciliatory strategy of the EEF during wartime gave way to a more confrontational stance. Wage rates were the initial point of conflict. In 1921–2 the employers took advantage of falling prices and rising unemployment to enforce the deepest wage cuts in the history of the trade, amounting to a reduction of over 20 per cent. Meanwhile, local firms were rapidly eliminating the wage inducements and other enticements that had been the norm during the 1910s. This was achieved in the face of union resistance and wildcat protest strikes.[18] The trend reversed to wage cribbing and undercutting of the association's minimum rate. The employers argued that to remain viable in the intensified competitive environment of the early 1920s and to attract orders they were compelled to slash production costs ruthlessly.

The costs reduction drive of 1921–2 was submerged by a parallel strategy of the engineering employers – an attempt to restore the supremacy of managerial control and prerogative in the workplace. On 7 April 1921, the EEF informed the engineering unions that they would initiate an industry-wide lock-out if the unions did not end all embargoes placed on overtime by union committees, drop the claim that unions were to be consulted before overtime was worked, allow apprentices to work on systems of payments by results (where they had worked on piecework prior to the war) and recognise the employers' rights to employ whom they chose on their machinery, without conditions being laid down by the union. This was almost a complete restatement of the principles of the 1898 Terms of Settlement.[19]

The AEU was determined to resist and in a national conference the

[18] Lancashire JSC, Minutes, 23 August, 4 October, 8 November, 6 December 1921; Oldham EEA, Minutes, 18 August 1921; Manchester EEA, Minutes, 6 February, 1 June – 10 August 1921. For example, apprentices went on strike at around half of the Manchester EEA firms when wages were cut and 'adult' bonuses removed from those over 18.

[19] See Shadwell, *The Engineering Industry*, pp. 51–3.

unions' interpretation of the Overtime and Nightshift Agreement was wholeheartedly supported. Initially, the employers decided to take no action to enforce their claims, but bide their time and allow the recession to erode further the financial resources of the unions. In November 1921, the employers returned to the question. A memorandum was drawn up defining managerial functions, asserting that the employers 'have the right to decide when overtime is necessary'.[20] The EEF received numerous expressions of solidarity from its members. In Manchester, the employers voted unanimously in favour of the memorandum.[21]

In a ballot in January 1922, the AEU rejected the claim that the employers had the right to decide unilaterally when overtime was to be worked or the right to introduce alterations in working conditions before the disputes procedure was exhausted.[22] This, the shop stewards argued, would effectively sanction overtime, which would amount to a 'betrayal of the unemployed'.[23] The employers argued that the adverse ballot challenged 'the whole principle of control' and forced them, in the national interest, 'to place the industry on a sound economic basis'.[24] The Manchester EEA stated that, by rejecting the memorandum, the AEU was directly challenging 'a principle of fundamental importance to industry; that is the right of the employers to exercise managerial functions in their establishments'.[25] The gist of EEF propaganda was to emphasise this challenge – that the unions were arrogating to themselves the right to manage industry – in order to maximise support. Allan Smith continually talked of the fight as one between the 'soviet system' and private enterprise.[26] The perceived challenge to the capitalist system of hierarchical managerial control was spelled out unequivocally in an EEF statement on 10 March 1922:

Let it be clearly stated that the overtime question is not the issue on which the parties have failed to come to an agreement, but is a matter, the solution of which cannot be achieved until the main issue has been settled. That issue is a refusal by the trade unions to continue the recognition of the employer's right to exercise

[20] Manchester EEA, Minutes, 3 November, 16 November 1921.
[21] Ibid., 5 December 1921.
[22] Ibid., 1 February 1922. The voting was 50,240 against accepting the memo and 35,525 for.   [23] *Manchester Guardian*, 7 March 1922, p. 9.
[24] Shadwell, *The Engineering Industry*, p. 57.
[25] Manchester EEA, Minutes, 16 February 1922.
[26] The transition in Smith's attitude from open support for Whitleyism in 1918 to his vociferous prosecution of the 1922 lock-out was noted wryly by a number of observers. See, for example, the editorial in *Manchester Guardian*, 13 March 1922, p. 7. The AEU district secretary for Liverpool wrote: 'those members who believed that as a consequence of the war, the demeanour and attitude of the employers would change must have experienced a rude shock; they will outrival even Herod. Their main argument is force – a so be it policy' (*AEU Monthly Journal*, April 1922, p. 45).

managerial functions in his establishment, unless with the consent and approval of the unions, which must be obtained prior to the initiation of any managerial act to which the union might feel inclined to take exception.

The position of the employers is, therefore, in defence of a right which, although encroached upon during the stress of war and during the post-war period, has never been officially challenged until now. That it has been challenged is no longer in doubt, nor the fact that it seeks to alter fundamentally the relation which has hitherto existed in the conduct of industry, and to establish a dual administrative control of the shops.[27]

Work in engineering firms was practically at a standstill because of the trade depression, so it was a perfect opportunity for an all-out stoppage as far as the employers were concerned. G.D.H. Cole observed:

It would suit the engineering employers just now to have a national lock-out. Orders are very slack. The AEU has paid away already over £2,000,000 in out-of-work benefit; one quarter of its 400,000 members are totally unemployed, and most of the rest are on short time. It is a moment, from the employers' point of view, for seizing the chance of administering a salutary lesson to the workers at less than no cost to the firms in the industry. A temporary shutting down will be good business from the purely commercial standpoint; it will be better business if it carries with it the defeat of the workers' organisations.[28]

The lock-out, which began on 11 March 1922, was supported by 98.5 per cent of the EEF voting power.[29]

In 1897, both sides lined up for the industry-wide lock-out with practically equal chances of success. In 1922, however, economic circumstances made an employers' victory highly likely from the very beginning. The AEU officials anticipated this and had recommended acceptance in the February ballot. Prior to the lock-out, around 92,000 members of the AEU were out of work and a great many more were on short-time. This had already seriously drained union funds, as Cole noted. The lock-out increased the number of AEU members unemployed to 141,000 in April and to a peak of over 160,000 in May 1922.[30] Such an additional burden on the dwindling reserves of the AEU was crippling. Furthermore, a year and a half of severe recession meant that very little was voluntarily donated to the AEU coffers from outside bodies and other unions to aid the struggle.

The Lancashire district reflected these developments in microcosm. Around 10,000 members of the AEU in the Manchester and south-east

[27] *Manchester Guardian*, 11 March 1922, p. 10.
[28] G.D.H. Cole in *Labour Monthly Magazine*, March 1922, reprinted in the *AEU Monthly Journal*, April 1922, p. 29.
[29] Voting figures reported in Manchester EEA, Minutes, 23 February 1922.
[30] *AEU Financial Report*, year ending 31 December 1922, p. 7.

Lancashire district were unemployed before the lock-out, and the stoppage threw another 19,000 out of work.[31] Nationally, the members of the EEF were loyal to the Federation line almost to a man. Only thirty-seven firms out of a membership of almost 2,700 were expelled for refusing to post lock-out notices.[32] The engineering employers' associations in Lancashire were solidly behind the Federation, locked out in unison on 11 March and sustained virtually a solid front thereafter.[33]

In comparison to the conflict in 1897–8, the 1922 lock-out passed very quietly in the Lancashire region.[34] This was partly because there were very few concerted attempts by the employers to bring in replacement labour for the AEU men and very little success in the odd attempts that did occur to entice blacklegging.[35] Moreover, whilst the lock-out disrupted production, most firms in Lancashire continued to run. Concerted attempts were made to retain supervisory personnel and the opportunity was taken to encourage such workers to join the Foremen's Mutual Benefit Society if they were not already members.[36] Apprentices were also kept on, and some firms were reported to have approached certain apprentices whom they had discharged during the apprentice strikes in Manchester (against the 1921 wage cuts), offering them reinstatement. Apprentices were utilised to complete skilled men's work to such a degree that the AEU decided to call out the apprentices officially towards the end of March 1922. Still, it was reported that by 30 March, whilst a few engineering firms in Manchester had stopped entirely, the vast majority were still running, work being done by the foundrymen, boilermakers and large numbers of operatives in the smaller engineering unions.[37]

---

[31] *Manchester Guardian*, 11 March, 13 March 1922; *AEU Monthly Journal*, March 1922, p. 27; April 1922, pp. 39–41; May 1922, pp. 25–8.   [32] Wigham, *Power to Manage*, p. 123.

[33] Rochdale EEA, Minutes, 12 March, 17 March, 20 April 1922; *Manchester Guardian*, 8 April 1922, pp. 10, 14; 10 April 1922, p. 9.

[34] T.I. Holt, secretary to the Manchester branch of the AEU, testified that the men had been quiet and well conducted throughout the first seven weeks of the dispute, despite the efforts of 'certain extremists' to induce them to be 'unnecessarily demonstrative' (*Manchester Guardian*, 1 May 1922, p. 8). The possible exception is Barrow-in-Furness, where extra police were drafted in to maintain order and two men were arrested and prosecutions brought by the local engineering employers' association. See *Manchester Guardian*, 15 May 1922, p. 8; 30 May 1922, p. 16; *AEU Monthly Journal*, June 1922, p. 33.

[35] *Manchester Guardian*, 6 April 1922, p. 6. No evidence has been found of Ferranti's wholesale labour replacement tactics of 1897–8 being repeated in 1922. Such tactics were to revive somewhat in the worst years of the recession, though labour replacement never assumed the strategic significance it had in the late nineteenth century.

[36] For a discussion of employers' strategies towards foremen see J. Melling, 'Non-commissioned officers: British employers and their supervisory workers, 1880–1920', *Social History*, 5 (1980), pp. 183–221, and K. Burgess, 'Authority relations and the division of labour in British industry, with specific reference to Clydeside, c. 1860–1930', *Social History*, 11, no. 2 (1986), pp. 211–33.

[37] *Manchester Guardian*, 30 March 1922, p. 8; *AEU Monthly Journal*, April 1922, p. 41.

The EEF not only locked out the AEU but scaled up the confrontation by demanding all the other forty-six or so unions employed in the works of their members declare their policy on the question of managerial prerogatives. Here the EEF was attempting to address a crucial weakness of the 1898 settlement, namely that some important unions were not parties to it, including the boilermakers and foundry workers. In what Wigham has described as 'among the most high-handed operations in the history of industrial relations', these unions were requested, in various ultimatums in March 1922, to sign the first three clauses of the EEF November 1921 Memorandum which the AEU had rejected.[38] Though there were criticisms of the strategy, the EEF was determined that the time was ripe for the 'encroachments' into managerial prerogative made during the war and after to be completely wiped out in the industry. The voting amongst the other unions in engineering was decisively against acceptance of the employers' terms by more than three to one.[39] They were therefore locked out from 2 May, raising the total out of work to around 250,000.

Several attempts were made at conciliation throughout March and April by the Ministry of Labour and the National Joint Labour Council (representing the Trades Union Congress and the Labour Party). When these attempts failed the Ministry of Labour appointed Sir William Mackenzie, KC, to hold a Court of Enquiry under the Industrial Disputes Act. The report, issued on 10 May, was more favourable than the employers had anticipated. Mackenzie agreed that it was imperative that the employers should have complete discretionary power to decide when overtime was to be worked within the 30-hours limit. Employers should also, Mackenzie suggested, have the right to introduce workshop changes, though more time should be allowed for prior consultation. Failing agreement, employers should introduce changes pending further discussion. Negotiations reopened on this new basis, though the AEU was initially not disposed to accept such terms.[40]

Meanwhile the EEF attempted to exert some pressure on those locked out by reopening the works of all member firms from 3 May to those who were willing immediately to accept the employers' terms. This tactic, however, proved abortive, nullified by worker solidarity, facilitated by mass picketing from a very early hour on 3 May and the days following.[41] By this time it was clear that the lock-out was causing much distress amongst the operatives. From the beginning of the lock-out, the AEU had

---

[38] Wigham, *Power to Manage*, p. 119.   [39] Shadwell, *Engineering Industry*, p. 57.
[40] *Report by a Court of Enquiry Concerning the Engineering Trades Dispute* (Industrial Courts Act), Cd 1653, 1922, pp. 19–21; Manchester EEA, Minutes, 24 April 1922, 15 May 1922.
[41] Manchester EEA, Minutes, 1 May, 8 May 1922; Oldham EEA, Minutes, 1 May 1922; *Manchester Guardian*, 2 May 1922, p. 9; 4 May 1922, p. 8; 5 May 1922, p. 12.

paid dispute benefit to its members at a rate of £1.00 per week. However, the drain on finances was rapid. From 2 May the union was forced to cut its payments by half and at the end of May funds were exhausted and all benefits stopped.[42] The Manchester, Preston and Oldham districts of the AEU reported that though the men were in 'splendid spirit' and determined to fight, problems were growing and many families were in dire difficulties.[43] Voluntary distress committees sprang up, whilst for the worst cases of poverty and destitution, appeal was made to local boards of guardians for relief under the Poor Law. The latter policy was generally successful in the early stages of the dispute. However, because the employers had made work available with the reopening from 3 May, outdoor relief was not granted thereafter.[44] The EEF circularised all its associations, informing them of this new position on Poor Law relief and suggesting that they organise deputations of rate-payers to any Boards of Guardians who were still illegally providing such benefit.[45] Manchester, amongst others, did just that. This tactic had a significant impact, turning the screw in a war of attrition. By mid-June 1922, the AEU district representative for Manchester bitterly reported on several unsuccessful attempts to secure outdoor relief and concluded: 'As a result, I find that in order to assist the employers in their attempt to starve our people, Boards of Guardians and Courts of Referees are doing all possible to prevent our members and their dependants from receiving from the Guardians relief to which they are entitled as citizens.'[46]

Clearly, under such conditions, the unions could not hold out indefinitely. On 17 May, the EEF proposed slightly amended terms, which, though they made no concessions on the overtime question, provided a face-saving formula for the unions on the issue of 'prior consent'. Ten days' notice was to be conceded to allow discussion prior to any contemplated change in working conditions which would 'result in a general displacement of one class of workpeople in an establishment by another'.[47] A return to work was agreed on these terms.[48] However, judicious victimisation and continuing trade depression resulted in almost 70,000

---

[42] *Manchester Guardian*, 29 May 1922, p. 9; 3 June 1922, p. 9.
[43] *AEU Monthly Journal*, June 1922, pp. 33–5.
[44] See the *Manchester Guardian*, 28 April 1922, p. 13 and 19 May 1922, p. 13. This decision was backed up by legal precedent in a decision of the Court of Appeal in the case of the *Attorney General* vs. *Merthyr Tydfil Guardians* in 1900. Indeed, when local Boards of Guardians requested advice on this question from the Minister of Health, Alfred Mond, he simply informed them of the decision in 1900 that relief could not be granted if work was available.   [45]   Manchester EEA, Minutes, 15 May 1922.
[46] *AEU Monthly Journal*, June 1922, pp. 34–5.   [47] Shadwell, *Engineering Industry*, p. 59.
[48] All the smaller unions accepted these terms on 2 June 1922. AEU members accepted the recommendation of their Executive and in a ballot voted 75,478 to 39,423 for a return to work.

members of the AEU remaining unemployed, with a commensurate haemorrhage in union membership, by the end of 1922.[49]

Beneath the apparent unity of the engineering employers during the lock-out there were divisions and some dissent, though this never assumed serious proportions and never undermined EEF strategy. The Manchester EEA placed on record that they thought the 3 May reopening was a tactical error, arguing that this would split the solid front of the employers and that some firms would gain an unfair competitive advantage.[50] An anonymous employer wrote to the *Manchester Guardian* criticising Sir Allan Smith as an autocratic, reactionary, nineteenth-century-style employer whose clumsy tactics had only embittered labour and prolonged the dispute.[51] It was claimed that there was a great deal of dissension amongst member firms but that 'class consciousness' was too strong amongst engineering employers for many of them to break ranks whilst the dispute was in progress. It was urged that this latent corporatist element within the Federation should emerge, take control of the organisation and plan 'constructive policies of co-operative progress'; further, that 'Progressive employers must insist upon a complete reorganisation of constitution, methods and personnel. A reorganised federation, instilled with the spirit of constructive endeavour, may save the industry by its efforts and industrial England by its example.'[52]

However, such a deviant policy was running against the tide in 1921–2. Significantly, the *Manchester Guardian* received a number of letters refuting the views of their disloyal comrade, championing the leadership of Smith and calling for a further offensive to slash production costs.[53] Fairly typical of this response was a letter from a representative of Armstrong-Whitworth's: 'We cannot compete with other countries under present conditions. Until these conditions are altered many firms in this country will not hold back. The cost of production must come down. Is it not better for the men that they should have somewhat less wages and be fully employed all the time, than that 30 per cent of their number should be unemployed?'[54] The evidence suggests that the great majority of engineering employers supported the confrontationist strategy of Smith and the EEF executive in 1922 and were firmly committed to both a concerted costs reduction drive and a relentless offensive to roll back encroachments into managerial authority. The key objectives were to

[49] For the strike settlement see *Manchester Guardian*, 3 June 1922, p. 9; 6 June 1922, p. 8; 14 June 1922, p. 7; *AEU Financial Report*, year ending 31 December 1922, pp. 7, 12–13; AEU membership fell by 25 per cent to 330,000 between 1920 and 1922.
[50] Manchester EEA, Minutes, 1 May 1922.
[51] *Manchester Guardian*, 16 May 1922, pp. 9–10; 22 May 1922, p. 3.
[52] Ibid., 16 May 1922, p. 10. [53] Ibid., 18 May 1922, p. 12. [54] Ibid., 13 June 1922, p. 7.

revive employers' prerogative to manage as they thought fit without union 'interference' on the shop-floor, to undermine industrial militancy, crush aspirations for workers' control and, critically, to extend the parameters of procedural control across the industry. The latter remained a key component in engineering employers' industrial relations strategy throughout the subsequent period.

Industrial relations after 1922

Recently, Zeitlin and McKinlay have placed the 1922 lock-out in perspective, persuasively arguing that this comprehensive employers' victory did not precipitate an extensive shift towards the rationalisation of labour management in engineering, or a thoroughgoing transformation in the division of labour.[55] This represents a very important and vital revision to our understanding of inter-war industrial relations. Nevertheless, it should not obscure the fact that 1922 did represent a pivotal success for engineering employers – one that was widely recognised as such at the time and one that critically influenced the tone of industrial relations thereafter. Despite a few voices of dissent, the EEF had united the industry, as in 1897–8, behind the defence of managerial prerogatives. The employers had made a sustained stand to redefine their managerial rights after the dangerous precedents of wartime. By mid-1922, the unions were bankrupt, morale was at a low ebb and the bargaining strength of the unions was severely undermined by the sudden and sustained membership decline, combined with the atrophying of workshop organisation and the corrosion of shop stewards' authority. Industrial relations were stabilised in the industry for more than a decade thereafter. Time lost through industrial disputes in the sector declined from 17.5 million days during 1922, to 6 million in 1923, 1.4 million in 1924 and then averaged only 183,000 days lost per year over the period 1925–34.[56] Moreover, the evidence for north-west England suggests that the employers' victory at the collective level critically facilitated the process at the point of production whereby employers reasserted their discretionary power and authority and intensified work, achieving significant productivity gains and the erosion of some time-honoured 'restrictive' (or, more correctly, 'protective') practices.

---

[55] McKinlay and Zeitlin, 'The meanings of managerial prerogative'; Zeitlin, 'Internal politics'; McKinlay, 'Employers and skilled workers'. See also A. Reid, 'Employers' strategies and craft production'.

[56] Mitchell and Deane, *Abstract*, p. 72. These are figures for the composite metals, engineering and shipbuilding sector.

The changed market circumstances induced by the economic slump encouraged the engineering masters to embark on a concerted costs reduction drive on the domestic, local and national level. The employers fully utilised the adverse trading conditions to retract many of the concessions won by labour over the previous decade. Further nationally negotiated wage cuts directly followed the settlement of the 1922 lock-out.[57] This created problems in some sections where product markets held up relatively well – for example in the Lancashire cotton spinning machinery-making trade in 1921–2. This prompted a number of resignations and some disloyalty from textile machinery manufacturers, who declared that such a provocative costs reduction offensive was inappropriate to their circumstances. However, decisive Federation action to neutralise a strike of AEU members in Lancashire textile machinery making shops in the autumn of 1922 (in support of a sectional wage rise) by threatening a full Federation pre-emptive lock-out stabilised this situation.[58] This illustrates a revival in the Federation's ability in the 1920s to contain the rolling, sectional strike.

As with the cotton industry, a serious attempt was made to roll back the wage drift which had characterised 1910–20. This involved a reassertion of discipline and control by the employers' organisations over the remuneration policies of members. The Lancashire sheet-metal workers, who had done relatively well out of the war and the boom in 1919–20, were one of the first groups to be attacked. The Bolton EEA posted notices in member firms informing the men that, after 1 April 1921, only the recognised standard rate for timeworkers on sheet-metal work would be paid and all extras and inducements above standard would be eliminated.[59] Sporadic protest strikes, lasting up to a month at some firms, failed to suppress this movement.[60] Similarly, the Manchester EEA initiated a wage cribbing offensive in an attempt to regain some degree of control over members' wage payments. Firms in the Ashton district which had previously increased the rates of sheet-metal workers without the authority of the association were instructed to abolish all extra payments and conform to the recognised district rate of pay.[61] Where strikes occurred, the member firms were refused financial compensation as a penalty for their previous disloyalty.[62]

---

[57] Of 16s 6d per week, in three stages in July, August and September 1922. Lancashire JSC, Minutes, 5 September 1922.
[58] Manchester EEA, Minutes, 3 October, 3 November, 1922; Oldham EEA, Minutes, 19 October 1921.   [59] Manchester EEA, Minutes, 5 April 1921.
[60] Ibid., 3 May 1921.   [61] Ibid., 11 July 1921; Oldham EEA, Minutes, 11 July 1921.
[62] Oldham EEA, Minutes, 3 October 1921; EEF, *Wage Movements*, p. 649; Lancashire JSC, Minutes, 6 February 1922.

During the war and the following boom, engineering firms offered all kinds of wage inducements under the guise of special bonuses, locality allowances, travelling and outworking grants and 'easy' piecework rates and systems of payments by results. These were all now rapidly swept away as the trend reversed to wage cribbing and even the undercutting of standard wages by firms struggling to remain marginally competitive. In 1924, the Liverpool EEA abolished the payment of double time for travelling on a Sunday and reverted to the Lancashire practice of single time.[63] Bonus schemes which had operated well in busier times were now considered too costly and summarily cancelled. Brooks and Doxey switched from piecework to daywork because of the exorbitant cost of the piecework prices negotiated in wartime.[64] Dobson and Barlow's 'superbonus' of 25 per cent disappeared, as did the lucrative bonus scheme for the Bolton patternmakers, after a short protest strike.[65] The patternmakers in Platt's lost their extra bonuses, whilst Holroyd's of Rochdale provoked a strike by withdrawing a bonus scheme which had been in operation in the foundry.[66] Lancashire outworking allowances were slashed in a local agreement in 1923, and at Leyland Motors special 'locality allowances' were cut from 4s 6d to 2s 6d per week.[67] Elsewhere, piecework prices were slashed without any pretence at changing methods of manufacture.[68]

Whilst the EEF (in combination with the NCEO) utilised every opportunity to raise public awareness of what they regarded as excessively high labour costs, the local engineering employers' associations co-ordinated the movement to reassert control over wage rates and slash labour costs at the regional level. In a circular as early as August 1920, the Lancashire JSC notified members:

that no system of payments by results other than that of straight piecework should be introduced until particulars of same had been submitted to and met with the approval of the local association, and further that where such schemes are already in operation particulars of the same should be obtained and sent to the secretary of the Joint Standing Committee.[69]

The Lancashire JSC in the 1920s and 1930s refused to approve any payments by results schemes unless these were linked directly to measurement of output. The employers' associations thus overtly encouraged

---

[63] Lancashire JSC, Minutes, 4 November 1924.   [64] Ibid., 6 December 1923.
[65] Ibid., 8 November 1921, 4 September 1923.
[66] Oldham EEA, Minutes, 17 November 1921; Rochdale EEA, Minutes, 7 February 1921.
[67] Lancashire JSC, Minutes, 8 May, 2 October, 6 November 1923.
[68] Ibid., 6 March 1928 (Dobson and Barlow); 6 November 1928 (Platt's – ring frame department.); 4 December 1928 (Holroyd's); 4 November 1930 (Vulcan Foundry – AEU); 16 April 1931 (Leyland Motors – labourers).   [69] Ibid., 10 August 1920.

payment by results, development of premium bonus systems and more systematic rate fixing.[70] In response, AEU shop stewards threatened a strike at Butterworth and Dickenson's in Burnley when ratefixers were introduced in 1933. Elsewhere in the north-west, there is some limited evidence of more systematic rationalisation, as at Ferranti's, where disputes arose over the introduction of motion study and the 'excessive' use of the stopwatch, and at Parkinson and Cowan (Gas Meters) Ltd, who were experimenting with variants of the Bedaux system of scientific management.[71] However, the evidence strongly suggests that traditional managerial techniques and wage payment systems continued to remain the norm in north-west England in the 1930s. In this sense, the Lancashire evidence supports Zeitlin's argument that engineering between the wars failed to provide fertile soil for American-inspired systematic management ideas. Rather, as in the cotton industry, work tended to be intensified and speeded up within the parameters of the existing technology and the traditional division of labour (this point will be returned to later).

Some areas clearly perceived the need to temper the costs reduction drive because of broader political considerations. As early as January 1925, the Manchester EEA argued: 'From the standpoint of other important factors, such as maintaining the present constitutional methods by giving support to the moderate labour leaders as against the activities of what is called the Minority Movement it might be considered expedient to concede some advance rather than have a serious dislocation of work.'[72] This strategy was embodied in the commitment of the EEF to the maintenance of formal union recognition through the collective bargaining and disputes procedures enshrined in the Terms of Settlement. Such recognition was kept, however, within bounds. The open shop principle was fiercely defended by the EEF between the wars – to the point of two lock-out threats in 1924 and 1926. Nor was the EEF willing to condone an extension of collective bargaining which took decision-making outside the industry, as exemplified in their opposition to the corporatist Mond-Turner talks and the reports that ensued.[73] The range of subjects open to collective bargaining was also prescribed. One issue that the engineering employers consistently refused to bargain over was that of labour

<hr />

[70] The Manchester EEA encouraged members to convert apprentices from time wages to piecework. See Manchester EEA, Minutes, 10 August 1921; Lancashire JSC, Minutes, 19 July 1921.
[71] Lancashire JSC, Minutes, 13 June 1933; Manchester EEA, Minutes, 2 November 1936, 19 July 1937 (Ferranti); Lancashire JSC, Minutes, 3 October 1938 (Parkinson and Cowan). [72] Manchester EEA, Minutes, 6 September 1927.
[73] Wigham, *Power to Manage*, pp. 131–3; Gospel, 'Employers' labour policy', pp. 180–97.

displacement as a consequence of rationalisation. Nor were apprentice issues subject to collective bargaining until the late 1930s.

The employers' counter-attack was characterised by a revival of anti-unionism and more coercive strikebreaking tactics. Where the formal disputes procedure failed to settle problems, market circumstances favoured more authoritarian options. Whilst the enquiry note appears to have fallen into abeyance, there was a revival of victimisation and labour replacement tactics. In at least three unconstitutional strikes in the 1930s the Lancashire engineering employers utilised the blacklist to victimise strikers and successfully replaced them with non-unionists.[74] All these cases were declared closed without the strikers being re-engaged.

The trade recession bottomed out over the period 1924–8 and no further attacks on wages or working conditions were made at the national level in engineering until the onset of the economic crisis in 1929–32.[75] Indeed, the improved trading environment of 1924–8 led to some upward wage drift. In the latter part of 1927, the EEF initiated a survey to ascertain the extent of wage escalation resulting from disloyalty to Federation agreements and association-negotiated wage standards. The returns indicated that a considerable percentage of skilled men were receiving higher wages than the standard rate and that this wage drift was particularly prevalent in Manchester and other towns in north-west England.[76] In their defence, the Manchester and Oldham EEAs argued that such extra wages were legitimate merit payments for long service, special ability and work.[77] The evidence suggests, therefore, that the costs reduction offensive in Lancashire had its limitations and even by the late 1920s a minority of firms continued to pay extra wage bonuses and inducements. Nor were such emoluments completely swept away by the slump of 1929. During the discussions over the implementation of the new EEF working rules in 1931 it was disclosed that some member firms had become very lax in observing collective agreements and that practices and customs contrary to what had been formally agreed were prevalent.[78]

With the economic crisis of 1929–32, orders collapsed to an all-time low and unemployment in engineering increased from 84,000 in 1929 to 280,000 by 1931. As a response, the EEF appointed a crisis committee to work out ways of further reducing costs and enhancing competitiveness. As an alternative strategy to the imposition of wage cuts, the EEF

[74] Lancashire JSC, Minutes, 3 May 1932, 6 September 1932, 3 October 1933, 7 March 1939.
[75] One manifestation of the improved trading environment was the concession in 1927 of a national bonus of 2 shillings per week to timeworkers to improve their position vis-à-vis pieceworkers.   [76] Lancashire JSC, 10 January 1928.
[77] Ibid., and see Oldham EEA, Minutes, 7 December 1927.
[78] Lancashire JSC, Minutes, 1 September, 6 September 1932.

proposed reducing production costs by an attack on agreed working conditions, including the overtime, shiftworking and piecework standard.[79] Reductions were imposed on 6 July 1931 and included a cut in the overtime rate from time and a half to time and a quarter for the first three hours, a cut in nightshift rates from time and a third to time and a sixth and a reduction in the basis for piecework from 33 per cent to 25 per cent above time rates. The objective was to return the trade more or less to the pre-1914 position. Proposals to extend working hours and increase the interchangeability and mobility of labour were, however, dropped.[80]

Throughout the inter-war years engineering employers' organisations undoubtedly remained the guardians of managerial prerogative. However, central policy could be interpreted differently at local level and evidence suggests that in north-west England employers were by no means rigid and inflexible across a range of issues impinging on managerial functions. No interference would be tolerated in the right of employers to determine overtime. However, sensitivity on the question of overtime whilst unemployment levels remained high was also urged upon federated employers.[81] Apprentices were refused collective bargaining rights and workplace discipline was sharply tightened in the 1920s.[82] However, the Manchester EEA allowed some sections (such as textile manufacturers) to pay over the agreed association apprentice wage scale and failed to control apprentice absenteeism in the 1930s. National policy on the closed shop was unequivocal, promulgating the inalienable principle that employers had the liberty to employ whom they chose and the right to expect trade unionists to work without objection with non-members.[83] Whilst the Manchester EEA formally subscribed to this policy there was no offensive initiated to break up the unionist shops in the district. Indeed, the established status quo was accepted – including the closed shop – in many areas. Despite falling union membership, some member firms apparently continued to sign pledges that they would not employ non-unionists in the 1920s.[84] In 1929, the Lancashire JSC noted that whilst employers' strategy in principle should be 'refusal to discriminate'

[79] The Manchester EEA had proposed an offensive to make such cuts as early as 1923. See Manchester EEA, Minutes, 3 May 1923.

[80] Lancashire JSC, Minutes, 4 November, 2 December 1930, 2 June 1931; Wigham, *Power to Manage*, pp. 133–4.   [81] Manchester EEA, Minutes, 31 August 1922.

[82] This included an organised campaign to reduce absenteeism – for example on Shrove Tuesday. See Manchester EEA, Minutes, 5 November 1921, 12 March 1925.

[83] Manchester EEA, Minutes, 10 August 1921. The EEF urged extra vigilance to oppose the closed shop and later, in 1926, to resist the extension of a principle which the AEU tried to establish in Barrow and Scotland whereby all vacancies which occurred in federated shops should be filled by unionised labour. See Lancashire JSC, Minutes, 4 May, 7 September 1926.   [84] Lancashire JSC, Minutes, 6 June 1930.

they recommended that much discretion should be exercised, especially in certain Lancashire districts where the closed shop was long established.[85]

Key points of conflict arose over the staffing of machinery and the pace of work. The change in the economic environment in 1921–2 made the engineering employers determined to claw back what they regarded as their managerial privilege to decide, without undue interference from the unions, who was to be employed on their machinery. Recent commentators have convincingly illustrated that the lack of technological renewal and slow pace of change in managerial practices resulted in only limited change in the division of labour in engineering and shipbuilding. However, what has been underestimated is the marked speed-up and intensification of work in the 1920s and 1930s, developments vividly caricatured in a Workers' Theatre Movement agitprop sketch in 1932:

> *Capitalist:* Speed-up, speed-up! Watch your step.
> Hold on tight, and show some pep.
> Move your hands and bend your body
> Without end and not so shoddy.
> Faster, faster, shake it up,
> No one idles in this shop.
> Time is money, money's power,
> Profits come in every hour.
> Can't stop profits for your sake,
> Speed-up, speed-up, keep awake.
> *Worker:* We are humans, not machines.
> *Capitalist:* You don't like this fast routine?
> Get your pay and get out quick,
> You speak like a bolshevik.
> Speed-up, speed-up, watch your step,
> Hold on tight and show some pep.
> *Woman worker:* My head, oh my head! I can't go on.
> *Capitalist:* You want time off, that's your game.
> Get your pay and get out quick,
> There's no place here for the sick.
> Speed-up, speed-up, watch your step,
> Hold on tight and show some pep.
> Number fifteen, number ten,
> I must fire two more men.
> Here's a youngster strong and willing.
> Will not find the pace so killing.
> To do more work for much less pay -
> That's the problem of the day.
> Speed-up, speed-up, work with me,

[85] Ibid., 9 April 1929.

Help bring back prosperity.
Speed them up and cut their pay,
Speed-up, speed-up, that's the way.[86]

The Lancashire evidence throws up numerous examples of this process in engineering and illustrates the pivotal role played by the employers' associations in facilitating work intensification. In the early 1920s, J.R. Lees Ltd, and J.P. Hall and Co. Ltd, (Oldham) doubled the workload of their AEU fitters and turners and slashed their total wage bills by switching from one machine tended by one operator to a ratio of two machines to each operator (with negligible technological innovation or reorganisation of work). This, the firms claimed, was simply returning to pre-1914 practice.[87] Employers' associations resisted union attempts to determine machinemen's wages by collective bargaining, and their efforts to declare that certain machines merited a skilled wage and the wages on others should be graded according to the operations involved. Conversely, employers' association strategy was to allow members to determine the wages of machine operators unilaterally and to pay them according to individual merit, responsibility and ability. In April 1921, the Lancashire JSC reminded its member associations:

of the practice recognised practically throughout the federation to the effect that owing to the different classes of work carried on in the industry and the varying types of tools employed, which called for varying degrees of skill from the workers, the rate of pay was based on the skill of the operator and the class of work etc., and not on the machine.[88]

Fairly representative of the union claims on the question of machine staffing was the attempt of the Burnley AEU to get an agreement with the Burnley masters which provided for certain machinemen to be paid by an agreed scale of wages for planing, drilling, milling and screwing. The Burnley masters threw out the claim, arguing that the only thing that was customary in the district was to pay unskilled men placed on machines 2 shillings over the labourers' rate. The Burnley employers stated that it was their intention 'to maintain the right to select, train and employ those whom they considered best adapted to the various operations carried on in their workshops and to pay them according to their ability as workmen and to the work being performed by them'.[89]

Between the wars, engineering employers increasingly introduced

[86] *Redstage* (Workers' Theatre Movement), September 1932, pp. 7–8. I am indebted to the late Steve Jones for this material.
[87] Oldham EEA, Minutes, 2 February, 28 June 1922.
[88] Lancashire JSC, Minutes, 5 April 1921.
[89] Burnley EEA, Minutes, 24 March, 31 March 1921.

labourers, semi-skilled men, juveniles and female workers to work which was previously performed by skilled men. In part, this process was facilitated by deskilling mechanisation and automation, particularly prevalent in the newer, more prosperous mass-production sectors of the industry (motor cars, electrical engineering, armaments) and epitomised by the introduction of the motor car assembly track. However, the economic circumstances of the inter-war slump made extensive capital reinvestment extremely difficult in the older, traditional textile machinery and heavy engineering sectors. Here the staffing changes often represented the direct employment of cheaper labour to what had been regarded as the preserve of craftsmen, combined with some limited changes in the way work was organised. The evidence for Lancashire suggests that such a process was a significant trend within what was a region dominated by traditional sectors of engineering, and that the most heavily depressed textile machinery making industry was amongst the foremost innovators in the deployment of their labour force.

Platt Brothers of Oldham provides a good example of this process at work. In 1921 Platt's replaced skilled AEU men on turret lathes with semi-skilled operatives.[90] In 1925 the company substituted 'machinemen' for turners on some processes.[91] In 1932, Platt's reorganised their fluted roller and gin crank departments at their Hartford Works, which resulted in a wholesale replacement of skilled men with semi-skilled, with a commensurate reduction in the total wages bill. When the unions asked Platt's to take into account the wages paid for the same class of semi-skilled work in Accrington and Rochdale, the firm refused.[92] Platt's also introduced women workers to gauging and viewing operations. They gave a guarantee, however, that this was not 'an attempt to insert the thin end of the wedge towards their introduction on machines'.[93] Such actions by Platt's were fully endorsed by their local organisation. The Oldham EEA made it clear that they envisaged a drastic decline in the number of skilled men employed in engineering and an increasing number of semi-skilled operatives and women.[94]

In north-east Lancashire similar changes were being introduced by the employers, with the agreement of their organisations. Butterworth and Dickenson, Burnley loom makers, were increasingly replacing their skilled fitters and turners with semi-skilled men and youths. In 1933, the firm reorganised by expanding the assembly department and transferring much of the work from the fitting department where most of the

---

[90] Oldham EEA, Minutes, 6 January 1921.
[91] Lancashire JSC, Minutes, 6 October 1925.
[92] Ibid., 21 September, 5 October, 21 October 1932.   [93] Ibid., 2 November 1939.
[94] Oldham EEA, Minutes, 27 April 1933.

men were skilled. This prompted bitter complaints from the AEU that the training and status of apprentices was impaired by the standard of work and supervision in the assembly room in Butterworth and Dickenson.[95] In another north Lancashire textile machine factory (Howard and Bullough, Blackburn) apprentices were substituted for skilled men on various processes, thus creating 'all-apprentice operations', a procedure which the firm claimed in 1930 was 'in accordance with standard practice'.[96] Walter Greenwood's popular novel *Love On the Dole* (1933) vividly illustrates such developments as they occurred in the Manchester district, including the common practice amongst employers of labour at this time to discharge apprentices once they had completed their time and could claim the full wage rate. Complaints came from the unions that the ratio of young workers to employed skilled men had increased dangerously.[97] Only one major engineering union – the sheet-metal workers – appears to have succeeded in retaining during the inter-war years the generous one apprentice to ten journeymen ratio agreed collectively during the First World War.[98] Hence, the 1920s and 1930s witnessed an increased proportion of young workers employed in engineering firms, and a declining proportion within this group of indentured apprentices.[99]

Engineering employers also replaced skilled craftsmen with female labour. Ferranti's substituted young women for men in some of their inspection departments, whilst Holroyd's of Rochdale introduced women in the foundry for work on small, plain repetitive cores.[100] J.P. Hall (Oldham) and the Lancashire Dynamo and Motor Company (Manchester) replaced apprentices, youths and in some cases skilled men with women in 1929.[101] Such developments were part of a quite radical change in the nature of the engineering labour force between the wars. Within federated firms, the employment of female labour held up relatively well, whilst the numbers of skilled craftsmen fell by almost a half between 1920 and 1932.[102] In 1939, the number of adult males employed in the Lancashire engineering industry was slightly less than the number

[95] Burnley EEA, Minutes, 25 August, 8 September, 2 November 1932, 16 March, 22 May 1933; Lancashire JSC, Minutes, 13 June 1933.
[96] Lancashire JSC, Minutes, 4 November 1930.   [97] Ibid., 24 March 1930.
[98] Manchester EEA, Minutes, 6 April 1936; Lancashire JSC, Minutes, 7 February 1939. On an earlier occasion the Manchester EEA had pressed the EEF to support an initiative to eliminate this restriction but the Federation had counselled inaction and refused official backing for such a campaign. See Lancashire JSC, Minutes, 3 March 1926, 10 January 1928, 4 December 1928.
[99] Of the total of 146,883 male employees aged under 21 in EEF firms in Britain in 1939, 83,592, or 57 per cent, were not apprentices.
[100] Lancashire JSC, Minutes, 6 October 1931 (Ferranti), 12 October 1926 (Holroyd's).
[101] Ibid., 7 May 1929.   [102] Wigham, *Power to Manage*, p. 303.

Table 9.3 *Proportion of skilled, semi-skilled and unskilled workers in EEF firms, 1914–33*

	Skilled	Semi-skilled	Unskilled
1914	60	20	20
1921	50	30	20
1928	34	53	13
1933	32	57	12

Source: Cited in Gospel, 'Employers' organisations', p. 50.

employed in 1920. The number of under-21-year-old males employed, however, rose by nearly 20 per cent and the number of females employed more than doubled between 1920 and 1939.[103]

By the mid-1930s the status profile of the engineering workforce was very different from that on the eve of the First World War. Limited rationalisation of work combined with more extensive reclassification of occupations and skills – downgrading jobs rather than genuine deskilling through alteration of task content – enabled labour costs to be slashed. Table 9.3, compiled by the EEF, clearly illustrates how employers perceived changes in skill levels. Whilst some sectors remained more immune than others to deskilling – notably machine tools, vehicles and aircraft – this represented a net loss of something in the region of 150,000 skilled jobs in British engineering over the inter-war period.

The supportive role of the industry employers' organisations played no small part in facilitating this process though they also, perhaps paradoxically, helped to limit work rationalisation. Broader considerations of maintaining stability in industrial relations and the association's role in maintaining fair competition drew many local employers' organisations into a more pragmatic interpretation of managerial prerogative, even on the staffing of machinery question. Within the parameters of the concerted employers' offensive to cut costs and reassert managerial prerogatives there was room for much local and sectional variation in policy. In

---

[103] May 1920, Lancashire: males over 21 – 101,784; males under 21 – 23,019; female workers – 6,133. October 1939: males over 21 – 100,798; males under 21 – 27,429; female workers – 12,356. Source: EEF, Numbers Employed Files. Significantly perhaps, the national figures register less change in this respect than those in the Lancashire region. Nationally, the proportion of the engineering labour force under the age of 21 stayed constant between 1920 and 1939, whilst the proportion of female workers rose from 8.3 per cent of the total to 9.3 per cent during the period 1920–39. In this particular respect, therefore, change should not be exaggerated.

1923, the EEF suggested to the Manchester EEA that they terminate a local agreement with the plate and machine moulders made in March 1919 and return to the pre-war practice of placing unskilled men on the work as required. In a sectional meeting of Manchester members employing plate and machine moulders a unanimous resolution was drawn up condemning this line of action: 'That in as much as the agreement had worked satisfactorily and the relations both between the association and the firms with this particular union were all that could be desired it was impolitic to take advantage of the present time by cancelling the agreement.'[104] Despite EEF protests, the suggestion to abrogate the agreement was rejected. In a similar case, a Manchester member firm, Royce Ltd, took it on their own initiative to place semi-skilled dressers and unskilled labourers on riveting, punching and shearing work previously done by boilermakers. The firm declared that under clauses of the 1922 settlement 'they had the right to introduce any class of labour upon any operation irrespective of what was the custom for the same operations in similar works in the district'.[105] In response, the boilermakers at the firm went on strike. Instead of supporting this initiative to test the strength of the 'Managerial Functions' agreement of 1922, the Manchester EEA refused all aid to the firm and rejected a recommendation to the EEF for financial assistance. The association argued: 'It was never the intention of the Federation that such an interpretation as the above should be construed into the agreement but that in putting into operation the agreement it should be done in a broad and reasonable spirit having regard to the recognised practice on any particular question.'[106] The 'recognised practice' in this case was clearly on the side of the boilermakers, as it was the custom in Lancashire for riveting, punching and shearing to be boilermakers' work. It was also noted that it had been extremely difficult to get the Boilermakers' Society to accept the Provisions for Avoiding Disputes earlier in the year and consequently it would be tactless to press such a provocative, raw assertion of managerial prerogative on the machine staffing issue at that particular time. Though at first reluctant, the member firm eventually agreed to carry out the recommendations of the Manchester association and boilermakers were put back on the work.[107]

The Lancashire JSC also proved that it was not entirely inflexible on the question of managerial prerogative on the machine staffing issue. In 1928, a sectional subcommittee of Lancashire textile machinery makers decided that a Manchester firm, Buckley and Crossley Ltd, was going too far in its proposal to manufacture flyers with unskilled labour. In all firms

---

[104] Manchester EEA, Minutes, 1 February 1923.   [105] Ibid., 22 November 1922.
[106] Ibid.   [107] Ibid., 11 December 1922.

but one, such work was done by skilled men. The Lancashire JSC, influenced by pleas of unfair competition, resolved that the firm could not be supported if its heavy-handed action resulted in a strike. In the event, the firm resigned from the Manchester association to have a free hand to alter its work practices. Significantly, however, the Manchester EEA and the regional federation had drawn back from an opportunity to spearhead deskilling and provide an unequivocal green light to member firms to transform their division of labour. Such conflicting messages from their associations must have gone some way towards maintaining the residual power of skilled male craftworkers in the industry even in the worst years of the slump. Evidence suggests that this was also the case elsewhere. McKinlay has demonstrated, for example, how the Clydeside shipbuilding employers' organisation failed to spearhead an attack on the traditional division of labour – partly because product markets dictated continuation of demand for traditional skills – and how the employers' strategy of maintaining an overstocked labour market was ultimately unsuccessful.[108] This may well have constrained somewhat the process of genuine deskilling. However, there were clearly other positive spin-offs for a more pragmatic and more corporatist strategy, notably in stabilising relations between capital and labour and in inducing consent to the labour cost-cutting and work intensification regime which characterised these years.

On other fronts, moreover, the engineering employers' associations were relentlessly advancing the interests of capitalist enterprise. Between the wars, the EEF played a significant role in a broader-based employers' anti-socialist movement. This movement had the dual role of more overtly propagandising capitalist, free-market ideology whilst also developing more formalised, centralised and covert victimisation mechanisms designed to keep labour activists out of the workplace. The former function was dominated by the NCEO, formed in 1919, within which the EEF was a major force.[109] However, evidence suggests that another organisation, the Economic League (formed initially as National Propaganda in 1919), played an important role in both the dissemination of anti-labour propaganda and the monitoring and blacklisting of activists between the wars. Furthermore, engineering employers and their associations had a high profile within the League.

The genesis, organisation, aims and policies of the Economic League (EL) have been examined in detail elsewhere.[110] The organisation was

---

[108] McKinlay, 'Employers and skilled workers', pp. 311–13, 321.
[109] See T. Rodgers, 'Employers' organizations'.
[110] M. Hughes, *Spies at Work*, Bradford: 1 in 12 Publications, diskbook, 1994; McIvor, 'Crusade for capitalism'; McIvor and Paterson, 'Combating the left'.

formed in 1919 by a group of right-wing industrialists and financiers, in collaboration with military and naval intelligence experts (notably Sir Reginald 'Blinker' Hall). Sir Allan Smith was present at the inaugural meeting, representing the EEF, as were Cuthbert Laws of the Shipping Federation and Evan Williams of the Mining Association. Arguably, the endorsement and influence of these powerful individuals and their respective organisations enabled the League to carve out a significant niche for itself within the employers' movement. Through its network of regional leagues the organisation championed private enterprise capitalism, disseminated anti-socialist literature, organised meetings and study circles and counselled against disruptive industrial action. It supported the government's strikebreaking activities during the 1926 General Strike and had an acrimonious and sometimes violent struggle with the NUWM during the 1930s. The EL also monitored the activities of what it regarded as 'subversive' individuals and organisations and, by the mid-1920s, had compiled a blacklist of labour activists. The key service that the League came to provide for employers thereafter was information on the politics and past activities of employees and job applicants. This was provided on request from subscribing firms and independently where the League felt that employers should be alerted to socialist or communist activities in their workplaces. This service was used extensively by engineering employers, aiding the collapse of the shop stewards' movement and the atrophying of workshop organisation between the wars.

One of the most active of the fifteen regional leagues was the Lancashire and Cheshire Economic League (LCEL) and, significantly, the basis of support for this organisation between the wars lay in the engineering sector. At least five of the members of the sixteen-strong LCEL executive committee in the mid-1920s were engineering employers, two of whom were members of the executive committee of the Manchester EEA and one, Major Challen, was the regional organiser for the Lancashire JSC. At one time or another in the 1920s and 1930s the Manchester, Oldham, Rochdale, Burnley, Blackburn and Preston EEAs voted to provide contributions directly from their funds for the EL. Manchester provided the most consistent support, creating a 3d per £100 wage bill levy upon member firms from which members had to contract out physically. Only a handful of firms took the latter option and between 1923 and 1939 more than £10,000 was forwarded from the Manchester association alone to the LCEL. No other outside organisation received support from the Manchester EEA on anything like this scale during these years. This is in marked contrast to the rather more ambivalent attitude of the cotton millowners to the League. Cotton had little representation upon the LCEL executive and there is no evidence of cotton spinning and weaving employers' associations organising financial levies upon their membership in support of this militant rightist organisation.

Rearmament and recovery, 1933–9

The engineering trade began a slow but steady recovery after the economic crisis of 1929–32. Unemployment began to fall in 1933 and by 1939 it had dropped to 6.6 per cent in general engineering and 4.4 per cent in the motors and aircraft sector. Union membership reached its lowest point in 1933 and began to climb thereafter. Membership of the AEU jumped from 191,500 in 1933 to 390,000 by 1939.[111] With the upsurge in membership came an increase in union confidence and a revival of militancy. Paralleling this was a recovery in employers' organisation and solidarity.

However, just as there had been significant regional and inter-regional variations in product market experience during the slump, so too there were variations in the recovery phase. The economic upturn was irregular and patchy, and this created tensions and exacerbated disagreements within the EEF. The earliest indication that trade was on the upturn in Lancashire came towards the end of 1934, when the Lancashire employers decided to defer their application for further reductions in the Lancashire outworking list.[112] The recovery gathered momentum through 1935 and 1936. By June 1935, it was already reported that the trade was suffering from a considerable shortage of craftsmen and the Federation urged members to take on more apprentices to increase the ratio of apprentices to journeymen.[113] However, in the north-west it was the large engineering companies in Manchester which were the first to benefit from the flow of orders for munitions and war-related equipment in 1936. Smaller companies outside Manchester continued in a depressed state until more equitable distribution of defence contracts late in 1938 and into 1939.[114]

Apart from inviting contracts from established firms, the government defence programme necessitated a considerable extension in Britain's capacity to manufacture war material, and aircraft factories and armaments works were established in Lancashire, as elsewhere, after 1936 to fulfil this need. The local employers' organisations viewed these developments with some trepidation. They feared that the accelerated demand

---

[111] Jefferys, *Story of the Engineers*, pp. 292–3.
[112] Lancashire JSC, Minutes, 6 November 1934.
[113] Ibid., 4 June 1935, 10 March, 7 July 1936.
[114] Lancashire JSC, Minutes, 14 June, 15 July 1938, 10 January 1939, 7 February 1939; Oldham EEA, Minutes, 20 April 1938; Manchester EEA, Minutes, 9 March, 29 May 1936, 11 April 1938.

for labour prompted by the new factories would lead to an increasing upward wage spiral. Given the intensifying skilled labour shortage in the later 1930s, the employers' associations were also concerned about the enticement of their labour force to the new factories. In Oldham, such fears were fully realised when the government in the early part of 1937 proposed the building of a 'shadow' factory for the manufacture of aircraft carburettors. The Oldham EEA recorded an urgent protest:

Oldham engineering industries depend mainly for their existence on export trade in which there is already a distinct sign of recovery. The new carburettor factory would require 25 setter-ups, trained to set up automatic machines. There is not a single setter-up of this type to be found in the Oldham district. It would require 200 capstan hands. Engineering firms in Oldham are unable to obtain a sufficient number of capstan hands for their own works. It would require 25 tool fitters. It is impossible to obtain any tool fitters in Oldham. These facts, in conjunction with the higher rates of wages generally paid in aircraft establishments would of necessity draw more vital key men away from the established industries of the town than could possibly be attracted to Oldham from other towns. This would result in depriving of employment hundreds of men at present employed in the town's industries and whose continuity of employment is dependent upon the work of key men.[115]

The government ignored the plea of the Oldham engineering masters and went ahead, production starting at the Woodstock factory, Oldham, in October 1937. Thereafter a number of complaints were received from member firms that many of their best operatives had been drawn into the new plant.[116] This presented a considerable threat to the association's control of wage rates in the district, which was only partially solved by the new firm agreeing to join the association in April 1939.[117]

The trade recovery of the later 1930s prompted a reversal of the predominant wage-cutting and cribbing trend of the previous dozen years or so and led to a significant softening of employers' labour relations policy, both at the local and the national level. From the doldrums of the 1929–32 period, relations between the unions and employers steadily improved. The costs reduction offensive ground to a halt and in the five years 1935–9 male engineering workers received four nationally negotiated wage rises totalling an increase of 10 shillings per week.[118] Improvements were also

---

[115] Oldham EEA, Minutes, 7 April 1937.
[116] Ibid., 22 October, 12 December 1938. The precise inducements were not known. Rumour had it, however, that semi-skilled men were being offered the skilled rate together with an additional output bonus and promises of continuous employment for four years.   [117] Ibid., 12 December 1938, 6 April 1939.
[118] Wigham, *Power to Manage*, pp. 138–43. Female workers did less well, receiving only two rises of 1 shilling each time. Evidently, patriarchal notions, especially the concept of unequal worth, persisted.

made in the rates paid for overtime and nightshifts, whilst the EEF recognised the inevitability of holidays with pay being granted in the trade, introducing the issue in the 1937 wages and conditions negotiations as an additional bargaining point.[119] Another indication of the marked change in industrial relations was the extension of collective bargaining rights to apprentices in 1937, after strike action which originated in the north-west. In Manchester and other towns in Lancashire, apprentices stopped work in the autumn of 1937, claiming a share of the 3s rise which had previously been conceded to the adults in 1935–6 and agitating for recognition of collective bargaining rights. To ensure uniformity in the Lancashire region, it was agreed in the Lancashire JSC to concede all apprentices a rise of 2 shillings per week on the wage-for-age scale lists from October 1937.[120] Later in the year, the EEF agreed to recognise the negotiating rights of the 120,000 or so apprentices in the trade, and on 22 December 1937 the first Apprentice Procedure Agreement was signed with the AEU. The voting of the local associations registered an 'overwhelming majority' in favour of this recognition.[121]

In Lancashire, however, considerable numbers in the trade were bitterly resentful of the increases in the costs of production which the EEF sanctioned over the period of 1935–9. The commercial trade of many member firms – particularly those in the textile machinery sector – remained depressed throughout this period and many firms outside the Manchester district did not benefit from orders under the defence programme until late 1938 or early 1939. Most of the associations in the north-west outside Manchester pleaded that trade just did not warrant the increases in wages and the concession of holidays with pay in 1935–8. At least, it was argued, the Federation should attempt to secure a long-term wage freeze if some concessions were given.[122] The Burnley EEA voted unanimously against the 1937 wage concessions and holidays with pay, and the Oldham association voted 88 to 18 against acceptance of the 1937 agreement.[123] In Manchester, significantly, it was only the two major textile machinery making firms, Brooks and Doxey and John Hetherington's, which voted against making some concessions to labour in 1937.[124] Only in late 1938, when commercial trade slumped to an all-time low, did the EEF respond to these protests and reject the engineering

---

[119] Lancashire JSC, Minutes, 2 March, 11 May, 9 August 1937.
[120] Manchester EEA, Minutes, 21 September 1937; Lancashire JSC, Minutes, 28 September 1937.
[121] Lancashire JSC, Minutes, 2 November 1937, 4 January 1938; Manchester EEA, Minutes, 1 November 1937.   [122] Lancashire JSC, Minutes, 7 January 1936, 6 July 1937.
[123] Burnley EEA, Minutes, 6 May, 9 August 1937; Oldham EEA, Minutes, 4 August, 1937.
[124] Manchester EEA, Minutes, 15 July 1937.

union's claim for further wage rises and improvement in working conditions.[125] During this whole period, there was considerable conflict on labour relations policy within the EEF between the firms producing for the home market, with the lucrative government rearmament orders, and those which continued to be dependent on the depressed export market.

The rearmament boom sharpened the skilled labour shortage in the later 1930s and prompted much upward wage escalation and the granting of unofficial wage enticements and inducements.[126] In Bolton, member firms complained in 1938 that they were losing their sheet-metal workers to companies where more attractive conditions were in operation. Two aircraft subsidiary firms in the Manchester district paying 'easy' piece-work rates were considered to be the worst culprits.[127] A number of Manchester firms also complained of enticement and of 'objectionable advertisements' in the press offering excessive rates – £7–8 per week – to skilled engineers.[128] Employers also protested that some employment exchanges were allowing operatives to register whilst they were still working, and were informing them of vacancies on armament work at higher wage rates as they occurred, thus allowing them to transfer without difficulty.[129] With tighter competition for operatives the customary 'enquiry' fell almost entirely out of use.[130] Evidence suggests that employers' associations were again increasingly losing control over actual wage rates paid by member firms, and that the wage drift was in an upward direction. The trade recovery encouraged employers' associations to be considerably more flexible in their labour relations strategy, particularly in defence of their managerial rights and prerogatives when a dispute threatened to stop production. The only factor which limited this flexibility was the intransigence of the employers who had not secured government contracts and were still suffering severely from the commercial recession.

Towards the end of 1937, the Manchester engineering employers became embroiled in a dispute with their labourers over wages. The labourers' unions complained that wages were lower in Manchester than in all the other major engineering towns in the midlands and the north-east and should be raised to a 30 shillings minimum.[131] The EEF agreed that there was some justice in the claim as 60 per cent of the engineering labourers in Britain were on a wage of 30 shillings or more and 75 per cent

[125] Lancashire JSC, Minutes, 1 November 1938.
[126] Zeitlin, 'Internal politics', pp. 72–4.
[127] Lancashire JSC, Minutes, 6 December 1938.
[128] Manchester EEA, Minutes, 2 November 1936, 5 April 1937.
[129] Lancashire JSC, Minutes, 7 March 1939.
[130] Rochdale EEA, Minutes, 15 April 1937.
[131] Lancashire JSC, Minutes, 2 November 1937.

received 29 shillings or more.[132] Skilled wages in Manchester were comparable to those in all other districts in Britain, so the anomaly deserved to be rectified. However, whilst the Manchester employers agreed to negotiate, the consensus view in the Lancashire JSC was opposed to any concession and managed to veto any action on the matter by the Manchester EEA. The local employers' associations argued that the commercial trade did not justify any increases in the cost of production and anticipated that a rise in Manchester would prompt a rise elsewhere to retain traditional differentials in the district. It was also feared that any concessions to the labourers would result in commensurate claims for increases to retain differentials from machinemen and all the semi-skilled hands. Moreover, most employers' associations reported that they had no trouble obtaining labourers at the existing rates of pay. This was in part due to the continued deep recession in the Lancashire cotton trade which kept the local unskilled and semi-skilled labour markets in surplus.[133] The victory of the depressed textile machinery manufacturers on the question of unskilled wage rates was, however, short-lived. The issue was deferred for three months, after which the Manchester EEA, under threat of a strike by their labourers, conceded a base rate of 30 shillings per week. Faced with a *fait accompli*, the other north-west local associations were obliged to follow suit.[134] The Lancashire JSC was forced reluctantly to acquiesce in these concessions, or face an intensification of the labour drain to Manchester.

The lack of consensus between organised employers in Lancashire was also made apparent in 1938 when rises in outworking allowances were discussed. The unions demanded a flat 15 shillings above the district time-workers' wage rate for those skilled workers sent out to work. The Manchester EEA was again the most vociferous within the Lancashire JSC in favour of giving some extra allowance and suggested that this should be equivalent to their average piecework earnings. To the textile machinery producers, this was simply an excuse by the Manchester engineering companies to establish yet another inducement to entice scarce skilled workers into the district. The EEF was approached but the Federation reply indicated that they felt the time was not opportune to be inflexible or to exert rigid controls on the members and tacitly agreed to ignore the proposals to compensate operatives when transferred to outworking.[135] The Manchester employers were left to settle the matter as

---

[132] Ibid., 7 December 1937.
[133] Manchester EEA, Minutes, 4 April 1938; Lancashire JSC, Minutes, 2 November 1937.
[134] Lancashire JSC, Minutes, 1 March, 5 April, 14 June, 8 September 1938; Manchester EEA, Minutes, 14 June, 4 July 1938.
[135] Manchester EEA, Minutes, 7 February, 4 April 1938; Lancashire JSC, Minutes, 14 June 1938.

they thought fit. This non-interventionist stance by the Federation was repeated when the Lancashire employers requested aid to challenge union limits upon apprentice numbers and defend the open shop principle.[136] Evidently, the message from the centre was that changed market circumstances necessitated the curtailing of offensive initiatives.[137] Caution, flexibility and pragmatism were now deemed necessary in order to avoid provoking widespread industrial discontent. The outbreak of the Second World War saw the engineering employers' associations already firmly locked within a defensive posture.

Conclusion

To sum up, there were evidently a number of dimensions to the engineering employers' campaign to reassert their control and authority in industrial relations between the wars. Labour costs were brought more effectively under control whilst managerial discipline on the shop-floor tightened. This offensive stopped short, however, of an outright attack upon trade unionism *per se*, led by the EEF. Indeed, by endorsing and extending collective bargaining through the official procedure the engineering employers were explicitly shoring up the unions, recognising, perhaps, the benefits of moderate trade unionism as a bulwark against less palatable alternatives. It was to undermine the possibility of the latter that the EEAs publicly courted trade union collaboration and peaceful coexistence, whilst, at the same time, covertly aiding the rooting out from their members' workplaces and subsequent blacklisting of militant shop stewards and other left-wing activists. Developments in engineering during the period 1914–20 dramatically increased the sensitivity of the employers' organisations in this sector to what they regarded as a 'subversive' presence within their workplaces and hence they remained in the vanguard of the movement to undermine socialist ideas and reconstruct capitalist hegemony between the wars.

Weakened by internal divisions, engineering employers and their organisations failed, it has been convincingly argued elsewhere, to spearhead any fundamental transformation in the division of labour, despite the opportunity offered by the slump and the employers' unequivocal victory in 1922. Deskilling was more limited and workgroup initiative and power less constrained in this industry than previous accounts have conceded. Clearly, organised capital in engineering was not omnipotent, nor was it operating in a vacuum. The evidence offered here from a regional

---

[136] Manchester EEA, Minutes, 3 April 1939; Lancashire JSC, Minutes, 7 February 1939.
[137] See Zeitlin, 'Internal politics', pp. 73–4.

perspective supports such an interpretation, with some caveats. First, fresh evidence is provided here of the fragmentation of employers' interests within this diverse industry in north-west England. Employer cohesion was undermined by relatively heterogeneous product markets and varied technologies – in marked contrast to cotton textile manufacture. In Lancashire there were quite fundamental distinctions in labour relations policies between the beleaguered textile engineering bloc and the more diversified Manchester engineering employers. This mirrored a fundamental division within the industry between the newer, consumer-orientated, more prosperous sector of engineering and the older, export-orientated, capital goods, declining sector. A gap also opened between national Federation strategy and practice in the localities, with local associations exercising much discretion in upholding prerogatives, developing pragmatic responses to individual circumstances, rather than taking principled stances. Over the period, conflicts of opinion and diverging product market experience set in train quite serious centrifugal tendencies, beginning a process of atomising industrial relations, returning the initiative slowly but inexorably back to the individual firm.

Nor, secondly, is there much evidence in north-west England of a managerial revolution between the wars. Rationalisation and scientific management were not openly promoted by the EEAs. What appears to have occurred was largely an intensification of labour within the parameters of existing technology, affecting the division of labour marginally rather than significantly. This paralleled developments in cotton manufacture. Whilst skilled engineering workers may have directly experienced relatively little change, there was, however, a significant increase in the proportion of the engineering labour force employed in 'semi-skilled' processing and a growing segment of it were women. This may well have represented regrading, however, rather than a unilinear process of deskilling. Nor was there much evidence of institutional support for the welfarist managerial option – growing in popularity, according to Fitzgerald and Jones, between the wars.[138] As Gospel has convincingly demonstrated, the collectively formulated substantive norms developed in the engineering industry focused predominantly upon wages and working hours, rather than loyalty-inducing 'fringe benefits'.[139]

However, all this does not amount to an impotent and hopelessly disunited employers' movement in engineering which played no significant

---

[138] H. Jones, 'Employers' welfare schemes and industrial relations in interwar Britain', *Business History*, 25 (1983), pp. 61–75; R. Fitzgerald, *British Labour Management and Industrial Welfare, 1846–1939*, London: Croom Helm, 1988, pp. 1–20, 247–8. See also S. Jones, 'Cotton employers and industrial welfare', pp. 64–77.

[139] Gospel, 'Employers' organisations', pp. 201–2.

role in industrial relations at the workplace, labour market or national level between the wars. By narrowing the focus to the impact of collective organisation upon competitiveness – via the division of labour – revisionist accounts have been overly negative, seriously underestimating the role played by organised capital in industrial relations. Recognition of the limits of employers' collective power and activities needs to be balanced by a more sensitive appraisal of just what it was that they achieved. With reference to engineering, several points deserve to be emphasised: first, membership data suggest that the organisational power and solidarity of the engineering employers was sustained between the wars. Secondly, the existence of a powerful employers' organisation did aid engineering employers in bringing labour costs under control in the 1920s and 1930s, though clearly this control fell short of being absolute and was undermined somewhat by the pressures of rearmament from c. 1935–6. Arguably, however, collective organisation helped prevent the concession of an even shorter working week in 1919 and, from 1920, the employers' organisations spearheaded a comprehensive costs reduction drive which slashed direct wage rates and, in 1931, cut labour costs by reducing overtime and nightshift costs. Thirdly, managerial authority was revived and workshop discipline restored during the slump years. Workers' wartime advances and the radical aspirations towards an extension of work control by the shop stewards were largely reversed in the 1920s. Many contemporary commentators have noted the quite markedly altered atmosphere on the shop-floor from the early 1920s on. This was a product of changed market circumstances, though the victory of the EEF in 1922 undoubtedly facilitated both these processes of cost cutting and the reimposition of managerial authority. The latter was further bolstered by a revival in the use of the lock-out threat and related, more authoritarian policies. Fourthly, the environment after 1922 was conducive to the more rapid extension within engineering – amongst the craft and non-craft sectors alike – of one element of 'scientific management' – payments by results wage systems. Significantly, the engineering employers' associations struggled to provide an industrial relations framework which allowed constituent members the freedom to tie wages more closely to production. This, in combination with the disciplining effects of the labour market and the undermining of the shop stewards' and workshop organisation, allowed the pace of work to be increased and customary workloads and craft privileges to be undermined.

Fifthly, and critically, the employers' organisations in engineering extended control over labour through a process of incorporation and accommodation of trade unions. The strategy formulated in the 1890s and pursued in the pre-war period was consolidated during and immediately after the First World War. Emphasis was laid upon channelling workers' claims and grievances through formalised and quite sophisticated collective bargaining and disputes procedures. On the one hand this system provided explicit recognition for unions in the industry and evidence that employers were willing to work with unions if they eschewed direct action and notions of worker control, acted responsibly, and adhered to the rules of the game. It imposed reciprocal obligations on both sides. However, the survival of this corporatist system after 1921–2 and through the inter-war recession bears testimony to its utility to the employers. By strangling district claims within the conference system, it effectively contained the classic trade union weapon of leapfrogging concessions. Significantly, the Central Conference was barren ground for union claims between the wars. However, the EEF was flexible and astute enough to prevent mass union defection from the formalised disputes procedure in the 1930s, even initiating some limited expansion of the system to incorporate women workers in 1932 and apprentices in 1937. The procedural and substantive norms provided security for employers and brought much stability to industrial relations.

Finally, on another front, the engineering employers' organisations engaged in activities designed to legitimise and induce ideological commitment to capitalist enterprise. Tactics here incorporated organisational support for the propaganda activities of organisations such as the NCEO and the Economic League and the more sinister policy of sacking and actively victimising the most vociferous critics of capitalism. The control mechanism here was overtly coercive. Whilst forcible strikebreaking via labour replacement may well have been in terminal decline from the late nineteenth century, its place was to some extent taken by more centralised, systematised and clandestine procedures to remove trade union activists from employment – to extirpate the 'socialist cancer' from the workplace. The success of such tactics between the wars is difficult to gauge. What is undeniable, however, is that the heavy involvement of the engineering employers – co-ordinated through their organisations – in the activities of the Economic League indicates a fundamental disregard for the rights of their workers as citizens.

Thus, engineering employers' organisations played a vital role in industrial relations in the 1920s and 1930s in so far as they spearheaded offensives designed to reduce costs and revive managerial authority, undermined the influence of socialist activists and militant shop stewards through victimisation, whilst bolstering a mode of moderate trade unionism which operated within the boundaries of what the employers regarded as acceptable behaviour. This is not to imply that craft workers in engineering were powerless, or trade unions impotent, or engineering employers' organisations completely solid and omnipotent in the 1920s and 1930s. Clearly, that was not the case. However, the evidence does suggest that there existed a very unequal relationship between capital and labour in this industry between the wars and that the employers' organisations played a significant role in structuring industrial relations and protecting capitalist interests during this period of economic recession.

Conclusion

This book has explored a somewhat neglected area of industrial relations history, discussing the emergence of employers' organisations and the labour relations policies formulated by such institutions up to the Second World War. It thus aims to make a contribution to the growing corpus of literature on industrial employers. Recent research has emphasised the variable nature of industrial relations across Britain and stressed the need for more work on the policies of employers at the industry and local levels in order to understand social relations better.[1] The comparative (three industries), regional (north-west England) perspective adopted here attempts to address this gap in the literature, providing an alternative focus to the national, single-industry studies that tend to dominate the literature and one that has thrown up some interesting and, I hope, quite meaningful results. At one level, this might be justified on the grounds that an extension of the empirical material available on the genesis, organisation and activities of what remain neglected institutions is welcome. Through absorption in internally generated association records and hence in the day-to-day activities of these organisations we have perhaps got a little nearer to what such bodies actually did, how they were structured, their patterns of growth and policy formulation, and the industrial relations strategies they pursued as they reacted to changing product market, labour market and political circumstances and to the challenge posed by the emergence of organised labour in the late nineteenth and early twentieth centuries.

The longevity of such institutions has been emphasised, though the apogee of employer organisation power and regulatory functions clearly lay in the period from around 1890 to the 1930s. By the First World War a formidable phalanx of employers' organisations existed across British industry. The First World War and its immediate aftermath further incubated class consciousness, creating a set of circumstances which critically enhanced employer solidarity, facilitating the emergence of a distinctive

[1] A. Reid, *Social Classes and Social Relations*, pp. 61–2.

employers' movement. Thereafter, however, the economic pressures unleashed by the inter-war recession and related changes in state policy and business structure released powerful centrifugal forces, working to undermine collective organisation and to relocate regulatory power at the level of the individual company, rather than the collective organisation. Such trends, evident in the 1930s, accelerated after 1945. After the Second World War, British employers' organisations increasingly shed their collective regulation of wages and working conditions and assumed advisory, pressure group and 'watchdog' functions.[2]

Apart from charting patterns of collective organisation and behaviour from a comparative and regional perspective, the text has also engaged in the current debates on the importance of employers' organisations in industrial relations and within British society. My interpretation is somewhat critical of accounts which regard capital as monolithic and omnipotent. Focusing on one region in some depth has brought into sharper focus the clusters of often competing interest groups which coexisted within employers' collective organisations and the great difficulties such associations had in reconciling these fragments and bringing competing, individualistic capitalists into some kind of meaningful union. Differences in business structure, product specialism and market experience were fundamentally important in this respect. Broadly speaking, employers within any given industry had common interests, as owners of capital, but these interests did not necessarily or always converge, as pluralist theory would have us believe, because of quite unique historical contingencies, not least diverging market experiences and differing levels of trade union implantation. Witness, for example, the conflicts of interest between cotton spinning and weaving, between Oldham (coarse and medium counts spinning) and Bolton (fine spinning), between the diversified Manchester engineering concerns and the textile machinery manufacturers of north Lancashire and between the building masters of Merseyside and the Manchester region. In such circumstances flexibility and pragmatism were important, indeed essential and characteristic components of British employers' organisations. Some studies have been overly deterministic, failing to recognise the possibility of autonomous activity – what Zeitlin has evocatively called 'strategic choices' – and a range of regional and sectoral divergences in the attitudes and policies of organised capital towards labour and trade unions.[3]

---

[2] See H.F. Gospel and G. Palmer, *British Industrial Relations*, 2nd edition, London: Routledge, 1993, pp. 67–91; H.F. Gospel, *Employers' Organisations and Industrial Relations*, Commission on Industrial Relations, London: HMSO, 1972; W. Brown, *The Changing Contours of British Industrial Relations*, Oxford: Basil Blackwell, 1981.

[3] Zeitlin, 'Labour strategies'; Zeitlin, 'Internal politics'.

Nevertheless, it remains true that external pressures intimately influenced employers' labour relations policies. Associational activity and behaviour was not preconditioned by economic or other forces; rather, actions were constrained, choices limited and possibilities prescribed by state intervention, unionisation, the nature of business organisation and developments in markets. A combination of such external pressures exerted a powerful centripetal force over the period *c.* 1880–1920, drawing employers together, incubating a sense of common interest and purpose, evoking class consciousness. Thus the period from the 1880s to the 1920s witnessed the proliferation of a complex matrix of employers' organisations, from the lowly local master builders' association combining a handful of small masters to the influential National Confederation of Employers' Organisations. Some of these were specialist single-function bodies, such as the free labour associations, whilst others combined industrial, commercial, political and ideological functions, such as the textile employers' federations. Their evolution took place at a particular stage in economic development, mirroring company amalgamation and merger, a component of the transition towards industrial concentration and the 'corporate economy'. Previous commentators have stressed the importance of mass trade unionism as a cementing force in this process, pressuring employers to counter with collective organisation and resistance. This was, indeed, a powerful stimulant to employer cohesion over these years. However, it has been argued here that there were two other forces which encouraged combination – a more hostile product market and a more actively interventionist state. It was the combination of these three powerful external forces – unions, the state and markets – which induced capitalists to eschew individualism and set up strong and representative collective organisations. The incentive to combine and externalise key aspects of labour relations was sharpened further by the nature of business enterprise in Britain, where typically small and medium-sized companies lacked (at least prior to the Second World War) the internal resources and organisational structures necessary to respond adequately to the challenge of labour.[4]

Reference has been made on a number of occasions to a strand of 'revisionist' historiography which regards British employers' organisations as characterised by disunity, ineffectiveness and impotency in the face of well-organised craft workers. How well does such a reappraisal stand up against the evidence for north-west England? The great strengths of the 'revisionist' interpretation are its effective destruction of the notion of a monolithic, all-powerful employer class and its persuasive

[4] See Gospel, *Markets*, pp. 16–7, 100–1, 181–2, for elaboration of this argument.

rejection of unqualified economic determinism. However, my argument here has been that such revisionism goes too far, that it in turn merits qualification and some reformulation. Concentrating, as it does, predominantly upon only one facet – the impact of industrial relations institutions on British competitiveness – this thesis has been too narrowly construed and is too negative in tone. The employer organisations in the north-west were characterised by their conservatism; rarely did they actively promote rationalisation of work. However, by concentrating on the relationship between skilled craft workers and employers such accounts have misrepresented industrial realities and underestimated the power and the dynamic role played by employers' organisations. This text has argued for a more balanced re-evaluation of British employers' organisations and their labour relations policies. In short, it challenges the notion that British employers' organisations were distinguished by weakness and disunity. In conclusion, several points might be made in support of this interpretation.

First, extrapolations are frequently being made within the 'revisionist' literature from a fairly narrow base – notably the metal manufacturing sectors of engineering and shipbuilding. Significantly, these are industries where trade union power and craft control clearly remained in evidence to the Second World War (and, arguably, through to the 1970s). However, the experience of such industries may well not apply across the economy as a whole – either in the case of Britain or elsewhere. Engineering was a particularly heterogeneous sector in terms of industrial structure and markets and effective combination was much more difficult and problematic than in more homogeneous industries, for example cotton textile manufacturing. We still know very little about employer behaviour, organisation and strategies across vast swathes of the British economy, including clothing, transport, chemicals, food processing, personal service, administration, commerce, finance and distribution. Until these gaps are filled, conclusions on collective employer behaviour must necessarily remain tentative rather than definitive. However, the range of collective activities thrown up in this regional study, across the gamut of labour market regulation, conflict management, political lobbying, the regulation of trade and product markets and the provision of mutual insurance suggests a much more vital role for such organisations than much of the literature implies.

Secondly, and to reiterate, the strength of British employer organisations prior to the First World War lay primarily at the local and regional level – a point raised but underemphasised in Tolliday and Zeitlin's preoccupation with the wider picture and the comparative perspective. The evidence for north-west England suggests that systems of internal discipline may well have been more pervasive and effective at the local level than these commentators give credit for.[5] The quantitative membership data presented and dissected in chapter 3, moreover, implies quite representative and powerful institutions. Furthermore, the evidence derived from at least one important manufacturing sector – cotton textiles – suggests stronger and more purposeful employers' associations exercising real control over many vital spheres of industrial relations, the labour contract and the labour market. Workers wielding a considerable degree of control over the labour process – including spinners and overlookers – were always only a very small, unrepresentative section of the textile manufacturing workforce. Moreover, whilst managerial authority and control over skilled workers was rarely complete, the degree of discretion exercised by craftsmen in British manufacturing industry was undoubtedly diminished by the late 1930s compared to c. 1880, whilst the autonomy of other work groups – women, clerical workers, unskilled and semi-skilled – remained severely constrained.[6] More importantly, perhaps, employer organisation facilitated work intensification within the parameters of existing technology and, more often than not, within the framework of the traditional division of labour. An example would be the way in which the engineering employer victories of 1898 and 1922 facilitated the diffusion of payments by results wage systems. Such effort intensification at the point of production was particularly marked in the inter-war period as overstocked labour markets empowered employers and organisations spearheaded a counter-attack to cut costs and reimpose workshop discipline.

Thirdly, whilst it is quite correct to stress the importance of government and trade unions as 'interlocutors' cementing employer organisation it is also the case that collective behaviour occurred without such pressures and, after c. 1890, continued beyond particular industrial relations crises. The impulse towards collaborative behaviour by employers was not entirely the product of knee-jerk defensive reactions to state and union interference. The very existence of employers' organisations dealing with labour matters before the First World War in such sectors as clothing, food, drink and tobacco, agriculture and even personal service, where unionisation was poorly developed, suggests, perhaps, a degree of class solidarity amongst employers irrespective of the binding agents of

[5] See McKenna and Rodger, 'Control by coercion'; McIvor, 'Employers' organisations and industrial relations', pp. 55–120.
[6] See, for example, J. Hilton's study, *Are Trade Unions Obstructive?*, London: Victor Gollancz, 1935; R. Price, 'Rethinking labour history', in J. Cronin and J. Schneer (eds.), *Social Conflict and the Political Order in Modern Britain*, London: Croom Helm, 1982, pp. 179–214.

worker organisation and government policy.[7] In this sense, as Magrath has argued for the wool industry, employers' organisations 'can be seen to be proactive rather than reactive'.[8] Foster and Woolfson have also recently demonstrated this to be the case in the British North Sea oil industry in the 1970s and 1980s.[9]

Fourthly, the revisionist interpretation plays down the utilisation by British employers' organisations of more draconian anti-labour methods that clearly represented naked pursuit of class interests. My argument in chapter 4 was that employers' organisations strengthened the ability of employers to neutralise the strike weapon and that strikebreaking techniques were changing in character over the period from 1880 to the 1920s, with labour replacement declining, whilst strike insurance schemes and covert victimisation became more popular employer weapons. These more clandestine and less openly provocative methods were invariably co-ordinated through industry employer organisations and supported in the 1920s and 1930s by the emergence of Britain's first centralised political victimisation agency, the Economic League (to which the mineowners and engineering employers' associations had particularly close links). This seedier, blatantly political, class-confrontational dimension of employer activities in the pre-Second World War period deserves due attention and reminds us of what employers' organisations essentially represented: aggregations of capital, albeit wracked by internal divisions, which succeeded in bolstering the authority of individual companies, thus enabling them to lord it over their workers more effectively, perpetuating injustice, inequality and exploitation of labour, though in more subtle and diversified forms as time went on. This dimension of associational activities was most sharply exposed in the employers' 'counterattacks' of the 1890s and 1921–33.

Thus, and this is my fifth point, over the period c. 1880–1939, the class identities of British employers were invariably being sharpened, rather than blunted, and this was most tangibly expressed in the emergence of a variegated and multi-functional matrix of powerful employers' organisations. Where it exists, evidence suggests that employers' associations proliferated in Britain in the period 1890–1920, that such bodies became increasingly representative of capital and that many had made the transition from transient to permanent and powerful structures capable of

[7] Ministry of Labour, *Eighteenth Abstract of Labour Statistics*, 1926, p. 191 for a full list of employers' organisations in existence in Britain.

[8] Magrath, 'Wool textile employers' organisations', p. 76.

[9] J. Foster and C. Woolfson, 'Safety cultures and national cultures: industrial relations in North Sea oil and gas' (unpublished paper, 'Management, Production and Politics' conference, Centre for Business History, University of Glasgow, 24–5 April 1992).

exerting a regulatory influence on labour markets. Certainly this appears to be the case for textile manufacturing, coal, engineering, building and shipping. This is not to imply that employers' associations were always dominant or always successful in achieving their objectives, but rather to argue that their role in the structuring of the British industrial relations system has been very significant – indeed much more important than many commentators suggest.

Due attention, however, has been devoted in the preceding pages to the weaknesses as well as the strengths and achievements of such organisations. Here, clearly, a balance has to be struck. Middlemas's conception of employers' organisations as governing institutions, or 'estates', seems as wide of the mark as the revisionists' over-zealous deconstruction exercise.[10] In reality, power and policy varied with product and labour market fluctuations and the actions of most employers' organisations were undermined, to a greater or lesser degree, by internal divisions, multiple interest groups, rifts between conciliators and confrontationists, doves and hawks. Divisions were based on ideological differences, or diverging product market experience or differences of company structure or on custom and practice. Competitive advantage was also a key centrifugal force, corroding solidaristic endeavours. Such divisions became particularly acute as the inter-war economic recession deepened and profitability came under intense pressure, particularly in the hard-pressed sectors of cotton manufacture and engineering in north-west England. I hope this study will help to dispel any lingering vestiges of the myth that employers were a holistic, homogeneous group. Apparent organisational solidarity often obscured deep-rooted intra-class schisms and fragmentation of interests which did erode the potential power of organised capital, as, for example, during the Brooklands (1892–3) and the more looms (1932) lock-outs in cotton.

Nevertheless, despite internal divisions, fragmentation and differences in form and structure, the evidence for north-west England strongly supports the view that British employers' organisations were invariably powerful and representative bodies which played an important role in forging alliances, defending class interests and structuring British industrial relations before the Second World War. Not least in helping to neutralise the sectional strike weapon, in minimising the real cost of labour legislation (such as the Workmen's Compensation Acts), and in promoting uniformity in the labour contract and labour markets, hence taking wages out of competition and removing many conflict-inducing anomalies. However, in the final analysis perhaps the most significant role of employers' associ-

[10] Middlemas, *Politics*, pp. 150–1.

ations lay in the initiatives they took to create, sustain and extend a more formalised, permissive industrial relations system – which might be theorised as an attempt to extend procedural controls over labour. This system was based on joint, collectively agreed regulation of wages and hours and increasingly comprehensive disputes procedures. This transition in labour management strategy evolved over time. Around 1880 most British employers' organisations were actively engaged in trying to break strikes forcibly and to extirpate trade unions, or, at the very least were trying to contain a moderate and tolerable mode of unionism to the small minority of scarce craft workers. The orientation of such employers' associations (take the ITEA for example) was generally authoritarian, with a whole arsenal of coercive, knee-jerk weapons – including victimisation, the importation of replacement labour and the lock-out – exploited to maintain workshop discipline and uphold unilateral managerial authority. As circumstances changed, this strategy became untenable and employers' organisations adapted to an altered social, economic and political environment. Faced with stronger and permanent trade unions, firmly implanted within a broader spectrum of industrial labour, such a strategic transition was vitally important in stabilising industrial relations. Increasingly, trade unions came to be accepted, recognised and accommodated within formalised disputes and substantive agreements, with the employers' organisations playing a pivotal role in forging and, especially, in sustaining such industrial relations systems. In cotton, building and engineering the employers' organisations converged in their commitment to maintain this formalised industrial relations system from the 1890s on. Indeed, multi-employer bargaining dominated the manufacturing sector by 1920. Significantly, whilst the employers' organisations spearheaded a counter-attack to cut costs and resuscitate eroded managerial authority during the inter-war recession, they continued to pursue accommodatory strategies *vis-à-vis* the trade unions, to maintain and even to extend collective bargaining, thus eschewing the clear opportunity offered by market conditions to root out trade unions altogether. By the end of our period under review, 1939, employers' associations had clearly come to accept unions as an integral and permanent part of the fabric of British society. This represented, in part, a pragmatic adjustment to events outside their control. However, it also constituted a strategic commitment to moderate, constitutional and economistic modes of trade unionism as a bulwark against more radical alternatives that challenged the very core of managerial prerogative, proprietorial control and capitalist endeavour. In defining the limits as well as the extent of the employers' inter-war counter-attack against labour, an illustration has been provided of how bureaucratic and corporatist tendencies deflected the logic of market developments.

The literature has emphasised the adverse impact upon economic competitiveness of such 'externalisation' of labour relations to employers' associations: fossilising multi-unionism; discouraging the development of more sophisticated and efficient internal management systems; constraining rationalisation at work; leaving space for the rigidification of 'restrictive' practices, with collective bargaining rarely tying wages directly to effort. What has been neglected has been the impact of organised capital upon society through labour market regulation, directed generally towards the employment of cheaper, less skilled labour and the victimisation of activists, and through the formulation of collectively negotiated wage rates and the maintenance of working conditions, which in turn influenced standards of living and occupational health. These organisations endeavoured to create an environment which allowed individual employers to maximise profits. They did this by regulating and cutting labour costs, intensifying workloads and, critically, by maintaining managerial prerogatives and a hierarchical form of organisation and control within the workplace. Exploiting a range of strategies, British employers' organisations played a key role in absorbing and neutralising the challenge posed by the rise of trade unions and, at least up to the Second World War, frustrated aspirations from below for direct workers' control of industry. Given the radical nature of the challenge of labour, particularly during the decade 1910–20, this was no mean achievement. It was the outcome of a continuing process of conflict between capital and labour within which employers' organisations critically bolstered the power of individual employers, came to accommodate trade unionism, and thus helped to sustain capitalism in Britain.

Bibliography

A PRIMARY SOURCES

1 EMPLOYERS' ORGANISATION RECORDS

1.1 Cotton

United Cotton Spinners' Association, *Annual Reports*; Rules and Membership Lists, 1886–8.

Cotton Employers' Parliamentary Association, Minutes, 1899–1911.

Federation of Master Cotton Spinners' Associations, *Annual Reports*, 1892–1939; Membership Lists, 1899–1939; Miscellaneous *Yearbooks*, Rules, Reports, etc.

Cotton Spinners' and Manufacturers' Association of North and North-East Lancashire, Minutes, 1866–9 and 1880–1939; Joint Minutes (with the cotton unions), 1881–1939; *Annual Reports*, 1935–9; Levy Book, 1912–39.

Accrington Cotton Spinners' and Manufacturers' Association, Minutes, 1896–1939; Levy and Subscription Books, 1912–39.

Ashton Master Cotton Spinners' Association, *Annual Reports*, 1891–1939; Minutes, 1891–1939.

Blackburn Cotton Manufacturers' Association, Minutes, 1877–1939; Letter Books, 1906–39; Membership List, 1899–1902; Ledgers, Subscription and Cash Books, 1903–39.

Bolton Cotton Manufacturers' Association, Minutes, 1894–1939.

Bolton Master Cotton Spinners' Association, *Quarterly Reports*, 1887–97 and 1933–9; *Annual Reports*, 1887–97 and 1933–9; Minutes, 1878–1939; Diary, 1886–1939; Levy Books, 1901–39; Miscellaneous Rules and Reports.

Burnley Cotton Manufacturers' Association, Minutes, 1894–1939; Ledgers and Cash Books, 1912–39.

Chorley Cotton Manufacturers' Association, Minutes, 1914–39.

Clitheroe Cotton Employers' Association, Minutes, 1906–39.

Colne Coloured Goods Manufacturers' Association, Minutes, 1888–1939; Ledgers, 1920–39.

Darwen Cotton Spinners' and Manufacturers' Association, Minutes, 1897–1930; Levy and Subscription Books, 1897–1928.

Glossop and Hyde Master Cotton Spinners' Association, Minutes, 1898–1920.

Great Harwood Cotton Masters' Association, Minutes, 1893–1924.

Manchester Master Cotton Spinners' Association, Minutes, 1892–1939.

Nelson Textile Manufacturers' Association, Minutes, 1891–1939; Ledgers and Cash Books, 1916–39.

Oldham Master Cotton Spinners' Association, *Annual Reports*, 1880–1939; Minutes, 1866–1939; Letter Books, 1870–1939; Membership Lists, 1890–1939; Levy Books, 1890–1939; Legal Opinions (Hesketh Booth, Solicitors) 1890–1912; Miscellaneous Rules, Reports, *Yearbooks*, etc.
Padiham Cotton Manufacturers' Association, Minutes, 1890–1939; Ledgers and Cash Books, 1890–1939.
Preston Cotton Manufacturers' Association, Minutes, 1894–1939; Letter Books, 1890–97; Ledgers, Levy and Cash Books, 1897–1939.
Preston Master Cotton and Flax Spinners' Association, Minutes, 1838–58.
Rochdale Master Cotton Spinners' Association, *Annual Reports*, 1910–38; Minutes, 1892–1907.
Stockport Master Cotton Spinners' Association, Minutes, 1892–1939.
Wigan Master Cotton Spinners' Association, Minutes, 1907–35.

1.2 Building
General Builders' Association, Minutes, 1865–71.
National Association of Master Builders (later National Federation of Building Trade Employers), *Annual Reports*, 1890–1939; Minutes, 1878–1939.
The Northern Centre, Minutes, 1898–1919.
Lancashire and Cheshire Federation of Building Trade Employers (later North-West Federation of Building Trade Employers), *Annual* and *Half-Yearly Reports*, 1914–39; Minutes, 1894–1939; *Yearbooks* and Membership Lists, 1913–39.
Ashton-under-Lyne Master Builders' Association, Minutes, 1900–16.
Bolton Master Builders' Association, Minutes, 1915–39.
Liverpool Master Builders' Association, Minutes, 1892–1939; Board of Conciliation Minutes, 1906–39; *Yearbooks*, 1909–39.
Manchester, Salford and District Building Trade Employers' Association, Minutes, 1901–39; Conciliation Board Minutes, 1906–18; Area Joint Council Minutes, 1918–39.
Middleton Master Builders' Association, Minutes, 1917–38.
Oldham Master Builders' Association, Minutes, 1889–1939; Conciliation Board Minutes, 1906–1918.
Preston Master Builders' Association, Minutes, 1892–1939; Area Joint Council Minutes, 1920–5.

1.3 Engineering
Iron Trades Employers' Association, *Annual Reports*, 1872–1899; *Record* (1900).
Engineering Employers' Federation, Minutes, 1896–1939; Correspondence Files, 1896–1939; Levy Registers, Subscriptions and Numbers Employed Files, 1899–1939; Individual Membership Files, 1896–1939; Central Conferences, 1898–1939; Wage Movement Indexes, 1898–1925.
Joint Standing Committee of Lancashire Engineering Employers' Associations, Minutes, 1918–39.
Association of Controlled Establishments (Lancashire), Minutes 1916–1920.
Blackburn Engineering Employers' Association, Minutes, 1935–39.
Burnley Engineering Employers Association, Minutes, 1899–1939.

Manchester Engineering Employers' Association, Minutes, 1897–1939; Cash Books, Ledgers, Journals, Levy and Subscription Files, 1897–1939.
Oldham Engineering Employers' Association, Minutes, 1906–1939; Levy Book, 1937–39.
Rochdale Machine Makers' Association, Minutes, 1897–1939; Cash Books and Ledgers, 1897–1939.

1.4 Other organisations
Economic League, *Annual Reports*, Bulletins, Pamphlets, Speakers' Notes, 1925–39.

2 NEWSPAPERS AND JOURNALS

Board of Trade Gazette
Bolton Evening News
Capital and Labour
Cotton Factory Times
Daily Worker
Economist
Engineer
Engineering
Forward
Glasgow Herald
Industrialist
Manchester Guardian
Master Builder
National Builder
Textile Manufacturer
Textile Mercury

3 TRADE DIRECTORIES

Aubrey and Co., Directory of Lancashire, 1938.
Barrett's Directories of Preston and District.
Clegg's Directory of Rochdale, 1916.
Cope's Bolton and District Directory and Buyers' Guide, 1930.
Cope's Directories of Preston, Blackburn and District.
Cope's Directories of Rochdale and Oldham.
Kelly's Trade Directories for Manchester and Salford.
Skinner's Cotton Trade Directories.
Tillotson's Directories for Bolton and District.
Worrall's Cotton Spinners' and Manufacturers' Directories.

4 PARLIAMENTARY PAPERS AND REPORTS

Board of Trade, Labour Department, *Annual Reports on Strikes and Lock-Outs*, London: HMSO, 1888–1913.
    Directories of Industrial Associations in the UK, London: HMSO, 1902–19, 1947.

Report on Collective Agreements between Employers and Workpeople in the UK, London: HMSO, 1910, Cd. 5366.

(later Ministry of Labour), *Abstracts of Labour Statistics*, London: HMSO, 1898–1937.

Board of Trade / University of Manchester, *An Industrial Survey of the Lancashire Area*, London: HMSO, 1932.

Chief Inspector of Factories, *Annual Reports*, London: HMSO, 1880–1939.

Departmental Committee on Accidents, *Report*, London: HMSO, 1911, Cd. 5535.

Departmental Committee on Compensation for Industrial Diseases, *Minutes of Evidence*, London: HMSO, 1907, Cd. 3496.

Health of Munitions Workers Committee, *Final Report on Industrial Health and Efficiency*, London: HMSO, 1918, Cd. 8696.

Memorandum by the Ministry of Health on Poor Law Relief in Connection with the Dispute in the Engineering Trade, London: HMSO, 1922, Cd. 1693.

Report by a Court of Enquiry Concerning the Engineering Trades Dispute (under the Industrial Courts Act 1919), London: HMSO, 1922, Cd. 1653.

Reports of the Commission of Enquiry into Industrial Unrest: No. 2 Division, North-West Area, London: HMSO, 1917–18, Cd. 8663; *Summary of Reports*, London: HMSO, 1917–18, Cd. 8696.

Royal Commission on Trade Unions, 1867–9, *First Report*, 1867, Cd. 3873; *Fifth and Tenth Reports*, 1867–8, Cd. 3980; *Final Report*, 1868–9, Cd. 4123.

Royal Commission on Labour, *Evidence Before Group C (Textiles, Clothing, etc.)*, *Minutes*, 1892, Cd. 6708; 1892, Cd. 6795; 1893–4, Cd. 6894.

Royal Commission on Labour, *Final Report*, London: HMSO, 1894, Cd. 7921.

Royal Commission on Trade Disputes and Trade Combinations, *Report and Minutes of Evidence*, London: HMSO, 1906, Cd. 2826.

Royal Commission on Trade Unions and Employers' Associations, 1965–68, *Report*, London: HMSO, 1968, Cd. 3623.

Committee on Industry and Trade, *Survey of Textile Industries*, London: HMSO, 1928.

B SECONDARY SOURCES

Alderman, G., *The Railway Interest*, Leicester: Leicester University Press, 1973.

'The National Free Labour Association', *International Review of Social History*, 21 (1976), pp. 309–36.

Allen, G.C., *British Industries and their Organisation*, 5th edn, Harlow: Longman, 1970.

Amalgamated Association of Card Blowing and Ring Room Operatives, *After Fifty Years*, Manchester: The Association, 1936.

Andrew, S., *Fifty Years' Cotton Trade*, Oldham: Oldham Standard, 1887.

Armstrong, E., 'Employers' associations in Great Britain', in Windmuller and Gladstone (eds.), *Employers' Associations*.

Ashmore, O., *The Industrial Archaeology of Lancashire*, Newton Abbot: David and Charles, 1969.

Askwith, G.R., *Industrial Problems and Disputes*, new edition, Brighton: Harvester, 1974.

Bain, G. and Elsheikh, F., 'An inter-industry analysis of unionisation in Britain', *British Journal of Industrial Relations*, 17, no. 2 (1979), pp. 137–57.

Bamberg, J.H., 'Rationalisation of the British cotton industry in the interwar years', *Textile History*, 19 (1988), pp. 83–101.

Banks, T., *A Short Sketch of the Cotton Trade of Preston over the Last Sixty Seven Years*, Preston: Toulain, 1888.

Bartrip, P. and Burman, S., *The Wounded Soldiers of Industry, 1833–1897*, Oxford: Oxford University Press, 1983.

Bean, R., 'Employers' associations in the port of Liverpool, 1890–1914', *International Review of Social History*, 21 (1976), pp. 358–76.

Blank, S., *Industry and Government in Britain: The Federation of British Industries in Politics, 1945–65*, Farnborough: Saxon House, 1973.

Bolin-Hort, P., *Work, Family and the State: Child Labour and the Organisation of Production in the British Cotton Industry, 1780–1920*, Sweden: Lund University Press, 1989.

Boothman, T.B., *The Bolton Master Cotton Spinners' Association, 1861–1961*, Bolton: BMCSA, 1961.

Braverman, H., *Labor and Monopoly Capital*, New York: Monthly Review Press, 1974.

Briggs, A. and Saville, J., *Essays in Labour History, 1886–1923*, London: Macmillan, 1971.

British Trade Association, *Planning*, 221 (May 1944), pp. 1–15.

Brown, K.D., 'The anti-socialist union', in K.D. Brown (ed.), *Essays in Anti-Labour History: Responses to the Rise of Labour in Britain*, London: Macmillan, 1974.

Brown, R., *Waterfront Organisation in Hull, 1870–1900*, Hull: University of Hull, 1972.

Brown, W., *The Changing Contours of British Industrial Relations*, Oxford: Basil Blackwell, 1981.

Browne, B.C., 'What employers may prevent and effect by united action', *The Engineering Magazine*, 20, no. 4 (January 1901).

Bullen, A., *The Lancashire Weavers' Union*, Manchester: Amalgamated Textile Workers' Union, 1984.

'Pragmatism vs principle: cotton employers and the origins of an industrial relations system', in Jowitt and McIvor (eds.), *Employers and Labour*.

Bullen, A. and Fowler, A., *The Cardroom Workers' Union*, Manchester: Amalgamated Textile Workers' Union, 1986.

Bullough, W., *The First Fifty: A Brief History of the North-West Federation of Building Trade Employers, 1894–1944*, Manchester: NWFBTE, 1944.

Burgess, K., *The Origins of British Industrial Relations*, London: Croom Helm, 1975.

The Challenge of Labour, London: Croom Helm, 1980.

'Authority relations and the division of labour in British industry, with special reference to Clydeside, c. 1860–1930', *Social History*, 11, no. 2 (1986), pp. 211–33.

Butterworth, E., *Historical Sketches of Oldham*, Oldham: J. Hirst, 1856.

Cadbury, E., *Experiments in Industrial Organisations*, London: Longmans, Green and Co., 1912.

Catling, H., *The Spinning Mule*, Newton Abbot: David and Charles, 1970.

Chapman, S., 'A historical sketch of the masters' associations in the cotton industry', *Transactions of the Manchester Statistical Society* (1900–1), pp. 67–84.

The Lancashire Cotton Industry, Manchester: Manchester University Press, 1904.

Church, R. (ed.), *The Dynamics of Victorian Business*, London: Allen and Unwin, 1980.

The History of the British Coal Industry, vol. III: *1830–1913*, Oxford: Clarendon Press, 1986.

Clarke, A., *The Effects of the Factory System*, London: Grant Richards, 1899.

Clarke, R.O., 'The dispute in the British engineering industry, 1897–98: an evaluation', *Economica*, 24 (1957), pp. 128–37.

Clegg, H.A., *The System of Industrial Relations in Great Britain*, Oxford: Basil Blackwell, 1970.

A History of British Trade Unions since 1889, vol. II: *1911–1933*, Oxford: Clarendon Press, 1985.

A History of British Trade Unions since 1889, vol. III: *1934–1951*, Oxford: Clarendon Press, 1994.

Clegg, H.A., Fox A. and Thompson A.F., *A History of British Trade Unions since 1889*, vol. I: *1889–1910*, Oxford: Clarendon Press, 1964.

Cohen, I., 'Workers' control in the cotton industry: a comparative study of British and American mule-spinning', *Labor History*, 26 (1985), pp. 53–85.

Coleman, D.C., 'Combinations of capital and labour in the English paper industry, 1789–1825', *Economica*, 21 (February 1954), pp. 32–53.

Collison, W., *The Apostle of Free Labour*, London: Hurst and Blackett, 1913.

Cronin, J.E., *Industrial Conflict in Modern Britain*, London: Croom Helm, 1979.

'Strikes, 1870–1914', in Wrigley (ed.), *A History of British Industrial Relations, 1875–1914*.

Cronin, J.E. and Schneer, J. (eds.), *Social Conflict and the Political Order in Modern Britain*, London: Croom Helm, 1982.

Currie, R., *Industrial Politics*, Oxford: Clarendon Press, 1979.

Daniels, G. and Jewkes, J., 'The post-war depression in the Lancashire cotton industry', *Journal of the Royal Statistical Society* (1928).

Davidson, R., *Whitehall and the Labour Problem in Late-Victorian and Edwardian Britain*, London: Croom Helm, 1985.

Denver, J., *Fifty Years History of the Manchester, Salford and District Building Trades Employers' Association*, Manchester: MBTEA, 1951.

Department of Employment, *British Labour Statistics: Abstract, 1886–1968*, London: HMSO, 1971.

Desmarais, R., 'Lloyd George and the development of the British government's strikebreaking organisation', *International Review of Social History*, 20 (1975), pp. 1–15.

Dickson, T., *Scottish Capitalism*, London: Lawrence and Wishart, 1980.

(ed.), *Capital and Class in Scotland*, Edinburgh: John Donald, 1982.

Dobson, C.R., *Masters and Journeymen: A Pre-History of Industrial Relations, 1717–1800*, London: Croom Helm, 1980.

Duncan, R. and McIvor, A.J. (eds.), *Militant Workers: Labour and Class Conflict on the Clyde, 1900–1950*, Edinburgh: John Donald, 1992.

Dutton, H.I. and King, J.E., *Ten Per Cent and No Surrender: The Preston Strike, 1853–1854*, Cambridge: Cambridge University Press, 1981.

'The limits of paternalism: the cotton tyrants of north Lancashire, 1836–54', *Social History*, 7, no. 1 (1982), pp. 59–74.

Economic League, *The Facts About Industry*, London: EL, 1929.

Edwards, R., *Contested Terrain*, London: Heinemann, 1979.

Elbaum, B. and Lazonick, W. (eds.), *The Decline of the British Economy*, Oxford: Clarendon Press, 1986.

Engineering Employers' Federation, *Wage Movements, 1897–1925*, London: EEF, 1926.

Decisions of Central Conferences, 1898–1925, London: EEF, 1926.

Thirty Years of Industrial Conciliation, London: EEF, 1927.

Realities and Problems, London: EEF, 1930.

Farnie, D.A., *The English Cotton Industry and the World Market, 1815–1896*, Oxford: Clarendon Press, 1979.

Farnie, D.A. and Yonekawa, S., 'The emergence of the large firm in the cotton spinning industries of the world, 1883–1938', *Textile History*, 19 (1988), pp. 171–210.

Federation of British Industries, *Twenty Five Years, 1916–41*, London: FBI, 1941.

Federation of Master Cotton Spinners' Associations, *Conciliation in the Cotton Trade*, Manchester: FMCSA, 1901.

The Fern Mill Dispute, Manchester FMCSA, 1911.

Fielding, G.B., *The United Kingdom Textile Manufacturers' Association, 1866–1966*, Manchester: UKTMA 1966.

Fitzgerald, R., *British Labour Management and Industrial Welfare, 1846–1939*, London: Croom Helm, 1988.

Foster, J., 'Combinations amongst Oldham cotton masters, 1830–1870', unpublished paper, *c.* 1964.

Class Struggle and the Industrial Revolution, London: Methuen, 1974.

Fowler, A., 'Trade unions and technical change: the automatic loom strike, 1908', *North West Labour History Society Bulletin*, 6 (1979–80), pp. 43–55.

Fowler, A. and Fowler, L., *The Nelson Weavers*, Manchester: Amalgamated Textile Workers' Union, 1984.

Fowler, A. and Wyke, T. (eds.), *Barefoot Aristocrats*, Littleborough: George Kelsall, 1987.

Fraser, W. Hamish, *Trade Unions and Society: The Struggle for Acceptance, 1850–1880*, London: Allen and Unwin, 1974.

Friedman, A.L., *Industry and Labour*, London: Macmillan, 1977.

Garside, W.R., 'Management and men: aspects of British industrial relations in the interwar period', in B. Supple (ed.), *Essays in British Business History*, Oxford: Clarendon Press, 1977.

Garside, W.R. and Gospel, H., 'Employers and managers', in Wrigley (ed.), *A History of British Industrial Relations, 1875–1914*.

General Union of Associations of Loom Overlookers, *Jubilee History*, Manchester: GUALO, 1935.

Glasgow Labour History Workshop, *The Singer Strike, Clydebank, 1911*, Glasgow: Clydeside Press, 1989.

'The labour unrest in west Scotland, 1910–14', in Duncan and McIvor (eds.), *Militant Workers*.

Goodrich, C., *The Frontier of Control*, new edition, London: Pluto Press, 1975.

Gospel, H., 'Employers' labour policy: a study of the Mond-Turner talks, 1927–33', *Business History*, 21 (1979), pp. 180–97.

'Employers and managers: organisation and strategy, 1914–39', in Wrigley (ed.), *A History of British Industrial Relations*, vol. II: *1914–1939*.

Markets, Firms and the Management of Labour in Modern Britain, Cambridge: Cambridge University Press, 1992.

Gospel, H. and Littler, C.R. (eds.), *Managerial Strategies and Industrial Relations*, Aldershot: Gower, 1983.

Gray, E.M., *The Weaver's Wage*, Manchester: Manchester University Press, 1937.

'Wage rates and earnings in cotton weaving', *Transactions of the Manchester Statistical Society* (1938–9), pp. 1–22.

Greenwood, W., *Love on the Dole*, new edition, Harmondsworth: Penguin, 1969.

Hannah, W.L., *The Rise of the Corporate Economy*, London: Methuen, 1976.

Harvey, C. and Turner, J. (eds.), *Labour and Business in Modern Britain*, London: Frank Cass, 1989.

Hay, J.R., 'Employers' attitudes to social policy and the concept of social control, 1900–20', in Pat Thane (ed.), *The Origins of British Social Policy*, London: Croom Helm, 1978.

Helm, E., 'The recent dispute in the Lancashire cotton spinning industry', *Economic Journal*, 3 (1893), pp. 342–5.

Henderson, H.D., *The Cotton Control Board*, Oxford: Clarendon Press, 1922.

Hicks, J.R., 'The early history of industrial conciliation in England', *Economica*, 10 (1930), pp. 25–39.

Hilton, J., *Are Trade Unions Obstructive?* London: Victor Gollancz, 1935.

Hilton, W.S., *Foes to Tyranny: A History of the Amalgamated Union of Building Trade Workers*, London: AUBTW, 1963.

Hinton, J., *The First Shop Stewards' Movement*, London: Allen and Unwin, 1973.

Hobsbawm, E.J., *Labouring Men*, London: Weidenfeld and Nicolson, 1964.

Labour's Turning Point, 1880–1900, 2nd edition, Rutherford: Fairleigh Dickenson University Press, 1974.

Hollingsworth, M. and Norton-Taylor, R., *Blacklist: The Inside Story of Political Vetting*, London: Hogarth, 1988.

Hopwood, R.E., *The History of the Lancashire Cotton Industry and the Amalgamated Weavers' Association*, Manchester: Amalgamated Weavers' Association, 1969.

Howe, A., *The Cotton Masters, 1830–1860*, Oxford: Oxford University Press, 1984.

Howe, E., *The British Federation of Master Printers, 1900–1950*, London: British Federation of Master Printers, 1950.

Hughes, M., *Spies at Work*, Bradford: 1 in 12 Publications, diskbook, 1994.

Hunt, E., *Regional Wage Variations in Britain, 1850–1914* Oxford: Clarendon Press, 1973.

British Labour History, 1815–1914, London: Weidenfeld and Nicolson, 1981.

Hutchinson, Z., *The Trusts Grip Cotton*, Independent Labour Party Pamphlets, no. 28 (1920).

Iron Trades Employers' Association, *Record*, London: ITEA, 1900.

Jacoby, S. (ed.), *Masters to Managers*, New York: Columbia University Press, 1991.

Jeans, J.S., 'Lessons of the great engineering strike in England', *Engineering Magazine*, 13, no. 6 (September 1897).

Jefferys, J.B., *The Story of the Engineers 1800–1945*, London: Johnson Reprint, 1970.

Jewkes, J. and Gray, E.M., *Wages and Labour in the Lancashire Cotton Spinning Industry*, Manchester: Manchester University Press, 1935.

Jones, H., 'Employers' welfare schemes and industrial relations in interwar Britain', *Business History*, 25 (1983), pp. 61–75.

'An inspector calls', in P. Weindling (ed.), *The Social History of Occupational Health*, London: Croom Helm, 1985.

Jones, S., 'Cotton employers and industrial welfare between the wars', in Jowitt and McIvor (eds.), *Employers and Labour*.

Jowitt, J.A. and McIvor, A.J. (eds.), *Employers and Labour in the English Textile Industries, 1850–1939*, London: Routledge, 1988.

Joyce, P., *Work, Society and Politics*, new edition, London: Methuen, 1982.

Kenefick, W., *Ardrossan: The Key to the Clyde*, Irvine: Cunninghame District Council, 1993.

Kirby, M., 'The Lancashire cotton industry in the inter-war years: a study in organisational change', *Business History*, 16, no. 2 (July 1974), pp. 145–59.

Kirby, R.G. and Musson, A.E., *The Voice of the People: John Docherty, Trade Unionist, Radical and Factory Reformer, 1798–1854*, Manchester: Manchester University Press, 1975.

Kirk, R. and Simmons, C., 'Engineering and the First World War: a case study of the Lancashire spinning machine industry', *Salford Papers in Economics*, no. 81/5 (1981).

Knowles, K.G., *Strikes: A Study in Industrial Conflict*, Oxford: Basil Blackwell, 1952.

Knox, W., 'The political and workplace culture of the Scottish working class, 1832–1914', in W. Hamish Fraser and R.J. Morris (eds.), *People and Society in Scotland*, vol. II: *1830–1914*, Edinburgh: John Donald, 1990.

Hanging by a Thread: The Scottish Cotton Industry, c. 1850–1914, Preston: Carnegie, 1995.

Laybourn, K., *A History of British Trade Unionism, c. 1770–1990*, Stroud: Sutton, 1992.

Lazonick, W., 'Industrial relations and technical change: the case of the self-acting mule', *Cambridge Journal of Economics*, 3 (1979), pp. 231–62.

'Industrial organisation and technical change: the decline of the British cotton industry', *Business History Review*, 57 (1983), pp. 195–236.

Lee, C.H., *British Regional Employment Statistics, 1841–1971*, Cambridge: Cambridge University Press, 1979.

'The cotton textile industry', in Church (ed.), *Dynamics of Victorian Business*.

Leng, P., *The Welsh Dockers*, Ormskirk: Hesketh, 1981.

Littler, C.R., *The Development of the Labour Process in Capitalist Societies*, London: Heinemann, 1982.

'A comparative analysis of managerial structures and strategies', in Gospel and Littler (eds.), *Managerial Strategies*.

Longworth, J., *The Oldham Master Cotton Spinners' Association, 1866–1966*, Oldham: OMCSA, 1966.

Lovell, J.C., 'Collective bargaining and the emergence of national employer organisation in the British shipbuilding industry', *International Review of Social History*, 36 (1991), pp. 59–61.

'Employers and craft unionism: a programme of action for British shipbuilding, 1902–5', *Business History*, 34 (1992), pp. 38–58.

Ludlow, J.M., 'The National Free Labour Association', *Economic Review*, 5 (1895).

'The Labour Protection Association', *Economic Review*, 9 (1899).

Lunn, K. (ed.), *Hosts, Immigrants and Minorities*, Folkestone: Dawson, 1980.

Macara, C.W., *Social and Industrial Reform*, Manchester: Sherratt and Hughes, 1919.

Modern Industrial Tendencies, Manchester: Sherratt and Hughes, 1926.

McCaffree, K., 'A theory of the origin and development of employers' associations', *Proceedings of the Industrial Relations Research Association*, 15 (1962), pp. 56–68.

McGuffie, C., *Working in Metal: Management and Labour in the Metal Industries of Europe and the USA, 1890–1914*, London: Merlin Press, 1985.

Macintyre, S., *Little Moscows*, London: Croom Helm, 1980.

McIvor, A., 'Employers' organisations and strikebreaking in Britain, 1880–1914', *International Review of Social History*, 29, part 1 (1984), pp. 1–33.

'A crusade for capitalism: the Economic League, 1919–1939', *Journal of Contemporary History*, 23, no. 4 (1988), pp. 631–55.

'Cotton employers' organisations and labour relations, 1890–1939', in Jowitt and McIvor (eds.), *Employers and Labour*.

'Work and health, 1880–1914: a note on a neglected interaction', *Scottish Labour History Society Journal*, 24 (1989), pp. 47–67.

McIvor, A. and Paterson, H., 'Combating the left: victimisation and anti-labour activities on Clydeside, 1900–1939', in Duncan and McIvor (eds.), *Militant Workers*.

McKenna, J.A. and Rodger, R.G., 'Control by coercion: employers' associations and the establishment of industrial order in the building industry of England and Wales, 1860–1914', *Business History Review*, 59, no. 2 (1985), pp. 203–31.

McKinlay, A., 'Depression and rank and file activity: the AEU, 1919–1939', *Scottish Labour History Society Journal*, 22 (1987), pp. 22–9.

McKinlay, A. and Zeitlin, J., 'The meanings of managerial prerogative: industrial relations and the organisation of work in British engineering, 1880–1939', in Harvey and Turner (eds.), *Labour and Business*.

McLean, I., *The Legend of Red Clydeside*, Edinburgh: John Donald, 1983.

McShane, H. and Smith, J., *No Mean Fighter*, London: Pluto Press, 1978.

Magrath, I., 'Protecting the interests of the trade: wool textile employers' organisations in the 1920s', in Jowitt and McIvor (eds.), *Employers and Labour*.

Manchester Studies, *Trafford Park, 1896–1939*, Manchester: Manchester Studies, 1979.

Marsh, A., *Industrial Relations in Engineering*, Oxford: Pergamon Press, 1965.

Marshall, J.D., *Lancashire*, Newton Abbot: David and Charles, 1974.

Mass, W. and Lazonick, W., 'The British cotton industry and international competitive advantage: the state of the debates', *Business History*, 32 (1990), pp. 9–65.

Melling, J., 'Non-commissioned officers: British employers and their supervisory workers, 1880–1920', *Social History*, 5 (1980), pp. 183–221.

'Scottish industrialists and the changing nature of class relations in the Clyde region, 1880–1918', in T. Dickson (ed.), *Capital and Class in Scotland*, Edinburgh: John Donald, 1982.

'Employers, industrial welfare and the struggle for workplace control in British industry, 1880–1920', in Gospel and Littler (eds.), *Managerial Strategies*.

'The "servile state" revisited', *Scottish Labour History Society Journal*, 24 (1989), pp. 68–85.

Merfyn Jones, R., *The North Wales Quarrymen, 1874–1922*, Cardiff: University of Wales Press, 1981.

Merttens, F., 'The hours and cost of labour in the cotton industry at home and abroad', *Transactions of the Manchester Statistical Society* (1893–4), pp. 125–90.

Middlemas, K., *Politics in Industrial Society*, London: André Deutsch, 1979.

Mitchell, B.R. and Deane, P., *Abstract of British Historical Statistics*, Cambridge: Cambridge University Press, 1962.

Mommsen, W. and Husung, H.J. (eds.), *The Development of Trade Unionism in Great Britain and Germany 1880–1914*, London: Allen and Unwin, 1985.

More, C., *Skill and the English Working Class, 1870–1914*, London: Croom Helm, 1980.

Morris, J.H. and Williams, L.J. 'The discharge note in the South Wales coal industry, 1841–1898', *Economic History Review*, 10 (1957–8), pp. 286–93.

Morrison, C.J., 'Short-sighted methods of dealing with labour', *Engineering Magazine*, 30, no. 1 (January 1914).

Musson, A.E., *Trade Union and Social History*, London: Cass, 1974.

National Federation of Building Trade Employers, *An Outline History of the National Federation of Building Trade Employers, 1878–1978*, London: NFBTE, 1978.

Pelling, H., *History of British Trade Unionism*, 4th edition, Harmondsworth: Penguin, 1987.

Phelps-Brown, H., *The Growth of British Industrial Relations*, London: Macmillan, 1959.

The Origins of Trade Union Power, Oxford: Oxford University Press, 1986.

Plowman, D., 'Employers' associations: challenges and responses', *Journal of the Industrial Relations Society of Australia* (1978).

Porter, J.H., 'Industrial peace in the cotton trade, 1875–1913', *Yorkshire Bulletin of Economic and Social Research*, 19 (1967), pp. 49–61.

'Wage bargaining under conciliation agreements, 1860–1914', *Economic History Review*, 23, no. 3 (1970), pp. 460–75.

'Cotton and wool textiles', in N.K. Buxton and D. Aldcroft (eds.), *British Industry between the Wars*, London: Scolar Press, 1979.

Postgate, R., *The Builders' History*, London: NFBTO, 1923.

Powell, C.G., *An Economic History of the British Building Industry, 1815–1979*, London: Methuen, 1982.

Powell, L.H., *The Shipping Federation*, London: SF, 1950.

Price, L.L., 'Conciliation in the cotton trade', *Economic Journal*, 11 (1901), pp. 235–44.

Price, R., *Masters, Unions and Men: Work Control in Building and the Rise of Labour, 1830–1914*, Cambridge: Cambridge University Press, 1980.

'Rethinking labour history: the importance of work', in Cronin and Schneer (eds.), *Social Conflict*.

Labour in British Society: An Interpretative Essay, London: Croom Helm, 1986.

Reid, A., 'Dilution, trade unionism and the state in Britain during the First World War', in S. Tolliday and J. Zeitlin (eds.), *Shop Floor Bargaining and the State*, Cambridge: Cambridge University Press, 1985.

'Employers' strategies and craft production', in Tolliday and Zeitlin (eds.), *The Power to Manage?*

Social Classes and Social Relations in Britain, 1850–1914, London: Macmillan, 1992.

Richardson, J.H., 'Employers' associations', in F.E. Gannett and B.F. Catherwood (eds.), *Industrial and Labour Relations in Great Britain*, 1939.

Roberts, R., *The Classic Slum*, Manchester: Manchester University Press, 1971.

Rodgers, T., 'Employers' organizations, unemployment and social politics in Britain during the inter-war period', *Social History*, 13, no. 3 (1988), pp. 315–41.

Rubin, G.R., *War, Law and Labour: The Munitions Acts, State Regulation and the Unions, 1915–1921*, Oxford: Clarendon Press, 1987.

Rule, J., *The Experience of Labour in Eighteenth Century Industry*, London: Croom Helm, 1981.

The Labouring Classes in Early Industrial England, 1750–1850, London: Longman, 1986.

Ryan, J., 'Machinery replacement in the cotton trade', *Economic Journal*, 40 (December 1930), pp. 568–80.

Sandberg, L., *Lancashire in Decline*, Columbus: Ohio State University Press, 1974.

Savage, M., 'Capitalist and patriarchal relations at work: Preston cotton weaving, 1890–1940', in L. Murgatroyd *et al.* (eds.), *Localities, Class and Gender*, London: Pion, 1985.

The Dynamics of Working Class Politics, Cambridge: Cambridge University Press, 1987.

Saville, J., 'The British state, the business community and the trade unions', in Mommsen and Husung (eds.), *The Development of Trade Unionism*.

Shadwell, A., *Industrial Efficiency*, London: Longmans, 1913.

The Engineering Industry and the Crisis of 1922, London: Longmans, 1922.

Singleton, J., *Lancashire on the Scrap Heap: The Cotton Industry, 1945–70*, Oxford: Oxford University Press, 1991.

Sisson, K., *The Management of Collective Bargaining: An International Comparison*, Oxford: Basil Blackwell, 1987.

Smith, A., *The Wealth of Nations*, new edition, Harmondsworth: Penguin Books, 1974.

Smith, J., 'Labour tradition in Glasgow and Liverpool', *History Workshop Journal*, 17 (1984), pp. 32–56.

Stearns, P., *Lives of Labour*, London: Croom Helm, 1975.

Thompson, E.P., *The Making of the English Working Class*, London: Victor Gollancz, 1963.

Todd, N., 'Trade unions and the engineering dispute at Barrow-in-Furness, 1897–8', *International Review of Social History*, 20 (1975), pp. 33–47.

Tolliday, S. and Zeitlin, J. (eds.), *The Power to Manage?* London: Routledge, 1991.
'Employers and industrial relations between theory and history', in Tolliday and Zeitlin (eds.), *The Power to Manage?*
'National models and international variations in labour management and employer organization', in Tolliday and Zeitlin (eds.), *The Power to Manage?*

Trades Union Congress, *Joint Committee Report on the Premium Bonus System*, London: TUC, 1910.

Trainor, R., *Black Country Elites: The Exercise of Authority in an Industrialised Area, 1830–1900*, Oxford: Clarendon Press, 1993.

Tressell, R., *The Ragged Trousered Philanthropists*, London: Panther, 1965.

Tripp, B., *Renold Chains*, London: Allen and Unwin, 1956.

Turner, H.A., *Trade Union Growth, Structure and Policy*, London: Allen and Unwin, 1962.

Turner, J. (ed.), *Businessmen and Politics: Studies of Business Activity in British Politics, 1900–1945*, London: Heinemann, 1984.

Vitkovitch, B., 'The U.K. cotton industry, 1937–54', *Journal of Industrial Economics*, 3, no. 3 (1955), pp. 241–65.

Walton, J.K., *Lancashire: A Social History, 1558–1939*, Manchester: Manchester University Press, 1987.

Ward, J., *Workmen and Wages at Home and Abroad, or the Effects of Strikes, Combinations and Trade Unions*, London: Longmans, Green and Co., 1868.

Ward, J.T. and Fraser, W.H., *Workers and Employers: Documents on Trade Unions and Industrial Relations in Britain since the Eighteenth Century*, London: Macmillan, 1980.

Webb, S., *Industrial Democracy*, London: Longmans, Green and Co., 1920.

Webb, S. and Webb, B., *The History of Trade Unionism*, London: Longmans, Green and Co., 1902.

White, J.L., *The Limits of Trade Union Militancy: The Lancashire Textile Workers, 1910–1914*, New York: Greenwood, 1978.
'Lancashire cotton textiles', in Wrigley (ed.), *A History of British Industrial Relations, 1875–1914*.

White, S., 'Ideological hegemony and political control: the sociology of anti-Bolshevism in Britain, 1918–20', *Scottish Labour History Society Journal*, 9 (1975), pp. 3–20.

Wigham, E., *The Power to Manage: A History of the Engineering Employers' Federation*, London: Macmillan, 1973.

Windmuller, J.P. and Gladstone, A., *Employers' Associations and Industrial Relations: A Comparative Study*, Oxford: Clarendon Press, 1984.

Wrigley, C.J. (ed.), *A History of British Industrial Relations, 1875–1914*, Brighton: Harvester, 1982.
'The government and industrial relations', in Wrigley (ed.), *A History of British Industrial Relations, 1875–1914*.
(ed.), *A History of British Industrial Relations*, vol. II: *1914–1939*, Brighton: Harvester, 1986.
'The First World War and state intervention in industrial relations', in Wrigley (ed.), *A History of British Industrial Relations*, vol. II: *1914–1939*.

'The trade unions between the wars', in Wrigley (ed.), *A History of British Industrial Relations*, vol. II: *1914–1939*.

Yarmie, A.H., 'Employers' organisations in mid-Victorian England', *International Review of Social History*, 25 (1980), pp. 209–34.

'British employers' resistance to "grandmotherly" government, 1850–80', *Social History*, 9, no. 2 (May 1984), pp. 141–69.

Zeitlin, J., 'The labour strategies of British engineering employers, 1890–1922', in Gospel and Littler (eds.), *Managerial Strategies*.

'From labour history to the history of industrial relations', *Economic History Review*, 40, no. 2 (1987), pp. 159–84.

'"Rank and filism" in British labour history: a critique', *International Review of Social History*, 34 (1989), pp. 42–61.

'The internal politics of employer organization: the Engineering Employers' Federation, 1896–1939', in Tolliday and Zeitlin (eds.), *The Power to Manage?*

C UNPUBLISHED THESES

Bennett, G.A., 'The present position of the cotton industry in Great Britain' (MA thesis, Manchester University, 1933).

Bullen, A., 'The Cotton Spinners' and Manufacturers' Association and the breakdown of collective bargaining in the cotton manufacturing industry, 1928–35' (MA thesis, Warwick University, 1980).

Dyson, R.F., 'The development of collective bargaining in the cotton spinning industry, 1893–1914' (Ph.D. thesis, Leeds University, 1971).

Furniss, C., 'Industrial unrest in Manchester and Salford, 1910–14' (MA thesis, Manchester University, 1971).

Gospel, H., 'Employers' organisations: their growth and function in the British system of industrial relations in the period 1918–1939' (Ph.D. thesis, London School of Economics, 1974).

Jones, F., 'The cotton spinning industry in the Oldham district from 1896 to 1914' (MA thesis, Manchester University, 1959).

McIvor, A., 'Employers' organisations and industrial relations in Lancashire, 1890–1939' (Ph.D. thesis, Manchester University, 1983).

McKinlay, A., 'Employers and skilled workers in the interwar depression: engineering and shipbuilding on Clydeside, 1919–1939' (D.Phil. thesis, Oxford University, 1986).

Magrath, I., 'Wool textile employers' organisations: Bradford, c. 1914–1945' (Ph.D. thesis, University of Hull, 1991).

Melling, J., 'British employers and the development of industrial welfare, c. 1880–1920' (Ph.D. thesis, University of Glasgow, 1980).

Paterson, Hugh, 'Industrial relations in Glasgow shipping, 1880–1914' (M.Phil. thesis, University of Strathclyde, 1991).

Riley, J.H., 'The more looms system' (MA thesis, Manchester University, 1981).

Smith, R., 'The history of the Lancashire cotton industry, 1873–96' (Ph.D. thesis, Birmingham University, 1954).

Thorpe, E., 'Industrial relations and the social structure: a case study of the Bolton cotton mule spinners, 1884–1910' (M.Sc. thesis, University of Salford, 1969).

Weekes, B.C.M., 'The Amalgamated Society of Engineers, 1880–1914' (Ph.D. thesis, Warwick University, 1970).

Williams, L.J., 'The Monmouthshire and South Wales Coalowners' Association, 1873–1914' (MA thesis, University of Wales, 1957).

Index

Printed in the United States
By Bookmasters